THE QUEST FOR

NATIONAL OFFICE

READINGS ON ELECTIONS

EDITED BY

Stephen J. Wayne
Georgetown University

Clyde Wilcox
Georgetown University

St. Martin's Press
New York

Senior editor: Don Reisman
Project management: Publication Services
Cover design: Irwin Hahn/Circa 86, Inc.

Library of Congress Catalog Card Number: 91-61129

Manufactured in the United States of America.
65432
fedcba

For information, write:

St. Martin's Press, Inc.
175 Fifth Avenue
New York, NY 10010

ISBN: 0-312-06242-7

 The text of this book has been printed on recycled paper.

Preface

It is necessary to get behind the scenes of a political campaign in order to learn what is happening, why it is happening, and what difference the campaign makes for the election, for the parties and the candidates, and for government. Political scientists try to make these discoveries with the hindsight of history. They tend to be more interested in the long-term social and political forces that shape events and affect decisions than in the shorter-term situations and personalities that dominate the news and may influence the vote. Journalists, on the other hand, focus on the story of the campaign, the people behind the story, the calculations of the candidates, and the immediate meaning of the election.

Each of these perspectives is important. Together they provide a comprehensive body of knowledge that enables us to understand and to assess the quest for office. We have therefore included both scholarly and journalistic selections in this book. Most of the chapters have at least one or two articles by political scientists to provide a framework for viewing the election and several others by journalists that describe and evaluate the process as they report from the most recent presidential and congressional campaigns.

The book's organization is parallel to that of *The Road to the White House: The Politics of Presidential Elections*, although it may be used alone or with other texts. Each chapter focuses primarily on presidential elections but also includes at least one reading on congressional elections. Our objective is to supplement the literature on national elections with descriptive and analytic readings about them.

A number of people have assisted us in compiling this collection. Eric Pages and April Morgan, Ph.D. candidates at Georgetown University, worked as our research assistants. They located and made valuable suggestions about many of the journalistic articles. Several political scientists—John A. Crittenden, Indiana State University; Samuel B. Hoff, Delaware State College; and Roy Young, San Jose State University—reviewed our chapter outline and helped us improve the selection of readings. We would like to thank them; Mike Buetow and others at Publication Services, Inc., for the editing of the manuscript; Don Reisman, political science editor at St. Martin's Press, for his encouragement and advice; and finally our wives, Cheryl Beil and Elizabeth Cook, and children, Jared and Jeremy Wayne, for their patience and support.

Contents

Introduction

There have been continuities and changes in the American electoral system. The continuities stem primarily from the system's constitutional underpinnings—the decisions by the framers to establish separate constituencies for members of the House of Representatives, the Senate, and the president and vice president; to give the states primary responsibility for the conduct of elections for federal officials; and to create an electoral college for the selection of the president and vice president. Those decisions have contributed to the basic structure of the electoral system and to the political tradition that has evolved from it.

Changes have occurred. A product of law and practice, these changes have been generated by the development of political parties, democratic reform movements, and advances in communications technology.

The creation and evolution of political parties have had a profound impact on the electoral process, affecting the nomination of candidates, their campaigns for office, and the qualifications and characteristics of those who seek elective positions. Parties have become the principal organizations for recruiting candidates; for shaping their policy positions; for developing allegiances among the electorate; and, if successful, for organizing and influencing those elected to office in their policy decisions.

The Constitution has been amended to rectify problems in electoral college voting, to extend suffrage, and to remove or reduce legal obstacles to voting. Laws have been enacted to encourage participation in the parties' nomination process; to regulate campaign finance; and, in the case of presidential elections, to subsidize nominations and fund the general election, and to equalize access to the media and use of media by the candidates in national elections.

Communications technology has also had significant repercussions for the electoral process. First, mass-produced newspapers and magazines and, later, radio and television have affected the information people have at their disposal and on which they make their electoral decisions. They have influenced the agendas of campaigns, the appeals and messages of candidates, and the images they try to project. They have also supplemented, and in some cases effectively replaced, the parties as principal links between the candidates and the voters.

Partisan reforms and technological innovations have worked to encourage participation, to equalize information, and to increase the importance of the individual candidates on the outcome of the elections. But in the process they have created tensions within the system between parties and the media, between candidates and the parties, and between candidates and the media.

The selections in this book explore those tensions and their impact on the electoral process.

The changes that have occurred in the political system have also produced a disparity between the original constitutional design and contemporary goals, needs, and operations. Some of this disparity has been intentional—for example, the attempt to make the political system more democratic and more responsive to the will of the majority. Some has been unintentional—the result of attempts by parties, candidates, and others to maneuver the laws and practices to their own political advantage.

Whether intentional or not, the changes that have occurred, either through law or practice, raise serious concerns for a democratic society. Suffrage has expanded, but turnout has declined. Parties are more responsive to their rank and file but less influential on the electorate, on the success of their candidates, and on their ability to govern and be held accountable. The mass media, particularly radio and television, bring the campaigns into living rooms and reach members of the electorate who might not otherwise be attentive to the election, but they provide limited information on which to base voting decisions. They have also vastly increased the cost of elections, affected the issues that are debated, and altered the way appeals and images are projected to the voters.

The articles in this book address these critical issues. They examine how the system works and the extent to which it meets its desired goals of facilitating majority rule yet allowing the minority to be heard and represented, of equalizing popular control and encouraging citizen participation, of inducing the most qualified candidates to run and providing them with an adequate forum for expressing their views, of enabling the electorate to make a rational judgment based on sufficient and accurate information about the candidates and their policy positions, and of providing public officials with guidance in making their policy decisions and holding them accountable for their actions. Striving to achieve these democratic objectives is essential if elections are to provide a critical link between the people and their elected representatives.

1. The Electoral System: An Historical Overview

Democratic systems are governed by rules that provide the framework for politics and government. With one major exception, the framers of the U.S. Constitution decided to give the states the authority to establish rules for federal elections. That exception was for the president and vice president.

The framers gave the states the power to conduct elections for federal officials to avoid the thorny issue of determining the qualifications for voting as well as to resolve the practical problem of how elections would be held and who would hold them. As a safeguard against the states' use of this authority in an unwise or indiscriminate way, they also gave the Congress the power to legislate on these matters if it chose to do so.

An exception was created for the presidency and vice presidency because those were the only elected offices with a national constituency. This meant that the delegates at the Constitutional Convention had to fashion a political compromise to create an equitable and workable electoral system that would be consistent with a republican form of government, not jeopardize the independence of the office, and, most importantly, select the most qualified person as president and the second most qualified as vice president. The electoral college system was their resolution of this compromise.

Although modified by amendment and by precedent, that system has framed presidential politics ever since. We begin this chapter with a reading by A. James Reichley that looks at the creation of that system, its initial design, and its principal alterations. In his analysis, Reichley assesses the strengths and weaknesses of the system, proposals for changing it, and makes his own recommendations on how to improve the election of the president.

Peter Baida's article on the fund-raising activities of Mark Hanna reminds us that concerns over the ethics and implications of fund-raising practices are not new. Hanna's activities led to the passage of the first of many laws that regulated campaign finance activity in the United States; that law banned direct corporate contributions to campaigns. In 1972 Richard Nixon's reelection committee solicited corporate contributions in ways that echoed Hanna's tactics. In response, Congress passed the Federal Election Campaign Act, which governs campaign finance today.

In the final reading Norman Ornstein examines the recent trend toward split government. He asks why there seems to be a permanent Democratic majority in Congress in a period when Republicans seem to have a lock on the White House. Although Americans have experienced divided government in the past, the current period is unprecedented. Since 1968 the party of the president has faced a hostile majority in the House for eighteen of the past twenty-two years. Ornstein argues that the Republicans would have done better in congressional elections had the Democrats more frequently won the presidency, for the president's party historically loses seats in Congress in off-year elections. In addition, he urges campaign finance reform to make congressional elections more competitive.

The Electoral System

A. JAMES REICHLEY

In this first selection A. James Reichley examines the creation of the electoral college system, its initial design, and its principal alterations. He notes the problems that have resulted in five traumatic elections—in 1860, 1876, 1888, 1912, and 1968—and asks whether these problems are sufficiently serious to change the system. His answer in general is that they are not, but he does suggest some improvements that could be made without upsetting the system's basic framework.

Elections are fundamental to any political system based on principles of democracy and republican government. Under democracy, elections in which all eligible voters may participate are the ultimate source of governmental authority. In a large, complex society like the United States, elections provide the chief means through which most voters influence the formation of government policy and exercise the rights and responsibilities of citizenship.

. . . The American electoral system is governed by rules that are basically majoritarian, with important modifications. At the federal level, the Constitution as originally enacted called for three election systems, each applying to one of the major governing units. The U.S. House of Representatives was to be apportioned by population, with Indians excluded and each slave counted as three-fifths of a person; members were to be chosen by the voting public as defined by the states in their requirements for "electors of the most numerous branch of the State Legislature." U.S. Senate seats were apportioned two to a state, with members to be elected by the somewhat more elitist mechanism of the state legislatures.

The president, heading the executive branch, and the vice-president were to be chosen through a complicated scheme based on what has come to be known as the "electoral college" (though the term does not appear in the Constitution). Members of the electoral college were to be elected in each state in a manner determined by its legislature, with federal public office-holders specifically excluded—thereby, it was hoped, placing the process at least one remove from ordinary politics. The number of electors would equal the state's total representation in the Senate and House (small states, therefore, being disproportionately represented, though much less so than in the Senate).

Source: A. James Reichley (ed.) *Elections American Style* (Washington, D.C.: Brookings Institution, 1987), pp. 1–21.

Electors would meet to vote, not as a collective body in the federal capital, but in their respective states, which it was thought would dampen electioneering. Each would vote for two persons for president, at least one of whom could not be an inhabitant of the elector's state. Ballots would be transmitted "sealed" to the president of the federal Senate, who would count them "in the presence of the Senate and House of Representatives." If one candidate had a majority of the total electors, he was elected president, with the runner-up vice-president. In case of a tie between two candidates, each of whom had a majority of electors (which was possible since each elector was to vote for two persons), the House would elect one of the two president, each state delegation voting as a unit and casting one vote. If no candidate had a majority in the electoral college, the House, again with each state casting one vote, would select the president from the five with the highest number of electoral votes.

The Founders do not seem to have expected that the president would always, or even usually, be chosen through majority support from the electors. This would be the case when a popular individual like George Washington was the clear national favorite. But when support was scattered among a number of candidates, the electors would in effect serve a winnowing function, leaving the final choice to the House (the more popular body, but operating in this one instance through a federal structure rather than by district).

All these public leaders were to be elected for fixed terms—two years for members of the House, six for members of the Senate, and four for the president and vice-president—giving them a measure of protection against transitory shifts in public opinion, but keeping them ultimately responsible to the people. The fourth major governing unit, the federal judiciary, was rooted in politics, through appointment by the president and confirmation by the Senate, but was made virtually autonomous by unlimited terms "during good behavior" and was not intended to be politically responsive.

Among the election systems called for by the Constitution, that for the House has changed the least, altered mainly by expansion of the electorate to include all citizens over the age of eighteen. The means of election for the Senate was sharply altered by the Seventeenth Amendment, moving voting authority from the state legislatures to the electorate as a whole. But it is the means for electing the president, the crux and apex of national leadership because of the chief executive's singular visibility and control over the administrative departments and agencies, that today probably differs most from the Founders' expectations.

. . . The Founders expected that the presidential electors would be public-spirited notables, not deeply involved in the rough-and-tumble of ordinary politics, who would cast their ballots much as the respected elders of a gentleman's club might participate in the choice of the club's presiding officer. Consistent with this view, the office of vice-president was designed primarily to provide a high public post for the individual judged by his peers to be the second most qualified for the highest office. The vice-president's availability to succeed a president unable to complete his term was for the Founders a secondary purpose. . . .

A CONSTITUTIONAL CRISIS

For the first two presidential elections, the system worked about as intended. Election of Washington as president and John Adams of Massachusetts as vice-president neatly symbolized the alliance between the planter class of the South and the merchant class and Puritan divines of New England that effectively dominated the new republic. The crucial middle states were not in the early rounds represented in the elected executive establishment. But the fact that the third-place finisher in both 1789 and 1792 was a New Yorker (John Jay in the first election and George Clinton in the second), and the practical power of Alexander Hamilton of New York as secretary of the treasury, seemed to point toward regional accommodation.

When Washington stepped down in 1796, however, the system began to operate differently than the Founders had planned. The two principal rivals for the presidency, Adams and Thomas Jefferson, instead of running purely on their personal merits, presented themselves as candidates of the two great factions known as Federalists and Republicans, that had begun, to the dismay of almost everybody, to form during Washington's second term. Adams was linked electorally with Thomas Pinckney of South Carolina, for whom Federalist electors were urged to cast their second ballots with the understanding that Pinckney would become vice-president. Republican politicians were unable to agree on a running mate for Jefferson, so Republican electors in different states gave their second votes to a variety of candidates. Adams carried all of New England, and Jefferson most of the South. The middle states split, New York, New Jersey, and Delaware going for Adams, and most of Pennsylvania for Jefferson. Adams eked out a narrow majority in the electoral college. But enough of the spirit of the Founders' intention survived so that twelve of Adam's seventy-one electors cast their ballots for candidates other than Pinckney. As a result, Jefferson finished second and became vice-president—following the Founders' design, but with the consequence that the president and vice-president represented hostile factions within the national government.

In 1800 the original system essentially collapsed, producing the young government's first constitutional crisis. The Federalists supported Adams for reelection, with General Charles Cotesworth Pinckney of South Carolina (Thomas's older brother) as his running mate. Republican members of Congress caucused in Marache's boardinghouse in Philadelphia and picked Aaron Burr of New York to form a slate with Jefferson—thereby forging a bond between the political establishments of New York and Virginia that would endure for almost two centuries, profoundly affecting the shape of

American politics. In the election New York switched sides, and both Republican candidates received majorities. This time, however, party unity held, so Jefferson and Burr were given identical votes.

Under the Constitution, the decision went to the House, in which eight state delegations were under Republican control, six were Federalist, and two were divided—thus neither party commanded a majority. Federalist House members supported Burr, hoping to keep out the hated Jefferson, split the Republican party, and perhaps share the fruits of victory if Burr should pick up the votes of a few Republican House members. Burr played a cautious game, declining to deal with the Federalists but avoiding the one act that would break the deadlock: his announcement that if elected president he would not serve. For thirty-five ballots both sides held firm. Then, as many began to doubt the very survival of the republic, the single member of the House from Delaware, a Federalist, declared he would vote for Jefferson, giving the Virginian the necessary majority.[1]

Aiming to avoid a similar impasse in the future, the Republican majority in the new Congress pushed through the Twelfth Amendment, requiring that the electors vote separately for president and vice-president. Signifying the trend from a primarily personal politics to a politics based on well-defined factions, the pool from which the House could select the president if no candidate won a majority in the electoral college was reduced from the highest five to the highest three.

During Jefferson's two terms, Republican leaders in Congress, now often called Democrat-Republicans to acknowledge the party's equalitarian ethos, increasingly functioned as the high command of a national party. In 1804 the party's congressional caucus chose George Clinton, boss of the powerful New York machine, to replace the mercurial Burr as Jefferson's running mate. In the next three presidential elections, the congressional caucus, in which all Democrat-Republican members of Congress were entitled to one vote, selected slates for president and vice-president. For each of these, the caucus appointed a committee of its members to manage a victorious national canvass. It seemed that national parties might form around the leadership of legislative factions, as was occurring at the time in Britain and has since happened in most democratic countries employing the parliamentary system.

EMERGENCE OF NATIONAL PARTIES

As matters turned out, however, legislative parties were not to become the focus of national politics in the United States. By 1824 the caucus had itself become a political issue, giving fuel to those who aimed to break the domination of the southern planter elite that had flourished under the

---

[1]John C. Miller, *The Federalist Era* (Harper, 1960), pp. 268–73.

administrations of Jefferson, Madison, and Monroe. The political power of the states, commanding campaign resources that evaded centralized control, was crucial in supplanting the caucus. But the ability of the president to exercise independent political clout far beyond that available to parliamentary premiers or prime ministers, at least before the rise of the welfare state, would probably in any case have been enough to assure a different structure for American politics.

Perhaps if the Federalist party has survived as a significant force in Congress, its legislative leaders might have been able to present themselves as the natural alternative to the political status quo. But in 1824 Federalists held only 12 percent of the seats in the House and 8 percent in the Senate. John Quincy Adams, son of the last Federalist president, was a Democrat-Republican, serving as secretary of state in the cabinet of President Monroe. Politicians desiring change needed some other fulcrum on which to hoist the political nation.

When the Democrat-Republican caucus convened in Washington in February 1824, only 66 of the party's 231 members of Congress attended. The caucus proceeded to award its presidential nomination to William H. Crawford of Georgia, secretary of the treasury in the Monroe administration and logical standard-bearer for the incumbent elite. The other major candidates, John Quincy Adams of Massachusetts, Andrew Jackson of Tennessee, and Henry Clay of Kentucky, were in no way deterred, and in fact used the caucus's designation as a symbol of oligarchic rule with which to bludgeon Crawford (much as insurgent candidates long after made party organization endorsement a liability for their slated opponents in many state and municipal elections).

Adams, Jackson, and Clay turned to their respective state legislatures to pass resolutions launching their candidacies. The resulting free-for-all produced a division in the electoral college of ninety-nine for Jackson, eighty-four for Adams, forty-one for Crawford, and thirty-seven for Clay. No candidate possessing a majority, the election once more went to the House. John C. Calhoun of South Carolina, originally a candidate for president, had switched to the competition for vice-president and was elected by a large majority in the electoral college.

Under the original provision of the Constitution allowing the House to choose among the top five presidential contenders, Clay, the political virtuoso of the day, might have been able as Speaker of the House to swing the prize to himself. But under the Twelfth Amendment, limiting the choice to the top three, he was removed from the pool. Clay backed Adams, who thereby was able to win a one-vote majority among the twenty-four state delegations in the House.

Jackson and his supporters were outraged, pointing out that he had not only been first in the electoral college but also led in the popular vote (though the significance of the popular vote was somewhat undercut by the fact that six of the twenty-four states still did not choose electors by direct election). When Adams appointed Clay secretary of state, the Jacksonians claimed to have evidence of a sordid political deal—a charge that clung to both Adams and Clay during the rest of their public careers.[2]

It is an interesting question why this accusation was so damaging. Under a multiparty system of the kind now found in many democracies, Adams and Clay could be said to have formed a coalition government. All four candidates identified themselves loosely as Democrat-Republicans, so no betrayal of party was involved. Between them, Adams and Clay had considerably more votes than Jackson, though less than a majority. But there clearly was a widespread feeling that Clay and Adams had employed a political maneuver to evade the will of the voting public, which already was seen as the real source of legitimacy for national leadership.

Shrewd politicians, notably Martin Van Buren of New York, took from the 1824 election the lesson that while the congressional caucus was no longer an acceptable means for proposing national leaders, the various state legislatures would not suffice as launch pads for presidential candidacies. In 1828, Jackson again ran on the basis of a resolution by the Tennessee legislature. But Van Buren and others put together a national party organization to manage the campaign. Jackson heeded the published recommendation of the United States Telegraph, a Washington newspaper, to accept Calhoun as his running mate. Adams was nominated for reelection by a convention of state political leaders in Pennsylvania. Both Jackson and Adams gathered endorsements from other state legislatures and public assemblies.

After Jackson's landslide victory, Van Buren and other Democratic strategists used federal patronage to build an efficient national party machine—a rarity, as it has turned out, in American political history. In 1831 the short-lived Anti-Masonic party, a curious amalgam of evangelical piety and populist class resentment, held the first national party convention in American history, in Baltimore, nominating candidates for president and vice-president. Clay and Van Buren took note. Within a year the recently formed National Republican party held a national convention to nominate Clay for president, and the Democrats met to endorse Jackson for reelection. Jackson's new running mate was Van Buren, replacing Calhoun, who had quarreled with Jackson over South Carolina's attempt to nullify the so-called Tariff of Abominations. The team of Jackson and Van Buren brought to the peak of fulfillment the program of agrarian democracy launched thirty years before by Jefferson.

For the next seventy-two years, from 1836 through 1908, . . . the national party convention operated as the effective selector of finalists in the competition for president. Since convention delegates were for the most part picked by state party organizations, the choice of presidential nominees

[2]Robert V. Remini, *Andrew Jackson and the Course of American Freedom, 1822–1832* (Harper and Row, 1981), pp. 74–99; and James F. Hopkins "Election of 1824," in Arthur M. Schlesinger, Jr., and Fred L. Israel, eds., *History of American Presidential Elections 1789–1968* (Chelsea House, 1971), vol. 1, pp. 349–81.

was made mainly by professional politicians, with some coaching from their financial backers.

The emergence of strong national parties in the 1830s reinforced the trend toward making presidential electors little more than tokens, elected at large in each state on slates picked by party leaders and pledged to support the party's national ticket. Before long, the idea of an elector exercising independent judgment, as the Founders had intended, began to seem contrary to the spirit of the Constitution. By 1832 all states except Maryland and South Carolina chose electors at large and through direct popular election. In Maryland electors were chosen by popular vote in congressional districts, and in South Carolina the choice was still made by the state legislature. In 1836 Maryland went to at-large elections. South Carolina, which for many years remained Calhoun's personal satrapy, chose its electors through the legislature until after the Civil War, when it too switched to at-large popular elections.

Since that time the system of choosing electors statewide by popular election has been almost universal. Individual electors, whose very names are unknown to most voters, retain the constitutional right to cast their ballots for whom they please, and a few, the so-called faithless electors, have in fact deserted the ticket they were chosen to support. But a strong moral assumption has developed that electors are ethically bound to vote for their party's national candidates. And state party leaders have of course taken care to pick persons of proven reliability as candidates for elector. In the entire history of the electoral college, fewer than twenty electors have been "faithless"—the most recent in 1976, when a Republican elector from the state of Washington voted, possibly with an eye to the future, for Ronald Reagan rather than Gerald Ford.

TRAUMATIC ELECTIONS

In only five elections since the party system formed in the 1830s has the national political order approached or reached constitutional crisis: 1860, 1876, 1888, 1912, and 1968. The first of these traumas was, of course, by far the worst, leading to actual disruption of the federal Union and four years of bloody civil conflict.

In 1860, four major presidential candidates competed in the general election: Stephen Douglas, representing the regular Democrats; John Breckenridge, representing a southern offshoot of the Democrats determined to preserve slavery; Abraham Lincoln, representing the recently organized Republicans, dedicated at a minimum to checking the spread of slavery; and John Bell, representing the Constitutional Union party, composed mainly of southerners who wished to avert the breakup of the Union. Lincoln, with just under 40 percent of the popular vote (not counting South Carolina, which still chose electors through the legislature), carried eighteen northern states, giving him a twenty-eighty-vote majority in the electoral college. By the time of Lincoln's inauguration in March 1861, seven southern states had seceded. Civil war followed....

During the first decade after the Civil War, the Republicans used the prestige associated with preserving the Union and their control of most readmitted southern states through support from former slaves to maintain national dominance. But by the election of 1876, national economic troubles and political scandal had made the Republicans vulnerable. White-supremacy Democrats had regained power in most of the South. Samuel J. Tilden of New York, the Democratic candidate for president, ran 3 percentage points ahead of Rutherford B. Hayes of Ohio, his Republican opponent, in the popular vote. On election night Tilden appeared to have won a clear majority in the electoral college as well. Early on the morning after the election, however, two strategists from the Republican National Committee and the editor of the *New York Times,* then a Republican paper, put their heads together and discovered that if Hayes won all the electoral votes of three southern states, Florida, South Carolina, and Louisiana, still controlled by Republican administrations, he would have a one-vote majority in the electoral college. Both parties launched all-out efforts, involving widespread vote fraud (at which the Republicans excelled) and voter intimidation (the specialty of the Democrats), to secure the electoral votes of these states.

Two sets of returns from each of the contested states were delivered to Congress, which at the time had no rule on how electoral votes were to be counted. A few days before the count was to begin, Congress established a special commission, composed of five senators, five representatives, and five Supreme Court justices, to decide all disputes. The congressional members of the commission were divided evenly between the parties, but as there were only two Democrats on the Supreme Court, three of the justices had to be Republicans (a political independent who had been expected to hold the swing vote resigned at the last minute to accept election to the U.S. Senate from Illinois), giving the Republicans a one-vote overall majority.

All disputes brought before the commission were settled along strict party lines. The Democratic majority in the House threatened a filibuster to prevent completion of the count, but this maneuver failed when southern Democrats, promised by Republican leaders that Democratic administrations would be allowed to resume control of all southern states, declined to support it. Hayes's election in effect was purchased at the price of Republican acquiescence in disfranchisement of blacks by white Democrats in much of the South.

Democrats at the time customarily referred to Hayes's victory as "stolen." The consensus among modern historians is that an honest count would probably have given Hayes the electoral votes of South Carolina and Louisiana, but that Tilden was entitled to the four votes of Florida, giving him a seven-vote majority in the electoral college. It is worth noting, however, that Tilden's majorities in many southern states were achieved with the help of ruthless intimidation of black voters, who undoubtedly preferred Hayes. An honest count of those voting, therefore, probably would have elected Tilden; but a free vote by all eligible voters might well have swung victory back to Hayes. . . .

In 1888 the winner in the popular vote again lost in the electoral college. Grover Cleveland, the incumbent Democratic president, ran almost a full percentage point ahead of Benjamin Harrison, his Republican challenger, in the popular vote. But Harrison, by winning narrow majorities in New York and Indiana, was able to assemble a majority of sixty-five in the electoral college. The Democrats cried foul, but their protest focused on alleged vote fraud in the two pivotal states rather than on Cleveland's popular lead. Again the disparity between the outcomes in the popular vote and the electoral college was not itself a significant source of controversy. (Four years later, Cleveland won a rematch against Harrison.)

In 1912 the general election contest for president among three major candidates—William Howard Taft, Republican; Woodrow Wilson, Democrat; and Theodore Roosevelt, Progressive—raised the possibility that for the first time since 1824 no candidate would achieve a majority in the electoral college. In the end, Wilson was supported by the great majority of Democrats, while Taft and Roosevelt divided the normal Republican vote almost evenly. Wilson, with only 42 percent of the popular vote, carried all but eight states and 435 out of a possible 531 electoral votes.

Roosevelt's failure to make much dent in the electoral college in 1912— he carried six states for eighty-eight votes—showed that even a highly popular third-party candidate could not capture the balance of power if he crippled one of the major party candidates while taking few votes from the other. In 1968 George Wallace, running for president on the ticket of the segregationist American Independent party, almost overcame this problem. Whether or not by deliberate strategy, Wallace won a substantial bloc of electoral votes in one region, the South, while leaving Republican Richard Nixon and Democrat Hubert Humphrey competitive in most of the rest of the nation. Though Wallace attracted a much smaller share of the popular vote than Roosevelt had done in 1912, and only about half as many electoral votes, he came much closer to putting himself in the position of kingmaker or throwing the election into the House.

This possibility was not much discussed during most of the campaign because Nixon was thought to be safely ahead. But when the count came in on election night, the division between Nixon and Humphrey in the popular vote was found to be very close. For several hours after midnight, Nixon hung just short of a majority in the electoral college. Television anchormen lectured their audiences on the constitutional and political horrors likely to result from an electoral college deadlock. Finally, as dawn broke along the East Coast, Illinois put Nixon over the top, and the prospect of a constitutional crisis was packed away for another day.

SHOULD THE ELECTORAL COLLEGE BE REPLACED?

. . . The fundamental objection to the electoral college is that it is undemocratic. Not only does it represent voters unequally (since smaller states are weighted disproportionately); it also interposes an elite body of practically anonymous electors between the voters and the actual election of the president. Critics of the electoral college further charge that the states' practice of casting their electoral votes on a winner-take-all basis, rather than in proportion to the division of the popular vote within the state, is anachronistic, springing from a time when states were far more meaningful to the lives of most Americans that they are today.

The combination of disproportionate weighting of states with winner-take-all, moreover, poses a constant threat that the loser in the popular vote may be elected president. That this outcome was accepted by the voters with relative equanimity in 1888, and even in 1876 under politically trying circumstances, has no bearing on today. The contemporary public would withhold moral legitimacy from a president who had finished second in the popular vote.

On the other side, the defense most often advanced for keeping the electoral college is simply that it is there. Many politicians and commentators who freely concede that if we were creating a presidential selection system today we would not produce anything remotely resembling the electoral college contend that it has in fact functioned reasonably well and enjoys the large asset of being familiar in both its strengths and weaknesses (the "devil-we-know" argument).

Furthermore, all the generally discussed alternatives to the electoral college have serious flaws of their own. Direct election of the president by the voters would increase the likelihood of a minority president—perhaps with as little as 30 percent of the vote, as occurs in some party primaries for governor in states where nomination by the dominant party almost assures election. Direct election with a runoff would lead to political turmoil and encourage the development of independent candidacies and small parties that could demand concessions for their support in the second round. Keeping the electoral college with modifications, such as choosing electors by congressional district rather than statewide, would not be worth the effort, and the modifications would not necessarily be improvements. (Under the district system, in 1960 Nixon would have won a narrow majority, though he was perceived as having finished second in the popular vote.) Switching to a parliamentary system of any kind is chimerical and would not suit a nation as large and diverse as the United States.

Some positive arguments have been advanced in favor of the electoral college. The procedure of winner-take-all by states makes it difficult for third-party candidates to win electoral votes, thereby strongly reinforcing the two-party system, which experience has shown works best for a complex country like the United States and probably for any democratic polity. The very fact that winner-take-all often converts a narrow victory in the popular vote into a decisive margin in the electoral college (as in 1948, 1960, 1968, and 1976) gives a much-needed boost to the winning candidate's public legitimacy. Disproportionate representation of the smaller states in the electoral college protects small-state interests, as the Founders intended. On the other hand, winner-take-all causes presidential candidates to devote most of their attention to populous urban states, heavy with electoral votes and also with economic and social problems. Presidents, therefore, are likely to build their political bases in big urban states, balancing the strength of rural and small-state interests in Congress. . . .

The electoral college, like the Senate, is rooted in the Founders' intention of forming a federal republic, not a pure majoritarian democracy. Can it be that the voters' apparent lack of interest in changing the electoral college indicates that most of the public have not moved so far from the Founders' intention as many commentators now assume? The states, it is true, do not now express community interests and values to the extent they did in the eighteenth and nineteenth centuries. But the states probably possess more social vitality, as shown by periodic waves of activism in state government, than intellectual elites imagine; and in any event they may serve as surrogates within the federal system for other bases of community: economic, vocational, ideological, and ethnic.

The one feature of the current system that genuinely risks disaster is the provision for election of the president, if no candidate wins a majority in the electoral college, by the House of Representatives with each state delegation casting one vote. Under this contingency, the president could be elected by representatives of so small a minority in the national electorate that democratic values would indeed be offended.[3] And, since support by an absolute majority of state delegations is required for election, the presence of even a few delegations evenly divided between the parties and therefore unable to vote could paralyze the selection process for an indefinite period. This problem could be cured by a simple constitutional amendment stipulating that the House in this capacity should act through a majority of its entire membership, as on most other matters. Why has not such an amendment been proposed and enacted? Because most politicians, perhaps sagely, fear to touch any part of the present system. If reform began, they are convinced, it could not stop short of some kind of direct popular election of the president, with attendant pitfalls.

[3]Theoretically, delegations representing the twenty-six least-populated states, including only 18 percent of the national population, could elect the president. A winning coalition of lightly populated southern and western states would be by no means beyond the realm of political possibility.

The Legacy of Dollar Mark Hanna

PETER BAIDA

During the 1988 presidential campaign the fundraisers for Bush and Dukakis received a good deal of press attention. One of the most famous fund-raisers in history was Mark Hanna, who raised then-record sums for Republican William McKinley in 1896. Writer Peter Baida describes Hanna's fund-raising tactics, arguing that Hanna set an important precedent that continues today.

More than any other man, "Dollar Mark" Hanna invented modern political fundraising. The campaign he organized for William McKinley in 1896 established how presidential elections would be financed through most of the 20th century. He proved that a big enough torrent of money could determine the outcome of an election. And it raised a troubling question the country has still not finished wrestling with: What should a democracy full of big private fortunes, bigger corporations and well-financed interest groups do about that fact?

Marcus Alonzo Hanna, who Theodore Roosevelt once said occupied "a position of power and influence . . . such as no other man in our history has had," married the daughter of a Cleveland coal and iron merchant in 1864. Over the next 20 years he made a fortune, mainly in iron and coal, but he also helped organize the Union National Bank, bought the *Cleveland Herald* and the Opera House, and helped develop Cleveland's street railway system. In 1885 his father-in-law's company, Rhodes & Co., was reorganized under the name M.A. Hanna & Co. Its successor still exists, headquartered in Cleveland, though its main business now is plastics.

Hanna was one of the new industrialists with whom the Republican party was allying itself late in the 19th century, and as he became rich, Hanna became political. In 1880 he organized a Business Man's Republican Club in Cleveland, raised funds and led torchlight parades of businessmen on behalf of the Republican nominee, James A. Garfield. His work won Hanna a place on the Republican state committee in Ohio. From there, he wanted to put a Republican—an Ohio Republican—in the White House.

Hanna had already liked Ohio Congressman William McKinley for his proven party loyalty. He liked him more when, as chairman of the House Ways & Means Committee in 1890, McKinley emerged as an ardent advocate of a protectionist tariff generally favored by business. Soon McKinley was governor of Ohio, and on his way to the presidency.

Perhaps Hanna also liked McKinley because the "Napoleon of Canton, Ohio" was not a terribly forceful man. As described by Kansas newspaperman William Allen White, he was "a kindly, dull gentleman . . . on the whole decent, on the whole dumb," a man who, "walked among men a bronze statue, for 30 years determinedly looking for his pedestal." Theodore Roosevelt was even less impressed. McKinley, he said, "had about as much backbone as a chocolate eclair."

And the chocolate eclair's opponent in 1896 was the legendary populist William Jennings Bryan, a tornado of a man, with a tornado's power to excite and potential to do damage. Bryan scared Hanna and many others as well. Bryan's oratory whipped his audiences into a frenzy of resentment against "the few financial magnates who, in a back room, corner the money of the world."

Free coinage of silver was Bryan's solution to all the nation's woes. The runaway inflation that sober men like Andrew Carnegie, Mark Hanna and Theodore Roosevelt expected to result from free silver terrified them. For all his doubts about McKinley's backbone, Roosevelt would run in the next election, in 1900, as his vice presidential candidate, to help save the nation from the silver-tongued easy money man who "would steal from the creditors of the nation half of what they saved."

Hanna spent $100,000 of his own money on preconvention expenses for McKinley—in today's dollars, well over $1 million. Even so, it was clear that this considerable spending would be only a tiny drop in the bucket that would be needed to put his man over. After the convention, as chairman of the Republican national committee, Hanna decided a campaign of education was needed. Deeply affected by the four-year depression just ending, the voters had to be shown that free silver would be a disaster.

Yet as Bryan poured his energies into a hectic whistle-stop campaign, McKinley sat on his front porch in Canton greeting visitors. It would be undignified, McKinley felt, to stump himself. "Looking for all the world like a benign undertaker," historian Thomas Bailey wrote later, McKinley "embalmed himself for posterity."

Fortunately, McKinley did not have to tour, because Hanna organized an army of speakers—1,400 of them—to do it for him. Moreover, in a kind of early equivalent of buying masses of television time, Hanna published and distributed an unprecedented volume of campaign literature. Over 100 million documents went out from the Chicago office, 20 million from New York. This in a nation of 71 million people, of whom that year 13.9 million would vote.

All this activity required organization. In earlier campaigns, as Herbert Croly, the founder of the New Republic, wrote in his 1912 biography of Hanna, the state committees had exercised much authority. But under Hanna, as it would be forever afterward for both parties, the national committee "became the general staff of the whole army. The State Committees carried out its orders."

But even more than organization, this campaign needed money. The old system—"voluntary" contributions from appointed officials dependent on the party for their jobs—was crude but effective: "Two percent of your salary is $——. Please remit promptly."

But it was not enough. Hanna transformed American politics with one simple change. Instead of soliciting party hacks, Hanna solicited the businessmen, who most wanted to see McKinley beat Bryan.

During the week of Aug. 15, the railroad tycoon James J. Hill introduced Hanna to New York's leading financiers. In raising money, Croly wrote, Hanna "always did his best to convert the practice from a matter of political begging . . . into a matter of systematic assessment." Banks were assessed according to capital. J.P. Morgan gave $250,000. And companies: Standard Oil gave $250,000; Chicago's giant meatpackers, $400,000.

Hanna certainly raised at least $3.5 million for McKinley—and maybe as much as $10 million. He himself never revealed the total figure. But even the low estimate was more than had ever been raised before. Multiply everything by 10 or 12 to get current dollars—in real terms, it was comparable to money raised for Richard Nixon in his 1972 campaign. The Republicans hugely outspent the Democrats—perhaps by as much as 20-to-1. And they won.

So most of all, 1896 ushered in big-money politics, at a time when the apparent power of big business was already making many American uneasy. Under McKinley's successor, Theodore Roosevelt, the Tillman Act of 1907 emerged, which barred corporations and banks from contributing to federal campaigns. Throughout the 20th century, the country would try reforms seeking to undo the political transformation Hanna had wrought.

Hanna died in 1904, at 67, three years before the Tillman Act. Once one of the most powerful men in America, today he is almost forgotten except in a series of cartoon images: Hanna the bloated plutocrat, covered with dollar signs and money bags, Hanna the puppetmaster political boss, pulling McKinley's strings. Hanna was more complex than the caricature of a Republican political boss—among other things he was an early advocate of collective bargaining and the right of labor to organize. But the cartoonists had touched one truth: He had put politics on a big-business basis, and for good or ill, politics—and the nation—would never be the same again.

The Permanent Democratic Congress

NORMAN ORNSTEIN

Republicans have held the White House for twenty-eight of the last forty years. Yet during that period from 1952 to 1992, the Democrats have dominated Congress. The same voters who elected Republican George Bush by a comfortable margin in 1988 reelected Democrats in the House and Senate. Why has this pattern of Republican control of the White House and Democratic control of Congress persisted for so many years? Political scientist Norman Ornstein considers why we seem to have settled on divided government.

One of the most enduring, puzzling, and contentious phenomena of modern American political life is the persistence of firm Democratic Party majorities in Congress even as the Republicans tighten their stranglehold on the White House. The enduring nature of the phenomenon can easily be seen with a few simple numbers. The Democrats have controlled the House of Representatives for thirty-six consecutive years, and fifty-six of the last sixty; they have run the Senate for fifty of the past sixty years. The Republican Party, meanwhile, emerging in 1952 from the desert of two decades outside the White House, has successfully held the presidency seven of the past ten terms, including three in a row and five of the past six. Since 1954, the United States has had eighteen years with a Republican president and a Democratic Congress, six years with a Republican president and Senate and a Democratic House, and only twelve years with a president and Congress of the same party.

The phenomenon has puzzled more than a few observers because it seems so irrational, even perverse. While coalition governments are common in parliamentary democracies, a stark division of powers not only between institutions but also between parties was nearly unknown in the parliamentary world until the recent French experiment with "cohabitation." Even seasoned American observers have a hard time understanding or explaining how voters can opt enthusiastically and overwhelmingly for a Republican president—who has campaigned by asking for a Congress he can work with—and then turn around collectively and choose by an equally overwhelming margin a Congress run by precisely the people he has asked them to reject. Indeed, the most common explanation has been that the electorate is not consciously making these choices, but is either forced by electoral mechanics or gulled by partisan congressional wiles to behave schizophrenically.

It is not surprising that the phenomenon of divided government breeds contention; neither Democratic nor Republican partisans are happy with the humiliation implicit in a long string of electoral defeats, or with the loss of power and position in major national institutions. Democrats, the Denver Broncos of American presidential politics, are fearful that several generations of their talented youth will be shut out of any opportunity to occupy high executive-branch office, leaving the party potentially without experienced elder statesmen into the twenty-first century. Meanwhile, Republicans, the Chicago Cubs of congressional politics, have not a single member of the House of Representatives who has ever been in the majority, with Republican Leader Bob Michel sharing (with colleague William Broomfield) the dubious distinction of a record-breaking thirty-four consecutive years in the minority.

There are many reasons to explore the phenomenon of the persistent Democratic Congress through an era of Republican presidencies. There is the scholarly puzzle—sorting through why it exists. Beyond this interesting if rather academic issue lie other serious political, constitutional, and policy questions. Among other things, the persistent Democratic Congress has led to increasing frustration, and resulting hostility, among conservatives toward the First Branch of government.

For many, this phenomenon has called into question the very legitimacy of the Congress itself. Since the phenomenon cannot be natural, the unnatural causes and consequences must have produced a chamber far removed from what the Framers intended, one so unrepresentative of the public's desires and wishes that it should be denounced, delegitimized, and defanged.

At the same time, the phenomenon has led to several new schools of constitutional thought. For decades, the staunchest defenders of Congress were American conservatives, who generally agreed with James Burnham, one of the leading figures in conservative thought, whose book *Congress and the American Tradition* was a forceful, well-documented, and persuasive defense of Congress's constitutional prerogatives against the presidency. In recent years, confronted by a presidency increasingly occupied by one friendly to conservatives and a Congress uniformly run by people and a party hostile to them, many conservatives have reread the constitutional scriptures and found new meaning in them, meaning that turns Burnham's book on its head.

This would be no more than an interesting and amusing example of situational constitutionalism (the exact opposite hypocrisy, of course, is found among newly energized liberal defenders of Congress) were it not for the fact that many conservatives now propose major constitutional reforms. Some, like the line-item veto, are designed to enhance presidential authority and to weaken congressional prerogatives. Others, such as a limit on congressional terms, are aimed more directly at altering the longstanding balance of power in Congress.

Beyond these kinds of struggles, though, the persistent pattern of power unquestionably has also altered political dynamics and party psychology in Washington, shaping our policy processes and their outcomes. For all these reasons, a careful examination of the permanent Democratic Congress is in order.

EXPLAINING THE PERMANENT DEMOCRATIC CONGRESS

American history has mostly consisted of alternating eras in which one party dominates, rather than continuing close competition between parties that frequently alternate in office. Most political historians divide the two centuries of American life into five distinct eras (or systems) of party dominance, each of which ended with a party realignment. Of course, the dominance was never pure and frequently involved different patterns for Congress than for the presidency, but it was still usually clear which party was in the majority in the country. The modern era of American politics is different. While scholars have disagreed about whether recent decades have been characterized by a realignment or a dealignment, the divisions in power among the parties and institutions are very unusual, particularly in Congress. The Democrats' string of eighteen consecutive terms of majority in the House is twice as long as any other string, for either party, since the Civil War.

Why this unprecedented rule for the Democrats? To Republicans and many other observers of American politics, this Democratic success—especially through the 1980s, when Republican party identification grew and Republican presidential control and popularity expanded—cannot be a natural phenomenon, or a reflection simply of Democratic political skill or Republican organizational failure. The key question for them is, why didn't national Republican popularity translate into congressional strength?

One of the most widespread and popular theories is that the powers and perks of incumbency in Congress, which have grown exponentially in the past two decades, have created a situation in which incumbents cannot be beaten except under the most extreme circumstances. Since the Democratic Party has more incumbents and controls the system of power and perks, it has been able, by dramatically increasing the incumbent advantage, to institutionalize its majority, insulating it from normal political pressures and, in effect, mesmerizing voters to the point that they cannot hear an alternative message.

This latter assertion is what gives particular bite to the incumbency explanation for contemporary Democratic dominance of the House. It suggests directly that the advantages of incumbents have grown so far beyond the "normal" or usual pattern that incumbents win even where voters really don't want them to—in other words, that the strong Republican tides in presidential politics would have washed over Congress if it weren't for the huge supply and size of the incumbency sandbags erected in the last several years.

Proof for this contention comes from the astonishing success rates for incumbent House members, particularly in the past two elections (98.0 percent and 98.4 percent, respectively); the growing number of House members winning elections by large margins; and a catalogue of the impressive perquisites, from staff to mailing allowances and television studios, available to lawmakers. In addition, incumbents have increasingly succeeded in raising the substantial sums of money needed to run modern congressional campaigns, especially money from organized sources like political action committees, while challengers have had an increasingly rough time.

The success rates for incumbents, the phenomenon of the "vanishing marginals," the perquisites of incumbency and the widening money gap— all are quantifiable and demonstrable. There can be no question that incumbency provides enormous advantages; it at least partially explains the phenomenon of Democratic one-party control. At best, however, it is an incomplete explanation. To begin with, reelection rates for incumbents in the House have been high for more than a century, and have averaged more than 90 percent for several decades at least; they changed little with the expansion in incumbent perquisites or the alterations in campaign financing. The mid-1950s, the late 1960s, and the mid-1970s each saw a string of elections with reelection rates in the mid-nineties, each followed by elections with more incumbent defeats. It is true that the mid-1980s cycle has a marginally higher level of incumbency success than previous ones and that the cycle is likely to persist through four elections, whereas in the past only three elections were usually strung together; but then the mid-1980s have also witnessed an unusually high and sustained level of voter satisfaction with the status quo.

Persistent high rates of incumbency reelection tell us that incumbency is a powerful tool. But its power goes back many decades, before this unprecedented Democratic string. We have unquestionably seen incumbency solidify as a political phenomenon. But a sharper change than we have seen would be required before we could credit the modern revolution in congressional support for Democratic congressional hegemony.

A major part in the revolution in incumbent advantage, moreover, has come not from mechanical advantages but from the political savvy, energy level, and drive of modern politicians—people who undeniably take advantage of the perks available to them, but who also know how to reach their constituents with communications, insights, concerns, and work products that will succeed. We have some evidence to suggest that the infamous class of 1974—the "Watergate Babies"—advanced and expanded the use of innovative political techniques to solidify their own sometimes precarious positions back home, with mobile district offices, twenty-four-hour constituent hotlines, and other modern marketing techniques. Whether they were pioneers or not, they and their contemporaries knew how to communicate and campaign. As the average age of members of Congress has de-clined (contrary to conventional wisdom, we have one of the least geriatric Congresses in modern times), the energy level has probably risen; combined with much more and more-regular jet transportation out of National Air-port, which lets lawmakers spend full weeks in Washington and still have a highly visible and energetic presence in their districts, we have a formula for incumbent popularity back home.

In a recent issue of *U.S. News & World Report,* Michael Barone reported on his visits to the districts of two Democratic House incumbents who have been regular targets of Republican campaign committees, Robert Carr of Michigan and Tom Downey of New York. Barone portrayed two ener-getic, intelligent, and attractive individuals who understand and respond to the local issues that matter most to their constituents, and whose style, openness, and drive overcome some of their liberal positions in the minds of many more-conservative voters. Carr and Downey would doubtless have more trouble without the staff, franking privilege, and other benefits avail-able to every incumbent—but even without the perks, Barone's reporting shows, they would not be easy to beat.

TESTING THE INCUMBENCY THEORY

Incumbents' advantages can be examined from many angles. As with Sher-lock Holmes's insight about the dog that didn't bark, the most significant evidence that bears on the role of incumbency may come from the seats that have no incumbents—the open seats. If the most pointed theory of incum-bency advantage is true—if Republican majorities have been thwarted by the shield of incumbency—then we should find major Republican successes *where those advantages are absent.* We don't.

If the incumbency theory holds true, there should be many seats pre-viously held by Democratic incumbents that go over to the Republicans when the incumbents leave those seats—and many fewer open seats held by Republican incumbents going over to Democrats when those seats open up. But the reality is the opposite. As Table I shows, since 1954 Republi-cans have won 77 open Democratic seats in the House of Representatives; Democrats during the same time period have won 101 open Republican seats—or 57 percent of the total party turnovers in the open seats. Repub-licans did do much better than their overall average in the tidal years of 1972 and 1980—but they did not distinguish themselves in the remainder of the seventies and eighties, including George Bush's victory year of 1988.

If the incumbency theory were correct, we should also see a pattern of GOP success in *special elections,* with seats opened up in the middle of the election cycle because of an incumbent's death or resignation. Since 1954 there have been 188 special elections to the House; the GOP's net gain from these elections has been four seats. Since Ronald Reagan's election in

TABLE I. Open House Seats Changing Party, 1954–1988

YEAR	D → R	R → D
1954	2	3
1956	2	4
1958	0	14
1960	6	6
1962	2	3
1964	5	8
1966	4	3
1968	2	4
1970	6	8
1972	9	5
1974	2	13
1976	3	7
1978	8	6
1980	10	1
1982	3	5
1984	5	1
1986	7	8
1988	1	2

Source: *Vital Statistics on Congress,* 1989–1990.

1980, there have been thirty-three special elections to the House; the GOP has made a net gain of one. In short, there is no evidence here for a GOP tide thwarted solely by incumbent advantages.

True, if there were no incumbent advantages, the race for majority in the House would be considerably tighter; Republicans, after all, have more or less kept parity with the Democrats in open seats. But that is like saying that if there were no seven-foot-tall players in the National Basketball Association, the Washington Bullets could win the championship. Incumbents could be outlawed from Congress, just as seven-footers could from the NBA, but until then guile and discipline are required to overcome their natural advantages.

Why haven't Republicans done better in open seats? Proponents of the incumbency theory often point to *gerrymandering,* the partisan drawing of the boundaries of congressional districts. The claim is that the redistricting process has been rigged to create safe seats for each party, so that the opposition can't win even when incumbents leave. It is true that the vast majority of open seats, like the vast majority of incumbents' seats, do not change party in a given election (a phenomenon that precedes this era of Democratic control). It is also true that more seats have become safe for both parties in recent decades. But many open seats still do change parties, and if the theory of an underlying Republican majority were correct, more of them would change toward the Republicans than toward the Democrats.

There are other explanations—starting with the parties' political will and skill. If latter-day incumbents are nearly impossible to beat, then political parties have to devise other strategies to win seats in Congress. They must target and challenge those incumbents who are vulnerable for reasons of age, scandal, inattention to constituent concerns, or voting record, and they must lay the groundwork necessary to win a district when an invulnerable incumbent leaves office. This means having an experienced, well-known candidate in place at the right time, with an experienced campaign team that knows the district's geography and politics.

The latter strategy means viewing congressional elections as investments; often it requires fielding and financing a candidate who cannot win, in order to build experience and name recognition for a second try. Republicans have consistently failed to do so. Consider, for example, the number of *uncontested seats*—seats held by one party where the opposition fails to put up even a token challenge. In most cases, obviously, seats go uncontested because incumbents are so strong that a challenger would have little if any hope of succeeding. But incumbents do not live forever; failing to challenge them means failing to create congressional campaign organizations and to cultivate viable candidates to run when the chance of winning increases.

From 1978 to 1988, on average, 14 percent of races for the House of Representatives went uncontested. Of these a total of 281 were held by Democrats—while only eighty-four were held by Republicans. In 1988 alone, fifty-eight Democrats were unopposed compared to only twenty Republicans. Most of the unopposed Democrats were Southerners, usually from conservative districts; it is no wonder that Republicans have at best a mediocre record at winning Southern open seats.

One of the races left uncontested in 1988 was that of House Speaker Jim Wright, despite the conservative nature of his Fort Worth district and the fact that the House investigation of allegations of ethics violations had begun well before the election's filing deadline. When Wright resigned in 1989 and a special election was held to fill the seat, Republicans had neither an experienced candidate with name recognition nor a competent staff in place. As a result, they narrowly lost an election that offered a golden opportunity for a major GOP victory; they now have much less chance to defeat the new incumbent, Democrat Pete Geren, in 1990.

Of course, few critics of incumbency advantages are motivated simply by partisan or ideological concerns. Many believe that incumbents from both parties in Congress have engaged in symbiotic, if not conspiratorial, behavior to harden their silos against any outside challenge. This, congressional critics charge, has so limited turnover in Congress that even the Supreme Soviet has more openness and fresh faces by comparison.

To one who walked the corridors of the Capitol in the late 1960s, the heyday of the senority system when greybeards were omnipresent, the idea that today's Congress is notably geriatric and unchanging is laughable. A glance at the House floor in the 101st Congress shows many more young faces than old—a casual impression of turnover that is borne out by the numbers. Turnover in Congress has many causes—retirements, runs at other offices, deaths, defeats in primaries—and the turnover in the past two decades has been high.

As House Speaker Tom Foley has pointed out, 93 percent of the House's members arrived after he did in 1965; 81 percent began serving after 1974, and 55 percent were first sworn in during the past decade. Since 1955, the average number of senior House members—those having served seven terms or more—has been 138, or 31.7 percent; the current number is 146, or 33.6 percent of the House. The number of senior lawmakers was much lower in the mid- and late 1970s, after many retirements and a series of elections in which more incumbents were defeated because many voters wanted change. The last few elections—1984, 1986, and 1988—reflect the cyclical changes typical of American politics: fewer retirements, since the pool of likely retirees is smaller; fewer incumbent defeats, since voters opt largely for the status quo. We do not require constitutional change to expect more retirements and more incumbent defeats in the early or mid-1990s, as the retirement pool is replenished and voters opt for change.

Certainly, as David Broder has pointed out, turnover does not mean competition, and competition has clearly declined in the House; fewer and fewer House seats are closely contested from one election to the next. This is a real and vexing problem, one that stems more from the difficulties of securing good challengers than anything else. I discuss some of the recruitment problems below, but it is worth emphasizing here that more competitive House elections will require new campaign-finance laws that make it easier for challengers to raise the money necessary to run serious races in large and diverse districts. The main thrust of most reformers, including Common Cause and the Democratic Party, is to limit spending on elections. Well-meaning or not, spending limits would almost certainly harm challengers, limiting their ability to get their messages across in districts that require sizable sums of money to do so.

Incumbent advantage could be dramatically reduced by forcing incumbents out through a constitutional amendment limiting terms of service. To do so would solve a problem, lack of turnover, that doesn't exist; would drastically shorten the institutional memory of the Congress, encouraging historical policy mistakes to repeat themselves; and would tremendously increase the clout of congressional staff, lawyers, lobbyists, pundits, bureaucrats, public-relations specialists, journalists, and other permanent denizens of the Capitol whose terms of service are not limited. It would probably bring into Congress a group of overly ambitious people viewing the job not, as the amendment's proponents believe, as a station on their way back to normal life in their communities, but as a stepping stone to higher office or major money. They would have little stake in the House as an institution, and little incentive to think about the broader and longer-term implications of their actions. Perhaps current members also lack those incentives, but a constitutional amendment should promise something more.

THE GERRYMANDERING THEORY

The evils of gerrymandering have been a favorite target of political reformers for decades; increasingly, they have been joined by Republican Party officials and conservative ideologues like the editors of the *Wall Street Journal*, who charge that gerrymandering has wildly distorted the House and made it an unrepresentative institution. Republicans and the *Journal* have been particularly exercised over the fact that the Democrats' percentage of seats in the House of Representatives has consistently exceeded their nationwide proportion of votes—evidence in their minds (not to mention their fundraising literature and editorials) of the unfair bias created by partisan Democratic gerrymandering.

There is no question that a clever and ruthless partisan who controls redistricting can wreak havoc on the opposition party. Democrats, led by Phil Burton, did so in California after the 1980 census; Republicans returned the favor in Indiana. But there are precious few additional examples that show clear-cut and extreme partisan advantages. Indeed, the single largest effect of redistricting around the country tends to be the bipartisan agreements in most states that end up protecting incumbents of both parties from the kinds of colossal shakeups that would create larger turnover.

As for the celebrated gap between votes and seats, its notoriety, along with the broader attack on gerrymandering, has stemmed largely from a misunderstanding of the inherent nature of the American political system, along with a lack of understanding of basic differences between Democratic and Republican voters.

The American political system, like the British system, is one of single-member, "first past the post" districts. Each has one winner, usually the one who captures the most votes (some have thresholds and run-off provisions). All such systems have a built-in votes/seats distortion: the party that gains a majority or plurality of the votes cast nationwide will almost certainly win a greater proportion of seats.

Why is this the case? Political scientists and mathematicians have written many books quantifying the reasons and the relationships. To be simple and brief, a first-past-the-post system means a lot of "wasted" votes—but fewer for the more successful party. Candidates who win with 51 percent of the votes "waste" a few of their votes; they needed only 50.1 percent to win. Candidates who lose with 49 percent of the votes "waste" all their votes; the result would have been the same if the candidates got zero.

In a system like ours, each party ends up with a lot of candidates who get 45 percent of the votes and end up with nothing, and a lot of candidates who get 80 percent of the votes and win when 50.1 percent would do. The variations, however, do not exactly cancel each other out. All things being equal, if a party in a two-party system captures 52 or 53 percent of the votes, that party is likely to end up with 55 or 56 percent of the seats, having been more efficient at translating its support into winning seats.

The skew can be even greater if a third party seriously contests an election. Margaret Thatcher's Conservatives, for example, won a staggering 58 percent of the seats in the British House of Commons—with barely more than 40 percent of the votes! (The *Wall Street Journal*, for some reason, has never questioned the Thatcher government's legitimacy on this basis.)

Through twenty-two elections in the United States since 1946, the average "bonus" for the majority party has been 6.2 percent more seats than votes. Since the "outrageous" gerrymandering after the 1980 census, the average bonus has been 6.0 percent—*less*, in other words, than the overall postwar average! On the one occasion in this modern era that the Republicans captured a majority of votes, they also took advantage of the built-in bonus. In 1946 Republicans captured 53.5 percent of the votes cast nationwide, and received 56.7 percent of the seats in the House, a bonus of 3.2 percent.

Why would the GOP bonus have been less? Other evidence suggests that Democrats generally tend to do better than Republicans in the votes/seats ratio—but not for malevolent reasons of gerrymandering. Rather, there are simple differences in the natural bases of party support. Democrats, not surprisingly, tend to attract votes more from poorer, worse-educated, and more minority-based constituencies than do Republicans. Their voters turn out less—and their districts, as a results, have lower turnout.

Assume that you have two fairly drawn districts of equal population, one a poor inner-city district that elects a Democrat, the other an affluent suburban district that elects a Republican. In the former district, 150,000 voters turn out; in the latter, 225,000. The Republicans have captured 60 percent of the votes cast in these two districts, but only 50 percent of the seats. Is that inappropriate? Not by most standards.

Table II shows the distribution, by levels of voter turnout, of contested seats won by the Republican and Democratic parties in the 1988 congres-

TABLE II. Contested House Elections in 1988

TURNOUT	DEMOCRATIC WINNERS	REPUBLICAN WINNERS
Less than 125,000	9	0
125,000–150,000	13	2
150,000–175,000	38	6
175,000–200,000	50	41
200,000–225,000	54	51
225,000–250,000	24	31
250,000–275,000	7	13
More than 275,000	7	11

Source: *Congressional Quarterly's Weekly Report,* May 6, 1989. There were seventy-eight uncontested elections.

sional elections. To summarize it, Democrats won 110 of their contested seats—54.5 percent—in districts where fewer than 200,000 people voted. Republicans won only 49 of their seats—31.6 percent—in such districts. In contrast, Republicans won 35.5 percent of their seats, fifty-five in all, in districts where more than 225,000 people voted; Democrats won only 19 percent of their seats, or thirty-eight, in such high-turnout places. The differences in party bases, and in the resulting district turnouts, alone account for many of the differences between seats and votes, leaving the natural bias of the first-past-the-post system to account for less than the standard formulae might suggest. Indeed, given that the average bonus in the 1980s was less than the forty-four-year norm, one might even argue that the Republicans, not the Democrats, won the redistricting wars of the past decade.

Bonus or no, the overall Republican problem in failing to win the House is best characterized by another set of numbers. Since 1952—the last time the GOP had a majority in the House—it has averaged only 45.3 percent of the votes cast nationwide. Except for 1956, when the Republicans captured 48.7 percent of the votes cast, the party has not exceeded 48 percent in the past thirty-six years. The GOP, in other words, has not come close during its entire period of minority status to winning a majority of votes for the House. During this same era, the Republican Party has averaged 53.1 percent of the votes cast for president. A prime explanation for this disparity is the quality of congressional candidates.

REPUBLICANS AND RECRUITMENT

In a broad sense, the Republican failure to win more House seats is directly related to a lack of success at candidate recruitment. Over the past several election cycles, the Republican Party has had great difficulty recruiting consistently top-flight candidates to run for the House of Representatives, either to challenge incumbent Democrats or to run for open seats. The reasons include:

- *the vicious cycle.* A party that is in the minority can offer potential candidates fewer incentives than the majority party, which can hold out the prospect of future subcommittee or committee chairmanships, extra staff, and other perks of majority status. The longer the GOP has been in the minority, the more remote look its chances of vaulting into the majority, and the more difficult it is to get ambitious people to be lured to run—and as a result, the longer it continues to occupy the minority.
- *the partisan culture.* While one must be careful about overgeneralizing, it is nonetheless clear that cultural definitions of career desirability and success vary between the parties. For the Republican Party's best

and brightest, the careers of choice are business, commerce, or the professions. Politics, especially in Washington, is not high on the list. For Democrats, a career in politics or government is much more highly prized. This difference is partly a matter of:

- *philosophy.* To a considerable degree, the Republican philosophical and political message for the past several decades has been, to put it simply, "Let's get government in Washington out of our lives." To recruit for Congress based on that message means saying to a prospective candidate, "Spend your life in government in Washington."

- *political reforms.* Well-intentioned, necessary, and important though they may be, there is no question that the web of conflict-of-interest and financial-disclosure requirements put into place in the 1970s and 1980s has made it more difficult to recruit people for public service in Washington, especially for elective office. The more complicated one's life and finances, the more sacrifices are now required to run for and to serve in high office, and the more likely one is to be reluctant to bare all for open public scrutiny. While this phenomenon affects both parties, Republicans, who tend to turn more to business executives and entrepreneurs, are affected more.

- *the GOP executive branch.* Many of the Republican Party's best and brightest who are interested in politics and public service have an alternative to running for Congress—namely, an appointive position in the executive branch. An appointment as an assistant secretary or deputy administrator of an agency may require financial sacrifice and Senate confirmation, but it involves more authority than minority membership in Congress and it does not require the fundraising, time commitment, and politicking necessary to run a competitive race for Congress—which still may not succeed. Ambitious and politically attuned Democrats, by contrast, have no executive alternative; for them Congress is the only game in town.

To be sure, the Republican Party's top political figures are aware of many of these problems, and they have taken steps to rectify them. Perhaps the most significant move was that of Ed Rollins into the top slot of the National Republican Congressional Committee (NRCC), where he has begun aggressively to target vulnerable Democratic incumbents, including those who may require two election cycles to defeat, and to recruit and finance top-flight candidates with name recognition and political skill, pledging to support them over more than one election, if necessary. This is a sharp departure from GOP practices of the past, and the change has not come easily; Rollins has been attacked vigorously by many Republicans more comfortable with the previous easy ways. But if Rollins is given the time and resources, his efforts are likely to bear fruit down the road.

At the same time, a number of Republicans like Jack Kemp, Vin Weber, Bill Gradison, and Newt Gingrich have been trying to find a more positive message for the Republican Party that goes beyond simply getting Washington off our backs and government out of our lives. These efforts may make for a more exciting message, and may increase the number of people eager to devote much of their lives to acting upon it.

At least some of the Republican support for the congressional pay raise in 1989, moreover, stemmed from the recognition that it would help recruit good candidates for Congress. And there is more openness in Republican ranks to significant changes in the campaign-finance laws that go beyond heavy-handed and unrealistic mechanisms designed simply to punish Democrats or to hobble incumbents; significantly, some of the proposed changes even involve tax credits—indirect public funds—to foster more competition in congressional elections.

All of these things should and will make a difference. But there is another, ironic, roadblock for the Republican Party to consider.

COUNTERCYCLICAL POLITICS

In the 130 years of American political history since the start of the Civil War, we have had eighty years in which the presidency and both houses of Congress were held by the same party, twenty-two years in which the presidency and one house of Congress were held by the same party, and twenty-eight years in which one party held the presidency and the other held both houses of Congress; the last arrangement, of course, has mostly occurred in recent years. But through each of these political arrangements, across different eras of modern American history, one relation has held almost universally constant: *the longer a party holds the White House, the worse it does in Congress.*

Every party has left the White House with fewer members of Congress than it had when it entered. The Republicans held the presidency from Lincoln's election in 1860 until Grover Cleveland's election in 1884. When Lincoln was inaugurated, his party held 59 percent of the House of Representatives; after the 1882 election (the last before the GOP's 1884 departure from the White House) it held 36.3 percent of the House. The GOP held the White House again from McKinley's election in 1896 until Wilson's election in 1912. It began this era of presidential control with 57.1 percent of the House; its last election in control left it with 41.3 percent. Woodrow Wilson, conversely, began his two terms as Democratic president with 66.9 percent of the House; after his sixth-year election, his party held 43.9 percent. (In every case, incidentally, the percentage took an additional sharp dive with the following presidential-election year.) Table III shows the figures from Warren Harding to the present.

Of course, part of what is reflected in these numbers is the well-known phenomenon of the midterm loss for the president's party: in every off-year election save one since the Civil War, the president's party has lost seats in

TABLE III. Presidents and Congressional Seats, 1920–1988

PRESIDENT	YEAR	PRESIDENT'S PARTY		OPPOSITION PARTY	
		Percent	Number	Percent	Number
Harding (R)	1920	69.5	301/433	30.2	131
Coolidge (R)	1922*	51.7	225/435	47.1	205
	1924	56.9	247/434	42.2	183
	1926*	54.5	237/435	44.8	195
Hoover (R)	1928	61.4	267/435	38.4	167
	1930*	49.2	214/435	50.6	220
Roosevelt (D)	1932	71.8	310/432	27.1	117
	1934*	73.8	319/432	23.8	103
	1936	76.4	331/433	20.5	89
	1938*	60.8	261/429	38.2	164
	1940	62.5	268/435	37.2	162
	1942*	50.7	218/430	48.4	208
	1944	55.8	242/434	43.8	190
Truman (D)	1946*	43.3	188/434	56.4	245
	1948	60.4	268/435	39.3	171
	1950*	53.9	234/434	45.8	199
Eisenhower (R)	1952	51.0	221/433	48.7	211
	1954*	46.7	203/435	53.3	232
	1956	46.2	200/433	53.8	233
	1958*	35.1	153/436	64.9	283
Kennedy (D)	1960	60.2	263/437	39.8	174
	1962*	59.3	258/435	40.7	177
Johnson (D)	1964	67.8	295/435	32.2	140
	1966*	56.9	247/434	43.1	187
Nixon (R)	1968	44.1	192/435	55.9	243
	1970*	41.5	180/434	58.5	254
	1972	44.4	192/432	55.3	239
Ford (R)	1974*	33.1	144/435	66.9	291
Carter (D)	1976	67.1	292/435	32.9	134
	1978*	63.7	276/433	36.2	157
Reagan (R)	1980	44.1	192/435	55.9	243
	1982*	38.0	165/434	62.0	269
	1984	41.9	182/434	58.1	252
	1986*	40.7	177/435	59.3	258
Bush (R)	1988	40.2	175/435	59.8	260

Source: *Congressional Quarterly's Guide to U.S. Elections,* Second Edition.
(*) indicates off-year election.

the House. But we also see two other phenomena at work: a party almost never regains as many seats in its president's reelection year as it lost in the previous off-year contest, and the losses in the second midterm election of a two-term president—the fabled "six-year itch"—are nearly always greater than in the first.

I lack the space in this article to explain in detail why the midterm-loss and six-year-itch cycles occur. Put in the simplest terms, though, when things are going badly, especially in the economy, as they often are in a president's second and sixth years, the public will blame the president's party; but when things are going well, as they usually are when an incumbent president gets reelected, voters are inclined to give a pat on the back to all incumbent office seekers. In off years, most presidents and their parties find themselves on the defensive; in presidential reelection years, presidents run by proclaiming that "things are good, let's keep them that way." Differences between turnouts and party coalitions in presidential and in off-year elections, as well as cycles of candidate recruitment, also account for midterm losses.

The cycle of presidential elections and off years has persisted for well over a century; yet in no other period of partisan dominance of the White House did the opposition party grab longstanding control over Congress. What makes the contemporary era unique? The roots lie in the 1930s and the 1950s, the Roosevelt and Eisenhower eras.

The drama of the Great Depression, coming after a decade of uniform Republican control, gave the Democrats a huge margin of power to work with in 1932. The Democrats had captured the House in 1930, after the 1929 crash; with the landslide of 1932, their edge increased overwhelmingly, to 72 percent of the membership. Both Woodrow Wilson and his successor, Warren Harding, had entered the White House with margins in the House of Representatives nearly as large—but they fell back dramatically in the off-year elections of 1914 and 1922, respectively.

1934 was different. For the only time in modern history, a president's party actually gained seats in the House in the off year. Democrats moved to 319 seats, or 74 percent of the total, and expanded to 331 seats, or more than 76 percent with FDR's reelection in 1936. (Democrats also held nearly 80 percent of the Senate after the 1936 election.) From that point on, the typical patterns took over—but the erosion in congressional numbers in the president's party came from such a huge base that the effect was limited. Democrats lost seventy seats in Roosevelt's "six-year itch" election of 1938, and lost another fifty seats in his last midterm election, 1942—but they still managed to retain a majority!

When it all finally caught up with the Democratic Party in 1946, after a full fourteen years in the White House, their loss of the House was narrow enough that they were able to regain control on the heels of Harry Truman's comeback victory in 1948. When Eisenhower won the presidency in 1952, he, unlike Roosevelt, had no party majority already in place from the preceding midterm election, and his coattails were too short to build any significant cushion against the coming midterm loss. Republicans lost the Congress in 1954, fell back by a huge margin in the six-year itch of 1958, and have been in a hole ever since. Every time they start to emerge from that hole, the counter-cycle of presidential politics deepens it a little more.

Without the large advantages of incumbents, and without modern redistricting, the outcomes of the last two decades in party control of Congress might still have been different. But they most certainly would have been different, and more advantageous to the Republicans, if the Democrats had won the presidency more often. (For obvious reasons, however, the Republican Party is unwilling to consider deliberately losing the White House in order to achieve the elusive goal of capturing the House of Representatives.)

FUTURE PROSPECTS

Does this then mean that the Republicans will not capture the Congress until the Democrats achieve a two-term presidency? Not necessarily. The GOP's commitment to the arduous and difficult tasks of building a candidate base, investing in districts where victory might be years away, and capturing a new philosophical excitement may pay off in the near future.

There are other favorable signs for the Republicans. The reapportionment and redistricting of the early 1990s are unlikely to result in a large partisan edge for either party, but by redrawing district lines for nearly all incumbents in the House, they may create new opportunities for turnover. For many reasons, including generational change, the trauma of new district lines, and changes in campaign rules, we are also likely to see more retirements from the House in 1992, leading to more open seats. If Congress enacts effective campaign-finance reform before then, a system that creates opportunities for challengers may enable more of them actively to contest seats. If the underlying, rumbling discontent in the electorate about Washington-politics-as-usual gets ignited by a catalytic event, such as the savings-and-loan scandal, the patterns of the past few decades may be broken, and large numbers of incumbents of both parties may find themselves unemployed.

These are all shaky, conditional statements, but they do indicate that the House may change significantly before the turn of the century. Would such a change be desirable? Beyond the obvious partisan considerations, many reformers, including such Democrats as James Sundquist and Lloyd Cutler, believe that the pattern of divided government is harmful, even pernicious. In terms of policy, however, political scientist David Mayhew has found no evidence of any real difference, in quantity or quality of outputs, between periods of unified and of divided government in America.

As for the American public, surveys for decades have consistently indicated that two-third of voters prefer having a president of one party and a Congress of the other. They are not losing sleep over our partisan institutional arrangements.

Nevertheless, the experience of the Senate, which the Republicans controlled from 1981 through 1986, shows that a change in party control can be healthy for both majority and minority—giving each side the perspective of the other, including the responsibility required to be in the majority and the frustration inherent in being in the minority. The Senate today, run by Democrats, operates better, in my judgment, than it would if the GOP had not won a majority a decade ago with Ronald Reagan's landslide. The House could benefit from the same change in perspective.

At the same time, the lengthy period of divided majorities, unprecedented in American history, has created damaging turmoil in the psyches of both parties. Schizophrenic government has led to schizophrenic parties. Democrats and Republicans are at the same time swaggering and uncertain, secure and paranoid. Each side is confident in its own hegemonic domain, but thrown off stride by its abject failure to extend its popularity and control to the other's turf.

Each party is fearful that it will make a mistake and lose its own empire— not just for one term, but for decades. And each side is hopeful that it can finally capture its rightful, complete majority, by forcing the other to make the fatal mistake. The result is passive-aggressive politics, the politics of avoiding blame. Each side is so concerned about avoiding a mistake, and so intent on tarring the opposition, that taking risks to make better policy is increasingly uncommon.

Conventional wisdom holds that the safer lawmakers are, the more willing and able they are to take risks and to cast unpopular votes. The reality, in the contemporary period, is the opposite. The safer are the seats in the House, the more skittish are the members. Changes that would bring more competition to House elections would help to break this pattern, even if they did not automatically result in a different majority party. Most desirable would be campaign-finance reform that would open up new sources of money to candidates and make it easier to run competitive campaigns, starting with generous tax credits and matching funds for individual in-state contributions, and some "seed money" mechanism to pay for start-up costs for fledgling challengers.

Campaign-finance reform of this sort is desirable, as is more real competitiveness in House elections. But there is no case to be made for significant constitutional reform. Like it or not, today's Congress legitimately reflects the electorate's wishes; it is not an artificial and illegitimate construct of a sneaky Democratic Party playing by its own set of rules. To win the House and break the pattern, Republicans need to change their outlook and their campaign approaches—not to alter the fundamental constitutional rules that we have used for two centuries.

Republicans tried the latter strategy once before; frustrated by Democratic dominance of the presidency under Roosevelt, the GOP pushed through the 22nd Amendment to the Constitution, limiting presidents to two terms. Ronald Reagan, among others, has forcefully underscored the self-defeating folly of that approach, arguing against its weakening of the presidency. It would be far better to mobilize to repeal the 22nd Amendment than to repeat the mistake by limiting tenure in Congress now that political currents have changed.

2. Campaign Finance

It is often said that money is the lifeblood of politics. Although congressional challengers may occasionally defeat their better-funded incumbent opponents, the incumbent advantage in congressional fund-raising is commonly cited as an explanation for the high reelection rates among Senate and, especially, House incumbents.

Among presidential candidates, access to sufficient money is vital. Activists in the campaign of Richard Gephardt in 1988 argued that the shortage of funds was critical in their candidate's poor showing on Super Tuesday. Gephardt himself later noted that instead of campaigning so diligently in Iowa, he should have spent some of his time raising funds.

Yet spending is not a sure guarantee of success. On Super Tuesday, George Bush won both in states where he spent the most money *and* in states in which he was outspent, but among Democrats only Jesse Jackson did well in states in which he did not spend substantial funds. The clear message from Super Tuesday is that well-known, popular presidential candidates can succeed without outspending their opponents, but money is necessary for unknown contenders to mount a campaign that will bring them name recognition and votes.

Congressional incumbents, their challengers, and those who have sought the presidency generally complain most loudly about the time spent raising money. In 1990, the median Senator raised more than $10,000 a week for six years to fund his or her reelection campaign, while the median House member raised more than $3,000 a week. In a survey conducted by the Center for Responsive Politics, a Washington-based research institute that studies campaign finance, more than half of the Senate respondents said that fund-raising significantly reduced their time for legislative work, and nearly half of the electorally safer House members reported that fund-raising had some effect on their legislative time. More than 86 percent of Senate staffers indicated that their fund-raising duties cut into the time they could devote to legislative duties.

Over the past three decades, the costs of elections have escalated sharply. Although we still spend less on national elections than we do to market common household products, critics charge that the high cost of campaigns may force candidates to take money that comes with some strings attached. Charles Keating, whose large gifts to several U.S. Senators lead to an ethics investigation, said that his contributions were intended to influence the behavior of these Senators. Most political science literature suggests that contributions from interest groups

(PACs) do not significantly influence legislative votes, but a survey by the Center for Responsive Politics found that a surprising percentage of members of Congress admitted anonymously that contributions had affected their votes. The sources of campaign funds are therefore an important issue for democratic governance.

Campaigns for the Presidents are funded differently from campaigns for Congress. Presidential candidates raise their funds primarily from individual contributors, and the first $250 of these contributions are matched by the federal government. Interest groups and parties are insignificant sources of direct funds to the candidate's campaign committees. In contrast, House incumbents raise more than half of their funds from interest groups and parties, and House challengers provide substantial portions of their funds from their own checkbooks.

The readings in this chapter focus on the sources of funds for presidential and Senate campaigns. In the first reading, Herbert Alexander details these sources for presidential candidates in their primary and general election campaigns. He shows the variety of ways that money reaches presidential campaigns—some directly, but much of it indirectly.

Edward Walsh describes in the second reading the importance of "seed money" in presidential campaigns. For unknown candidates like Bruce Babbitt (former Democratic Governor of Arizona), early money was essential to any hope he had of winning an upset victory in the early contests. Such an upset might have given him the momentum to raise additional funds and attract volunteers.

The next two readings, by Charles Babcock and Richard Morin, detail where and when Bush and Dukakis raised their funds during the primaries. Both candidates assembled fund-raising teams who personally solicited their friends and colleagues for gifts. Bush and Dukakis raised substantial sums in gifts of $1,000, the maximum allowable by law. Yet the sources of these funds differed.

Clifford Brown, Lynda Powell, and Clyde Wilcox describe the contributors who gave at least $200 to presidential candidates in 1988 and compare those with givers of "serious money" in 1972. They report that those candidates with an expressed ideological appeal solicited contributions primarily through direct mail, while moderate candidates more frequently built personal networks of fund-raising.

Finally, Charles Babington describes the fund-raising empire of Senator Jesse Helms. Helms has raised enormous sums for his Senate reelection bids, and his PAC and foundations are major sources of funds. Like ideological presidential candidates, Helms raises his funds primarily through the mail. His appeals on ideology attract contributors across the country.

Financing the Presidential Elections, 1988

HERBERT E. ALEXANDER

Money enters presidential elections through a variety of channels. During the primaries, candidates solicit their constituencies for contributions, which are then partially matched by the federal government. In the general election, an equal subsidy goes from the government to both major parties, but this is supplemented by independent spending by PACs, communications by labor unions to their members, and "soft money" funds for each party. Professor Herbert Alexander has written a series of books on campaign finance, the most recent of which is Financing the 1988 Election *(with Monica Bauer). Here he describes the sources of funds in the 1988 election.*

In the 1970s the laws regulating federal election campaign financing in the United States underwent dramatic changes. In regard to presidential campaigns, enactments including public funding, contribution limits, expenditure limits and disclosure requirements were intended to minimize opportunities for undue financial influence on officeholders and to make the election process more open and competitive. The laws have accomplished some of their aims, but they also have had some unintended, and not always salutary, consequences. The degree to which the laws have failed to achieve their intended effects testifies at least as much to the inventiveness of political actors in circumventing the laws and to the intractability of election campaign finance in a pluralistic society as to the deficiencies of the laws themselves.

The Federal Election Campaign Act of 1971 (FECA), the Revenue Act of 1971, and the FECA Amendments of 1974, 1976, and 1979 thoroughly revised the rules of the game for political candidates, parties and contributors. For presidential campaigns, the laws provided for public matching funds for qualified candidates in the prenomination period, public treasury grants to pay the costs of the two major parties' national nominating conventions, and public treasury grants for the major party general election candidates. They also established criteria whereby minor parties and new parties and their candidates can qualify for public funds to pay nominating convention and general election campaign costs.

The public funds, earmarked through a federal income tax checkoff, were intended to help provide or to supply in entirety the money serious candi-

Source: Adapted from Chapters 2 and 3 of Alexander and Bauer, *Financing the 1988 Election*, 1991: Westview Press, Boulder, CO.

dates need to present themselves and their ideas to the electorate. In the prenomination period, public funding was intended to make the nomination process more competitive and to encourage candidates to broaden their bases of support by seeking out large numbers of relatively small contributions matchable with public funds. In the general election period, flat grants to major party candidates were intended to provide the basic money needed soon after the nominating conventions, to be supplemented by national party coordinated expenditures on behalf of the presidential ticket.

Contribution limits and expenditure limits also were enacted, although the Supreme Court subsequently ruled that spending limits are permissible only in publicly-financed campaigns. These laws were intended to control large donations with their potential for corruption, to minimize financial disparities among candidates, and to reduce opportunities for abuse. Finally, laws requiring full and timely disclosure of campaign receipts and expenditures were put in place to help the electorate make informed choices among candidates and to make it possible to monitor compliance with the campaign finance laws by establishment of the Federal Election Commision.

Four presidential elections have now been conducted under the FECA, its amendments and its companion laws, a sufficient experience from which to draw some conclusions about the impact of the laws and to determine whether they have had their intended effects. The costs to the voters, the taxpayers and the candidates' campaigns, have been considerable. An assessment is in order of how well the public funding system for presidential campaigns, and the accompanying expenditure limits, served the candidates and the American people.

THE 1988 PRESIDENTIAL COSTS

In the 1987–1988 election cycle, political candidates and committees at all levels—federal, state and local—spent $2.7 billion on political campaigns. About 18.5 percent, or $500 million, was spent to elect a President. . . . Drawing together all reported expenditures, some $233.5 million was spent by and on behalf of candidates seeking nomination (through June 30, 1989), $42.1 million related to the two major party conventions, and $208.3 million in the general election period. Miscellaneous spending accounted for the remainder of the $500 million total.

While the 1988 spending was high, when seen in perspective in Table 1, the long-term trends are not so alarming. When adjusted for inflation since 1960, the costs of presidential campaigns have increased only by a factor of four, whereas aggregate unadjusted costs have risen almost seventeen-fold from 1960–1988.

The $500 million costs, however, represent a whopping 54 percent increase from the 1984 cost of $325 million. With no incumbent running in 1988, the presidency was wide open for the first time in 20 years.

The intense competition for nomination in both parties combined cost

TABLE 1.   Presidential Spending: 1960–1988
(Adjusted for inflation, 1960 = 100)

Year	Actual Spending[a]	CPI (1960 Base)	Adjusted Spending[a]
1960	30.0	100.0	30.0
1964	60.0	104.7	57.3
1968	100.0	117.5	85.1
1972	138.0	141.2	97.7
1976	160.0	192.2	83.2
1980	275.0	278.1	98.9
1984	325.0	346.8	93.7
1988	500.0	385.4	126.5

Source: Citizens' Research Foundation
[a] All spending figures are in millions and include prenomination, convention, and general election costs.

about $212 million in candidate spending, twice that of 1984, when there was no Republican challenge to President Reagan's renomination but a competitive Democratic contest. General election spending rose over 1984 mainly because of the infusion of large amounts of soft money raised and spent in each major party campaign. Inflation and entitlements for eligible parties to hold the 1988 conventions, and for candidates in the prenomination and general election phases, began to eat up the balances of the Presidential Election Campaign Fund, supplied by dwindling income-tax checkoffs. America's system of public funding is not yet in jeopardy but 1988 demonstrated many problems that need fixing.

. . . There has been no change in federal election law sine 1979 but most of the presidential election provisions have not been changed since 1974. There is one exception, however: amounts of public financing and expenditure limits were adjusted to changes in the Consumer Price Index—but not enough to keep pace with the escalation of campaign costs at a much higher rate than inflation. Table 2 demonstrates the amounts of public funding and expenditure limits as adjusted from 1976 to 1988.

The problems in 1983 have spurred both increased public concern and the attention of President Bush and the 101st Congress. On June 29, 1989, President Bush proposed to the Congress a series of election reforms, and there were scores of legislative bills introduced in the Congress. An evaluation of how well or poorly the election law operated in 1988 will help focus policy makers on trouble areas requiring revision of the Federal Election Campaign Act as it relates to presidential campaigns.

PRENOMINATION CAMPAIGNS

The major problem manifested in the 1988 prenomination phase of the presidential selection process was the inflexibility of the law to respond to highly-competitive campaigns in both parties and events such as Super

Table 2. **Major Party Presidential Campaign Expenditure Limits and Public Funding: 1976–1988 (in millions)**

YEAR	PRENOMINATION CAMPAIGN					NOMINATING CONVENTION	GENERAL ELECTION CAMPAIGN				
Year	National Spending Limit		Exempt Fund Raising		Overall Spending Limit		Public Treasury Grant		National Party Spending Limit		Overall Spending Limit
1976	$10.9	+	$2.2	=	$13.1	$2.2	$21.8	+	$3.2	=	$25.0
1980	14.7	+	2.9	=	17.7	4.4	29.4	+	4.6	=	34.0
1984	20.2	+	4.0	=	24.2	8.1	40.4	+	6.9	=	47.3
1988	23.1	+	4.6	=	27.7	9.2	46.1	+	8.3	=	54.4

Tuesday. March 8th was almost half a national primary—20 states for the Democrats and 17 for the Republicans. The candidates had to be selective in marshalling and allocating their resources in order not to leave themselves too short for the rest of the long presidential season. Thus candidates could not spend the $5 million minimum that most experts said was necessary in order to campaign effectively in those numbers of states, or to purchase spot announcements in the 50 or more media markets.

If Bob Dole or Pat Robertson had remained competitive with George Bush through the California primary and up to the time of the Republican Convention, the leading spenders would have been unable to expend much money in ensuing primaries and caucuses without exceeding the overall expenditure limit that the law imposed—$23.1 million plus a 20 percent overage of $4.6 million for fund-raising costs, totaling $27.7 million per candidate. Even without such competition, Bush had to curtail his schedule a month before the convention in order to conserve his spending sufficiently to avoid violating the election law. In contrast, Michael Dukakis's opposition is seeking nomination was mainly Jesse Jackson, whose middling spending did not push toward the upper limits as the Bush, Dole and Robertson competition raised the ante for the Republicans.

Within the $27.7 million total limitations are sublimits in each state based on population size. These limitations on how much a candidate could spend in each state have become wholly unrealistic in this day of media-dominated, regional presidential campaigning. They forced candidates to engage in subterfuges that made a mockery of the law, and further confused the funding picture.

Consider the psychological stake of winning in the first two contests: in Iowa, where the spending limit was $775,217; and in New Hampshire, where the limit was $461,000. Candidates found ways to assign spending to their national headquarters or to surrounding states or to fund-raising costs, a separate accounting procedure. For example, autos were rented in Massachusetts for use in New Hampshire and credited against the larger Massachusetts limit. The Federal Election Commission allowed for 80 percent of the television time purchased on Boston stations, reaching 80 percent of the New Hampshire population, to be allocated to the Massachusetts limit, where the primary was not held until Super Tuesday. Richard Gephardt put tag-end requests for contributions on his television ads and allocated half the costs to fund-raising; thus the expenditures were not credited against the New Hampshire limits. By sanctioning such allocations, the FEC allowed the candidates to avoid exceeding the state limits. And in any case, documented excessive spending only brings an FEC fine in the amount of the overspending, months after the event, and is considered by pragmatic candidates as a cost of "doing business." As L. Sandy Maisel has written, "Certainly the intent of the law was not to create incentives for candidates to cheat on the state-by-state limits, because the consequences of being caught cheating were less serious for a campaign than the consequences of losing a caucus or primary."

The ultimate absurdity of the state limits, however, can be found by adding them all up. For the 50 states, this produced a total of $70 million, almost three times the $27.7 million national limit (including fund-raising costs) candidates could legally spend.

In the 1988 prenomination campaigns, the major party candidates spent $212 million; matching funds, as shown in Table 3, amounted to $67.2 million, accounting for 31 percent; thus the United States Government was the largest single contributor. In addition, independent expenditures were $3.5 million for all candidates, $3 million of that on behalf of George Bush; and $656,179 was spent in negative campaigning in opposition to various candidates. Independent expenditures on behalf of Democratic candidates were only $81,681, but the negative spending in opposition to Democratic candidates was $638,637, including $395,974 against Michael Dukakis, the frontrunner, and $163,755 against Jesse Jackson.

George Bush and Michael Dukakis had two common characteristics: they had the most money early, and they had enough money to sustain their campaigns throughout. George Bush's successes were more related to his status as Vice President, to his impressive resume, and to the political obligations people owed to him, than to his spending; he won decisively on Super Tuesday despite being outspent in 12 states....

In the Democratic contests for nomination, the seven candidates all needed exposure. Dukakis had the most money, enabling him to win by spending the most money; money gave Dukakis staying power through the long campaign season. Jesse Jackson had much more money than in 1984, but received notable media attention throughout, with the consequence that his spending was less important than for others; he won or came in second in several primaries or caucuses where he was outspent.

TABLE 3.   Payouts from the Presidential Election Campaign Fund

Prenomination	
Republicans	$35,496,466
Democrats	30,767,102
National Alliance	938,798
Total	$67,202,367
Conventions	
Democrats	$9,220,000
Republicans	$9,220,000
Total	$18,440,000
General Election	
Bush-Quayle	$46,100,000
Dukakis-Bentsen	46,100,000
Total	$92,200,000
Total Paid Out	$177,842,367

Source: Federal Election Commission, as of July 19, 1989.

Pat Robertson in 1988 showed what George McGovern did in 1972, that a minority with strong feelings, if activated by an effective organization and supported by sufficient resources, can win or do well particularly in caucus states, at less cost than is necessary in primary states. Jackson also had an intensely loyal following but less effective organization and fewer resources than Robertson.

One analysis of Super Tuesday indicates that the Democratic big spenders won in 62 percent of the states on that day, whereas the big spender won in only 24 percent of the Republican contests that day.

As Clyde Wilcox has suggested, "campaign spending matters most when little-known candidates contest the nomination, and matters considerably less when the candidates are well known and when free media provide voters with sufficient information to make up their minds."

GENERAL ELECTION CAMPAIGNS

The Democratic nomination went to Dukakis in mid-July, giving him an extra month before Bush's nomination in mid-August. Dukakis had to spread out the use of his money over a longer time until the November election, but Bush was able to concentrate his general election spending over a shorter period. Bush's major media spending did not begin until mid-September, after he took the lead in the public opinion polls from Dukakis' pre-convention status.

Spending on media in the prenomination campaigns totaled about 6 percent of the $212 million expended. But in the general election, the Bush campaign spent more than $30 million on media, the Dukakis campaign less than $30 million, but both near 50 percent of the public grants they received. In a sense, general election public funding amounts to a major transfer of funds from the government to the broadcasters. Of course, the broadcasters provided significant additional free time in the form of the presidential debates, daily coverage, and special programs. . . .

Soft Money

In the general election phase of the presidential selection process, the most notable financial phenomenon was the search for soft money. Soft money is raised and spent outside the restraints of federal law and is determined by state laws, many of which are less stringent than federal law. Efforts by the campaigns to raise soft money became as competitive and as high profile as the search for votes on November 8.

Soft money was sanctioned by the 1979 Amendments to the Federal Election Campaign Act. It was raised and spent in the 1980 and 1984 presidential campaigns, but the money was raised in low-key efforts, not the high-visibility competitive ways as in 1988, and in smaller amounts, as shown in Table 4.

TABLE 4.   Soft Money Expenditures: 1980–1988 (in millions)

| | PARTY | |
YEAR	Republican	Democrat
1980	$15.1	$4.0
1984	15.6	6.0
1988	22.0	23.0

Source: Citizen's Research Foundation

Both parties at the national level sought through parallel fund-raising efforts carried on by the candidates' prenomination campaign operatives soft money contributions to supplement the public funds each presidential and vice-presidential ticket received: $46.1 million, plus $8.3 million the national parties could spend on behalf of the ticket, to be supplemented by however much hard and soft money the parties raised and spent. Money was raised centrally at a frantic pace as if no public funding or expenditure limits existed. It was raised not by the parties but by the same Bush and Dukakis finance people who raised the candidates' prenomination funds. And it was raised in large individual contributions—much in excess of the federal contribution limitations—some as much as $100,000 each; the Republicans claimed 267 contributors of $100,000 or more, while the Democrats counted 130 individuals who gave or raised $100,000.

Robert A. Farmer, Treasurer of the Dukakis-Bentsen campaign, started the drive for soft money by announcing an effort to raise $50 million in such private donations. Farmer admitted this to be a strategic error because it triggered a Republican response in the form of Team 100, which raised $22 million in soft money.

Michael Dukakis put a $100,000 limit on soft money amounts that would be accepted, and refused to accept any from corporations, labor unions or PACs. However, before Dukakis was nominated, the Democrats had accepted soft money from corporate and labor sources for help in funding the Democratic National Convention. Most Republican soft money contributions were from individuals—one disclosed as high as $503,263 contributed by former Ambassador to Hungary, Nicholas Salgo—but some were corporate. Some Republican soft money was raised in amounts as low as $1,000 for tickets to the Gala Luncheon at the Republican National Convention. The costs of the Gala were part of the Republican soft money expenditures. So both conventions used up some of the soft money expenditures for 1988 shown in Table 4 . . . . Additional hard money (within the restraints of federal law) in the tens of millions was raised and spent by both Republicans and Democrats on combined hard-soft money activities related to the presidential campaigns. And additional soft money was raised and spent locally by state and local party committees in amounts not included in the national soft money totals. . . .

Thus the 1988 general election period, in which candidate spending limits were set by law at $46.1 million, found more than twice as much spent, mainly by combinations of candidate and party committees at the state and local levels. The erosion of the effectiveness of the contribution and expenditure limits represents a return to big money—public and private, hard and soft, candidate and party. It threatens the general election public funding concept, that full public funding would be provided, with minimal national party participation, and effective expenditure limitations. Public funds were intended to help provide or supply in entirety the money serious candidates need to present themselves and their ideas to the electorate. Such public money also was meant to diminish or eliminate the need for financing from wealthy donors and interest groups, thereby minimizing the influence contributors possibly could exert on officeholders. And, of course, public funding was designed to relieve candidates of the need to engage in fund-raising; instead, they helped to raise soft money. If soft money expenditures do violence to the rationale for public funding, the whole election law framework is opened to doubt.

Moreover, when presidential candidates accept public financing for the general election campaign, they agree not to raise private funds nor to spend more money than permitted under the expenditure limits. Yet the presidential candidates speak at events at which soft money is raised, and their finance staffs from the prenomination campaigns help to raise soft money and direct its disbursements in key states. Some observers believe this is a violation of the law.

There is much criticism of soft money, but it plays an important role in both voter outreach and party renewal. Its use is required by federal law to be restricted to spending related to voluntary activities. Its purpose is to allow state and local party committees to undertake such activities as registration and get-out-the-vote activities, phone banks and the like—widely accepted functions which attract citizen participation, highly valued in a democracy. Soft money also can be used for items such as bumper strips and local canvassing materials. With more money available in 1988, the definition of voluntary activity was broadened by experience to include joint state headquarters and related expenses shared with presidential campaign operatives in key states. In contrast, the public funding provided by tax checkoffs to the candidates was used directly on advertising by the presidential tickets. To some extent, soft money expenditures freed up more of the public money for advertising, travel and other expenditures directly associated with the presidential campaigns.

Three Parallel Campaigns

In the 1988 general election, the campaigns both expressed a need for a level playing field. As a result, the campaigns sought to supplement spending beyond the expenditure limits through the use of soft money. But soft money was only one component of spending outside the candidates' expenditure limits. Analysis of the presidential general election period demonstrates that

TABLE 5.   Sources of Funds, Major-Party Presidential Candidates, 1988 General Election (millions)

	Sources of Funds	Bush	Dukakis
Limited Campaign			
	Federal Grant	$46.1	$46.1
Candidate controlled	National Party	8.3	8.3
Unlimited Campaigns			
	State and Local Party	22.0[a]	23.0
	Labor[b]	5.0	25.0
Candidate may coordinate	Corporate/Association[b]	1.5	1.0
	Compliance	4.0	2.5
Independent of candidate	Independent Expenditures[c]	6.8	6
Total		$93.7	$106.5

Source: Citizens' Research Foundation

[a] Includes money raised by the national party committee and channeled to state and local party committees.

[b] Includes internal communication costs (both those in excess of $2,000, which are reported, as required by law, and those less than $2,000, which are not required), registration and voter turnout expenditures, overhead, and other related costs.

[c] Does not include amounts spent to oppose the candidates: $2.7 million against Dukakis, $77,325 against Bush, and $63,103 against Quayle.

at least three distinct but parallel campaigns were conducted, either by each candidate or on each candidate's behalf. Amounts of each component are shown in Table 5.

In the first campaign, spending was limited by law to the flat-grant amounts—$46.1 million that public funding provided. This money was supplemented by national party coordinated expenditures of $8.3 million. The total of these public and party funds—$54.4 million—was entirely within the control of the major-party nominees and their campaign organizations. Identical amounts were spent by the Bush-Quayle and Dukakis-Bentsen campaigns in these categories. . . .

In the second campaign, spending was provided for but not limited under the law. Some of it was directly controlled by the nominees and their campaign organizations, and some was outside their control. Even those funds outside their direct control, however, could be coordinated with spending by the nominees. This second campaign was financed in part by funds raised under FECA limits from private contributions to pay the legal, accounting, and related costs the organization incurred in complying with the law. It also was financed in part by soft money funds spent by state and local party committees—in almost identical amounts by each major party. In addition, funds were spent on the nominee's behalf by labor unions, trade associations, and membership groups on partisan communications with their own constituencies and on nominally non-partisan activities directed to the general public; for example, it was reported that Senator Alan Cranston (D–CA) raised $12 million for tax-exempt groups carrying out voter registration and turnout drives among Democratic-leaning groups. This parallel spending could be coordinated with spending by the nominees' campaign organizations.

In the third campaign, spending also was provided for but not limited under the law. Under *Buckley v. Valeo,* individuals and groups are permitted to spend unlimited amounts to advocate the election or defeat of specific candidates as long as these independent expenditures are made without consultation or collaboration with the candidates or their campaigns. The advantage to the Bush campaign in independent expenditures was notable, in contrast to the $2.8 million spent in opposition to Dukakis.

These three parallel campaigns illustrate why expenditure limits are illusory in a pluralistic system with numerous openings for disbursement sanctioned by law or court decisions. Such developments demonstrate the difficulties in attempting to regulate money strictly in the American political arena. When freedom of speech and association are guaranteed, restricting money at any given point in the campaign process results in new channels being carved through which monied individuals and groups can seek to bring their influence to bear on campaigns and officeholders.

With totals of $93.7 million for or on behalf of Bush, and $106.5 million for or on behalf of Dukakis, as shown in Table 5, it is apparent that the candidates' spending limitations, plus those of the national party, are not effective. Moreover, the felt need for additional spending by both campaigns was apparent.

The total amounts spent in the major-party general election campaigns were remarkable, not only for the aggregate amounts raised and spent on behalf of the candidates, but also because the Democratic candidate was the beneficiary of more spending than was the Republican. This stark reversal from all presidential elections in the twentieth century occurred for several reasons: (1) unlike 1980 or 1984, the Democrats spent the full amount of party coordinated expenditures, $8.3 million; (2) unlike 1980 or 1984, the Democrats spent slightly more than the Republicans in soft money; and (3) the Democrats continued their advantage of strong labor spending in parallel campaigns, amounting to $25 million. Indeed, the Democrats achieved more than their long-sought-after level playing field; they had a slight advantage in actual dollars spent. . . .

The high rate of growth in spending has resulted in a level of government payouts which exceeds the amount of revenue generated by the tax checkoff. From 1976 through 1987, the approximate percentage of tax returns checking off money for the Presidential Election Campaign Fund has ranged from a high of 28.7 percent in 1980 to a low of 21 percent in 1987. Based on estimates of future spending and revenue collection, the FEC projects that the 1992 campaign will exhaust available funds, and that by 1996 the system will be unable to meet costs.

The More Seed Money, the Better the Harvest: At the Bottom of Heap, Babbitt Struggles to Raise Funds on Phone

EDWARD WALSH

Campaign professionals refer to early money as "seed money," because it is thought to grow. Early money helps candidates hire the campaign professionals who can manage a solid campaign and who can also help the candidate to attract further contributions. Journalist Edward Walsh describes the process of obtaining seed money, and its importance for presidential candidates.

Bruce Babbitt stared out the window of a corner office 24 stories above Fifth Avenue. To his left, Karen Kapler, a Florida-based political consultant working for his presidential campaign, was on the telephone tracking down a potential contributor. To his right, Muffie Meier, the campaign's deputy national fund-raising director, was doing the same.

Babbitt smiled wanly, muttering about "the absurdity of all this." He had just finished lunch in the conference room of the sleek offices of Ware Travelstead, a New York real estate developer and one of his supporters. Over lunch he had discussed "big issues with the best minds on Wall Street," Babbitt said. "Then I walk in here and beg someone for a thousand bucks."

A target located, Kapler handed the telephone to the former Arizona governor and long-shot Democratic presidential hopeful. The man and his wife had already given $250 each to the Babbitt campaign. The candidate's task was to squeeze another $750 each out of them, to get them to "max out" to the limit of a $1,000 contribution.

"Hello," Babbitt said cheerfully, using an easy first-name familiarity with his listener. "I'm in Manhattan, passing the tin cup. . . . "

This is how it is to run for president retail style. Among the 12 presidential candidates in both parties, Babbitt's campaign is one of the poorest. As of Sept. 30, [1987], the lastest period covered by Federal Election Commission (FEC) reports, his campaign reported $1.4 million in contributions, $35,973 in cash and $339,113 in debts. His candidacy has been kept afloat with $557,000 in loans from a bank in Phoenix.

Source: *The Washington Post*, December 5, 1987: Al. Reprinted by permission of *The Washington Post*.

The collateral for the loans is the federal matching funds that Babbitt will receive beginning in January. Most of the money will go right back to the bank, and the Babbitt campaign will remain strapped for cash as the marathon presidential campaign approaches the first true tests of strength in the Feb. 8 Iowa caucuses and Feb. 16 New Hampshire primary.

Massachusetts Gov. Michael S. Dukakis (D) should not have any loans to repay when his campaign receives a much larger infusion of federal matching funds. As of Sept. 30, the Dukakis campaign reported $7.6 million in contributions, $4.2 million in cash and $280,066 in outstanding debts.

But even Dukakis' success as the leading Democratic fund-raiser pales in comparison to the top Republican, Vice President Bush, who reported $12.6 million in contributions, $4.8 million in cash and $570,241 in outstanding debts as of Sept. 30. Former secretary of state Alexander M. Haig Jr., low man on the GOP fund-raising totem poll, reported $898,190 in contributions, $86,348 in cash and $100,377 in outstanding debts.

At this stage, the rich get richer. Since the Sept. 30 report, the Bush campaign estimates it has taken in an additional $5 million and expects to raise a total of more than $18 million by the end of the year. Senate Minority Leader Robert J. Dole (R–Kan.) raised $7.7 million by Sept. 30 and claims an additional $4 million since then. Dukakis raised $1 million in October and is easily over $9 million in total receipts, with several major fund-raising events still to come, according to campaign aides.

Other campaigns, however, are being stretched, joining Babbitt in the line of borrowers. Among those who have been forced to borrow because of cash flow or deeper problems are Rep. Richard A. Gephardt (D–Mo.), Sen. Paul Simon (D–Ill.), Haig, Republican Marion G. (Pat) Robertson and Rep. Jack Kemp (R–N.Y.).

Republicans historically have been more successful at political fund-raising than Democrats and this year is no exception. As of Sept. 30, Bush and Dole had raised a total of $20.2 million between them, $2.3 million more than the combined fund-raising of the six Democratic contenders — and the gap is probably widening.

At least three factors appear critical to fund-raising in presidential campaigns and are illustrated by the success of Bush and Dole. One is the perception that the candidate has a good chance of being nominated. Bush and Dole appear so far ahead of their rivals that the GOP contest is coming to be seen as a two-man race long before the first votes are counted.

In contrast, the Democratic picture remains extraordinarily muddled, making it more difficult to pick a likely winner. For the purpose of pre-election year fund-raising, it doesn't matter much whether these perceptions turn out to be accurate.

A second factor is incumbency. Bush holds the nation's second-highest elective office and Dole, if not elected president, will remain a powerful senator. The Democratic field includes only one officeholder with a strong, established fund-raising base, Dukakis, who still will be governor if he loses the presidential race. Babbitt is out of office. Jesse L. Jackson has never held office. Although Gephardt has risen high in the House Democratic leadership, neither he nor any of the other Democrats can rival Dole's position at the center of power on Capitol Hill.

Finally, Bush, 63, and Dole, 64, have a combined 58 years in national Republican politics beginning with their elections to the House in the 1960s. Both are former Republican National Committee chairmen and both have either held or run for national office before. In the course of their careers, they have worked tirelessly for the GOP and its candidates, accumulating political and personal debts that are now being called in.

The Democratic candidates are younger, less well known and less well connected to party leaders. This is not exactly, to use one of the political world's sports metaphors, "a level playing field," and all of these factors are reflected in the candidates' fund-raising. Money is more than the fuel that drives presidential campaigns. Long before the first votes are cast, money — or its absence — has helped to shape the strategies, styles and internal dynamics of the campaigns, and begun to separate the candidates into those who are perceived as "viable" contenders—and therefore perhaps worth a maximum contribution—and those who are not.

"What will 8 million buy you?" asked Bob Farmer, Dukakis's campaign treasurer and chief fund-raiser. "We have offices in 38 cities. We have 240 paid staff, 14 in Florida and Texas, 10 in North Carolina, 18 in Minnesota. We're the only Democratic candidate with a national campaign."

"There is also the advantage of time," he added. "We can get started three or four months earlier [in the March "Super Tuesday" primary and caucus states that follow Iowa and New Hampshire]. We have our act together."

In style at least, the Dukakis operation is beginning to take on something of the look and the insulation of a full-blown, national presidential campaign on the march. On a recent trip to Texas, Dukakis and his aides flew in a chartered jet from Dallas to College Station to Austin while three reporters chased the candidate in a twin-engine prop aircraft, also arranged by the campaign.

At Texas A&M University in College Station, Dukakis was surrounded by about a dozen aides, including an advance party that had smoothed the way. Watching his boss answer questions from students, Nick Mitropoulos, Dukakis' executive assistant, expressed awe over how the campaign's fund-raising prowess had allowed it to buy the technical expertise that was beaming the event by satellite television to 50 other colleges in 25 states.

Meanwhile, Babbitt told a small audience of supporters in New York that "I get off a [commercial] plane occasionally carrying my own bag not because I want to emulate Jimmy Carter but because no one is with me." At the national campaign headquarters in Phoenix, Babbitt aides track the accumulating "frequent flyer" miles, celebrating whenever the candidate earns a free trip.

If the well-financed candidates are already embarked on national campaign extravaganzas, Babbitt is running a two-state sideshow. More than 75 percent of his spending was allocated to Iowa and New Hampshire. Of the three other states where the Babbitt campaign reported spending, two border Iowa.

It was the lack of cash—which has turned out to be even worse than anticipated—that dictated the two-state strategy, just as it dictated the dispatch of Chris Hamel, one of Babbitt's top aides who ordinarily might have a lofty title and broad responsibilities in Phoenix, to Des Moines more than a year before the caucuses.

"Every dime we get is going in there [Iowa]," said Elaine Kamarck, deputy campaign manager for Babbitt. "We're going to have as much money there as anyone."

Kamarck has now seen presidential politics from both ends of the fundraising barrel. In 1984, she worked in former vice president Walter F. Mondale's Democratic campaign, which, like the Bush operation today, wallowed in contributions.

The differences, she said, are mostly on the national level, not in the first two critical states. For her, it means staying in the houses of supporters, not fancy hotel rooms; it means dealing largely with volunteers, so that "you can't have your ordinary temper tantrums, working with people who are doing it for love, not money," and it means scrambling for the meager resources that are left after Iowa and New Hampshire take their cuts.

"I called Iowa recently with sugar dripping out of my voice to ask them to send 50 bumper stickers to Ohio," Kamarck said.

Beyond strategy and style, political money has real political consequences, at least until the first votes are counted. The size of a campaign treasury is one of the few measurable commodities before voting starts. The ability to raise large amounts of cash in contributions of $1,000 or less gives a candidate instant credibility, which leads to heavier press coverage of the campaign, which leads to more contributions.

"Money begets money," said Robert Beckel, Mondale's campaign manager, who argues that "money is far more important in the early preliminaries, before the voters get in it, than it is after the voters get in."

"It's a self-reinforcing problem," said Kathy Bushkin, who was Gary Hart's press secretary in 1984. "If you don't have money, you can't do the things that help you get money. If you can't prove the campaign is moving, it's hard to convince people to give."

Bob Farmer understood this psychology. He turned first to Dukakis' Massachusetts network. "I sat down with 300 people, one on one for an hour, and asked them, 'Would you exercise your network for Michael Dukakis?'" he said. "The secret is the number of gray-haired people willing to get committed. There are a lot of 22-year-old fund-raisers. We have a lot of people with pot-bellies and little or no hair."

Two-thirds of Dukakis' initial contributions came from Massachusetts, a far more congenial fund-raising location than Babbitt's base in sparsely populated, Republican-dominated Arizona. Dukakis also turned to his unique ethnic base among his fellow Greek Americans, who have provided more than 15 percent of his campaign funds.

The result, contained in the Dukakis campaign's first FEC report for the period ended June 30, was $4.6 million in contributions, triple the collection rate of his nearest Democratic fund-raising rival. Dukakis was off and running.

Just the opposite psychology took hold in the Babbitt campaign. After clearing $750,000 from a dinner in Phoenix in February, its next largest event, in Connecticut in June, netted $30,000, according to Lauren Post, the campaign's national fund-raising director. Money was already tight when the Democratic candidates gathered in Houston July 1 for their first nationally televised debate, where Babbitt's awkward performance earned him the media title of the evening's biggest loser.

"The Houston thing haunted us for months," Post said.

After Houston, Babbitt was firmly entrenched in the bottom tier of the Democrats and sometimes simply left out of media accounts of the race or assumed to be not long for the campaign.

The disaster was written in the third quarter FEC report for all to see. Between July 1 and Sept. 30, Babbitt reported $551,815 in contributions, while Dukakis scooped up $3.4 million and the four other Democrats reported contributions of more than $1 million each.

The reality was even worse. Of the contributions Babbitt claimed—$262,000—was the second of the three loans his campaign has received and $35,000 came out of his own pocket. Babbitt, one of the wealthiest of the Democratic contenders, and members of his immediate family have given $50,000 to the campaign, the maximum allowed by law. The real total of third quarter contributions to Babbitt's presidential quest was $249,358.

"Everybody thought he was a loser, that it would be throwing money away," Post said of this low point. "It was very discouraging. It was frustrating. People often thought he wasn't worth $500."

When Babbitt first started running for president months ago, he said he viewed the campaign as a great "national seminar" in which, at worst, he would learn a great deal about the country. He has learned about the intricacies of agricultural policy in the Midwest, the chemical composition of acid rain in the Northeast, the technical capabilities of nuclear weapons systems.

He also has learned a few things about the more mundane aspects of life.

"I'm learning things I never knew when I had a secretary when I was governor," Babbitt said. "Four out of every five phone calls you make, the person is not there. If you don't have a place where the phone call can be returned, you waste an enormous amount of time."

It was this realization, plus the increasingly desperate fund-raising situation, that led to a change in tactics and brought Babbitt to Travelstead's midtown Manhattan office late last month. Instead of trying to raise money on the run—popping in and out of airport telephone booths between flights—since late summer Babbitt, operating out of a fixed base, has devoted one or two days a week almost exclusively to fund-raising.

While Farmer is planning a major fund-raising dinner for Dukakis here next Wednesday, Babbitt has no choice but to continue with what he calls "root-canal therapy," going one-on-one with potential contributors of from $250 (the maximum contribution the federal government will match) to the $1,000 total limit. Michael McCurry, his press secretary, estimates that it takes $90,000 to $120,000 a month just to keep the campaign alive. Babbitt must raise about half that amount, much of it on the telephone.

"There's no substitute for the candidate asking," Kapler said. "It's so much easier to say no to somebody else."

On Babbitt's first afternoon in New York, Kapler and Meier, the deputy fund-raising director, placed 105 telephone calls across the country. Babbitt talked to 30 people, and others called back the next day. He worked off a list prepared by his staff with the names of potential contributors, what they do, how much they have given in the past, perhaps a personal note such as friendship with Babbitt's wife, Hattie.

The take for the first afternoon's work is more than $10,000 in individual commitments and promises to raise $35,000 in addition. That night, at a cocktail party in a Park Avenue apartment, Babbitt raised $1,500.

Since so much of political fund-raising at this stage is psychological, Babbitt is relentlessly optimistic on the telephone. He brags often about his Iowa and New Hampshire organizations.

"Hi, Larry," the candidate says to a Texas lawyer. "Pretty good. We've had a couple good weeks. Things are moving. . . . I need 1,000 people to provide me with a thousand bucks. I understand. Let me make a counteroffer. The first $250 is matched by the federal government. . . . I really do have a message. I think I have a good shot."

Babbitt gets the $250 pledge and has other successes. A prominent New York investment banker pledges $1,000 and the check is in Meier's hands an hour later. But fund-raising is an acquired skill for Babbitt, as it is for many politicians, and he still needs coaching.

"And his wife. What about his wife?" Meier whispers urgently as the candidate winds up a conversation with a contributor.

In another call, Babbitt doesn't even get around to asking for money as he chats with a high school classmate of his wife.

"It's the first time I finked out on you all day," he says sheepishly to Meier and Kapler. "It wasn't a big money call."

"It's the second time, but that's okay," Kapler replies.

In the last three months of 1983, Hart's presidential campaign raised $330,130. In March 1984, after Hart had finished a distant second to Mondale in Iowa and first in New Hampshire, the same campaign took in $8.2 million in one month.

"I would exchange the momentum of a good finish in Iowa for $10 million," said Beckel, speaking from the perspective of the battered Mondale campaign that barely survived Hart's unexpected challenge in 1984.

Next year, after the New Hampshire primary comes Super Tuesday, mostly in the South, where the front-runners are already hard at work organizing. But Beckel argues that after the first two states "presidential politics is not a field business. It's a momentum, expectations and media business."

"Ten million dollars is small change when you're talking about 20 states," Beckel said. "We had all that much money going in and we were broke after the New Hampshire primary.... It's important and good to have, but all the money these front-runners have won't be worth much if they lose in Iowa and New Hampshire."

"What saved Walter Mondale was not his money or his organization," Kamarck added. "What saved Mondale was 25 years as a real, true leader in the Democratic Party. You can't buy the kind of loyalty Mondale had."

Meanwhile, McCurry and other senior Babbitt aides are playing the underdog role to the hilt. It was the principal reason that they allowed a reporter to observe Babbitt in the decidedly unpresidential business of asking for money.

At this stage, it also helps to have a sense of humor, a quality that Meier, a gregarious woman, enjoys in abundance. Early one morning last week Babbitt met with some of his New York supporters. The discussion turned serious as Babbitt explained how he is trying to sharpen his campaign message. "I'm always searching for a metaphor, a parable," he said. "I'd rather have a crisp image than a $1,000 check."

At that, Meier collapsed against a nearby wall in mock exasperation.

"You're fired," she told the amateur fund-raiser and would-be president.

Bush's Money Machine: Cadre of Friends Helps Raise $29 Million

CHARLES R. BABCOCK AND RICHARD MORIN

George Bush and Michael Dukakis both raised substantial amounts of money early in the election process. Both built pyramid networks of fund-raisers, who solicited contributions from their friends and encouraged them to solicit from their friends. Both primarily sought large contributions. Yet Bush and Dukakis relied on different networks, and their constituency base was quite different. Journalists Charles Babcock and Richard Morin describe their fund-raising practices. They note that Bush built a network through the Republican party, while Dukakis solicited within his home state of Massachusetts and from Greek Americans.

To Bobby Holt, a West Texas friend and fund-raiser for Vice President Bush, the wildly successful fund-raising operation that has produced $29 million for Bush's presidential campaign can be described in one sentence: "You stroke 'em, you pluck 'em, you thank 'em."

With the primary season ending and Bush's nomination assured, records of that fund-raising effort and interviews with some of those who did the stroking, plucking and thanking produce a portrait of the very model of a modern political money machine. It played to the candidate's strength—the friends and associates he has nurtured over his career in the oil business and Republican politics—as well as traditional sources of large contributors, from Wall Street to Palm Beach to Beverly Hills.

In raising the $29 million, the Bush operation:

Persuaded 17,000 individuals to give the maximum $1,000 donation, a record $17 million that surpassed even Ronald Reagan's fund-raising prowess. Bush also took the time to sign thank-you notes to each of these and about 3,000 other donors of $500 or more.

Concentrated on the wealthy pockets in large states that historically produce political funds. Texas led the way with $2.8 million, followed by California with $2.4 million, Florida with $2.3 million and New York with $2.2 million. The campaign also collected $38,800 from Guam, American Samoa and the Northern Mariana islands and $12,150 from Americans living abroad. A computer analysis of the addresses of major donors shows, not surprisingly, that the Upper East Side Manhattan ZIP code 10021— which leads the nation in political giving—produced the most cash for

Source: "Bush's Money Machine," *The Washington Post*, May 15, 1988: Al. Reprinted by permission of *The Washington Post*.

Bush, $373,460 through March. A Greenwich, Conn., ZIP code was next, followed by another one in Manhattan, one in Cincinnati—scene of a large luncheon—and one in Palm Beach, Fla.

Used a large network of personal friends to solicit widening circles of acquaintances and business associates. For instance, a luncheon at the Waldorf Astoria hotel in New York a year ago that produced $950,000 had two chairmen, a special chairman, 14 general chairmen and 54 vice chairmen. And Wally Ganzi Jr., who runs Palm restaurants in several cities, said he has passed out to nearly 1,000 donors autographed pictures of Bush and each individual.

The thoughtful and methodical Bush touch of the personal thank-you note and the autographed picture is symbolic of the highly organized campaign fund-raising operation.

"George Bush has been running for president since 1976," Rodney Smith, who was finance director of New York Rep. Jack Kemp's campaign, said admiringly. "He's been all over the country. He's a very likable person and he follows up with notes. He has developed a cadre of friends and now he's reaping the benefits of 10 years of work."

Nurturing those personal contacts over the years has been important to Bush because most of his government experience was in appointed positions and, as vice president to Reagan, it could be said he didn't have a natural constituency of his own.

Bruce S. Gelb, vice chairman of Bristol Myers and cochair of the Bush finance committee in New York, recalls that Bush was reminded of this when he first ran for president in 1979 and was "an asterisk" in the polls. "He said, 'I have a very big family with a lot of friends.' And he has made a lot of friends, lasting friends, and that is the rock core of his constituency," Gelb said. "Fund-raising starts at home. You tell you family, your friends, your business associates."

Many of Bush's friends, the 350 members of the Bush finance committee, were in Washington last week to get another personal thank you from the candidate, a dinner at his home Tuesday night and a sales pitch Wednesday to raise $27 million more for the national and state parties to use in this fall's election.

This new money will go to the national and state parties because Bush's general election campaign—along with that of his Democratic opponent—will be financed with public money. Each of the major candidates will receive about $46 million for the fall campaign.

The Bush fund-raisers include Holt and Ganzi, Gelb and former ambassador Walter Curley in New York, developers Alex Courtelis of Miami and Don Bren of California, lawyer Michael Galvin of Chicago, Tim Timkin, who runs a ball bearing company in Canton, Ohio, and John Hathaway, head of Wild Boys Land and Cattle Co. of Huntsville, Ala.

These names all are familiar to Fred Bush (no relation to the vice president), the 39-year-old deputy finance chairman of the campaign, who has been in constant touch with state fund-raisers around the country. Since the maximum individual contribution is $1,000, "the whole idea is working networks and cross-fertilization," he said.

Holt, vice chairman of the finance committee to Houston's Robert Mosbacher, said in an interview it is especially important to thank donors "so they feel part of the team." He was reluctant to say how much he had raised one-on-one for Bush, but estimated he and his contacts have brought the campaign $1.5 million "or something like that."

Federal Election Commission records show that through March the Bush campaign had raised more than $29 million—$21.5 million in individual donations, another $6.9 million in federal matching funds (up to $250 of each donation is matched dollar-for-dollar from a special federal fund) and $640,000 from political action committees.

More than 200 oilmen like Holt are identifiable in the list of donors of $500 or more to the Bush campaign, including at least two dozen Pennzoil employees and two dozen "independent oilmen." Holt said "wildcatters" like himself favor Bush because the vice president ran an oil company in Texas and understands the industry, not because of specific stands such as Bush's pledge to kill the windfall profits tax on oil.

A computer analysis of the Bush donors, arranged by occupation and employer, shows significant numbers of lawyers, investors, self-employed entrepreneurs and retirees.

For example, 49 members of the Los Angeles law firm of Latham & Watkins, which has represented some defense contractors, donated more than $35,000 to Bush. William Long, a former Pentagon official who runs the firm's Washington office, said he held a dinner here for Bush and a New York partner raised funds for a luncheon there. "Obviously, when you raise money you solicit your colleagues," he explained.

Bush, who has come out in favor of cutting the capital gains tax from 28 percent back to 20 percent, is popular with stockbrokers and investors. The best evidence of that is a $550,000 lunch at the Vista Hotel on Wall Street last December, just six weeks after the Oct. 19 stock market crash. The key organizer was Henry Kravis, a specialist in "leveraged buy outs."

The Bush donor lists are peppered with $1,000 donations from the securities industry. For instance, $25,000 came in contributions from officials of the Lazard Freres & Co. brokerage firm in New York, another $20,000 from employees of the Alex. Brown & Sons securities firm in Baltimore.

Some of the Alex. Brown officials were among the group that paid $1,000 to attend a dinner at the home of a colleague, J. Carter Beese, 31. That event raised about $110,000, the campaign's largest event in Maryland.

There are fewer identifiable contributors from major manufacturing companies, though at least 17 Bristol Myers officials, colleagues of New York fund-raiser Gelb, are listed. So are 21 employees of Eli Lilly, the Indianapolis drug manufacturer where Bush was a director.

Fred Bush said he believes it is easier for individuals to solicit money from peers, such as law or accounting partners, or financial house colleagues. Corporate executives may ask subordinates to give, but don't want to appear to be pressuring them, he said.

More than half the major donors to the Bush campaign are not identifiable, because they did not furnish their occupation and employer to the campaign and FEC rules only require that the committee ask for the information once in writing. This "best efforts" rule has been in place for several years after campaigns complained about the cost of having to go back to donors again and again to request the information.

Bush's donor lists are not the least informative. Among former Republican rivals, about 68 percent of Kansas Sen. Robert J. Dole's major donors are unidentified by occupation and employer as are nearly 56 percent of Pat Robertson's. Democratic Rep. Richard A. Gephardt of Missouri failed to disclose this information for 63 percent of his large givers. Jesse L. Jackson's reports did not identify about 46 percent of his campaign's major donors. Massachusetts Gov. Michael S. Dukakis had the most complete disclosure, with 31 percent of the givers unidentifiable by profession and place of business.

At times, even those who listed their occupation for the Bush report were not very specific. Through March, for instance, 283 listed "attorney" and another 78 said "lawyer." There were 101 who listed "investments" and 50 who said "investor." There were 283 "self-employed," 457 "retired," 600 "homemakers," and 179 "housewives." Also listed was "a great actor" (James Stewart) and a "singing cowboy" (Gene Autry), two teachers and one $1,000 donor who listed "unemployed."

Bush's fund-raising team started out in late 1985 with an ambitious plan that was surpassed last month. It set goals for each state and sent out weekly printouts showing how well everyone was doing. "That helped the spirit of competition," Fred Bush said. "State chairmen took this very seriously. I would get calls after the printouts were received, with someone saying, 'Are you sure you deposited all the money from that event?'"

One easily surpassed fund-raising goal was getting 15,000 contributors to give the maximum $1,000, he said. Direct-mail donors added nearly $4 million more to the Bush bank accounts. There are about 100,000 donors to the campaign overall, with the average contribution $211.

The $600,000 target for PAC contributions was passed without a special focus on collecting such special-interest money, according to Fred Bush. "We just sent a list of the PACs in a state to the state chairmen," he said. An analysis by Public Citizens' Congress Watch determined that PACs from the banking and financial industry gave more than $125,000 to the Bush campaign, with oil and energy companies next with nearly $70,000.

The campaign tried to keep its fund-raising costs to about 20 cents on the dollar, Fred Bush said, so the emphasis was placed on selling $1,000 tickets to about 100 fund-raising events around the country.

The top draw was the luncheon at the Waldorf Astoria hotel in New York a year ago that raised $950,000. The second largest Bush event was held last June at the Galleria Hotel in Houston and collected $750,000. Next was a dinner at the Chicago Hilton in October, the night the vice president announced his candidacy. That event collected $625,000. Illinois state finance chairman Galvin, 35, a partner at Winston and Strawn, said about eighty people representing various industries helped him sell tickets.

By the time New York developer Donald Trump sponsored a $600,000 event at the Plaza Hotel last month, the campaign had raised the maximum allowed for the primaries. So the campaign got about 450 of those who attended to permit their $1,000 checks to go toward a separate compliance fund to pay legal and accounting costs for the fall election.

The campaign raised $520,000 in Massachusetts, Dukakis's state. It also raised $484,000 in the District of Columbia, all at dinner parties in the homes of supporters, with the largest a $180,000 event hosted by real estate executive Joseph Gildenhorn. Maryland supporters of the vice president raised $483,000 and those in Virginia added $469,000.

Greek Americans, Home State Boost Dukakis' Coffers

CHARLES R. BABCOCK AND RICHARD MORIN

In raising almost $24 million in his run for the presidency, Gov. Michael S. Dukakis with unprecedented success has tapped the deep pockets of two neighborly constituencies—fellow Greek Americans around the nation and residents and business people of his native Bay State, election finance records show.

Massachusetts donors have contributed more than $6.5 million and Greek Americans more than $3 million.

Dukakis' take from in-state contributors is almost double the amount he amassed in any of his four campaigns for governor—a success some of his former rivals for the Democratic nomination find easy to explain.

Said Rep. Richard A. Gephardt (D–Mo.): "You've got to be a sitting governor. Then you've got the lawyers and the landfill operators and the bond dealers. They don't love you enough to give $1,000, but they've got to do it."

Robert A. Farmer, Dukakis' chief fund-raiser, said in an interview that his fund-raisers do not solicit state contractors in any "systematic" way, but added that there is "a fine line" between appropriate fund-raising and unacceptable pressure on a contractor.

He said the campaign does not accept contributions from donors whose business is dependent on state government. "We are very sensitive to the possibility for abuse," he said. "Michael Dukakis has a reputation of running a very pristine, squeaky-clean fund-raising operation" that includes rules against accepting political action committee (PAC) money, money from state lobbyists, or more than $100 from any state employee.

A computer-aided analysis of contributors shows that the campaign received a boost from Massachusetts donors in the early days, when Dukakis was not well known nationally.

While barring PAC money, the campaign accepted hundreds of thousands of dollars from some types of professionals: lawyers in Massachusetts, some whose firms do business with the state as bond or corporate counsel, gave more than $400,000; developers and contractors, including some with state contracts, gave at least $140,000.

At least fifty major donors were from firms with state work or that are qualified bidders. The group included two leading Dukakis fund-raisers, individuals from three dozen firms on the state public works bid list, the head

Source: "Greek Americans, etc." *The Washington Post*, May 29, 1988: A1. Reprinted by permission of *The Washington Post*.

of an advertising firm with a state lottery commission contract, several officials of a major construction company, and the owner of a janitorial service.

The campaign accepted $98,200 from employees of Wall Street brokerage and investment firms, though Farmer said the campaign was not going to Wall Street because its firms underwrite state bond issues.

Farmer, a retired businessman and chief fund-raiser for Dukakis's last two gubernatorial campaigns, said the key to his success was getting 900 people around the country to agree to raise at least $10,000, through friends and business associates.

These networks have attracted 85,000 donors, including about 7,000 who have given the maximum $1,000 contribution. Through April, the campaign had collected $16.5 million in individual donations. Nearly two-thirds came from donors of $500 or more, and $2.4 million came in smaller direct-mail donations. Federal matching funds totaled $6.8 million, and nearly $400,000 came from the Dukakis for governor campaign committee.

Many of Dukakis' $1,000 donors and the campaign's three largest fund-raising events were in Massachusetts, including one that cleared $2.1 million last June. Sixteen of the top 20 zip codes of donors also were in Massachusetts.

Last fall, the campaign broadened its base, using key individuals and Massachusetts "ambassadors" to tap traditional Democratic money spots such as New York, California, Florida, and the Washington area.

In March, just after Dukakis' loss to Jesse L. Jackson in Michigan, the groundwork paid off, with three $200,000 fund-raisers that week. One, at the Georgetown home of Elizabeth and Smith Bagley, raised more than $250,000 from a group she described as "very much the Washington Democratic establishment crowd." The host committee included at least 20 registered lobbyists who paid $1,000 each to attend.

Meanwhile, campaign officials said, Greek Americans have poured in their support, often in smaller sums, accounting for at least 20 percent of the funds from individuals and a greater share of the donors. One $50-a-ticket Greek fund-raiser in Astoria in the borough of Queens last summer, organized by New York restaurateur Taso Manesis, raised more than $125,000. Three events sponsored by Tina and Andrew Manatos of Bethesda collected about $130,000 from several thousand Greek Americans in the Washington-Baltimore area.

Top Dukakis fund-raisers include Boston developer Alan Leventhal, the national finance chairman; Peter Bassett, a Boston hotel chain manager who heads the Greek-American drive with key help from Manesis and Clay Constantinou, a New Jersey lawyer; Nadine Hack of New York; Marvin Rosen of Florida; John Battaglino, a Boston businessman who has spent the past year nearly full time as the campaign's "ambassador" to California; and the Bagleys in Washington.

A key early fund-raiser in New York was Michael del Giudice, former chief of staff to New York Gov. Mario M. Cuomo (D) and a partner in Lazard Freres & Co., an investment banking firm. Last fall, Massachusetts picked Lazard Freres as fiscal manager for a multibillion-dollar road and tunnel project in Boston, a contract criticized by the state inspector general's office as open-ended before the selection.

Del Giudice said his firm's proposal on the Massachusetts job had nothing to do with his Dukakis fund-raising efforts. Several of the firm's partners support Vice President Bush, campaign records show.

Farmer said it would be "inappropriate" to take donations from people dependent on state business. "The line you have to draw is, is it an important part of their business? If it is, we won't accept their contributions, let alone . . . no one who is doing a lot of business with the state is collecting for us."

The Boston Herald has reported that two members of the finance committee do business with the state. John Keith is a developer whose companies had received millions of dollars in loans and subsidies from the state housing finance authority. Farmer said he recruited Keith, did not think he was dependent on the state for his livelihood, and has not been asked to do a favor for him.

Battaglino, who sold his chain of college bookstores two years ago and heads the drive that raised $2 million in California, also has had state contracts, with state colleges.

Another $1,000 donor with state contracts is John M. Connors Jr., chief executive of Hill, Holiday, Connors, the largest advertising firm in New England with $300 million in billings. He said his firm, which employs John Sasso, Dukakis' former campaign manager, has about $13 million in competitively won contracts with the state lottery commission and tourism office, about 4 percent of his business. "We hardly depend on it and there was no pressure to give," he said.

Farmer said the state does not let managing partners of accounting firms solicit their employees because they bid on state audits.

He said the campaign systematically solicited the state's law firms after former senator Paul E. Tsongas collected more than $35,000 from his firm in the early days. Farmer said he and Paul Brountas, a close Dukakis friend and adviser, then met with the managing partners of all the major firms and asked them to solicit their colleagues. The effort produced about $400,000, including $142,065 from four Boston firms.

Francis X. Meaney, managing partner of Boston's Mintz, Levin, Cohn, Ferris, Glovsky & Popeo, said his firm's "original inspiration was to help the campaign get off to a fast start. There was enthusiasm about having a native son back in the White House." Records at the Federal Election Commission show that 35 individuals from the firm gave a total of almost $28,000 to Dukakis. Meaney said that the firm is bond counsel to the state treasurer's office, but that state business is less than 1 percent of its income and had "zero" effect on the decision to back Dukakis.

When Dukakis first discussed presidential fund-raising in 1986, Farmer said he could raise $6.5 million, including matching funds, by the time of the Iowa caucuses. He raised twice that.

Farmer said that when he began the effort in the spring of 1987, he targeted $1,000 donors in Massachusetts—where Dukakis had just raised $3 million for his 1986 reelection bid—as well as in New York and California. "If you can't raise money in your home state, you ought not to be in the ball game," he said.

"What I do," Farmer said, "is sit down with people of status, influence, and prestige and ask them to exercise their network for Michael Dukakis. . . . People give because they don't want to say no to people who ask them. People give to people."

Kristin S. Demong, the campaign's finance director, added that from the start, "We tried to go after people who have networks and they are usually business people. We do hold people accountable, like they have made a business decision," she said. "We call them up and ask: Where are you on your commitment? You owe us $8,000 or whatever. We don't put a lien on their house. It's more of an incentive." The campaign takes pains to award top fund-raisers, while those who don't deliver don't get to the inner circle.

Farmer and Leventhal started building their networks March 30, 1987, a month before Dukakis declared his candidacy. They set up in the newly renamed Presidential Suite in Leventhal's Meridien Hotel and went one-on-one for days, persuading new and old Dukakis supporters to sign on.

The Boston Globe later reported how they approached Gerald D. Cohen, a local developer and former Dukakis advance man. "Gerry, I don't know how rich you are," Farmer said. " 'Do' your wife, mother-in-law, think of your family, then employees. Who's doing your construction?"

Leventhal added: "Your land brokerage, your contractor on a major job, major subs, electrical contractor. They're giving and raising the money for you. They give because you've given them a lot of money over the years."

Cohen solicited his business associates. "I haven't gone to them and twisted arms," he said. "I asked them [to contribute]. If they didn't give, they didn't give." One of his main contractors did not, he recalled with a chuckle.

Asked about his quotes in the Globe about soliciting contractors, Leventhal said, "You ask those you have relationships with." He said he did not think this put pressure on the businessman. "That's not the way we operate." He said his company has 4,000 employees and he has never asked any of them to donate to the campaign.

While Farmer and Leventhal fielded 350 solicitors in Massachusetts, Steven Grossman, a Boston businessman active in Jewish fund-raising circles, was seeking support among Jews nationally at the request of Dukakis' wife, Kitty. He said in an interview that he had worked with her in sponsoring a $1 million fund-raiser in Boston in 1985 for the Holocaust museum.

He said that although Sen. Joseph R. Biden Jr. (D–Del.) had a head start in Jewish fund-raising, there was room for support for Dukakis. The early work paid off, Grossman said, with successful fund-raisers recently in Cleveland and Portland, Ore., sponsored by contacts from those days.

Farmer's most impressive achievement was the $2 million event at the Park Plaza Hotel in Boston last June 15. Analysis of contribution records shows that the campaign took in nearly $2 million that month in donations of $500 or more, 70 percent from Massachusetts.

The home-state money was especially critical because at the time, a national Gallup survey showed that four of five Democrats didn't know who Michael Dukakis was.

The amount of Greek-American support surprised Farmer. "I never anticipated the passion," he said. "Going to a Greek-American event is like going to a Jesse Jackson rally."

Bassett, who is coordinating the effort, said the campaign identified potential supporters through fraternal and church groups and networks of friendships. For instance, Constantinou, organizer of several $100,000 fund-raisers in New Jersey, contacted a boyhood friend from Cyprus, John Charalambous of Virginia Beach.

Charalambous, who runs several restaurants, sponsored a $100-a-ticket event in February the night of a Democratic debate in Williamsburg. More than 1,000 people attended and the evening cleared $135,000, Bassett said.

Vic Raiser, finance chairman of the Democratic National Committee, said Farmer has revolutionized fund-raising for the party. "He is as much a psychologist as a fund-raiser," he said, praising Farmer for bringing in a wide variety of people and making them feel part of the campaign. "And he and his crew are like locusts," Raiser said. "They are very thorough and efficient."

Serious Money: Presidential Campaign Contributors and Patterns of Contribution in 1988

CLIFFORD W. BROWN, LYNDA W. POWELL AND CLYDE WILCOX

In the presidential primary season, the ultimate source of most campaign money is individual donors. Political Scientists Clifford Brown, Lynda Powell, and Clyde Wilcox are currently working on a book on individual contributors in presidential elections. They describe the various constituency bases for the presidential candidates of both parties in 1988. They conclude that some candidates solicited from national networks of political activists, others built contributor bases in their home state, and still others used direct mail to market their ideological position.

It has long been known that contributors to presidential nomination campaigns are an elite group, and this is especially true for those who contribute serious money, which we define as contributions totaling more than $200. For example, among those who contributed such amounts to presidential candidates in 1988, fully 56 percent came from families with incomes over $100,000, and more than a quarter came from families with incomes of $250,000 or more; these latter percentages were even higher for Bush contributors (44 percent) and Dole contributors (50 percent). And, although contributors to Jackson and Robertson were substantially less affluent than contributors generally, still 54 percent of Jackson contributors and 44 percent of Robertson contributors enjoyed family incomes of $50,000 or more.

Futhermore, 78 percent of those contributing more than $200 in 1988 are college graduates (the exact same percentage for a comparable sample in 1972); 43 percent in 1988 had advanced degrees.

Contributors of serious money are also generally advanced in their careers (66 percent are above the age of 45, 31 percent above the age of 60); they are disproportionately white (in fact, 62 percent of Jackson's contributors of more than $200 were white); and disproportionately male: although reporting procedures create problems in terms of establishing the gender of contributors (single contributions may be made in the names of spouses), by our estimate, 72 percent of the contributors were male—a percentage

Source: Clifford Brown is an Associate Professor of Political Science at Union College, Lynda W. Powell is an Associate Professor of Political Science at the University of Rochester and Clyde Wilcox is an Assistant Professor of Government at Georgetown University. Reprinted by permission of the authors.

almost identical to the 75 percent found in 1972. Jackson, with 53 percent men, 47 percent women, was the only candidate in 1988 whose contributors of serious money were more than 40 percent female.

Presidential contributors as a group are also very active politically: 50 percent rate themselves as strong partisans, 35 percent say they have *spoken personally* to their senators or representatives in Congress or to the President for the purpose of attempting to influence an act of Congress, 40 percent say they have worked for presidential candidates in some or most elections, and 40 percent for political parties. In addition, 8 percent have held public elective office, 18 percent public appointive office, and 17 percent party office.

Furthermore, 49 percent of those who contributed serious money to presidential candidates in 1988 say they make such contributions in most elections (and an additional 31 percent say they have done so in some elections, for a combined total of 80 percent who can be said to be more than casual contributors).

Given the high level of political activism of those who contribute serious money to presidential candidates, it is important to ascertain why these people participate in politics. The following table presents the percentages who say each listed motive is a "very important" reason for participating in politics in 1972 and in 1988:

	1972	1988
A way of influencing policies of government	54%	45%
Might make a difference to the outcome of an election	47	47
Helps fulfill my sense of community obligation	46	34
Personal friendship for a candidate	28	34
For business or employment reasons	12	12
Enjoyment of the friendships and social contacts	11	5
It is expected of someone in my position	9	8
Political activity gives me a feeling of recognition	3	5

Generally speaking, there is not much difference between the two years, with the "purposive" motives of influencing the policies of government and making a difference to the outcome of an election ranking highest, followed by fulfilling a sense of community obligation and personal friendship for a candidate.

The differences between the two years may be explained, in part, by the different mix of candidates. For example, higher percentages of contributors say influencing the policies of government is very important in the case of "ideological" candidates such as Wallace (61 percent), McGovern (65 percent), Jackson (61 percent), and Robertson (61 percent), than in the case of more "centrist" candidates, such as Nixon (45 percent), Bush (44 percent), Dukakis (44 percent), Dupont (37 percent), and Dole (31 percent).

Turning to patterns of contribution, we have found that in 1988 the candidates perceived to be most extreme on the liberal/conservative scale, and whose supporters by one measure were also the most extreme (Jackson, Robertson, Kemp, and Simon) were successful in raising large percentages of their total contributions (from those who gave more than $200) through impersonal first contacts with their contributors—mostly direct mail, which means that direct mail is still alive and well as a fund-raising option for candidates on both ends of the liberal/conservative scale.[1]

Second, we found that the rest of the candidates studied (Babbitt, Bush, Dole, Dupont, Dukakis, Gephardt, and Gore) relied primarily on personalized contacts to make the first approach to their contributors of more than $200: this despite the campaign finance rules enacted in the 1970's, which tend to encourage direct mail, and despite the growth of an extensive direct mail industry partly in response to such rules.

Personal networking was at least as important as direct mail in raising serious money in 1988: 51 percent of those who contributed more than $200 were first contacted personally by someone they knew; an additional 17 percent were contributors who received a request in the mail for someone they knew personally; only 33 percent were asked by someone they did not know personally, most of the latter requests being by mail.

In terms of dollar totals from those whose contributions totaled over $200, about two-thirds of the money raised by all candidates came from contributors first approached directly by someone they knew personally. Less than a fifth of the money came from those who were intitially contacted through impersonal means by someone they did not know.

As far as the winners are concerned, 59 percent of Bush's contributions of more than $200 came from contributors first solicited by direct personal contact; for Dukakis, it was 65 percent (by contrast, in the case of Robertson it was 15 percent, with 65 percent coming from contributors first contacted impersonally by someone they did not know).

Lest it be argued that to focus on contributions of more than $200 is to focus on a narrow segment of the contributing public: well over half of the money raised from individual contributors came from this source in the case of Babbitt, Dukakis, Gephardt, Gore, Bush, Dole, and Dupont.

These results confirm that money coming from networks based on personal relations (where those who solicit support know personally those from whom the support is solicited) are at least as important in the presidential nomination fund-raising process as are direct-mail and other impersonal fund-raising techniques.

Furthermore, we have also found that personalized fund-raising networks may have some strategic advantages over direct-mail networks. Although the results vary some by candidate, contributors first approached personally

---

[1] Simon relied much less on impersonal means of successful solicitation than did the other three candidates, and was much closer to the "centrist" candidates in this regard.

by someone they knew generally were wealthier than those first approached by mail, and they gave more. Also, they tended to be younger than those approached impersonally (although this finding might not hold true for candidates with special appeals to young people).

Finally, contributors approached personally are more willing themselves to solicit money from others: among those who were first approached in person by someone they knew, 40 percent solicited funds from others on behalf of presidential candidates, compared to 29 percent for those who were first approached through the mail by someone they knew, and only 18 percent for those first approached through the mail by someone they did not know.

Thus for every contributor first identified through personal contact, there is a much higher "multiplier effect" in terms of identifying new contributors than is the case for direct mail: the personal contact method of raising money seems much more amenable to pyramiding.

When it comes to building a network of personalized contributors, however, the opportunities for a candidate to succeed in doing so depend upon the strategic resources that candidate has to begin with. In 1988, we found three rather different resources.

First, we found that several candidates relied heavily upon contributions from their own state to form a nucleus of their fund-raising efforts: Simon (41 percent), Dukakis (32 percent), Gore (30 percent), Babbitt (29 percent), and Gephardt (29 percent) were the leading examples of this in terms of the estimated percentage of contributions of more than $200 coming from their home state. In each of these cases, over two-thirds of their in-state contributors of more than $200 were first contacted by someone they knew personally, either directly, or by mail.

One political implication of this is that candidates from the "mega-states" have a major resource to utilize in mounting a campaign: Babbitt, Gore, and Gephardt, although they raised impressive percentages of their money in their own states, all suffered from the fact that their states were small or medium-sized.

To illustrate the potential role of a mega-state financial power base: the amounts of money raised by candidates for governor in 1990 in states like California and Texas comfortably exceeded half the amount needed (when added to its matching funds) to reach the federal campaign expenditure limit for a presidential nomination campaign.

Also, the 1988 data show that in-state personal-contact fund-raising efforts can successfully reach the potential contributors who are not necessarily closest to the candidate ideologically: only 42 percent of those first contacted by someone they knew personally on behalf of a candidate from the same state gave to the ideologically most proximate candidate (compared to 61 percent among all contributors who did so, and 70 percent for out-of-state contributors who were first contacted by impersonal means by someone they did not know). Thus in-state personal-contact fund-raising efforts seem to have the potential to tap contributors from a wider ideological spectrum than is the case with direct-mail contacts, either in-state or outstate.

Second, in addition to the mega-state financial "power base," we also found that ranking congressional office can enable a candidate to assemble an impressive cadre of "special interest" contributors—those who also are regular contributors to PAC's (although direct contributions by PAC's themselves are not a major factor in presidential nomination funding totals). Dole, in this case was the most successful, but by no means only, practitioner: 72 percent of his contributors also gave to a PAC in 1987–88, and 42 percent say they give to PAC's in most elections. These are the highest percentages for any candidate. In the case of Bush, it was 48 percent who gave in 1987–88, and 31 precent who give in most elections; in the case of Dukakis, it was 34 percent who gave in 1987–88 and 21 percent who give in most elections.[2]

Moreover, half of Dole's contributors say that they participate in politics at least as much for business and employment reasons as to affect the outcome of an election, the highest for any Republican.

Being a candidate heavily dependent on PAC contributors, however, did not provide Dole with in-depth support, at least by one measure. We asked respondents if they, in turn, had solicited money from others on behalf of a candidate. Thirty percent said they had. In the case of Dole, however, it was only 18 percent—the lowest for any candidate. By contrast, more than 30 percent of Babbitt's, Bush's, Dukakis', Gephardt's, Gore's, Jackson's, and Simon's contributors solicited money on their behalf from others. Dole also ranks last (among those with large enough sample sizes to measure) in terms of the percentage of those who were themselves solicited in person, and who, in turn, solicited from others: his pyramid was the flattest.

These results seem to suggest that Dole's money (more than that of any other candidate) was "opportunity money" contributed by PAC contributors (no doubt because of his office), who were not enthusiastic enough about his candidacy to beat the bushes on his behalf.

Third, and perhaps least generic, there was the Bush candidacy, also heavily reliant on personal-contact methods of fund-raising, which assembled a national financial network grounded in Republican Party loyalists. For example:

- 63 percent of Bush contributors say they are strong Republicans, compared to 56 percent for Kemp and Robertson, 47 percent for Dupont, and 42 percent for Dole.
- 23 percent have held a party position, compared to 17 percent for Kemp, 15 percent for Robertson, 14 percent for Dole, and 11 percent for Dupont.

[2]Large percentages of Robertson's (48 percent) and Jackson's (43 percent) contributors also contributed to PAC's in 1987–88. Not only are there traditional "legislative" PAC's, but also ideological PAC's. See Alexander, *Financing Politics*, 3d edition (Washington D.C. 1984), 108–110.

- 15 percent have held a public elective position, compared to 8 percent for Kemp and Dupont, 4 percent for Dole, and 1 percent for Robertson.
- 23 percent have held public appointive office, compared to 16 percent for Dupont, 14 percent for Kemp, 13 percent for Dole, and 4 percent for Robertson.

Bush also ranks highest among Republicans in terms of the percentage of contributors who themselves solicited contributions from other people, which suggests that his pyramiding efforts were the most successful of any candidate.

It would seem, then, that Bush built a large and deep network of financial contributors from within traditional Republican Party sources, and thus came to represent the traditional Republican party organization far more than did any other candidate. Presumably Bush's years of political and governmental experience, former campaigns, the Vice Presidency, and the services of professional fund-raisers all contributed to his ability to build this network.

Thus, we are seeing a fragmentation of the presidential fund-raising process. Ideological causes, mega-state power bases, congressional leadership positions, and in-depth national party networks are all sources from which presidential nominees can raise adequate funds to mount a sustained campaign effort throughout the primary season.

While it is not surprising that fund-raising strategies and sources of contributions vary widely, given the different political backgrounds of the candidates and the types of campaign they wage, what is most interesting about 1988 is that mass-based means of raising money (which were encouraged by the reforms of the 1970's) seemed to have been overshadowed by personal networking techniques, often operating in-state.

The implications for the future are that sitting governors (and perhaps well-networked senators) from large states, as well as those who occupy top leadership positions in Congress, can (through networks built around the resources of their offices) raise money in strategically equivalent amounts to the money that ideological candidates can raise through direct mail—despite the limits on size of contributions—and apart from independent expenditures.

Senator Alms

CHARLES BABINGTON

Senators routinely complain that they must raise thousands of dollars a week for six years in order to fund their reelection efforts. One of the most successful fund-raisers in the Senate is Jesse Helms. Senator Helms raised record amounts of money in his 1984 and 1990 reelections. Writer Charles Babington describes the Helms fund-raising empire, how it works, and why it has been so productive.

The Moral Majority has closed its doors. Conservative direct-mail wizard Richard Viguerie has sold his Virginia office building to Sun Myung Moon's Unification Church. The Fund for a Conservative Majority, which ranked among the nation's four richest PACs in the first three elections of the 1980s, now can't crack the top fifty. These are hard times for right-wing fund-raisers. With the Berlin Wall in pieces and the ever accommodating George Bush as president, the movement has lost its momentum. But there's one far-right fund-raiser who's comfortably surviving the cold war thaw: Senator Jesse Helms of North Carolina.

Helm's direct-mail operation remains among the nation's biggest, boldest, and wealthiest. The 1990 Helms for Senate Committee—which is only one arm of his money-raising organization, headed by the National Congressional Club in Raleigh—has so far hauled in $5.6 million through $10 and $20 checks from donors all over the country. (Less than 20 percent of Helms's money comes from North Carolina.) That puts it roughly on schedule with his 1984 campaign, which set the all-time Senate record by raising $16 million. Helms beat Governor Jim Hunt that year. This year he easily defeated two minor Republican challengers in the May 8 primary and now awaits a June 5 Democratic runoff to see whether his opponent will be former Charlotte Mayor Harvey Gantt or Southport District Attorney Michael Easley.

Helms still succeeds where other conservatives fail because he has replaced the bogeyman of Marxism with the horrors of homosexuality, AIDS, and "perverted art," and because he carefully synchronizes his fund-raising letters with his Senate speeches (broadcast nationwide by C-SPAN). Beyond that, his direct-mail formula has barely changed: Announce a new campaign crisis every week. Ask the same people for money often enough

Source: *The New Republic*, May 28, 1990. Reprinted by permission of *The New Republic*, (c) 1990, The New Republic, Inc.

Staff writer Charles R. Babcock and researcher Colette T. Rhoney contributed to this report. Senior computer analyst Edward Dolbow contributed to this report.

to make a televangelist blush. Launch a bitter, highly publicized Senate fight just when the money operation needs to hit high gear. (In 1984 it was the Martin Luther King holiday battle; this year it's arts funding.) And lace nearly every letter with racial code words. Sometimes his writers put it all in one sentence. "Since Jesse refuses to compromise conservative principles, the union bosses, Jesse Jackson's crowd, the radical feminists, and the homosexuals are all out for Jesse's political hide!" said one of the dozens of letters that have flooded our home since we sent $10 to get on the Helms mailing list in mid-1989.

Helms was a pioneer of political direct mail. When he and Tom Ellis, a Raleigh lawyer, founded the Congressional Club to retire the debt from Helms's 1972 victory, mass-mail fund-raising was virtually unheard of among Senate candidates. Today other conservative direct-mail operations, such as the National Conservative Political Action Committee, are better known. But NCPAC is nearly $4 million in debt, and it raised only $328,000 last year. The Congressional Club, meanwhile, was the nation's richest or second-richest PAC in four of the five election cycles of the 1980s. Although the club recently showed a debt of about $700,000 (stemming from its 1987–88 slump), it raised more than $1.4 million last year. And Congressional Club revenue doesn't include the income of its affiliated groups. Most of the club's income is plowed back into fund-raising, always building and refining the mailing lists that fuel the Helms political engine.

The director of the Congressional Club, Carter Wrenn, won't divulge how many letters his operation churns out, or which ones are the most lucrative. You can walk right into the club's headquarters, but you need a security code to enter the rooms where the mass-mail machines hum. Still, the length of the Congressional Club's mailing lists (and ambitions) aren't total mysteries: Helms said he sent out more than a million copies of his 1985 letter urging conservatives to buy CBS stock and become "Dan Rather's boss."

Some of the Helms direct-mail strategy is readily apparent. For example, the campaign constantly varies the size, shape, and color of its envelopes, not to mention its stamps, aware that even dedicated conservatives will sometimes throw away a letter, unopened, if they realize it's only another solicitation. Some letters resemble government mail, with envelopes promoting savings bonds or warning of fines for unauthorized use. An October letter came by certified mail, requiring the recipient to sign for it but giving no hint of its contents. "If I have inconvenienced you in any way, I sincerely apologize," it said. "But I need your help urgently." A hand-addressed Christmas card last year said: "I hope you'll do something special to say 'Merry Christmas' to Senator Helms—and send him a special contribution." It then noted that Gantt is among "the state's leading black politicians." The letter then took swipes at three other blacks: Jesse Jackson, Virginia Governor Doug Wilder, and Ron Brown, the chairman of the Democratic National Committee.

In fact, nearly every Helms letter describes a black person or institution as part of the enemy. Through the years—as a Raleigh radio and TV commentator in the 1960s, and a senator since 1973—Helms's attacks on "the so-called civil rights movement" and "forced busing" have not been lost on Tar Heel voters. When he denounces "the bloc vote in North Carolina," everyone gets the point. A recent Helms letter said, "One reason Jesse Jackson is campaigning against me is because I opposed the national holiday for Martin Luther King. Because I wanted all Federal Government and FBI files about King made public.... And for that matter, don't you agree the American people are entitled to know the whole truth about a certain Senator and what really happened at Chappaquiddick?"

When the Raleigh *News and Observer* ran a long article last September outlining Helms's "well-worn pattern" of injecting campaigns "with the divisive politics of race," Helms called the story a smear. Yet his campaign staff reprinted it and mailed it to thousands of potential donors, after first highlighting, and occasionally quibbling with, fourteen passages. "The liberals flat-out paint Jesse Helms as a racist," said the accompanying letter, in case anyone missed it.

Most of the letters are signed by "Bill Bennett, finance co-chairman." Helms describes Bennett as "a nice young man" from Raleigh. The senator shrugs off the suggestion that people might confuse him with that other Bill Bennett, the drug czar, who maintained his official residence in North Carolina until recently.

Perhaps the biggest boost to Helms's fund-raising has been C-SPAN's telecasting of Senate proceedings—which Helms initially opposed. He says C-SPAN watchers call his office constantly, saying, "Go get 'em, Jess," when he takes the floor to denounce gay activists, welfare programs, or funds for "deviant art." But Helms insists it's not his doing when his mass-mail team sends a letter on the heels of such events. "This business of saying, 'Well, Helms is doing this because of politics,' it just isn't so," he told me. "I don't operate that way. Now, my folks down in Raleigh, they pick up on an issue. What are they supposed to do?"

When Helms began his attacks last summer on the National Endowment for the Arts and its funding of homoerotic photos, the fund-raising potential was obvious. In an interview at the time, he said his political operatives in Raleigh "were highly commendatory about this. But I don't know if they've got any plans. As long as they tell the truth about it, it's OK."

They had plans indeed. An August 18 letter said: "Please rush Jesse Helms a special contribution of $29 today!... He needs you to support his legislation to stop the liberals from spending taxpayers' money on perverted, deviant art!... All Jesse's legislation would do is stop radical, left-wing artists from getting government money to pay for attacks on Christianity and so-called 'art' that promotes immorality and homosexuality!" The letter, from Bennett, said some federally subsidized photographs "are so utterly disgusting I can't even describe them. Mrs. Helms saw some of the pictures. 'Lord have mercy, Jesse, I'm not believing this,' she said and slammed the book shut!" Eight months later the NEA controversy still primes the money-raising pump. An April 26 letter (on pink stationery) from Helms's daughter Jane Helms Knox says, "The mean-spirited ultra-liberal news media viciously attacked my Dad for opposing the waste of your tax dollars to fund obscene, homosexual 'art.' "

Despite the desperate tone of the letters, federal campaign records show that thousands of people send money to Helms week after week. When *The News and Observer* recently interviewed twenty-five people who had sent him at least two dozen checks since mid-1987, it found their average age was eighty. Earlier I had asked Daisy Wigent, a retiree in Albuquerque, New Mexico, why she once sent Helms sixteen checks for $10 each over a six-month period. "Well," she said. "to me he seems like a sincere man in all his House committees and so forth."

Those sold on Helms's sincerity might note that last fall—when he was outpacing all his opponents twelve-to-one in fund-raising—his campaign issued an "absolutely urgent" call for more money to answer "left-wing radicals." "Frankly," the letter said, "Senator Helms's campaign could be won or lost in the next few weeks. . . . The next smear could hit any day!"

3. The Political Environment

Political campaigns do not occur in a vacuum. Candidates and their managers are aware of environmental conditions that may affect the outcome of an election. One party will have a numerical advantage over the other. Various social and political groups will be active, with important consequences. These social groups will differ in their size and in the proportion of their members that turn out to vote; these differences may in turn lead to specially targeted voter mobilization efforts. Social groups also differ in their loyalty toward a particular party and its candidates. Astute campaign managers assess these environmental factors early in their planning.

Perhaps the most important environmental condition for American national elections is the party balance. Between 1860 and 1932, the party balance had shifted several times, in relatively consistent intervals of thirty-two to thirty-six years. Since the New Deal realignment of the 1930s, more Americans have considered themselves Democrats than Republicans. These shifts in party balance, called realignments, have attracted considerable scholarly interest and have led researchers to develop several theories to explain the apparent regularity of changes in the party balance. If realignments occur at regular intervals, we are substantially overdue for a change that would create a Republican majority. Scholars and journalists have spent considerable time and effort explaining why the realignment is late and speculating as to whether it will ever come.

In the first reading, Everett Carl Ladd suggests that the expectation of an imminent party realignment may have deflected attention from more gradual shifts in political attitudes and the party balance. He points to several important changes in the party system, including the decline of the Democratic New Deal coalition, and the emergence of a "two-tier" system where different dynamics apply to presidential elections and sub-presidential elections. Instead of waiting for a realignment, he suggests that we should take stock of these actual changes that have occurred.

During the 1980s, a growing gender gap in voting has attracted attention from journalists, scholars, and party strategists. Although the gender gap is not large, its recent emergence has puzzled many experts and has led Republican strategists to ponder survey results in an attempt to win more women's votes. In the second reading, Evans Witt discusses what Republicans have concluded from these surveys. He breaks the "women's vote" into several distinct categories—younger, married, working women; older, single, working women; and others. He concludes that the gender gap is larger among the young, and that it will probably grow over time. Witt's article was written in 1985, after the second Reagan election. In 1988, Bush began the campaign facing a large gender gap, but his campaign targeted women voters with both the "kinder, gentler" theme and the crime issue. Bush pollsters discovered that many women felt that the Reagan administrations had been insufficiently compassionate toward disadvantaged elements in society, and the "kinder, gentler" theme was aimed to rectify that image. Women were also concerned about violent crime, and Bush's emphasis on crime deterrence helped close the gender gap. Yet even after substantial investments in narrowing the gender gap, women's votes were evenly divided between Bush and Dukakis, while Bush won by a large margin among men.

White, evangelical Christians also changed their voting pattern during the 1980s, and by 1988 they were one of the most loyal Republican social groups. They rallied to Jimmy Carter in 1976, but in 1980 they split their vote between Carter and Reagan, and in 1984 they voted for Ronald Reagan in record numbers. The changing voting patterns among white evangelicals is of vital political import, for they are disproportionately located in crucial Southern states that Democrats must win if they hope to recapture the White House. Lyman Kellstedt shows that religion was an important factor in the 1988 election, for highly religious Protestants voted for Bush in higher numbers than their less committed brethren. Kellstedt sees potential discord in the evangelical-mainline Protestant Republican coalition, however, for evangelicals generally endorse the conservative social agenda of Republicans, while mainline Protestants do not. This tension suggests the potential for further shifts in the religious composition of the parties.

Although voter turnout has declined fairly steadily in American elections for many years, it has not been constant across social groups. Explanations of electoral outcomes often hinge on turnout differences between parties and among social groups. In the final reading in this chapter, Ruy Teixeira focuses on turnout in the 1988 election. He explores the impact of differential turnout rates across racial and class lines, concluding that although higher rates of participation among blacks, Hispanics, blue-collar workers, and the poor would have helped the Democrats, Bush won the election because he appealed more broadly to the citizenry, not because his supporters were more likely to vote.

The Uselessness of Realignment for Understanding Change in Contemporary American Politics

EVERETT C. LADD

For nearly two decades political scientists and political professionals have been searching for evidence of a major, permanent shift in partisanship that would make the Republicans the majority party. We refer to this type of change as a realignment. Political scientist Everett Carl Ladd suggests that while we have been searching for this massive change, we have ignored important shifts in the attitudes and partisanship of the electorate.

WHAT IS "REALIGNMENT"?

Three sets of definitions of the phenomenon [of realignment] have been in circulation: (1) the dictionary meaning, which is the most general; (2) the understanding common in media discussions; and (3) the predominant political science usages, which are the most elaborate and hence the narrowest. The *Random House Dictionary of the English Language* (2nd edition, unabridged) defines "alignment" as "a state of agreement or cooperation among persons, groups . . . with a common cause or viewpoint." Realignment occurs, then, when such an alliance is significantly changed or, inferentially, when conflict among competing alliances is transformed. This simple construction would have provided a far better starting point for disciplinary research than those that have in fact held sway.

Journalistic definitions pivot on the idea of a new majority party. The question the press has posed untiringly after every Republican victory since Eisenhower's first, "But is it a realignment?" in fact asks: Has the GOP supplanted the Democrats as the majority party? Since in every instance the correct answer has been "No," these press accounts have for the most part concluded complacently. In effect: "The Republicans won, but the long-awaited realignment has yet to occur. Whether the GOP will succeed eventually, or the Democrats' New Deal coalition be revitalized remains to be seen." Already a bit silly in 1972, this perspective had become ludicrous by the 1980s.

V. O. Key, Jr., the discipline's "Father of Realignment," wrote three key realignment pieces in the 1950s, not just the two *Journal of Politics*

Source: *Polity*, Spring 1990, Volume XXII #3, pp. 511–525. Reprinted by permission of the author and *Polity*.

works so often cited. His first was an essay in *The Virginia Quarterly Review,* published during the 1952 campaign. In it he introduced the term "party realignment" and described some of what realignment entails. His starting point was the pivotal historical role played by catastrophe. "For almost a hundred years," Key wrote, "catastrophe has fixed the grand outlines of the partisan division among American voters." First, it was the Civil War that "burned into the American electorate a pattern of partisan faith that persisted in its main outlines until 1932." The Depression was the second great realigning catastrophe.

But Key immediately went beyond this formulation, arguing that in fact it was not the Depression itself that established a Democratic majority, nor was it the opportunity the collapse gave them to show they could govern well that was decisive. The Democrats became the majority party when they developed convincing answers to problems long manifest but theretofore addressed only in part. Thus, party competition was transformed by "the New Deal's fulfillment of the hopes of these many streams of progressive agitation . . . ." Here, a decisive reformulation of policy is the key element in realignment.

Key also introduced the term "secular realignment": "The New Deal should not be credited with the entire accretion to Democratic strength. In part the Democrats merely recruited potential converts who had been accumulating under the effects of long-term demographic trends and were awaiting political activation." The sources he cited were industrialization, urbanization, and the gradual political incorporation of the last great wave of European immigration.

Key's initial formulation in "The Future of the Democratic Party" was a promising start. The U.S. party system was seen to have been permanently reshaped by a few massive sociopolitical events which left deep imprints on Americans' collective memories. But realignment has also involved the emergence of new social needs and breakthroughs in partisan responses to them, as well as demographic shifts that gradually transform the electorate. These diverse developments surely help determine winners and losers, and in certain periods they have come with special force. But in his first formulation of realignment, Key did not envision any fixed pattern or singular model.

By itself, Key's next piece in the series, "A Theory of Critical Elections," need not have been a step backward conceptually. It was, as he stated, "an attempt to formulate a concept of one type of election . . . *which might be built into a more general theory of elections"* —not a mature theory of partisan change. Key discerns

> a category of elections in which voters are . . . unusually deeply concerned, in which the extent of electoral involvement is relatively quite high, and in which the decisive results of the voting reveal a sharp alteration of the pre-existing cleavage within the electorate. Moreover, and perhaps this is a truly differentiating characteristic of this sort of election, the realignment made manifest in the voting in such elections seems to persist for several succeeding elections.

Unfortunately, as we know, American political science proceeded to build on this modest foundation an elaborate conceptualization of realignment as the centerpiece of a more general theory of partisan change. Many things besides Key's suggestions caused this to happen. The New Deal's burst of partisan change was alive in analysts' minds. It was the one such occurrence political scientists of the time had experienced personally. The vividness of the specific instance helped it masquerade convincingly as the general rule. With more perspective, we can now see that the massive shifts in the party system and voting alignments in the 1930s were in fact *sui generis*. In many essential structural regards, nothing like the New Deal transformation had ever occurred before, nor have they since.

For other reasons, a discipline seeking the neatness, precision, and predictability it naively attributed to "science" could not resist realignment's beguiling simplicity. We were highly susceptible. I remarked in a convention paper fifteen years ago that "it is truly a case of Key sneezing and political science catching a cold. . . . "

CHANGE AND THE CONTEMPORARY PARTY SYSTEM

I have argued for some time that, by focusing on the emergence of a new majority party in the New Deal model, the concept "critical realignment" detracts attention from other changes in parties and elections which are of fundamental importance. Anyone who hazards to write about current political developments will receive ample training in the need for humility. Of this I am confident because, in 1980, I authored an article entitled, "Why Carter Will Probably Win." Nonetheless, I insist that the general outlines of a new party system, fundamentally different from that of the New Deal era, have been evident for some time. This system is really not envisioned by the realignment perspective. As the Watergate election balloting was taking place in the fall of 1974, I attempted the following summary of the new system's notable features:

1. The Democrats have lost the presidential majority status which they enjoyed during the New Deal era, as new lines of conflict have decimated parts of the old coalition, but the Republicans have not attained presidential majority status. There is no majority party in the presidential arena.

2. There has been an inversion of the old New Deal relationship of social class to the vote. In wide sectors of public policy, high SES groups are now more supportive of equalitarian (liberal) change than are the middle to lower SES cohorts (within white America), and as a result liberal (often, although not always, Democratic) candidates are finding higher measures of electoral sustenance at the top of the socioeconomic ladder than among the middle and lower rungs. This inversion follows from very basic changes in the structure of conflict in American society and is likely to be long term.

3. The Republican coalition has experienced serious erosions, and is weaker now than at any time since the days of the Great Depression, probably weaker, in fact, than at any time since the party's rise during the Civil War era.
4. A "two-tier" party system has emerged, with one set of electoral dynamics operating at the presidential level, and yet another at sub-presidential contests.
5. The electorate is far more weakly tied to political parties now than at any time in the past century, and, as it has been freed from the "anchor" of party loyalties, it has become vastly more volatile.
6. The communications function—whereby party leaders communicate with the rank and file, and the latter in turn send messages up to the party leadership—has historically been a great raison d'etre for political parties in egalitarian systems; but this function has increasingly been assumed by other structures, notably those organized around the mass media of communication.
7. A major new cohort of activists has assumed vastly increased importance in the electoral arena, a cohort whose position is closely linked to the growth of the intelligentsia in postindustrial America.

The second observation was an overextrapolation from certain tendencies then evident in public opinion data. The third either did not belong at all, if taken simply as a commentary on short-term conditions where the Republicans were besieged; or it was flat-out wrong, if seen as a long-term projection. Point seven was too limited; the changes in elite composition and outlook extended far beyond the element identified.

Still, much of the formulation seems about right. A new party system had appeared, though it did not include the emergence of a new majority party. Voter ties to political parties were weaker than in the past, a factor which had important implications throughout the system's operations. The composition and outlook of party elites had shifted markedly from what they were in the New Deal years. Split outcomes were not accidental occurrences in the new system but an essential feature of it. The Democrats had lost their presidential majority status, to which we would now add that the Republicans have secured majority status presidentially, though by no means elsewhere. The structure of campaigning had been transformed, especially by the dramatic enlargement of the mass media's role in political communication—a role played out independently from the political parties and even in opposition to them institutionally. By no means a realignment these developments surely reflected whopping, highly consequential, largely irreversible changes.

Each succeeding U.S. party system has been ushered in by the dynamics of a new societal era; the current system is no exception. While no one term can ever adequately identify an era's distinguishing characteristics, for the present one "postindustrial" is very helpful. Many, though by no means all, of the important social changes experienced by the U.S. in recent decades are captured by the idea of postindustrialism's emergence.

Influences of the postindustrial setting on the party system are varied and profound, and easily traced. An electorate with high levels of formal education, for example, which receives its political information largely through national communications media of great institutional autonomy, must be far less dependent on political parties for cues and direction than were its predecessors.

Similarly, vast growth in occupations involved in creating, manipulating, and disseminating ideas, as opposed to producing things, has transformed the labor force. Organized labor, which developed in the industrial era, became a major economic and political force during and immediately following the New Deal as union membership soared. In 1989, however, after much of postindustrialism's transformation had been completed, unionized workers were scarcely half the proportion of the labor force they were 35 years earlier; inevitably, labor had become a far more feeble element in national politics generally, and in the Democratic coalition specifically.

Other important changes in the larger society are related more tangentially to the coming of postindustrialism. The collapse of the "Jim Crow" system of racial separation and gross discrimination in the South since World War II has, for example, had enormous political implications. Of special importance given our focus here, the enfranchisement of black Americans and their entry en masse into the Democratic coalition transformed party competition in the South. Such features of the postindustrial setting as greatly expanded affluence and extended access to higher education undoubtedly contributed to the growing perception of categoric discrimination as illegitimate. But, obviously, many other things were at work, among them: the development of a political base for blacks in large northern states, which gave them leverage; the population shift within the South itself from rural to urban areas, where black political organization could be achieved more easily and extralegal violence against blacks with greater difficulty; the initiatives of the civil rights movement; etc.

Similarly, changing generational experiences only partially attributable to postindustrialism have reshaped the party system since the New Deal era. Those who came of age politically at the time of the Great Depression, when the immediate comparison of presidential leadership centered on Republican Herbert Hoover and Democrat Franklin Roosevelt, remain even today notably Democratic in their party attachments. Once the youngest cohort in American politics, the Depression Generation is now the oldest. The Republicans fare much better among those who have come of age politically in the late 1970s and 1980s, for whom the most vivid comparison is that of Democrat Jimmy Carter to Republican Ronald Reagan.

Quite apart from how we categorize their sources, we can see massive shifts in social needs, problems, and interests in the contemporary era, which have in turn transformed the ideational substance of political conflict. The intense conflict over abortion is only the latest manifestation of the high salience social or moral issues have attained in the past quarter century. Social issues had been relatively submerged in the New Deal years, though they had loomed large in earlier eras. Now, they have not only again come to the fore, but derive from new sources and have taken new form. Historically, immigration loomed large are a source of cultural tensions, but it is little implicated in the ascendance of social issues today. Cultural class conflict, organized around different levels of formal education and attributable to jarringly different world views thus transmitted, forms the core of today's moral disputation.

When the New Deal parties were taking form, Adolf Hitler was just coming to power in Germany, and Soviet communism seemed to many, including some idealistic Americans, a system rich in promise. The world has changed much since then, and so has how we view it. Quite apart from the arguments over specific programs and policies, the intellectual climate has changed enormously. Not many in the U.S. or abroad are now inclined to see the road to economic salvation running through increased interventions of the state. Call it capitalism, free enterprise, or market-centered economy, the idea has a following whose breadth and depth would have been unimaginable fifty years ago.

In the U.S. during the New Deal, the idea of "more government" seemed to be linked to that of "progress." Committed to the expanded state, the Democratic party thus derived enormous political sustenance. Today things have changed greatly. The suggestion sometimes advanced in the late 1970s and early 1980s that Americans had swung philosophically *against* government was nonsense, but certainly they had become and still are far more *uncertain* about the merits of expanding it. The exceptional ambivalence of today's public on many policy questions but especially on those of government's proper role, deeply influences the present status of the parties. It is a major source of the Republican revival.

Systematic attention to the many dimensions of social change and their partisan consequences lies beyond the reach of this essay. But there is little real dispute that, in the last quarter century, a new societal era has become manifest in the United States. The New Deal coalition and other features of the party system of the preceding era could not possibly have survived this transformation. They have not, save for the fact that residues of earlier systems always remain in their successors.

The realignment perspective requires us to ask why the partisan "Big Change" has not occurred (and when will it). Thus it continues to tease us with the promise that an enormously complex reality will submit to a very simple and highly parsimonious theoretic organization. But the political world stubbornly refuses to comply. It requires of us the task—laborious and prosaic—of charting the many shifts that have occurred in the party system and of seeking *their diverse sources and implications*.

What the Republicans Have Learned about Women

EVANS WITT

When political scientists discussed gender differences in the 1950s, they noted that women were more conservative than men. During the 1980s, women and men increasingly diverged in the attitudes, partisanship, and vote choice, but in this case women are more liberal than men. Men are more likely to support Republican candidates than women, and Republican strategists have considered various strategies to increase their share of the women's vote. Writer Evans Witt discusses what Republican pollsters have learned about the gender gap. Republicans have identified discrete groups of women and men that differ most in their attitudes and have targeted appeals to narrow the gender gap.

Early in October 1985, the Republican National Committee sponsored the first of a series of three-day workshops across the country aimed at the working women of America. There were sessions on managing money, managing time, managing the family, Jazzercize, and—*almost incidentally*—on politics.

Why is the Republican party spending $200,000 for such meetings, which are life-style seminars in everything but name?

Because of the "gender gap."

Many thought that the gender gap had been buried along with Walter Mondale beneath the 1984 Reagan landslide. Even the addition of Geraldine Ferraro as the first woman ever on a national political ticket could not win a majority of women's votes for the Democrats, much less turn around the election.

Republican politicians and strategists have publicly belittled the impact of the gender gap, suggesting the real problem is that Democrats have a gender gap among men. After all, didn't Reagan win forty-nine states in the 1984 election even while taking 6 percentage points less of women's votes than men's?

But privately, GOP professionals have been working to analyze the party's problems with women and to craft solutions. Amid all the talk of realignment and party-switching, women remain among the groups least responsive to the GOP's appeals. And if the Republicans are to become the majority

Source: *Public Opinion*, (October/November 1985): pg. 49–52. Reprinted with permission of the American Enterprise Institute for Public Policy Research, Washington, D.C..

party in the nation for the next several decades, women must be a big part of that majority.

WOMEN'S GROUPS

The "gender gap" was the phrase popularized by feminists groups to describe the lingering troubles Republicans and President Reagan have been having with women. Beginning with the 1980 campaign, Reagan has received lower ratings and fewer votes from women that he has been winning from men. Some of that negative attitude has rubbed off on GOP candidates at the state level.

In the 1980 balloting, Reagan easily won the men's vote by a 56 percent to 36 percent margin over incumbent Jimmy Carter, the Associated Press-NBC News exit poll of voters found. But women split their votes 47–45 percent between Reagan and Carter. The differences between men's and women's voting behavior was labeled the "gender gap." Democrats sought to exploit it, while Republicans looked for ways to heal it or reduce its political impact.

As with any political strategy, there are many different ways to look at the Republicans' response to the gender gap. One can listen to the politicians on the stump and read the position papers. Or one can talk to the party professionals and the political consultants for their views. Or one can look at hour upon hour of political commercials and dissect the networks' political coverage with an eye on what campaigns *wanted* the camera to see.

One way to examine the GOP's gender gap strategy is to look at the polls that were conducted to guide the politicians' tactics. The numbers tell a fascinating story of past techniques; and they suggest what might happen next.

But political pollsters conduct their surveys for their clients, not for the public. That means their clients see the results and the public does not. Decision/Making/Information, President Reagan's main polling firm, is no exception. Dr. Richard Wirthlin, the DMI chairman who serves the White House incumbent as his personal pollster, gives an engaging portrait of what his surveys are showing. Rarely, though, does he or any other private pollster release all the raw numbers from political surveys.

But a different window into the strategies of the Reagan campaign, the Republican party, and those often supporting the GOP, has been opened. Wirthlin's firm—through a subsidiary—did a series of polls that focused on women in 1983 and 1984 for the American Medical Association Political Action Committee, one of the oldest, largest, wealthiest, and most sophisticated PACs in the nation. Pete Lauer, executive director of AMPAC, said the polls were conducted to help the PAC make its decisions and to guide the candidates it supported who didn't have the time, money, or inclination to ask these questions themselves.

Neither Ronald Reagan's campaign nor the GOP had any part in the polls, but DMI's and Wirthlin's explorations of the women's vote for Reagan guided the methodology. And the survey analysis followed the same patterns of those done for the GOP.

The DMI analysis begins with the proposition that women are not a homogeneous group—a point that has been central to the GOP counterattack on the gender gap since 1981. By aggregating the results of dozens of national surveys, DMI vice president Cathy Chamberlain concluded that the most helpful guides to women's political attitudes are age, marital status, and employment outside the home. The DMI analysis combined women into eight groups based on six categories, with those under forty-five categorized as younger women and those forty-five and over categorized as older women. The category of married women included only those currently married with a living husband, with all other women identified as not married. Working women were defined as those working full time or part time outside the home.

At least part of this analysis is an extension of earlier work on the gender gap. Working women's negative attitudes toward Reagan, for example, were obvious in 1980. And Marty Plissner of CBS News laid out the case for a "marriage gap" two years ago in *Public Opinion*, finding that unmarried voters tended to be more Democratic than married voters. It is important to look at the women who are in each DMI subgroup, for the different pressures and experiences they have faced have shaped their political views.

- **Younger, married, working women:** This group represents 20 percent of all women. Eighteen percent of them have college or advanced degrees. They rank second in family income, with 22 percent reporting annual earnings over $40,000. Eighty-one percent have children, and 57 percent have children under twelve at home. This group gives family financial support as the primary reason for working. Only 21 percent say they work for a sense of personal achievement.
- **Younger, single, working women:** This includes 15 percent of all women. Though this subgroup ranks fifth out of eight in income, with only 6 percent making more than $40,000 a year, their prospects are bright; 20 percent of them college graduates. Even though not currently married, a substantial 46 percent have children, and 34 percent have kids under twelve at home. Thirty-two percent of this group are separated or divorced. Twenty-five percent have professional or technical jobs, and 52 percent have white-collar jobs. Eighty-two percent say that they work from financial necessity.
- **Younger, married women who are not working:** This takes in 13 percent of all women. Young children are the predominant feature of this subgroup. Ninety-four percent have children, and 81 percent have children under twelve at home—the highest percentage of any group. They rank third in family income, and 11 percent hold college degrees. Sixty-two percent plan to enter the workforce in the near future. For

six out of ten of these women, the presence of small children at home explains why they are not working. (One in ten don't work because their husbands don't want them to.) Fifty-three percent of them call themselves conservatives, and 39 percent say they are liberals.

- **Younger, single, not working women:** This group is a mere 5 percent of all women. It is concentrated between ages eighteen and thirty-four, and about half are students. About half have children, and 85 percent have only a high school education or less. Forty-five percent of them are separated, divorced, or widowed. Eighty percent plan to work, though 22 percent have no desire to work outside the home. Twenty-one percent of them earn $5,000 or less (26 percent refused to say how much they earn). They split their ideological allegiance right down the middle—41 percent liberal and 41 percent conservative.

- **Older, married, working women:** Ten percent of all women fall into this group. These women are at the top in income, with 27 percent having family incomes over $40,000. Seventeen percent are college graduates. While almost all—98 percent—have children, only 4 percent have any under age twelve still at home. Two-thirds of the group are between forty-five and fifty-five. This group also enjoys the highest professional employment level; 28 percent are in professional or technical fields, and 15 percent are in management or own their own business. Thirty-two percent of these women work for a sense of achievement. Six in ten of them are conservatives.

- **Older, single, working women:** This includes 6 percent of women. This is the least financially well-off group of working women and the second least well-off among all women, with two-thirds reporting incomes under $15,000 a year. Fourteen percent are college graduates. Forty percent of them are separated or divorced, and 44 percent of them are widowed. Thirty-two percent are employed in blue-collar fields, and most of the group report they work from financial necessity. They divide evenly ideologically—41 percent conservative and 41 percent liberal.

- **Older, married, not working women:** This describes 19 percent of all women. Three-quarters of this subgroup are fifty-five or older. Five percent are college graduates, and 38 percent did not get a high school degree. Only 4 percent have children at home under age twelve. Half describe themselves are retired and half as housewives. Forty percent have household incomes of less than $15,000 a year. Fifty-nine percent call themselves conservatives and 25 percent liberals.

- **Older, single, not working women:** Comprising 12 percent of all women, this is the least well-off subgroup, even though 10 percent are college graduates. A majority of them did not complete high school. Seventy-six percent are widowed. Most are over age sixty-five, and most (76 percent) have incomes of less than $15,000 a year. Thirty-seven percent earn less than $5,000 a year. Sixty percent say they are conservative, and only 19 percent say they are liberal.

THE EFFECTS

Separating women into eight groups for analysis makes sense only if those groups differ in their attitudes and their political behavior. And they do. Their vote for Reagan in 1984 varied by as much as 31 percentage points from group to group (see Table 1).

The DMI poll said women voted for Reagan by a 57 to 43 percent margin over Walter Mondale, while men voted for the GOP incumbent by a 60 to 40 percent edge. These figures are consistent with those from the CBS News/*New York Times* exit poll of voters in 1984. That survey found men voting for Reagan by 67 to 37 percent, while women backed him 56 to 44 percent. The DMI numbers were also consistent with the CBS/*New York Times* survey in saying unmarried women split 49 percent for Reagan and 51 percent for Mondale, while married women went 60 to 40 percent for Reagan. [Table 1 shows] the DMI breakout of women.

The patterns of the vote in the DMI subgroups are not easy, straight-line equations. But a close examination shows the value of the analytical approach.

Perhaps the easiest way to understand the table is to start with the larger categories and work down. Married women, for example, were substantially more pro-Reagan than single women. And non-working women were more tilted in the GOP direction than were working women.

But then look how the categories interact: Women who were both single and working were two of the most pro-Mondale groups. And there were some surprises: Older married women who don't work were one of Reagan's strongest groups. But older married women who work outside the home were more evenly split.

Lest anyone believe that these margins indicate most women rejected the Ferraro candidacy—rather than the Democratic ticket of which she was

TABLE 1.   Women's 1984 Vote for President

	Reagan	Mondale	Reagan minus Mondale
Younger, married, working women	61%	39%	+22%
Younger, not married, working	50	50	Even
Younger, married, not working	64	36	+28
Younger, not married, not working	33	66	−33
Older, married, working	55	45	+10
Older, not married, working	41	59	−18
Older, married, not working	62	38	+24
Older, not married, not working	56	44	+12

part—other DMI findings supply ample evidence. Overwhelming majorities from each subgroup agreed that Ferraro showed women can compete for the nation's highest offices, and majorities agreed that the Ferraro candidacy was a victory for women.

The Republicans can take less solace from the congressional vote in 1984, which in the DMI poll pretty much followed the party registration or partisan identification of the subgroups. Women voted 55–45 for the Democratic candidates, while men voted 53–47 for the Democrats [see Table 2].

As with the presidential vote, this four-dimensional pattern is difficult to visualize, and it differs somewhat from the presidential vote pattern. The underlying themes, however, remain the same: Single women are more pro-Democratic than married women. Working women are less favorable to the GOP than non-working women.

But here the power of partisan identification—and the lack of the pull of Reagan as the candidate—gave Democrats the margins. Among older married women who don't work, for example, the GOP could eke out only a split. And among their working counterparts, the Democrats swept by 18 percentage points.

The 1983 DMI survey tried to gauge the impact of two key feminist issues—abortion and the proposed Equal Rights Amendment—on the voting behavior of the various subgroups. While such questions may not be a reliable guide to how an individual will vote, they do provide a good indicator of the perceived importance to women of various issues in contrast to other findings.

Republicans might take heart from an earlier DMI question that found women putting the ERA at the bottom of their list of most important problems for women. But the results of the direct questioning on the ERA and abortion show the GOP has a problem with significant groups of women on the feminist issues.

TABLE 2.   Women's Vote for Congressional Candidates, 1984

	Rep.	Dem.	Rep. minus Dem.
Younger, married, working women	48%	52%	−4%
Younger, not married, working	45	55	−10
Younger, married, not working	50	50	Even
Younger, not married, not working	35	65	−30
Older, married, working	41	59	−18
Older, not married, working	25	75	−50
Older, married, not working	48	52	−4
Older, not married, not working	51	49	+2

On the ERA, for example, 39 percent of the young, single, working women said they would change their vote to oppose a candidate who did not support the ERA. Only 5 percent said they would change their vote to oppose a candidate who supported the ERA. Thus the pro-ERA bias among the group was 34 percentage points. In contrast, among older, married, non-working women, 14 percent would switch their votes in a pro-ERA direction, while 15 percent would switch in the anti-ERA direction.

Those two groups were also at the ends of the spectrum on the voting impact of the abortion issue. Thirty-six percent of the younger group would swing their votes in support of a candidate who backs women's right to choose an abortion, while 22 percent would go in the other direction. That's a "pro-choice" bias of 16 percentage points. But among the older, married, non-working women, 16 percent would swing their votes in the "pro-choice" direction, while 33 percent would switch to vote for the "pro-life" candidate—an anti-abortion edge of 17 percentage points.

Whatever the attitudes on those two issues, large majorities of each subgroup rated the women's movement as having a positive impact on this country and as having made them more aware of their own potential as women. In addition, the women's judgments were that the movement would have continuing and growing impact in the future.

The DMI surveys did not ask directly about an issue that some argue is critical to understanding the differences between men's and women's attitudes—war and peace. Kathleen Frankovic of CBS News has written elsewhere that the war issue, not women's issues, best explains the gender gap in 1980. Unfortunately, we cannot gauge its effect from this set of surveys.

A persuasive explanation for variations in women's political behavior among subgroups is that women's experiences and expectations vary.

More young women, for example, say they have personally faced sex discrimination than older women. The 1984 DMI survey found about a third of the younger women reporting such an experience, while only 18 percent of the older group did. Nearly two out of five younger, single, working women experienced discrimination. And working older women are more likely than non-working older women to report discrimination.

Asked whether men and women have equal opportunities in America today, the majorities in every subgroup of women said no. But more than two-thirds of those under 45 perceive discrimination, compared to just over half of those among the older group.

In addition, a somewhat finer analysis finds that the most feminist of the women are in the twenty-five to forty-five year old age bracket. These women came of age politically and professionally while the latest version of the women's movement was surging onto the political stage. Their expectations for their lives were certainly shaped by that movement in the turbulent 1960s and early 1970s.

The interaction of the burden of child-rearing and child care seems to play an important role in how these groups of women view the world. Having small children does not necessarily make one more conservative—or more liberal—but the responsibility of children interacts with the woman's personal and professional expectations to shape her political views (and almost certainly with a man's expectations as well).

Women not only say they have experienced discrimination, they also say their expectations have been shaped by that experience. Four out of ten women believe their opportunities are limited by their sex. Single women are more likely to believe this than married women, particularly those over age forty-five. About a third of the women with college or advanced degrees feel limited as well.

Discrimination and limits on their achievements are a personal, everyday experience for many women, a reality that shapes their political attitudes. And this reality rebounds against the GOP among women. Many women see the Republicans as insensitive to their concerns. By big margins in every group, the women pick the Democrats as more sensitive than the GOP, and that perception clearly translated into votes for the Democrats in 1984.

All this indicates the GOP problem with women will not just fade away and that it will probably get worse.

Younger working women are a growing part of the American scene, both socially and politically. Many do not vote now while they are getting their personal and professional lives on track, but they will become a crucial political force in the near future. As they age and settle down, these younger women will still be shaped by the memories of their early personal, professional, and political experiences—as they replace a more conservative generation of women from which Reagan and the Republicans have drawn significant support.

Thus, women are still missing from the Republicans' grand design for realignment. The GOP must find a way to attract the support of women, particularly younger working women, if that grand design is ever to become a reality.

Religion and the U.S. Party System

LYMAN A. KELLSTEDT

During the 1980s, Republicans sought to increase their share of the vote among white evangelical Christians. Although Jimmy Carter captured a fair share of the evangelical vote in 1980, in both 1984 and 1988 evangelicals supported Republicans in record numbers. Professor Lyman Kellstedt has written a number of articles on evangelical politics. In this brief piece, he discusses changes in the relationship between religion and voting in the 1980s and explores what these changes augur for future electoral politics.

Questions about religious commitments are typically not included in election surveys. Though the Christian Right has thrust religion to the forefront of public debate, the development of survey measures to monitor linkages between religion and politics on the general public level has not kept pace with events. The only information regularly obtained marks respondents as Protestant, Catholic, or Jew. As a result, the role of religion gets poorly handled in explanations of contemporary political behavior. This situation needs to change. We need to ask about the specific denominations to which Protestants belong—permitting us to classify them into religious families that in fact behave quite differently politically, such as the establishment Congregationalists and the "new breed" Pentecostals. The many religious families can then be categorized into broader religious traditions—mainline and evangelical Protestant. More generally, we need measures of church attendance, religious salience, and doctrinal concerns, if we are to explore properly the impact of religious commitments on political behavior.

Here, I want to review briefly what we know about the relationship between religion and politics, using data from the National Election Studies (NES), University of Michigan. The NES have asked specific denominational preference since 1956. Other religion measures were added in the 1980s to permit examination of relationships between religious commitments and political behavior. Beginning with this year's congressional election study, an even more complete set of religious measures will be available through the NES.

Source: This article first appeared in the November/December 1990 issue of *The Public Perspective*, a bi-monthly magazine produced by the Roper Center for Public Opinion Research at the University of Connecticut, Storrs, CT.

TABLE 1.   Party Preference and Presidential Vote of Religious
Groups, 1980–88 (Whites Only)

		PARTISANSHIP		
	Jews	Catholics	Mainline Protest.	Evang. Protest.
1980	1.25*	2.46	3.24	2.46
1984	1.73	2.58	3.37	3.12
1988	2.26	2.89	3.40	3.16
		PERCENT REPUBLICAN VOTE		
1980	44	57	68	63
1984	31	57	71	75
1988	27	54	64	70

Source: Surveys conducted by the Institute for Social Research at the University of Michigan
for their National Election Studies series.
* Party identification scores are means for the groups. Scores for individuals range from zero
(strong Democrat) to six (strong Republican). A score of 3.0 would place a group equally
between the two poles; scores above 3.0 show that the group leans Republican, scores
below 3.0 that it is Democratically inclined.

RELIGIOUS GROUP POLITICS

Table 1 compares religious groups in terms of their party identification and
presidential vote. Jews identify as Democrats and vote accordingly. Catholic
identification with the Democratic party has declined, from the high level it
occupied throughout most of US history, but it remains substantial. When
it comes to voting, though, Catholics have gone Republican in the last
three presidential contests. Mainline Protestants, the old Republican core,
still show strong Republican support.[1] Evangelical Protestants maintained
their historical identification with the Democratic party through 1980, even
though they voted for the Republican candidate in every presidential election since 1956, expect 1964. In recent years, evangelicals have changed
partisan preferences as well and joined the Republican coalition. This swing
of evangelicals to the GOP is not just a southern phenomenon; it took
place among northerners, and among both younger and older voters. Much
of the recent persistent talk about realignment centers on younger voters
and southerners. It should also focus on the change among evangelicals.

RELIGIOUS COMMITMENT AND POLITICAL CHOICE

Did religiosity remain an important political variable in the 1988 election?
Many thought not. Ronald Reagan, who had galvanized evangelicals, was

[1]Mainline Protestants include most Presbyterians and Methodists, Congregationalists, Episco-
palians, Lutherans, and assorted other denominations. Evangelical Protestants include Baptists,
Pentecostals (e.g., Assemblies of God), Holiness denominations (Nazarenes, Salvation Army),
Anabaptist, Reformed and most non-denominational Protestants. Coding details available from
the author.

TABLE 2. Religiosity and Political Behavior in 1988 (White Protestants Only)

	MAINLINE PROTESTANTS, RELIGIOUS COMMITMENT		EVANGELICAL PROTESTANTS, RELIGIOUS COMMITMENT	
	Low	High	Low	High
Partisan Identification	3.37	3.86	2.97	3.51
Percent Vote for Bush	63	75	65	78

Source: 1988 NES Survey.
* The means and percentages are adjusted to control for the effects of region, age, sex, and education. Differences between evangelicals and mainliners and between high and low religious commitments shown in the table are "real" differences, not the result of the aforementioned variables.

no longer on the ticket. Pat Robertson had lost badly in the primaries. The Moral Majority had disappeared. But analysis of the data indicates that, in fact, religiosity was still a key determinant. Table 2 shows white Protestants broken into those of high and low religious commitment according to an index which is a composite of frequency of church attendance, the perceived importance of religion, and a measure of evangelical identification.[2] (We see that for both mainline and evangelical Protestants, Republican identification and the Bush vote were significantly greater for persons of high religious commitment.

Evangelicals of high commitment were a key component of the Republican coalition. It's not surprising that the Bush campaign made strong efforts to recruit leading evangelicals (such as Jerry Falwell) even before the primary season in 1988 and to court the group as a whole in the fall campaign.

THE "RELIGIOUS FACTOR" IN POLICY DIFFERENCES

Both evangelical and mainline Protestants are significant components of the Republican coalition. Reagan and Bush united the two behind their presidential candidacies in the 1980s. Can the two groups continue to co-exist, or will intra-party wrangling between them become intense? The 1988 NES survey results indicate that the coalition is indeed fragile. Mainline and evangelical Protestant Republicans both identify as conservatives (the latter much more so if their religious commitments are high), and have similar views on government's role in economic life. They part company, however, on attitudes toward social issues—notably on abortion. Evangelicals are more favorable to a social issue agenda and to a pro-life position than

[2] A high score on the church attendance item is given to respondents who attend on a greater than weekly basis. A high score on the measure of religious salience was assigned to those who attached a "great deal" of importance to their faith. High scores on the evangelical identification measure are those who believe in an "inerrant" Bible and identify as born-again Christians. To be placed in the "high" religious commitment category, respondents must meet two or more of the above criteria—a demanding test of religious commitment.

TABLE 3. Religiosity and Issue Stands among White Protestant Republicans (in Percent)

	MAINLINE PROTESTANT REPUBLICANS, RELIGIOUS COMMITMENTS			EVANGELICAL PROTESTANT REPUBLICANS, RELIGIOUS COMMITMENTS		
	Low	High	Total Group	Low	High	Total Group
Identify as "Conservative"	54	58	55	43	74	56
Favor Government as Guarantor of Jobs	12	4	11	11	8	10
"High" Scores on Social Issues' Index†	17	49	22	28	72	46
Abortion: Pro-Life*	29	66	35	55	87	68
Pro-Choice	41	14	37	26	7	18

Source: 1988 NES Survey

† High score on the social issues' index include negative attitudes toward homosexuals and feminists, traditionalist stands on women's issues, opposition to a law protecting homosexuals, and favorable attitudes toward anti-abortionists and school prayer.

*Pro-life includes those who oppose abortion in all circumstances, or support only where the mother's health is endangered or where rape is involved. "Pro-choice" favors abortion without restrictions.

mainliners (Table 3). Highly religiously committed respondents within both evangelical and mainline groups take these positions—though highly committed evangelicals are more decisively inclined to them. The more salient social issues become, the harder it will likely be for the GOP to bridge its evangelical-mainline split.

Registration and Turnout

RUY A. TEIXEIRA

After each of their defeats in 1980, 1984, and 1988, Democratic activists have debated the best strategy to recapture the White House. Many southern Democrats have urged the party to become more moderate on domestic and foreign policy issues. Others have urged the party to recapture its populist heritage and attempt to mobilize blacks, Hispanics, the poor, and workers to higher rates of turnout. Writer Ruy Teixeira argues that although higher turnout among these groups would help the Democrats, it would not be enough to win the Presidency.

The 1988 votes are in, and two things stand out: (1) the Republicans won the presidency yet again, albeit by a more modest margin than in 1984; and (2) voter turnout continued its post-1960 downward trend. At just about one-half of the voting-age population (VAP), the 1988 turnout is the lowest since 1924 and dips below a low turnout mark set by the 1948 Dewey-Truman election.

The votes had barely been counted before we heard a familiar refrain from the losing side: "If only turnout had not been so low, if only more people had been registered, if only more blacks/Hispanics/poor people had voted—then we could have won the election." To the extent this claim is believed, it suggests a Democratic strategy focused on "more of the same, but more voters." The other interpretation of the election assumes that the Democrats lost because people didn't support them, so a different sort of politics is in order. A lot rests on which version of recent events is the accurate one.

IF ONLY MORE BLACKS AND HISPANICS HAD VOTED...

We know that overall turnout in November was about 50 percent. That figure is easily arrived at by dividing the numbers of votes cast by the VAP. The turnout of different groups *within* the population is more difficult. Election officials do not count "black votes" and "white votes" and "rich votes" and "poor votes"; they count "votes." This makes it impossible to calculate black turnout or white turnout, for example, in a straightforward way.

Source: *Public Opinion*, (January/February 1989): 12–13, 56–58. Reprinted with the permission of the American Enterprise Institute for Public Policy Research, Washington, D.C..

The author wishes to thank Leonard Bloomquist of Kansas State University, Curtis Gans of the Committee for the Study of the American Electorate, Keating Holland of CBS News, Jerry Jennings of the Census Bureau, Lett Jensen of Bates College, and Neil Maslansky of *Public Opinion* for data and helpful discussions that contributed to this article.

Exit poll data, though, make it possible to calculate indirect estimates of these different turnout rates. First, we assume that the demographics of a given exit poll reflect the demographics of actual voters (10 percent black, 85 percent white, for example). Then, based on the overall number of votes cast, we infer the number of actual voters who were black, white, and so on. This can be compared to the size of these groups in the voting-age population to derive specific group turnout rates.

This procedure and final exit poll data from the CBS News/*New York Times* survey allows us to estimate 1988 turnout rates by race and by different income groups in the population. Whites had the highest estimated turnout at about 52 percent, while blacks were at 46 percent, and Hispanics at 23 percent. It is worth noting that this black-white turnout differential of six points is no larger than the black-white differential in the 1984 election, and in fact, closely approximates it.

The high turnout groups were those with $25,000 or more in family income: 64 percent for those with between $25,000 and $35,000; and 57 percent each for those with between $35,000 and $50,000 and those with over $50,000 in family income. The low turnout groups were those with under $25,000 in family income: 46 percent for those with between $12,500 and $25,000 and only 31 percent for "the poor," those with under $12,500 in family income.

Thus, there appear to have been substantial turnout differentials between different races and income groups in the 1988 election. It should be emphasized that these estimates are based on a highly imperfect procedure that is subject to a number of sources of error (especially sampling error), and that these results cannot be regarded as definitive. The definitive results are not available until the Census Bureau releases results from its November survey. This said, it is still the best, and virtually the only, procedure we have to compare the turnout rates of different groups immediately after an election.

Assuming for the moment that these estimated differences in turnout are close to the real differences, it would appear that the "if only" analysts have a case. There *were* substantial differences in turnout between different racial and income groups, with the low turnout groups tending to be the ones that voted heavily Democratic. Blacks, for example, voted about 85 percent for Dukakis, while Hispanics cast 69 percent of their ballots for Dukakis, and the poor, 62 percent (the next lowest income group split about evenly between Bush and Dukakis).

The real question, however, is how many additional votes the Democrats would have gained if these groups had voted in larger numbers. It is necessary to look at race and income separately because of the considerable overlap between the poor and blacks/Hispanics. The net Democratic gain is shown [in Table 1] under three different higher turnout scenarios: (1) if black and Hispanic turnout had each been the same as that of the general population; (2) if black and Hispanic turnout had each matched white

TABLE 1. Net Democratic Gain from Increased Black and Hispanic Turnout

	Blacks	Hispanics
Matching turnout in general population	610,000	1,396,000
Matching turnout among whites	862,000	1,483,000
Exceeding white turnout by 10 points	2,349,000	1,991,000

Source: Author's estimates based on final 1988 CBS News/New York Times exit poll data and Census Bureau's Projections of the Population of Voting Age, for States; November 1988 (Senes P-25, No 1019).

turnout; and (3) if black and Hispanic turnout had each been *higher* than white turnout by ten percentage points.

If black turnout had matched turnout in the general population, the Democrats would have netted about 610,000 additional votes. If black turnout had matched that of whites, the net Democratic gain would have been about 862,000 votes. And if black turnout had somehow been ten points higher than whites, the Democratic gain would have amounted to about 2,349,000 votes.

Dukakis lost the election by over 6,900,000 votes, which means that even if blacks had turned out in much larger numbers than they did or even much larger numbers than they are ever likely to, Dukakis still would have lost. This suggests that Dukakis's problem was not turnout but his overall level of support among the population.

This story is borne out by the figures for Hispanics. If Hispanic turnout had matched turnout among the general population, the net gain for the Democrats would have been about 1,396,000 votes. If Hispanic turnout had matched that of whites, the Democrats would have netted 1,483,000 votes. Finally, under the unlikely scenario that Hispanic turnout exceeded white turnout by ten points, the Democrats would have gained 1,991,000 votes. (These estimates are probably high since they are based on a turnout gap between Hispanics and other races that is inflated by the large number of Hispanic aliens. If only citizen-eligible Hispanics were taken into account, the turnout gap would be much smaller and so would the effects of closing that gap.)

Hispanics could not have won the election for Michael Dukakis either. In fact, both Hispanics *and* blacks had voted at rates ten points higher than whites, the overall net gain for the Democrats, 4,340,000 votes, would still have fallen far short of the number Dukakis needed for victory.

CLASS AND THE 1988 ELECTION

It could still be argued that the Democratic turnout problem was not so much a race problem as a class problem. Only an estimated 31 percent of poor people voted in the 1988 election. But they voted for the Democratic ticket at a 62 percent rate, the only income group that voted solidly

TABLE 2.   Net Democratic Gain from Increased Turnout Among the Poor[1]

Matching turnout in general population	1,898,000
Matching turnout among the rich[2]	2,566,000
Exceeding rich turnout by 10 points	3,549,000

Source: Author's estimates based on final 1988 CBS News/*New York Times* exit poll data, Census Bureau's *Projections of the Population of Voting Age, for States; November 1988* (Senes P-25, No 1019) and March 1988 Current Population Survey.
[1] Less than $12,500 in family income.
[2] More than $50,000 in family income

Democratic (partially a reflection of the large number of blacks and Hispanics included in this category). What if the poor had turned out at higher levels? Specifically, what if poor people's turnout had followed these three scenarios: (1) poor turnout matched turnout in the general population; (2) poor turnout matched turnout among the "rich," those with $50,000 or more in family income; and (3) poor turnout actually exceeded turnout among the rich by ten points.

The net gain for the Democrats under these scenarios appears in Table 2. If turnout among the poor had been 50 percent, the same as among the general population, the Democrats would have netted about 1,898,000 voters. If poor turnout had matched rich turnout, the net gain would have been 2,566,000 votes. Finally, if the poor had managed to turn out at a level ten points higher than the rich, the Democrats would have gained about 3,549,000 voters. This is still far short of the 6,900,000 needed to overtake the Republicans.

Once again the results are clear. Even if poor people had turned out at much higher rates, Michael Dukakis would still have lost the 1988 election. Some Democrats may have an understandable urge to trade in the current electorate for a new one, but it isn't advisable. They lost the presidency because they didn't have enough support in the nation as a whole, not because enough of their people failed to show up at the polls.

OTHER SCENARIOS FOR INCREASED TURNOUT

These results seem clear enough at the national level. It could still be argued, however, that the electoral college makes national results less important. What is key are the state-level results, and therefore, increased black or Hispanic turnout in enough key states could conceivably have swung the election for the Democrats. I tested this theory by looking at a number of states, including California, Illinois, and Pennsylvania, where the election was close, and estimating the state-level effects of increased black/Hispanic turnout.

I found no evidence that reasonable increases in minority turnout could have swung these states for the Democrats. That is, when I estimated the net Democratic gain accruing from a ten-point increase in black or Hispanic turnout in each of these states, it was still not enough to change the outcome in any of them. This does not completely disprove the theory since I did not look at all states, but it does cast considerable doubt on its plausibility.

Now, none of this is to say that nonvoters could not *technically* have won the election for the Democrats. If every black in the United States had voted in 1988—that is, if turnout among the black electorate were 100 percent—the Democrats would probably have won the presidency. Or, if turnout among the poor had been a mere twenty points higher and every one of these additional poor people voted Democratic—that is, 100 percent for Dukakis, 0 percent for Bush—this, too, would have been enough to swing the election for the Democrats. But none of this will ever happen.

These fantastic scenarios, however, do illustrate an important point about turnout. When people say "turnout is the solution" they are usually basing their assessment on the kind of implausible assumptions described above. They envision either preposterously high turnout increases for their favorite group, or preposterously high voting rates for their favorite candidate among new voters, or both. Under more realistic scenarios—such as the ones described in this article—the turnout solution just doesn't work.

The implausibility of increased turnout as the solution to the Democrats' problems is further underscored by looking at one last scenario. What if they gave an election and everybody came? The CBS News/*New York Times* postelection survey has the answer for us. This survey investigated the presidential preferences of both voters and nonvoters. The result: if nonvoters had voted in the 1988 election, George Bush would still have won the election—except by a bigger margin! Even allowing for possible winner bias (the tendency of respondents to say they voted for the known winner), this result suggests rather strongly that turnout did not decide the 1988 election; voter preferences did.

Turnout may not be the key for the Democrats, but it is not completely irrelevant either. On the contrary, increased turnout among certain groups would clearly help the Democrats. Targeted registration and turnout activities have much to recommend them as parts of a winning strategy. But increased turnout cannot by itself be that winning strategy, as the figures presented above show conclusively.

IMPACT OF REGISTRATION/TURNOUT GROUPS

In this context it is worth taking a look at the activities of groups that put a great deal of effort into registration and turnout. I would include here such groups as Human SERVE, Southwest Voter Registration Education Project, Midwest-Northeast Voter Registration Education Project, and the National Coalition for Black Voter Participation, among others.

The claims of these groups are hard to pin down, but they seem to have two basic objectives: (1) to increase voter registration among their target groups (generally, the poor or minority groups) and thereby increase turnout; and (2) by increasing turnout among their target groups, to serve the political agenda of these groups (generally, Democratic). How much success have they had with these objectives?

This is not an easy question to answer. It is difficult to ascribe responsibility for any observed increases in registration to a particular group or groups, using official statistics or census data. We basically have to take their word for it when a group claims it signed up certain numbers of voters.

Assuming that their figures are accurate, these groups do appear to have had some success in the 1984 election. In that election the four groups mentioned above signed up over a million and a half new voters, while other nonpartisan groups of a generally liberal bent signed up over two million additional voters. Presumably, this enhanced turnout was among groups most favorable to the Democrats: blacks, Hispanics, and the poor.

On the partisan-impact side, however, there is much reason to doubt the efficacy of these efforts. To begin with, the efforts of liberal groups were roughly counterbalanced by registration efforts on the conservative side (Republican party, Christian right), so the overall net gain for the Democrats from registration activities may have been very small.

But even if there had been no conservative countermobilization, and if every one of the registrants claimed by the liberal groups had actually voted, and every one of them had voted for Mondale, he still would have lost badly to Reagan. In fact Mondale lost so badly that if every black in American had been registered, turned out at the polls, and voted for him, he still would have lost by more than seven million votes.

The most that can be said for registration drives in the 1984 election is that they might have prevented Reagan's margin from being even larger than it was. And, as pointed out above, there are reasons for doubting even that.

What of the 1988 election? On the face of it, registration groups would appear to have had little effect since the registration rate of the population actually went down 2.2 percentage points. This means that registration failed to keep pace with growth in the voting-age population. This compares rather poorly with 1984, when the registration rate actually went up 3.2 points.

It's hard to see in these circumstances how the groups under discussion could have had much partisan impact on the election outcome. Nor is there much evidence of such partisan impact. There are no success stories in individual states, for example, that seem to correlate with Democratic victories. In fact, only three states (Nevada, Arizona, and Virginia) showed registration increases, all of which went heavily for Bush; the District of Columbia also showed a registration increase, but there the outcome was never in doubt.

It is possible that without these groups' activities, registration and turnout would have gone down even further, especially among Democratic-leaning groups, and Dukakis would have lost by a bigger margin than he did. But this seems cold comfort, given the high aspirations of these groups.

Thus, it appears that registration activity was too anemic to have been much of a factor in the 1988 election. Could it have been a factor if it had been less anemic? What if, for example, the success of the 1984 registration drives had been duplicated?

To test this, I first assumed that the normal avenues of voter registration had added enough new voters to the rolls to keep pace with population growth. This keeps the registration rate at its 1984 level. Then I assumed that registration groups succeeded in adding another 3.2 percent of the electorate to the rolls (the registration increase in 1984), and that every one of these additional registrants was a member of a Democratic-leaning group. The results, allocating the new registrants equally among blacks, Hispanics, and the poor: a net gain of about 2,384,000 for the Democrats, once again far short of the 6,900,000 needed to overtake the Republicans.

Thus, even under a very generous series of assumptions, registration drives would not have changed the outcome of the 1988 election. This means that not only were the registration groups apparently unsuccessful in their efforts, but even *had* they been successful—indeed, spectacularly successful—it wouldn't have made much of a difference.

FUTURE OF VOTER TURNOUT

The more than three-point drop in voter turnout in the 1988 election continues a downward trend that started after 1960. This latest drop in voter participation makes it clear that turnout trends are linked, not to the difficulties of voter registration, but rather to a generalized withdrawal from the political world by larger and larger segments of the electorate. This is because, while registration has become progressively easier, turnout has continued to go down, including the drop observed in the last election. This clearly invalidates the arguments of those, like Frances Fox Piven and Richard Cloward, who attribute all problems with voter turnout to the registration system.

Another indicator that voter registration does not lie at the heart of the turnout decline phenomenon is that the turnout rate of registrants has also been declining over this period. Exactly how much is a matter of some controversy, though it could be as high as the thirteen-point decline shown by state registration and turnout figures.

It should be noted that figures based on Census survey data (which go back only to 1968) suggest a much smaller decline. Some, like Piven and Cloward, claim these are the "true" figures and that any attempt to use state data is hopelessly flawed due to the inflation of turnout rolls with the names of those who have died or moved away, but who have not been purged from the rolls. There is no doubt such inflation exists, but their argument hinges on the idea that this inflation has been increasing over time, thereby producing the declining turnout rate of registrants observed in state data. This contention is not consistent with the available evidence: some states have tightened up the procedures they use to purge the voter rolls, and some have loosened them, a mix that wouldn't lead to a steadily declining turnout rate.

Furthermore, the assumption that the Census data are by definition correct is open to question. A careful look at the way the Census calculates registration rates suggests it is open to biases of unknown scope. This is because the registration rate is derived by simply adding reported voters to reported nonvoters who say they are registered and dividing by the number in the sample. The problem is that some of these reported voters are nonvoters of unknown registration status. It can be shown mathematically that, depending on the true registration status of these misreporting nonvoters, the turnout rate of registrants derived from Census data could be inflated by as much as ten points. This is not to say it *is* off by ten points, but simply to illustrate that the Census data have their problems as well and are by no means a perfect guide to the changing turnout rates of registrants.

In light of all this I am inclined to believe that the turnout rate of registrants has dropped fairly substantially over time, though the exact magnitude may lie somewhere in between the state figures and the Census figures. This suggests that there is little cause for optimism on the turnout problem since even those who have taken the trouble to register seem increasingly disinclined to vote. It also suggests that faith in registration reform as an easy solution to the turnout problem is misplaced (see Teixeira, "Will the Real Voter Please Stand Up?" July-August 1988, *Public Opinion,* for a discussion of the limited effects of registration reform).

Faith in the partisan impact of increased turnout is probably also misplaced. As we've seen, simply bringing more of certain groups to the polls is not a quick and easy solution to the Democrats' problems. Because of this I am inclined to be skeptical that the Democrats (or the Republicans, for that matter) will move to "solve" the turnout problem in a big way since the marginal benefits of increasing turnout, especially among the general population, would probably not be enough to repay the costs. Instead, I would expect them to move to more and more precisely targeted activities among certain groups in certain states.

This puts the turnout problem squarely in the lap of society as a whole. This is appropriate since the problem appears to originate in the way politics is conducted in our society. Unfortunately, at this point we do not know the precise origins of this political problem, though the hypothesized causes are many: the influence of the media and polls; the role of television advertising; the decline of the political parties; the conduct of campaigns; the quality of candidates; generalized disconnection from politics; decreased sense of civic duty; the erosion of traditional forms of political consciousness. More work is needed to specify which among this rogues' gallery of political suspects are truly contributing to low and declining turnout.

Beyond this, perhaps we need to decide: is the turnout problem worth solving? What are the societal benefits that would accrue to increased turnout, and how does that compare to the costs of attaining it? In particular, do we want a "participatory democracy," to borrow a phrase from the sixties, or will a "de-participatory democracy" do just as well? The choice is ours.

4. Presidential Nominations

Perhaps no area in the quest for public office has changed as quickly and as comprehensively as the presidential nomination process. Since the end of the 1960s party rules have been revised for the selection of delegates to the nominating conventions, congressional statutes and Supreme Court decisions have affected campaign fund-raising and expenditures, and media coverage of campaigns, particularly by television, has revolutionized the process by which the electorate learns about the campaign.

Each of these changes was designed to improve the political process, to make it more democratic. And they have. But they have also produced unintended consequences that have hurt the parties, readvantaged monied interests, and elevated style over substance in electoral campaigns.

The reforms in party rules have encouraged more people to participate in their party's selection process. They have decreased the ability of political bosses to influence the nomination and have produced convention delegates who are more representative of their party as a whole. Minorities are better able to exercise influence than in the past. Even the pool from which presidential candidates are drawn has changed. Today it is not necessary to be a party insider or a well-known national politician to gain the nomination.

But the reforms have also hurt the parties, particularly the Democrats. They have weakened the position of party leadership at both the state and national levels. They have encouraged factions to develop within the parties. Although intended to make the parties more responsive to their rank and file and to make the candidates they nominate more acceptable to party supporters, the reforms have produced a process susceptible to domination by those with extreme political views.

How did these unintended consequences result? Some of them were the product of skillful manipulation by the nomination seekers. Politics is the art of bending the rules to one's own advantage. Strategy and tactics do make a difference and do affect the outcome, particularly during the nomination phase of the electoral process. But the environment in which the elections occur has also changed, and this new environment has affected the parties as well. The readings in this chapter discuss these changes and their impact on the nomination process.

Party rules for delegate selection are not neutral. When contests are held, which candidates are eligible as delegates, and who votes and how those votes are apportioned can all affect the outcome. Candidates who understand the rules can take advantage of them. This is why their strategy and tactics are so important. They provide the operational game plan: what to emphasize, when, how, and to whom.

All the readings in this chapter deal with some aspect of the strategy and tactics. They indicate what works and what does not work, based on the experience of the 1988 presidential election. Unfortunately for the planners of the next election, the rules will undoubtedly change again, as will the political and financial environment in which the contest will occur. Strategy and tactics will have to change as well if they are to be successful.

In the first reading, Rhodes Cook provides an overview of the 1988 presidential nomination process. Cook sees the campaign in stages, each affecting the one that follows. His sequential perspective emphasizes early planning. The campaign begins well before the first contest and may effectively conclude well before the last.

One of the rules of contemporary presidential contests is that aspirants must position themselves well to maximize their strength and take advantage of any problems their opponents may encounter. Michael Dukakis followed this rule successfully in his 1988 quest to win the Democratic nomination.

Front-runners have another reason for constructing an elaborate campaign apparatus early on and for designing an effective strategy with multiple scenarios. They want to prevent a misstep or a bad break from dooming their chances. This is why George Bush's advisors decided to build a fire wall around his support in the southern states. Fearing that he might lose one or two of the very early contests (which he did), they wanted to be in a position to prevent further erosion, keep the campaign on its feet, and reap the initial benefits that Bush brought to the nomination process as Ronald Reagan's vice president.

The object of the early contests is to gain media coverage. As Dr. Robert Lichter notes in the reading that ends the chapter, the first caucuses and primaries receive disproportionate media attention. For candidates who are not well known, this attention, if associated with electoral success—winning contests or simply doing better than expected—can be *the* critical factor in giving them a chance to win. Money, volunteers, popular support, and more media coverage (albeit more critical coverage) follow the likely winners.

In recent years the presidential selection process has become increasingly frontloaded. More states have been holding their primaries and caucuses toward the beginning of the process in order to exercise more influence over who the nominees will be. In 1988 this frontloading reached new heights on Super Tuesday, the first day that the Democratic party permitted most states to hold their nomination contests. Sixteen primaries and five caucuses were conducted on that day.

Such a large number of elections so early in the process presented the candidates with unusually difficult problems: how to raise sufficient funds to mount effective campaigns in so many states at the same time, how to target an appeal to so many diverse voters, and how to maximize their delegate vote with limited resources. Journalist R. W. Apple, Jr. of *The New York Times* discusses these problems, the candidates' resources, and the strategies that proved most successful on Super Tuesday in a short article that appeared toward the end of the nomination process. He notes the objectives of those who designed these early contests and wonders whether those objectives were achieved and whether additional reforms are desirable.

Although primary elections have dominated media coverage and public attention, candidates must also compete in caucuses. About one-third of the delegates are selected in these multistaged contests. Caucuses require a different strategy than primaries: They reward organization and commitment rather than mass appeal. Democrat Jesse Jackson and Republican Pat Robertson did surprisingly well in these contests in 1988. Rhodes Cook and Dave Kaplan tell how these candidates used their "invisible armies" to dominate caucuses and to establish their political base. The strategies that produced success for these "candidates of passion" will probably not be lost on nor easily imitated by more mainline contenders the next time around.

In the long and arduous quest for office, candidates often are stressed to the limit. Some break. Exhausted and sick, Senator Joseph Biden misstated his academic record when challenged by an opponent's supporter. Pat Robertson employed "funny facts" to support his positions and then denied he used them; much to his chagrin, his remarks were recorded on tape. During the 1972 New Hampshire primary, front-running Democratic candidate Senator Edmund Muskie of Maine lost his composure and cried while responding to allegations about his wife made by a conservative newspaper publisher. Each of these events seriously damaged these candidates' standing in the eyes of the voters.

How does it feel to be a candidate? What is it like to run and lose? Former 1988 Democratic candidate Bruce Babbitt tells part of his story: what he thought went wrong and how the problems he encountered might be overcome by future aspirants for the nomination.

We began this chapter by suggesting that the nomination process has changed a great deal and therefore candidates have had to adapt their strategies and tactics to these changes in order to be successful. Coverage of the nomination process by the mass media has contributed to the new environment in which primaries and caucuses occur. Rhodes Cook uses a fishbowl analogy to describe the visibility of the process. Prior to the 1960s, that analogy would not have been appropriate.

The media do more than provide visibility. They affect the agenda of the campaign. What they emphasize, how they treat the candidates and issues, and whether their coverage is fair and balanced affect the campaigns of the candidates and contribute to the outcome of the nomination. Television in particular has had a major impact. Robert Lichter assesses this impact in his examination of the evening news on the three major networks during the 1988 nomination process. The picture presented by Lichter goes a long way to explain why many of the democratic objectives have not been realized: why turnout is low, why the electorate is unimpressed by the candidates and their campaigns, and why the eventual nominees have such difficulty generating enthusiasm in the general election.

The Nomination Process

RHODES COOK

Rhodes Cook, correspondent for the Congressional Quarterly, *provides an overview of the presidential nomination process. He sees it as a dynamic and open process, but one that dictates that all candidates take the same general approach at the beginning of the campaign. All of them need to begin their quest early, concentrating on the media and trying to generate a bandwagon effect. In examining the stages of the process, Rhodes suggests that success comes to those who understand these stages and adopt appropriate strategies for dealing with them.*

One of the striking features of the presidential nominating process is its ongoing change, with aspects of both the parties' rules and the calendar order of primaries and caucuses noticeably different from election to election. Compared to nominations, the process of electing a president is a model of stability, with a one-day, fifty-state vote every fourth year on the first Tuesday after the first Monday in November.

The major impetus for change in the nominating process has come from the Democrats, who began revising their delegate-selection rules after the party's tumultuous 1968 convention in Chicago, at which Vice President Hubert H. Humphrey was nominated without having run in a single primary state. Convention delegates in 1968, as in previous elections, had been chosen mostly by established party leaders within each state, in many cases during the year before the election.

When liberals, opposed to the war in Vietnam, cried foul at Humphrey's nomination, party regulars grudgingly agreed to create a commission to review the party's nominating rules. The McGovern-Fraser commission (named for its leaders, Sen. George McGovern of South Dakota and Rep. Donald Fraser of Minnesota) undertook an overhaul of the process that has yet to be completed. Rewriting their rules every four years since 1968, the Democrats have transferred power in their nominating process from party kingmakers to citizens at the grass roots. The overwhelming majority of convention delegates now are chosen in primaries that are open to any and all voters who call themselves Democrats. Since the 1970s, there has been a steady growth in the number of primaries—from seventeen in 1968 to thirty-seven in 1980 and, after a brief downturn in 1984, up to thirty-eight in 1988.

To a significant degree, the Republican nominating process also has been changing since 1968. In many states where Democratic-controlled legisla-

Source: Michael Nelson (ed.) *The Elections of 1988* (Washington, D.C.: Congressional Quarterly, 1989) pp. 26–39. Reprinted by permission of Congressional Quarterly, Inc.

tures have established presidential primaries for their party, the Republicans have been pushed to hold a primary as well. When southern Democrats decided they would try to maximize their influence over the party's 1988 nomination by having all their region's presidential primaries on the same day (March 8, the much-heralded Super Tuesday), Republicans—operating in the minority—were almost powerless to stop them.

THE WEIGHT OF THE PRIMARIES

The effect of the proliferation of primaries cannot be understated. In 1968, when party and elected officials still controlled the nominating process, the relatively small number of primaries played little more than an advisory role in helping them make up their minds. Democratic leaders were interested to find out through the 1960 primaries, for example, that Massachusetts senator John F. Kennedy, a Roman Catholic, could win votes from religiously conservative Protestants in states like West Virginia. In 1968 former vice president Richard Nixon used the primaries to demonstrate to Republican leaders that, even though he had lost the 1960 presidential and the 1962 gubernatorial election in California, voters did not see him as a "loser." But in both cases, party leaders decided how much weight should be attached to the verdict of the primaries.

Now that primaries dominate the nominating process, candidates spend as much time courting grass-roots party activists in Iowa and New Hampshire as they do the governor of New York or the state party chairman in California. The national party convention no longer determines the nominee; rather it serves mainly as a backdrop for the coronation of the candidate who emerges on top in the primaries.

Even the Democratic party's efforts to "undemocratize" the presidential nominating process by restoring, at least in part, a role for party leaders has had little effect. Beginning in 1984 the party created several hundred "superdelegate" slots for Democratic members of Congress and state party leaders. These delegates do not have to run in their state's primary or caucus and can vote for any candidate they wish. Although the superdelegates occupied roughly 15 percent of the seats at the 1984 and 1988 Democratic conventions, they did not steer the nominating contest in a direction of their own choosing. Almost unanimously, they fell in line behind the frontrunner in the primaries, former vice president Walter F. Mondale in 1984 and Dukakis in 1988.

Although the ranks of participants in the nominating process are far larger than twenty years ago, those who vote in the primaries still are only a fraction of the number who cast ballots in the November presidential election. In 1988, 35 million votes were cast in the primaries—23 million on the Democratic side, 12 million on the Republican—compared to more than 91 million in the general election. Activity in the states that choose their delegates in party caucuses (caucuses, like primaries, are open to all party members but they require that participants attend a meeting rather than just pull the lever in a voting booth) probably did not involve more than 2 million additional voters. One of the characteristics of the smaller primary and caucus electorate, most analysts agree, is that the nominating process is more apt to be dominated by ideological activists—liberals in the Democratic party, conservatives in the Republican party.

THE ONLY STRATEGY: START EARLY

The modern nominating process frequently is described as "wide open." Many candidates can run, and it is impossible to predict with much certainty who will win.

When it comes to devising a strategy to win a party's presidential nomination, however, the modern process is anything but wide open. Candidates have no choice but to adopt nearly the same approach—start early, organize early, and try to put the opposition away before the primary season is more than a few weeks old.

In this respect, as in many others, presidential politics once was very different. As late as 1968, candidates had plenty of flexibility in deciding how to run their campaigns. They could enter the race early or late; they could run in some or all of the limited number of primaries that were held or they could skip them all. Still, it was difficult for anyone outside a small circle of established political figures to be considered seriously for president.

The sanctity of the small circle of prospective candidates and the strategic flexibility of candidates within that circle were destroyed by the reforms that followed the Democrats' 1968 convention. As power moved from party committee rooms to the grass roots, the barriers to running for president came down. Party "outsiders," George McGovern in 1972 and Jimmy Carter in 1976, proved conclusively by sweeping to the Democratic nomination that the nominating process was beyond the control of any power bloc within the party. McGovern had his base in the insurgent anti-Vietnam War wing of the party; Carter was a one-term former governor of Georgia. Neither was particularly well known when they began their campaigns.

But McGovern and Carter understood the dynamics of the revamped nominating process and, unlike their opponents, made major efforts in Iowa and New Hampshire. Both ran well in those early contests, gaining a bonanza of favorable media attention and a surge of publicity, financial contributions, and organizational volunteers that carried each of them to further primary victories and, ultimately, to the nomination.

The imperative to start campaigning early is a legacy of McGovern and Carter that has come to dominate the entire process. It is an imperative that obsesses not only the candidates but also the states. In an effort to increase their influence in the nominating process, a growing number of states have moved primaries and caucuses to dates near the beginning of the delegate-selection season. In 1968 only New Hampshire held its primary before the middle of March; in 1984, seven states did, and in 1988 there were twenty. Add another ten or so caucus states—including Iowa—that held their events by mid-March 1988 and it is easy to see why candidates in 1988 were gearing up earlier than ever.

THE NOMINATING PROCESS: AN OVERVIEW

Although the nominating process has continued to evolve during the last twenty years, some basic patterns have developed that give it an unmistakable five-stage structure.

The first stage is the "exhibition season," the period that lasts from the day after a general election to the start of primary and caucus action more than three years later. The exhibition season is a time for potential candidates to test the political waters, raise money, and begin to organize their campaigns around the country, wooing important individuals and interest groups and honing basic campaign themes.

The second stage is the "media fishbowl," in which the voters finally get involved and those in Iowa and New Hampshire begin to winnow the field of candidates. Third is Super Tuesday, the crowded day of primaries and caucuses in early March for which only the best-financed candidates can prepare adequately. The fourth stage of the nominating process is the "mop-up" stage, the spring primaries in which each party's nomination is clinched. Whether the mop-up stage concludes in harmony or bitterness may affect the nominee's chances in the general election.

The fifth and final stage is the "convention" stage, the month or more after the primary season ends in early June, when attention shifts to discussions of the party platform and the party's nominating rules for the next campaign, as well as to the choice of vice president. Culminating the fifth stage—and the nominating process—is the convention itself, the four-day summer gathering of politicians and media from around the country at which nominations are ratified and the party tries to show its most attractive face to the world.

The Exhibition Season

During the long exhibition season candidates can exert the most control over their destiny. The exhibition season is a building and testing period, in which candidates are free to fashion campaign themes and to discover which constituencies are receptive to their appeals.

The candidates are not entirely free, however: they must spend much of their time raising money in the relatively small amounts permitted by the Federal Election Campaign Act (FECA). Prior to the passage of the FECA in 1974, well-connected candidates could raise campaign funds quickly by tapping a handful of large contributors. The current system slows down the fund-raising process by placing a $1,000 limit on individual contributions and a $5,000 limit on contributions from political action committees (PACs). The FECA also allows only individual contributions of $250 or less to be matched by public funds. Indeed, even candidates who do not participate in the public financing system still are bound by the FECA's contribution limits.

Two kinds of candidates have special advantages when it comes to raising money for the campaign—those with national stature and those who can compensate for the absence of such stature through their access to a lucrative fund-raising constituency. In 1988 Republicans Robert Dole of Kansas, the Senate minority leader, and Vice President Bush clearly had national stature and were able to raise all the money the law allowed. Although they were not well known nationally (at least not in political circles), Dukakis and the Reverend Pat Robertson were nearly as successful as Bush and Dole in early fund raising. Robertson, for many years the host of "The 700 Club" on television, tapped into the fundamentalist Christian community in his quest for the Republican nomination, and Dukakis was able to exploit his Greek heritage and his status as the sitting governor of a populous state. Dukakis drew a rich lode of financial support from his fellow Greek-Americans around the country and from residents of Massachusetts and those who did business with the state.

As the exhibition season neared its close at the end of 1987, Bush ($18.1 million), Robertson ($14.2 million), Dole ($13.2 million) and Dukakis ($10.2 million) were the front-runners in collecting individual campaign contributions, much of which the federal government would match under the FECA. As a result, when the voting in the early primaries and caucuses began, they were free to campaign full time while their rivals still were hunting for money. In addition, they were financially in position to compete in more of the myriad early primaries and caucuses than their rivals.

Jockeying for Position.   The exhibition season is about more than money; it is also the time for candidates to woo the support of interest groups that can provide their campaigns with organizational muscle. In recent years, Democratic candidates have sought the support of the AFL-CIO, the National Education Association (NEA), the National Organization for Women (NOW), and other liberal groups that can provide a campaign with active support at the grass roots. In 1988, however, Republican presidential candidates matched the Democrats at the interest group game, making stops at numberless meetings of conservative organizations in quest of the grass-roots help their activist members could provide.

As Mondale discovered in 1984, too close an identification with interest groups can be a mixed blessing. Support from the AFL-CIO, the NEA, and NOW was a boon to Mondale in caucus states, where turnout is traditionally low and a candidate's organizational strength is crucial. But the interest group endorsements also enabled Mondale's rivals to label him the "special interest" candidate, a charge that particularly hurt him in primaries that took place outside the heavily unionized, industrial Northeast and Midwest.

In 1988 Democratic candidates were more coy than Mondale had been. They solicited the help of interest group activists, but avoided making a full-court press for the public endorsements of their national organizations.

The Early Bench Marks. The bench marks of candidate success during the exhibition season are campaign fund-raising reports, public opinion polls, straw votes at state party gatherings, and, in 1988, press reviews of the candidates' performances in the plethora of debates that dotted the preprimary calendar.

These early bench marks are the less-than-perfect harbingers of what will happen in the primaries and caucuses that follow. Success at meeting some of the challenges of the exhibition season is difficult to quantify—notably, the building of organizations that can turn out the vote in Iowa and New Hampshire and the development of campaign themes that can appeal to the voters there. The quantifiable bench marks are sometimes irrelevant by the time the voting actually takes place.

Polls taken before the presidential election year rarely reflect much more than "name identification," the share of the voters who have heard of each candidate. Straw votes at state party gatherings reveal the preferences of only the most dedicated political activists. Fund-raising problems during the exhibition season are not always insurmountable—they often will disappear if the candidate wins an early primary or caucus.

Still, even well-constructed campaigns can find it difficult to survive without some success in the widely monitored early bench marks. Candidates who are not receiving favorable debate reviews or who are not among the leaders in public opinion surveys must survive the scarcity of media attention and volunteer help needed to succeed. Without a cadre of talented and hard-working supporters in the early primary or caucus states, some candidates are essentially out of the race before the first vote is cast.

The Media Fishbowl

The exhibition season is a model of order and decorum compared to the topsy-turvy media fishbowl stage of the presidential nominating contest that follows. For long-shot candidates, this turbulent period is the one remaining chance to make a breakthrough and emerge as a serious contender. To the front-runner, the media fishbowl offers the opportunity for an early knockout and a quick finish to the campaign.

The delegate-selection contests that are most closely watched during the media fishbowl stage are in Iowa and New Hampshire. These two states have had competition for the coveted lead-off spot in recent years: in 1988 Republican caucuses in Michigan, Hawaii, and Kansas were held before the February 8 precinct caucuses in Iowa. (Michigan Republicans, hoping to grab the media spotlight from Iowa, actually began their caucuses in 1986!) But the early Republican events were conducted in a confusing fashion and received scant attention.

It is during the media fishbowl stage when the electronic and print media probably have their greatest influence. Their interpretations of who won and who lost various delegate-selection contests help to winnow the field of candidates. Low vote totals are fatal; but the media can describe even candidates who run fairly well as losers if they do not do as well as they were expected to do. Conversely, a candidate who does not win, but does better than expected, is likely to be portrayed as a winner.

Robertson, for example, received reams of favorable media attention when he finished second in the Iowa caucuses with 25 percent of the vote simply because no one expected him to do that well. But the media generally regarded Illinois senator Paul Simon's second-place finish on the Democratic side, with 27 percent of the caucus tally, as a loss because he had been given a fair chance of winning before the vote. Poor media reviews, damaging enough in their own right, also can mean dwindling finances if they discourage potential contributors, which in turn can force a candidate to fold the campaign within days of the Iowa vote.

In every recent presidential nominating campaign, the requirements for success in the media fishbowl have been the same: a candidate must "win, place, or show" in Iowa and New Hampshire. Since 1976 every Democratic and Republican nominee has won at least one of the two states and finished no lower than third in the other. McGovern, the Democratic nominee in 1972, was widely perceived to have been the winner in Iowa and New Hampshire: even though he lost both states to the early front-runner, Maine senator Edmund S. Muskie, he ran much stronger (and Muskie much less strong) than had been expected.

Many Democrats complain that Iowa and New Hampshire are inappropriate places for their party to start its nominating process. Both are widely unrepresentative of the party and the nation—neither has big cities or a sizable minority population, and they nearly always vote for Republican presidential candidates in the general election. (Iowa has voted Republican in eight, and New Hampshire in nine, of the last ten presidential elections.) Moreover, in Iowa and New Hampshire relatively small numbers of voters have an enormous effect on the nominating process. In Iowa, roughly 235,000 voters turned out for the Democratic and Republican caucuses in 1988, and about 280,000 voters participated in the Democratic and Republican primaries in New Hampshire. In comparison, more than 5 million voters participated in the California primary on June 7, but they had little influence on the nominating process because both parties' contests already had been settled by then.

Still, many in the political community regard Iowa and New Hampshire's small populations as a virtue rather than a vice. Because both states can permit a candidate to overcome low name identification and limited financing with personal effort and an effective organization, they have carved out reputations as launching pads for long-shot candidates. New Hampshire, in particular, lacks strong interest groups such as labor, which can skew the race to the candidate they support. Finally, Iowa and New Hampshire test the candidates' ability to compete in two totally different systems of delegate selection—the small-turnout world of the Iowa caucuses, where the key to success is either a passionate message or a superior organization, and the proportionately larger-turnout world of the New Hampshire primary, where a candidate must demonstrate broad acceptability among a wider range of voters.

Super Tuesday

The big prize for the winner in Iowa or New Hampshire is not delegates, but momentum. A win in Iowa provides a candidate with a boost in New Hampshire, and a win in New Hampshire can boost a candidate in the states that immediately follow. One of the big questions in 1988, however, was what would happen to this momentum once it hit Super Tuesday on March 8, only three weeks after the New Hampshire primary.

Super Tuesday was not wholly a 1988 phenomenon. A small-scale southern primary took place in early 1980 and 1984 that involved three states—Alabama, Florida, and Georgia. But weary of taking a back seat to the early media fishbowl events and of being saddled with northern liberal presidential nominees who seemed to be a drag on the ticket, Democratic state legislators across the South expanded the event to include almost every state in the region. A few states in other regions joined in, with primaries in Massachusetts and Rhode Island and caucuses in several western states.

No one was quite sure what the effect of Super Tuesday would be. Many southerners hoped that it not only would force candidates to come to the South and "talk southern," but also that it would reduce the Iowa and New Hampshire events to the status of small-scale warm-up acts. Others argued that Super Tuesday could just as easily enhance the influence of Iowa and New Hampshire. A burst of momentum based on a victory in one of those two states, critics suggested, could enable the winners to sweep through the vast block of states that were voting on March 8.

Which prediction was right? In a sense, both were. On the Republican side, Vice President Bush, who had rebounded from an Iowa loss to win New Hampshire, swept the South on Super Tuesday and essentially wrapped up the nomination. But the Democratic race became more muddled. The two candidates with southern ties—Tennessee senator Albert Gore, Jr., among white voters, and Jackson mainly among blacks—emerged with strong showings on Super Tuesday that enabled them to challenge Rep. Richard A. Gephardt, D–Mo., and Dukakis, the winners in Iowa and New Hampshire, respectively.

The Mop-up Stage

In recent elections, the last twelve weeks of the primary season often have been anticlimactic. The period from mid-March to early June is the mop-up stage of the nominating contest: the front-runner concentrates on the gradual accumulation of enough delegates to make a nominating majority, and the other surviving candidates try desperately to catch the front-runner.

In the not-too-distant past, the situation was entirely different. The spring solstice was the beginning, not the end, of the nominating process. In 1968, for example, Sen. Robert F. Kennedy of New York entered the Democratic presidential contest in mid-March in the wake of Minnesota senator Eugene J. McCarthy's strong showing against President Johnson in the New Hampshire primary. The eventual nominee in 1968, Hubert Humphrey, entered the race more than a month later.

But a late start no longer is feasible, partly because the FECA now makes it so difficult to raise money quickly and partly because there are not as many delegate-winning opportunities available for a candidate who starts late. Almost half the states had voted by mid-March 1988, and filing deadlines had passed in a number of the later-voting states, including delegate-rich New York and Pennsylvania.

Even for those who already are in the race, recovery from early defeats is difficult. Theoretically, a candidate could make a comeback after Super Tuesday. A number of populous states have yet to vote. In addition to New York and Pennsylvania, these include Illinois, Ohio, New Jersey, and California. To "backload" the process further, Democrats in 1988 moved the selection date of their roughly three hundred congressional superdelegates from a week before the Iowa caucuses to April 19–20. Still, no candidate in recent years has mounted a successful comeback during the mop-up period. Since 1976 the candidate who had amassed the most delegates by mid-March has won the party's nomination. Both major party candidates continued this pattern in 1988.

The mop-up stage poses challenges even to the front-runner, however. Not the least of these is money. The public financing system establishes state and national spending limits. The individual state limits are of little concern after the media fishbowl stage because only in Iowa and New Hampshire do candidates usually spend close to the maximum allowable amount. But the national limit—nearly $27.7 million in 1988—may be a problem, especially for the early leader who spent heavily in the exhibition season to organize nationally. Indeed, a challenger who did not spend money early because the money was not available may now be able to outspend the front-runner in the closing primaries.

By itself, a monetary disadvantage is not fatal to the front-runner in the mop-up stage or afterward. The front-runner who continues to receive favorable media treatment need not depend on spending large sums of money. For example, Jackson outspent Dukakis by $1.5 million to $1.2 million in the largest of the late primary states in 1988—Pennsylvania (April 26), Ohio (May 3), and California and New Jersey (June 7). But Dukakis easily won all four events.

Although the nominee may be all but chosen when the mop-up stage begins, the way the race ends can be important in the November general election. Front-runners—and most party leaders—want the nominating contest to end quickly and without acrimony so that the competing forces will have time to mend fences and the victor will have time to develop a strategy for the general election. The longer the battle for the nomination drags on, the less chance the party has to win.

The mop-up stage also can be crucial to the long-term political future of the runner-up. It is important to finish respectably enough to remain a major player on the national scene. Bush did that in 1980, defeating Ronald Reagan in several late primaries, including Pennsylvania and Michigan. Bush's late spurt helped to earn him the vice-presidential nomination.

On to the Convention

Even if the nominating *contest* is effectively over by the end of the primary season in early June, the nominating *process* is not. If the race has been bitter, the losing side may mount a last-ditch fight at the convention over issues such as the delegates' credentials—as McGovern's foes did in 1972—or convention rules—as Reagan did against President Gerald R. Ford in 1976 and Sen. Edward M. Kennedy of Massachusetts did against President Carter in 1980. But whether the political hatchets from the primaries and caucuses have been buried, the period leading up to the conventions is also the opening round of the fall campaign. The front-runner's decisions no longer are geared toward nomination, but toward election.

The preconvention period is concerned with image, issues, and strategy: image, in terms of how the front-runner is mending fences with the defeated rivals, especially the concessions that may have to be made as the price of a united party; issues, as the views of the nominee and the other candidates are reflected in the party platform; and strategy, as shown in the nominee's choice of a vice-presidential running mate. Because a front-runner usually selects someone who will buttress the ticket's support in a state or constituency group where the presidential nominee's own appeal is weak, the vice-presidential selection can be the first real clue to the fall campaign strategy.

Different Playing Fields

Democratic and Republican candidates play basically under the same rules when it comes to the calendar of primaries and caucuses and the campaign finance laws that regulate fund raising and spending. But the two parties' candidates are on different playing fields when it comes to winning delegates. The Republican party allows a winner-take-all system of delegate selection in its various state primaries and caucuses; the Democratic party is more oriented to proportional representation, with the delegates divided to reflect each candidate's share of the primary or caucus vote. The result is that a Republican candidate who registers a string of early successes in the media fishbowl and Super Tuesday states, as Bush did in 1988, is more apt to score a quick knockout than a Democratic candidate who gets off to a similarly fast start.

On Super Tuesday alone, Bush won every delegate at stake in six southern primary states, including those in the two most populous, Texas and Florida. In contrast, virtually every Democratic delegate chosen that day was allocated on the basis of proportional representation, further delaying the emergence of a clear winner on the Democratic side. Subsequent Democratic primaries in Illinois, Pennsylvania, and New Jersey were modified winner-take-all contests that offered the victorious candidate the chance to reap a large windfall of delegates. But those states stood virtually alone as exceptions to the Democratic rule of proportional representation. . . .

How America Voted:
Early and Often,
and Mostly by the Old Rules

R. W. APPLE, JR.

Many people believe that Super Tuesday was a natural consequence of the frontloading of the nomination process that has been occurring since the 1970s. Not only does this frontloading dictate certain strategies and tactics, it also benefits those who begin their campaign with national recognition and support. New York Times *reporter R. W. Apple, Jr. explains why this is the case, what the lessons of Super Tuesday are, and what this indicates the impact of a national or regional primaries would be on the quest for office.*

As 1988 began, there were the usual complaints about Iowa; it is too atypical, people said, too small, too old and too full of tightly knit communities to function as a testing ground for the country as a whole.

Maybe so. But this year, it didn't much matter, because the winners in Iowa (Senator Bob Dole of Kansas for the Republicans and Representative Richard A. Gephardt for the Democrats, for those with short memories) didn't last. Iowa's role this time was mainly to awaken Vice President Bush to the dangers of overconfidence and to give Gov. Michael S. Dukakis enough votes to fight on.

As 1988 began, people were complaining about New Hampshire; it has too much influence, they said, for a place even less representative than Iowa. That accusation proved to have some point, since New Hampshire—young and increasingly fueled by high-tech industries—chose a pair of local boys (Dukakis of Massachusetts and Bush of Connecticut and Maine) and gave them a momentum that carried them through the nominating marathon.

As 1988 began, people were complaining about Super Tuesday, the cluster of primaries, mostly in the South, whose sponsors designed them to produce a more conservative Democratic nominee, preferably a Southerner, in the belief that that was the formula for victory in November. The critics said it would put a premium on money and television skills, because "retail" campaigning over so vast an area would prove to be utterly impracticable.

In the event, the critics' forecast was proved correct, but the outcome was not noticeably altered. Grouping the primaries in the region seemed to produce winners who might have been expected to do well in the area anyway: the Rev. Jesse Jackson and Senator Albert Gore Jr. of Tennessee, and an outsider, Governor Dukakis, who chose his targets carefully, spent his money wisely and had effective ads.

If Super Tuesday had any significant impact, it came in the Republican race, by permitting Vice President Bush to close out his rivals early.

So what did we learn about how the system works and doesn't work? Lots of things, but here are a half-dozen that spring quickly to mind, most of which have applied in some degree to other recent campaigns, too:

1. Money counts. Each party seems sure to nominate the man who raised the most money early. Money buys staff, advertising, credibility; most important, it provides the wherewithal to keep going after a defeat or two, as in the case of Mr. Dukakis's setbacks in the Illinois and Michigan voting.
2. States that lack a caucus tradition, unlike Iowa, often produce a skewed result because of poor or at best imbalanced turnout. They tend to attract "activists," meaning liberals in the Democratic Party and conservatives in the Republican Party. No serious politician in Michigan believes Jesse Jackson could have won a primary there by anything like the margin he won in the caucuses, if he could have won at all.
3. In a multicandidate field like that of the Democrats' this year, with no obvious front-runner, victory goes to the candidate who can most significantly reach outside his geographic base. Mr. Dukakis did so during the Super Tuesday voting on March 8, in Texas and Florida, which in retrospect constituted two of the decisive tests of the campaign.
4. Candidates skip New Hampshire at their peril. It didn't work for Senator Henry M. Jackson of Washington in 1972 or for former Gov. Edmund G. (Jerry) Brown Jr. of California in 1976, and it didn't work for Mr. Gore this year either. He got his Super Tuesday victories, but he never managed to establish his credibility elsewhere.
5. Basic tactics still matter; Mr. Dukakis spent his time and money in the right places on Super Tuesday and Mr. Gephardt spent his in the wrong places, with predictable results.
6. The random or unexpected often matters more than anything else, as in Mr. Dole's fatal moment of fury on television in New Hampshire over a Bush commercial or the corruption of Mr. Gore's New York campaign by Mayor Koch's intemperate, noisy attacks on Mr. Jackson.

Do we need yet another bout of "reform" on the heels of the Democrats' repeated efforts of the last two decades, most of which the Republicans have accepted? There is no agreement whatever within political circles on that subject, except perhaps for an ill-defined notion that the process is too big, too costly and too sloppy.

Something also needs be done to give it more substance. It is noteworthy that Mr. Dukakis and Mr. Bush not only raised more money than their rivals but also kept their messages much more bland.

But it is not easy to suggest just how those goals might best be achieved. Remedies that seem sure-fire often are not; there were far more debates than ever before this year, but they didn't seem to accomplish much.

A series of Super Tuesdays, regional or otherwise, is perhaps the most widely discussed "solution," but surely that would give even more of an advantage to the candidates with money. So would a national primary.

In most Western European countries, the money problem is overcome by limiting or forbidding paid political advertising and requiring television and radio stations to make free time available to the parties, but that, most legal scholars say, would raise huge constitutional problems here.

The fact is that there is not much of a constituency right now for changing the electoral process. There never is, except when some particularly nasty scandal, like Watergate, or some particularly nasty fight, like the Democrats' in Chicago in 1968, concentrates minds. For now, with both parties poised to nominate candidates with both feet on the middle ground, the present system doesn't look too dreadful to those who bother to examine it.

In 1988, Caucuses Have Been the Place for Political Passion

RHODES COOK and DAVE KAPLAN

Although presidential primaries dominate the nomination process, they are not the only way in which delegates are selected. In 1988, 35 percent of delegates were chosen in caucuses. Operating by different rules and requiring different strategies, this method of delegate selection rewards those candidates who have the best organized and most intense supporters attending and dominating the local meetings. In the selection that follows, Rhodes Cook and Dave Kaplan describe the caucus selection process, its strengths and weaknesses, and which candidates benefited most from it in 1988. There will be fewer Democratic caucuses in 1992.

The Democratic and Republican presidential nominations essentially were resolved weeks ago. But if there had been fewer primaries and more caucuses this year, both Vice President George Bush and Massachusetts Gov. Michael S. Dukakis might still be struggling to nail down their nominations.

If primaries were the place to demonstrate broad acceptability, caucuses were the place for passion, and it was there that Bush and Dukakis encountered their stiffest resistance.

Fortunately for both candidates, more than 65 percent of the delegates to the Democratic and Republican national conventions were elected in primaries, where both Bush and Dukakis fared well. On the eve of the four-state primary vote June 7, Bush has swept 32 of 33 Republican primaries, while Dukakis has won 17 of 32 primary contests on the Democratic side. Both decisively won primary contests in the megastates of Florida, Texas, New York, Pennsylvania and Ohio.

But it has been a different story for Bush and Dukakis in the lower-turnout world of the caucuses, where the frequently long meeting hours turn participation into a test of commitment. It was in the Republican caucuses where religious broadcaster Pat Robertson's "invisible army" was most evident, and it was in the Democratic caucuses where the Rev. Jesse Jackson made some of his most impressive showings.

DIVIDENDS OF DEVOTION

Unlike a primary election, which is a single event held on a single day, a caucus process can extend over several months, usually beginning with first-

Source: *The Congressional Quarterly Weekly Report*, Vol. 46, (June 4, 1988): 1523, 1525, 1527. Reprinted by permission of Congressional Quarterly, Inc.

round mass meetings open to the voting public and concluding with district and state conventions where national convention delegates are chosen.

Robertson, who did not come close to winning a primary in 1988, won first-round caucus action in three states—Alaska, Hawaii and Washington; he finished second—but ahead of Bush—in two other caucus states, including Iowa; and he ended up with most of the national convention delegates in Nevada, even though he was not the first-round caucus winner there. Robertson probably would have scored even more caucus successes had his campaign not run aground in the March 8 Super Tuesday primaries.

Meanwhile, Jackson was the only candidate in either party to win first-round caucus action in every region of the country—Delaware and Vermont in the East, South Carolina and Texas in the South, Michigan in the Midwest and Alaska in the West.

As both Jackson and Robertson learned, a candidate with a passionate, but limited, cadre of supporters can be overwhelmed in a primary, where turnout often represents 35–40 percent of a party's registered voters.

But in caucuses, where participation rarely exceeds 5–10 percent of a party's members, candidates with motivated support often finish first. "Caucuses do tend to measure intensity of support in a way that primaries do not," says Michigan Democratic Party Chairman Rick Wiener.

In short, a few votes can go a long way in the caucuses. When Jackson won the March 26 Michigan caucuses with barely 100,000 votes, there was a burst of speculation that he could become the Democratic nominee. Ten days later, it took nearly 500,000 votes for Dukakis to win the pivotal Wisconsin primary, which opened the door for his march to the nomination.

JACKSON'S SECOND EFFORT

But even harvesting a small number of votes can be difficult in the caucuses, where party rules are murkier than in primaries. In caucuses, it is not simply the number of supporters a candidate has that counts, but also *where* those supporters are.

Jackson did not reap many delegates from caucus states in 1984, and he complained loudly that the process was undemocratic and unfair. Even though he was favored by more caucus participants in Mississippi and Virginia than any of his rivals, he ran third behind Walter F. Mondale and uncommitted forces in both states in the measurement that counts—the selection of delegates to the next stage of the caucus process.

The problem for Jackson in 1984 was that his support was too concentrated to win him a share of the delegates proportionate to the share of participants who backed him. In many predominantly black precincts, he turned out hundreds of supporters where only 10 or so would have been needed to dominate the selection of caucus delegates. But in many predominantly white precincts, he had no support at all.

This year, the Jackson campaign consciously set out to broaden its base in the caucus states, by reaching beyond the black community to liberal union members and issue-driven activists who largely had been in Mondale's corner in 1984. "They are all easily identifiable," says Jackson's delegate selection coordinator, Steve Cobble, "and the caucus process tends to enhance [their value]. It's one place where intensity actually counts."

However, Jackson's caucus coalition of blacks, liberal activists and the economically threatened was not quick to coalesce behind him. In Iowa, his effort to woo struggling farmers and blue-collar workers was blunted by Missouri Rep. Richard A. Gephardt's campaign blitz extolling the virtues of populism and economic nationalism. And Jackson's effort to attract students and liberal activists was undercut by Illinois Sen. Paul Simon's cerebral appeal. Jackson got only 9 percent of the Iowa caucus vote.

But once Gephardt and Simon started to fade, Jackson began to soar in the caucus states by drawing to himself what Larry Lamb, the communications director of the Minnesota Democratic Party, has described as the "Democratic spirit vote."

As a result, Jackson's success in the caucuses has transcended race. That was not often the case for Jackson in primary contests. Except for Puerto Rico, none of his seven primary victories this year was in a place where the population was less than 19 percent black.

But Jackson won the caucus action in several states—notably Alaska and Vermont—where there is virtually no black base at all. And he scored his biggest headlines of the year by winning the largest caucus state, Michigan, which is only 13 percent black.

TOP-DOWN, OR BOTTOM-UP

One of the criticisms of the caucuses is that they are vulnerable to domination by insurgent candidates, who can overwhelm the party regulars with a small cadre of voters.

That complaint was rarely heard in the first half of this century, when caucuses were the insiders' paradise. From Theodore Roosevelt's challenge to President William Howard Taft for the GOP nomination in 1912 to Tennessee Sen. Estes Kefauver's bids for the Democratic nomination in the 1950s, insurgents had to make their case in the primaries; caucuses were the party establishment's domain.

That began to change in 1964, when conservative Republicans supporting Barry Goldwater flooded the Republican caucuses, spearheading the conservative takeover of the GOP. Four years later, liberal activists in the Democratic Party, angered by Hubert H. Humphrey's ability to win the party's presidential nomination without competing in a single primary state, forced a major overhaul of their party's rules. As an outgrowth, the Democratic caucuses were opened to greater grass-roots participation, while the proliferation of primaries was implicitly encouraged.

Since then, there have been essentially two routes to success in the caucuses. One is for a candidate to mobilize around the passion of his message or his personality, as Jackson did this year, as Ronald Reagan did in pursuing the Republican nomination in 1976 and 1980, and as George McGovern did in seeking the Democratic nomination in 1972.

The other way is for a candidate to build an organization closely connected to party leaders across the country and their interest group allies, as Humphrey did in 1968 and Mondale did in 1984.

Dukakis' caucus campaign this year more closely approximated the Humphrey-Mondale model. By and large, the Massachusetts governor cultivated the support of political heavyweights within a state, then sent in campaign staffers to help organize.

Operating with a smaller budget, Jackson developed more grass-roots-oriented operations. "The Dukakis campaign was more top-heavy," says Jennifer Wallace-Brodeur, deputy director of Vermont's Democratic Party, in describing the caucus campaign in her state. "It was mostly legislators, the governor, and statewide officials. But in terms of knowing the towns, Jackson did a much better job."

That was not the case in every state, though. Dukakis' late flourish helped him finish with more caucus state victories (10) than Jackson, including six wins in the West, the lone region of the country where caucuses are still the dominant method of delegate selection. Still, Jackson drew more popular votes than Dukakis in first-round, mass-level caucus voting in 1988—a 37-to-32 percent edge in the 17 states and territories where Democrats tabulated a popular vote.

A BAD YEAR FOR THE CAUCUS

Focusing on how the 1988 candidates performed in the caucuses tends to obscure a larger question about the caucus as a political institution: Is it a dying breed?

This year was not a particularly good one for the caucus. There were fewer caucus states than at any time since the current primary-dominated era of presidential nominations began two decades ago, and the attention that caucuses drew often was negative.

Iowa came in for particular criticism. The nation's best-known caucus state drew potshots from one of the Democratic candidates (Tennessee Sen. Albert Gore Jr.) and from elements of the media; they criticized the state's Democratic caucuses as an unrepresentative test dominated by liberal interest groups. And it did not enhance the credibility of Iowa's caucuses that the two winners—Democrat Gephardt and Republican Sen. Robert Dole of Kansas—were both out of the race by the end of March.

On the Republican side, the Michigan GOP caucuses featured vicious infighting between the supporters of Bush, Robertson and New York

Rep. Jack F. Kemp, who first allied with Robertson before switching to Bush. At the GOP state convention in January, the Bush and Kemp forces elected one delegation, while Robertson's forces met separately and elected another.

Nor was the situation much calmer in Hawaii. Faced with a rush of registrations by Robertson voters in late January, local Republican leaders postponed the caucuses, then agreed to go ahead with the vote a week later after a barrage of negative publicity.

But the Democrats have also had some bickering of their own. Jackson's campaign has challenged the results of the Kansas caucuses, claiming they were conducted unfairly. While Jackson beat Dukakis in the popular vote taken at the first-round mass meetings, Dukakis won more delegates to the second-level district conventions and has ended up with nearly twice as many national convention delegates from Kansas as Jackson.

SECOND THOUGHTS

The intraparty bickering has prompted some caucus states to think seriously about shifting to a presidential primary in 1992. "There's a ton of sentiment to go back to a primary," says Kay Mettner, caucus coordinator for the Kansas Democratic Party. And in Michigan, legislation to establish a primary for 1992 already has passed one house of the Legislature.

In some caucus states where sentiment is not so crystallized, there still seems to be plenty of interest in a primary. "Some of the same pressures that are working in other states are working here," says former Colorado Democratic Chairman Floyd Ciruli, citing the need felt by some party officials for a delegate-selection system that would have a "quicker reporting process, numbers to grab onto and greater participation."

The problem of getting tangible results is a particularly vexing one in GOP caucus states, where many state parties do not even take straw votes to gauge voter sentiment. While Democrats do record votes at nearly all levels of their caucus process, the results are not always tabulated quickly.

The major complaint about the caucus process, though, is that it does not involve enough voters, and that the low turnouts are not as representative of voter sentiment as a higher-turnout primary.

The disparity between primary and caucus results has been evident in the three states this year where Democratic voters have been able to participate in both systems. In Idaho and Vermont, the primary was a non-binding "beauty contest," with delegates elected through a separate caucus process, while in Texas, both the primary and the caucus were for delegate-selection purposes. In all three states, Dukakis was the primary winner. In Texas and Vermont, Jackson won the caucuses. In all three, the primary turnout was at least eight times higher than the caucus turnout.

COMMITMENT, COST ARE VIRTUES

The caucuses, though, have their staunch defenders, who believe a caucus has party-building attributes a primary cannot match. They note that several hours at a caucus can involve voters in a way that quickly casting a primary ballot does not. Discussion of issues and party business often takes place at caucuses, and once the meetings are over, the state party has lists of thousands of voters who can be tapped to volunteer time or money, or even run for local office. These lists can be particularly valuable to parties in the twenty-two states where voters do not register by party.

And, many caucus supporters note, while the multi-tiered caucus process is often a chore for the state party to organize, a primary costs money, and many cost-conscious state governments are looking for ways to cut spending rather than increase it.

The result is that leaders in a number of caucus states are not talking these days about switching to a primary, but about joining with nearby states in forming a regional event for 1992 that would attract more attention from the candidates and the media. That is a particular possibility in the Rocky Mountain region, where this year's first-round caucus action extended all across the calendar . . . .

"The caucus system is alive and well and extremely popular, at least with the local party," says Jim Hansen, chairman of the Idaho Democratic Party rules committee. "It may be confusing to the media, but we love it."

A Candidate's Farewell

BRUCE BABBITT

Campaigns are educational. Voters learn about issues, managers learn about strategies and tactics, and candidates learn about style, character, and appeals. After ending his candidacy for the 1988 Democratic nomination, former Arizona governor Bruce Babbitt recounted the lessons he had learned from his unsuccessful campaign and on the basis of them offers advice to those who aspire for their party's nomination the next time around.

I've never paid much attention to television. Never watched much, and never thought much about how I looked on screen. I hardly expected that TV would provide both the low and high points of my campaign for president.

The first televised Democratic debate, last July in Houston, was a disaster for me. I had no sense of the medium at all. Simple things—keeping my head steady, looking straight into the camera and holding my gestures "high and tight" in the camera frame—had seemed to me trivial.

They weren't trivial, as I soon found out. Most of my reviewers looked to the animal kingdom for analogies. *Time* said I looked "as comfortable on television as a moose being pelted with buckshot." The New Republic asked, "Is this man about to bite the head off a live chicken?" Two days later, flying from Los Angeles to Phoenix, I read that some enterprising politico had hooked up 85 Iowans to a computer, to which they had signaled their reactions as they watched the debate. The verdict: I was the big loser. It stung.

So I did what any candidate in my position would do. I hired a consultant. I paid good money to find out I was creasing my forehead incorrectly. I tend to frown when I concentrate, which made me look unhappy on TV. The consultant, Michael Sheehan, taught me to do "eyebrow pushups" to "open up" my face and tried to keep me in the mood by repeating, "Bruce, you're *so happy* to be here." I had my doubts, sometimes, but darned if it didn't work.

The damage from Houston was immediate and extensive. That Sunday, I called Grace Zimmerman, an Iowa county treasurer, to ask for her support. There was a long, uncomfortable pause, and she said: "I'm watching a woman from *NEWSWEEK* on television, and she just got through predicting that you're going to drop out of the race." Thanks, *NEWSWEEK*.

Things picked up in December, when Tom Brokaw hosted the first network debate. In the dressing room beforehand, while the NBC technician was making me up, Jesse Jackson snuck up behind me and began playfully powdering my face. It helped cut through the tension. I knew I had to

Source: *Newsweek* (February 29, 1988): 24, 26. Reprinted by permission of the author.

do something dramatic at that debate. For weeks I'd been hammering my opponents about their silence on the federal budget deficit. Everybody knew we'd have to raise taxes and cut spending to balance the budget, but nobody was willing to come out and say so. That seemed to me the emblem of a much deeper failure: most politicians like to quote John F. Kennedy, but very few ask the voters to do anything for their country.

Halfway into the debate, Dick Gephardt gave me a pretty good opening. "I think it's time to stand up," he said, " and say ... what it is we're going to do to get this budget balanced." I bent back my microphone and I *did* stand up. Then I asked if any of my rivals would stand up with me for the truth on taxes and spending. Afterward, Paul Simon leaned over, one performer to another, and said, "Congratulations, Bruce, you'll have the lead in tomorrow's story."

People said it was a gimmick, planned in advance. Of course it was. So what? Supporters of Andrew Jackson ("Old Hickory") planted hickory poles at rural intersections all over America. That was a gimmick too. As gimmicks go, mine had some substance. And for a while it seemed to be working. On West End Avenue in Manhattan, a truck lurched to a halt and the driver rolled down his window. "Keep on standing, Bruce," he yelled at me. "I'm with you." For the rest of the campaign, I rarely left an audience without asking them to stand, and I rarely got fewer than half of my listeners on their feet.

In January, the press kind of rushed me for ten days, writing very favorable articles. Then reporters got self-conscious and the story became "Why is the press falling all over Bruce Babbitt?" I was accused of being the "media darling," which is something like being called "teacher's pet" in the first grade, with one important difference: your first-grade teacher had real control of your fate. Whatever power the media may have, its favors never translated into votes in Iowa or New Hampshire.

But I made a mistake as well. I let myself be stereotyped by a single plank in my platform, and I never fully communicated the "up" side of my campaign. That positive message included my plans for "workplace democracy," which would increase American productivity by giving workers more say in the running of their businesses and more money when they help make things run right. As it was, I became the Man Who Dares to Raise Taxes, and rarely got beyond that.

Oddly, one issue that was supposed to kill me didn't. I have long supported a "needs test" for federal spending, so benefits are targeted on the people who need them most. I thought I might break my pick on that one, but people understand the idea of asking the affluent to bear a bigger burden. I occasionally asked audiences to raise their hands if they thought millionaires should have their social-security benefits fully taxed. When the hands went up, I'd ask them what about people making $100,000? $90,000? $80,000? They usually bailed out on me around $50,000, which is about $20,000 higher than I proposed. But they bought the principle.

A modern presidential candidate comes close to living in a world where every waking hour is recorded on videotape, and I actually encouraged that as a way of drawing attention to my campaign. I've had cameras come into my bedroom while I was still woozy in the morning. I had cameras with me when I went to buy a Christmas tree with my kids. I remember the time a documentary crew . . . filmed an NBC crew . . . filming me . . . as I watched myself on the monitor. The whole scene was in danger of spiraling, Escher-like, into infinity.

One of the few places interesting dialogue went un-broadcast, ironically, was onstage during the TV debates. In one New Hampshire encounter, I got indignant with Al Gore when he accused me of having a "Republican" tax plan. It was a testy exchange. But later, while others were talking, Gore leaned over to say he hoped I wasn't really upset. I said "Naw." Then there were the chance meetings on the road. On a late-night flight from Des Moines to Chicago, Gary Hart advised me earnestly to think twice before taking on campaign debt. On another red-eye flight before Thanksgiving, Paul Simon offered avuncular encouragement at a time when he was soaring in the polls. Dick Gephardt and I once shared a ride in a horse-drawn carriage, of all things, but for some reason we couldn't connect: the conversation kept returning to the flowers we were passing along the shores of Lake Michigan.

What did I learn from the campaign? The most important lesson, I think is one *not* to learn. It hasn't gone unnoticed that in 1984 Fritz Mondale said he'd raise taxes, and he lost. In 1988 I said we'd have to raise taxes and cut spending, and I lost. Many people take my failure as further proof, if any were needed, that the American people will not respond to a tough and honest message.

I think that is nonsense. There's room for tough ideas in presidential campaigns. But if you've got them, you'd better lay them out early, and you'd better find creative ways to advance them. Mondale waited to raise the tax issue until after he was nominated. That's too late. I had another problem, which is that I was a virtual unknown, and I think it was a bit much to ask the voters to accept both a new messenger and a challenging message at the same time. But I feel certain that voters will rise to a challenge in the long run, particularly if it comes to them from a more familiar figure. One of the remaining contenders, perhaps? I'm allowed to dream, aren't I?

How the Press Covered the Primaries

S. ROBERT LICHTER

Most political scientists think that the media have the greatest impact on voters at the beginning of the nomination process when the least is known about the candidates. In the final reading in this chapter, media analyst S. Robert Lichter, Director of the Center for Media and Public Affairs, examines how the three major commercial networks covered the primaries and caucuses. He discusses which issues received the most coverage, which candidates received the best coverage, and how television coverage affected the momentum of the campaign.

Critics have been accusing the media of distorting the electoral process ever since television became a prominent political actor. The three most persistent complaints about TV news are: (1) Television provides saturation coverage of the horse race and ignores policy issues; (2) The networks favor liberals over conservatives, or Democrats over Republicans; (3) Television bestows precious momentum on some candidates and withholds it from others by its sometimes arbitrary coverage.

How do these charges stack up against the evidence this time around? To find out, we turned to the Center for Media and Public Affairs and its ongoing content analysis of TV news election coverage. We examined all 1,338 election stories on the ABC, CBS, and NBC evening newscasts from February 1987 through the final primaries on June 7, 1988. On each charge there was some evidence to support the critics but not enough to clinch their case.

MAKING AN ISSUE OF ISSUES

There's no doubt that television loves the horse race and dislikes the issues. The medium thrives on excitement, conflict, and contests that are structured like sports events. All of these are built into elections but must sometimes be teased out of policy debates. Virtually every study of election coverage has noted (if not decried) the primacy of horse-race news, and ours is no exception. As Table 1 shows, over 500 stories dealt with the horse race, two and one-half times the number that addressed policy issues. And that figure doesn't include over 300 discussions of campaign strategies and

Source: *Public Opinion* (July/August 1988): 45–49. Reprinted with permission of the American Enterprise Institute for Public Policy Research, Washington, D.C..

TABLE 1. Top Five Story Topics

	STORIES
Horse race	537
Campaign issues	312
Strategy and tactics	280
Policy issues	215
Candidate politics	88

Source: Center for Media and Public Affairs, election news coverage, February 1987–June 7, 1988.

tactics, which also outdistanced the policy debate. Even when TV went looking for issues, it found more ephemeral campaign matters than enduring policy concerns—things such as disputes over the current behavior of candidates, like Hart's sexual escapades or Bush's impromptu debate with Dan Rather.

Yet all the attention to the horse race and the daily campaign agenda failed to drive issue coverage off the airwaves. The issue coverage may look thin by comparison to the contest coverage, but 215 stories can take in quite a lot. Table 2 lists the top ten policy issues in order of the number of stories in which each was mentioned. Some of these were only passing mentions, but others involved extensive discussions. (The latter was required for an issue to be considered a story topic.)

The Iran-Contra affair was brought up in over 100 election stories, reflecting questions over Bush's role. Then came the "big four" economic issues of 1988—taxes, trade, unemployment, and the state of the economy—along with Central American policy. Close on their heels came issues that emerged after the campaign was in full swing (like the drug problem) and others that simmered slightly more slowly throughout (like the budget deficit).

Each of the top ten issues came up in over fifty stories, and a total of twenty-five issues in at least twenty stories. That total doesn't include discussions of these issues aired outside the context of election coverage. The moral is that when you run well over 1,000 stories that take up over

TABLE 2. Top Ten Issues

	STORIES
Iran-Contra	114
Taxes	97
Unemployment	85
Economy	83
Central America	78
Trade	73
Drugs	68
Education	58
Civil rights	57
Budget deficit	55

thirty-five hours of airtime, you can cover the horse race *and* the issues, at least all the issues the candidates want to talk about.

That raises a rarely noted problem with criticism of runaway horse-race news. Pundits and political scientists may be the only ones who complain about the lack of issue coverage. The candidates complain instead that the media don't carry their "message," a message usually calculated to fuzz over distinctions on policy issues and to avoid alienating potential supporters. Nor is it clear that average viewers usually thirst for more thorough and detailed debates on the INF treaty or the Middle East peace process. If they did, MacNeil and Lehrer would pass Rather, Brokaw, and Jennings in the Nielsen ratings.

The deeper problem with complaints about horse-race coverage is that the critics are asking the media to do just what they criticize it for doing otherwise—to shape the campaign agenda by forcing the candidates to march to the media's tune. The media don't discuss policy issues in greater depth at least partly because the candidates don't, and the candidates don't because it's frequently counterproductive. It just didn't pay for Walter Mondale to be so forthright about raising taxes, and Dick Gephardt discovered this year how quickly his trade proposals became a lightning rod for criticism. Policy debates can even backfire on journalists, as Dan Rather learned when he tried to force a reluctant George Bush to discuss Iran-Contra policy.

Horse-race news predominates because it flows from news values. It concerns what just happened and what's about to happen. That's also why campaign issues outstrip policy issues. The candidates' daily behavior on the campaign trail is less predictable, hence more potentially newsworthy than their stump speeches. In sum the critics don't want to let journalists be journalists. But do they really want journalists to be more like political scientists?

TELEVISION'S TILT

The scholars may grumble about horse-race coverage, but it's partisan bias that brings cries of outrage from the politicians and their supporters. Conservatives have been the quickest to cry foul, and they got some support from a controversial study by Edith Efron claiming network bias against Richard Nixon in 1972.

They also drew sustenance from the 1980 Rothman-Lichter survey of media elites, which found that four out of five major media journalists vote for the Democratic presidential candidate. That same year, however, a study directed by Michael Robinson failed to add fuel to conservative complaints. It found that liberal favorite Ted Kennedy had more negative print and broadcast coverage than Jimmy Carter in the primaries, and Carter got worse press than Ronald Reagan in the general election. But Robinson's study of the 1984 election found dramatic differences in the networks' treatment of the two tickets. While Mondale and Ferraro each received slightly more positive than negative spin, Reagan's spin index was ten to one negative, and Bush had the dubious distinction of getting *only* negative spin. And in a study of the 1984 primaries, Henry E. Brady and Richard Johnston found that Jesse Jackson received the most positive wire service coverage among the Democratic contenders.

With this mixed bag of findings as prelude, we examined the good and bad press meted out to the various candidates for 1988. Specifically, we coded every assessment of each candidate as either positive, negative, mixed, or neutral. We included only judgments about whether a candidate would make a good president, not whether he is likely to become president.

By this definition good press was CBS's Bruce Morton's closer on Jesse Jackson campaigning in Illinois: "He's neon and fireworks. All the rest this week have been pastel." Bad press was political analyst Kevin Phillips calling George Bush "an overstuffed resumé" on NBC. Even after excluding mixed and neutral statements, we coded 1,823 clearly positive or negative statements on the fourteen announced candidates—1,062 for the Democrats and 761 for the Republicans. The results are of more than academic interest.

This has been a banner year for charges of media bias. Columnist Mark Shields accused journalists of "pervasive intellectual elitism" for rejecting Gephardt's trade proposals. Pat Robertson was moved to "thank the Lord" that "most Christians read neither the *New York Times* nor the *Washington Post*." Columnist Dorothy Gilliam traced some of Jackson's bad press to "the veiled demons of racism and white supremacy." And Bob Dole complained that Republicans were subjected to a "double standard" of negative coverage by journalists who "see the world through liberal-colored glasses."

How do the claims of bias stack up against a systematic content analysis? Table 3 shows the percentage of good press received by each candidate, and the average score for candidates from each party. The left-hand column includes assessments from all sources who appear or are quoted on the air, the best overall portrait of how each candidate was treated. The right-hand column considers only nonaligned sources like reporters, election analysts, and voters. It excludes the candidates, their families, and their campaign staffs. This is often done in academic studies to highlight the sources that reflect the greatest journalistic discretion and carry the most influence on public opinion.

Among Democrats Jesse Jackson stands out for favorable press—he received the most positive coverage of any major candidate from both partisan and nonpartisan sources. Apart from the early days when Bruce Babbitt was the media favorite, Jackson headed the field during every phase of the campaign. Michael Dukakis's coverage hovered near the average for all candidates. Dukakis, Gephardt, Gore, and Simon all received nearly equal amounts of good and bad press. Gephardt was the only one to fall below

TABLE 3.   Good Press

	ALL SOURCES		NONPARTISAN SOURCES	
Jackson	74%	(250)*	75%	(167)*
Dukakis	55	(249)	58	(107)
Gephardt	48	(164)	63	(54)
Gore	54	(56)	45	(22)
Simon	53	(57)	75	(12)
Babbitt	89	(37)	86	(21)
Biden	54	(61)	39	(28)
Hart	38	(188)	21	(121)
All Democrats	57	(1062)	56	(532)
Bush	50	(379)	49	(127)
Dole	64	(181)	65	(59)
Robertson	49	(122)	37	(46)
Kemp	58	(50)	64	(22)
Haig	67	(15)	50	(6)
DuPont	50	(14)	17	(6)
All Republicans	54	(761)	49	(266)

Note: * = Number of clearly positive or negative evaluations of candidates' desirability.

the 50 percent mark, but that reflects attacks from other candidates, as his 63 percent positive rating from nonpartisans attests. Hart's dismal rating didn't improve after he reentered the race in January.

Among Republicans Dole easily outdistanced both Bush and Robertson. Bush's ratings were mainly negative throughout the campaign, except for a brief spurt to 65 percent positive during the New Hampshire primary run, the only time that he was not the front-runner. Robertson, in contrast, received favorable early press—about two to one positive through New Hampshire. After that he was done in by controversies over his "funny facts" and received the worst press of any candidate still in the running—over two to one negative.

Was there a partisan bias? When we compared the two parties' overall good press/bad press ratios, the result was a slight edge for the Democrats—56 percent good press versus 53 percent for the Republicans. After extensive coverage of fourteen candidates over more than a year of campaigning, a partisan difference of only 3 percent looks more like balance than bias.

That impression is reinforced by focusing on the category that might be expected to produce the most partisan tilt—assessments of the candidates' issue positions. On the issue of "the issues," the level of good press dropped substantially for both parties. But the Democrats retained their 3-percent margin, by 40 to 37 percent positive evaluations.

When the comparisons focused on nonpartisan sources, however, the gap between the parties widened somewhat. The Democrats held steady at a 55 percent positive rating, while the Republicans dropped to 48 percent. And when we narrowed the focus to comments by journalists themselves, the gap widened further. The Democrats received 65 percent good press from journalists' on-air evaluations, compared to 51 percent for Republicans. So reporters and anchors spoke favorably of the Democrats nearly two-thirds of the time that they ventured assessments, while they found favor with Republicans only half the time.

Journalists, themselves, however, accounted for about only one in seven assessments that were broadcast. Most of their comments were directed toward the candidates' performances as campaigners rather than their professional qualifications, personal qualities, or issue stands. This was in keeping with a general tendency by journalists to direct their on-air opinions toward the horse race rather than the candidates' desirability.

All in all the evidence for Senator Dole's charge of bias is less than compelling. Democrats were favored over Republicans, but by margins that ranged from trivial to modest.

MEDIA MOMENTUM

Finally, what about the media's vaunted role in bestowing precious momentum on winners or "hot" contenders in the early primaries? Iowa winners Dole and Gephardt have been asking the same question. It's not that TV news abandoned its tradition of frontloading. More stories were broadcast about Iowa and New Hampshire this year than all the other primaries put together, although those two states selected only 2 percent of the parties' convention delegates. Moreover, frontloading did have a measurable impact. Both Dole and Gephardt jumped 12 percentage points in the New Hampshire tracking polls the day after the Iowa vote. Similarly, Jesse Jackson climbed ten points in the polls during the month after New Hampshire, during which he received extremely favorable coverage. It's just that these modest gains pale before the 31-percentage-point gain by Gary Hart in ten days after his better-than-expected 1984 Iowa finish.

What caused big mo' to downshift into this year's little mo'? Two explanations stand out. First, non-media factors placed a cap on the benefits available to the would-be media candidates. Dole and Gephardt both had to battle opponents who had advantages in New Hampshire. Bush's tie to Reagan became a plus there, and Dukakis already had a positive image among his home state's next-door neighbors. As for Jackson, analysts and partisans have heatedly debated whether his appeal is limited by his race or his ideology. That such limits exist is not debated.

Second, what television gave with one hand, it took back with the other. Gephardt received the most negative coverage of the major Democratic contenders after Iowa. Dole's ill-chosen remarks the night of the New Hampshire vote became a major "mediality" (an event whose impact is vastly inflated by media attention) by resurrecting the "mean Bob Dole" story. By avoiding such blunders, Jackson gained the same lasting benefit that Hart did in 1984—a new prominence whose payoff may come in future elections. One of momentum's benefits is deferred compensation.

As in earlier elections, the media were dealing the cards in 1988. But it's not just the hand you're dealt, it's how you play it that counts in politics. Whatever else has changed in the age of mediated elections, you've still got to know when to hold 'em and know when to fold 'em.

5. National Nominating Conventions

National nominating conventions have existed since the 1830s. Then and now they continue to perform many of the same formal functions. They choose their party's standard bearers, decide the platform on which their nominees will run, and adopt rules and procedures for the conduct of the meeting. In addition, they have always been seen as a unifying force, bringing their partisans together and orienting them toward the presidential campaign.

In appearance, contemporary conventions bear a resemblance to those of the past. The seeming chaos of the sessions, the interaction of party officials and rank-and-file supporters, and the banners, balloons, and other regalia all recall a time when delegates at national conventions made important decisions for their parties. Although the appearance is similar, however, the changes in nominating conventions have been as dramatic as the changes in party rules. In fact, the changes in party rules, combined with the new modes of communicating to the electorate, have altered the principal roles of national nominating conventions in the presidential selection process.

Today, conventions are big, public extravaganzas. They are designed primarily to demonstrate the party's enthusiastic support of its presidential nominee—who had effectively won the nomination in the caucuses and primaries prior to the convention. Conventions now ratify the people's choice rather than determine it, as they did in the past.

Conventions have another important, new role. In addition to healing a party divided by the nomination process, the convention offers a podium for launching the general election campaign. With the major television networks tuned in and the American public watching, the conventions take on the character of huge pep rallies, carefully scripted, with party leaders as the star performers. This public relations aspect of the campaign has become increasingly important for three reasons: it is the last and only time the parties will communicate directly to the voters during the campaign, except through paid advertisements; it is the time when a majority of the American public begins to pay attention to the election and thus might be influenced, even persuaded by what they see and hear; and it represents a golden opportunity to set the campaign agenda, to emphasize the most favorable issues for the party and its nominee, and to articulate the themes and appeals that will be reinforced throughout the campaign.

To achieve these objectives, conventions must be artfully staged and written. The speakers must read their lines and the audience must cheer at the right time. Dissent must be kept to a minimum. If all this is accomplished, the convention may achieve the objective of helping the party and its candidates in the fall campaign. If this is all that occurs, however, the convention is likely to be a real bore. Television viewership will decline. The audience that remains will be the true believers, those partisans who have already made up their minds.

Naturally, the news organizations that cover conventions have different objectives. They wish to convey an exciting, newsworthy event, so they emphasize conflict, drama, and human interest. To get the large picture, they cover what goes on inside the convention hall as well as outside of it. Most media coverage creates a natural tension between those who plan and run conventions, who wish to emphasize unanimity, and those who report on them, who wish to show disagreement and dissent.

The readings in this section focus on that tension and how it has affected the evolving role of conventions. The first selection, by journalist Warren Weaver, Jr., describes the old and the new Democratic conventions. In discussing the multiple ballots of the past and the divisions of the present, Weaver explains why contemporary Democratic candidates wish to avoid public dissent as much as possible.

In the next reading, Professor Byron Shafer summarizes the principal changes in nominating conventions and the reasons those changes occurred. According to Shafer, each convention is really two conventions. There is the convention that takes place on the floor of the meeting hall, in which the elected delegates participate and perform their legally designated roles; and there is the convention seen on television, orchestrated and scripted by the parties and mediated by the media, that is designed to influence the public. Much of what goes on in the convention is intended to serve one of these two simultaneous purposes: to make decisions on party matters and to provide a partisan message to the electorate.

A political convention is a gathering of people. Who they are determines who is nominated, how the meeting is conducted, what issues are emphasized, and the extent to which the party and its nominees can project a national appeal. The next two selections focus on the delegates who attend national conventions. Martin Plissner and Warren Mitofsky provide a demographic portrait of them, one that reflects the attempts of both parties to select people who are representative of their party's rank-and-file supporters. Journalist Maureen Dowd provides a glimpse of the human dimension in her chronicle of a day at the 1988 Republican convention.

Turning from the delegates to the candidates, we next examine their convention objectives: to win and to present a united front. To achieve these dual goals in a meeting of thousands of people, some of whom may not be enamored with the prospective nominees, it is necessary to have a large and tight organization, one that can impose discipline on its supporters. Andrew Rosenthal describes Michael Dukakis's organization at the 1988 Democratic convention. The Dukakis operation is typical of the efficient, modern-day operations that leading candidates create to take no chances.

From the perspectives of those who plan the convention, those who participate in it, and those who will see it on television, such matters as the content of the party's platform, the choice of the presidential nominee, and the general appeal to the electorate are usually foregone conclusions. The only suspense at the convention surrounds the choosing of the vice presidential nominee.

By tradition, the choice of the vice presidential candidate is that of the presidential nominee. Although this is a very important decision, in recent years it often has not been made with a great deal of forethought or information. A primary aim of the decision-making process has been to achieve surprise with the consequence that the backgrounds of potential nominees have not been adequately examined. Another problem has been the tendency of presidential candidates to select their running mates on the basis of their electoral appeal rather than on their qualifications to serve as vice president, and if the need arose, as president. The dual objectives of achieving surprise and balancing the ticket have resulted in selection of vice presidential nominees who have been subjected to considerable public scrutiny and criticism. The choice of Dan Quayle in 1988 is a case in point. In a reading on vice presidential selection, Gerald Boyd, a reporter for *The New York Times*, discusses the calculations that went into George Bush's decision to choose Dan Quayle as his running mate, a decision subsequently criticized by the media, by members of his own party, and by the opposition.

The final readings in this chapter concern the televised convention, the one most Americans see. Jeremy Gerard views this coverage as declining in large part because of the predictability of what goes on. From the perspective of those who report the news, conventions are becoming much less newsworthy. Jonathan Rauch describes how one television correspondent, Ann Compton, tried to overcome this problem by her coverage of Jesse Jackson. Robert and Linda Lichter present a content analysis of convention coverage by the three major networks. As we might expect, pomp and personality, enthusiasm and criticism, and good news and bad news all emerge from their analysis.

As Ever, the Democrats Would Prefer a Contest

WARREN WEAVER, JR.

National nominating conventions have changed a great deal. They used to be contentious events in which the delegates debated and fought before they eventually determined who the nominees would be and on what platform they would run. The reforms in the nomination process have rendered contemporary conventions placid by comparison. Lamenting the changes, New York Times reporter Warren Weaver Jr. describes the bygone days when Democratic conventions were marked by major battles over rules, procedures, candidates, and policy.

Hubert H. Humphrey never tired of proclaiming Democratic dedication to "the politics of joy." Fellow Democrats of various stripes have long insisted that, win or lose, love feast or fistfight, they have a lot more fun nominating their Presidential candidates than do the Republicans. More noise, more disorder, more gleeful fratricide.

Truth to tell, however, the Democrats have not had much political fun at a national convention in a quarter-century or more. There was plenty of ugly action at the 1968 brawl in Chicago and some clever manipulation in Miami in 1972, but both the resulting nominees, Hubert H. Humphrey and George McGovern, went down to defeat, and their conventions have had to share the blame....

Over the years, political convention fun has, by definition, required a close contest. But the Democrats haven't needed more than one ballot for any nomination since 1956, when Adlai E. Stevenson startled the delegates, who had chosen him on the first ballot, by throwing open the Vice Presidential selection. Senator Estes Kefauver led on the first roll-call, and Senator John F. Kennedy on the second, but delegates began switching votes and Senator Kefauver won on the third ballot. In hindsight, the outcome probably strengthened Mr. Kennedy's 1960 Presidential bid; running for Vice President, he would have had to share the blame for the Eisenhower wipe-out that November.

Democratic nominations for President have required more than one ballot on just two occasions in the last 64 years. In 1932 it took a series of preliminary floor victories and four ballots to turn back challenges by Alfred E. Smith and Speaker John Nance Garner and nominate Franklin D.

Roosevelt. In 1952, it took three ballots to draft Governor Stevenson of Illinois over Senators Kefauver of Tennessee and Richard Russell of Georgia. Mr. Stevenson, incidentally, was the first and last candidate to be drafted since the Republicans chose James Garfield in 1880. Modesty long ago ceased to be a marketable political commodity.

One reason the Democrats have avoided multi-ballot conventions since 1924 may be that their convention in New York that year ran a record 17 days and required 103 ballots to nominate John W. Davis, whose name does not ring down the corridors of political history. The rules, not changed until 1936, required a two-thirds majority to nominate. Four years before Mr. Davis, a 44-ballot Democratic convention had chosen James M. Cox, another man whose fame was not lasting. Neither did very well at the polls.

The 1924 convention was notable also as the first to be broadcast by radio, which may be what gave durability to Franklin D. Roosevelt's nominating description of Mr. Smith as "the happy warrior." But since television made its first coast-to-coast broadcasts in 1952, it has been the medium of choice for political conventions. Over the years, gavel-to-gavel coverage came to be interspersed with network-manufactured events to break up the tedium. This time, the networks have decided to provide coverage only in prime time, with shows consisting partly of events in progress, partly of other material.

As the Republicans have done for years, the Democrats are looking this year to show-business professionals to give color to their convention, hiring a team of Hollywood consultants to stage their Atlanta gathering. The result is likely to be a better show for the home audience with no notable increase in political fun for the delegates.

There is not, for example, likely to be anything like the "voice from the sewer" episode that enlivened, even influenced, the Democratic convention of 1940 in Chicago. The delegates had just heard a message from President Roosevelt, saying he had no desire for a third term and freeing the delegates. The stunned silence was broken by a voice on an off-stage microphone chanting "We want Roosevelt!" Delegates picked up the chant—some said it sounded as if it originated beneath the stage—and the draft was on. The voice was later reported to have been that of an aide of Chicago Mayor Edward J. Kelley, one of the city's legendary bosses.

Nor is it likely that the Atlanta convention will bear any resemblance to the Chicago gathering of 1968. That year, violence between antiwar protesters and the police outside convention hotels gave the nominee, Mr. Humphrey, one of the worst launching pads for a campaign in party history. On the convention floor, the battle came into unforgettable focus when Senator Abraham Ribicoff, nominating Mr. McGovern, referred to "Gestapo tactics in the streets of Chicago," and the cameras caught Mayor Richard Daley reacting with obscenities.

The violence helped produce changes in party rules that greatly reduced the power—at least at conventions—of the party bosses. There were more blacks, more women and a generally more liberal tone in 1972, when the Democrats nominated George McGovern.

That convention also produced one of the most memorable episodes of inside baseball. In a credentials challenge that boiled down to a head-to-head contest with the Humphrey camp, the South Dakota Senator's strategists deliberately switched votes so that Humphrey supporters would win by a large margin. Had the McGovern strategists pulled out all stops, they might have won this relatively minor floor fight. But then they would have faced a challenge on the issue of what constituted a majority on subsequent issues. The McGovern forces had a majority of delegates present and voting, but may not have had a majority of all those elected. Clearing that procedural hurdle, they controlled the convention.

McGovern aides did not advertise the strategy, and at least one television anchorman interpreted the maneuver as a defeat rather than a victory for the Senator.

It doesn't happen often, but in 1980 the platform debate was the political highlight of the Democratic convention. It was clear early in the session that President Carter would defeat Senator Edward M. Kennedy's challenge to his renomination, but stubborn Kennedy backers, pressing for philosophical victory, pushed amendment after amendment and got a number of them adopted. The debate ran 17 hours over two days and was climaxed by a rousing speech by Mr. Kennedy. When the convention closed with the traditional gathering of candidates and party leaders on the rostrum, Senator Kennedy's participation was almost perfunctory, foreshadowing political problems for President Carter. . . .

The Convention and a Changing American Politics

BYRON SHAFER

Why and how have conventions changed? Professor Byron Shafer explains their evolution and the role they play in contemporary electoral politics. In the past, conventions were the centerpiece of the nomination process, making the critical decisions for the national party; today these decisions have been made by the process that precedes the quadrennial meetings. This has not rendered conventions obsolete, but merely changed their principal objective to that of launching the general election campaign. Shafer describes the components of this new objective and the politics it generates.

For its audience, the charm of a national party convention remains a mix of what it has always been. There is the element of momentous decision, of course. Even in an era when the convention merely ratifies rather than makes its central decision, that act still confirms one of two possible alternatives for the most important political office in the United States, and perhaps the world. There is the element of contention and conflict too. Few conventions occur without some evident struggle—over platform, over rules, perhaps over the presidential nomination itself—and that struggle acquires the intrinsic attraction of disputes which are larger than those of daily life. Finally, there is the element of sheer spectacle as well. If this is the aspect most satirized in conventions, it still possesses an almost automatic, visceral fascination—the proverbial cast of thousands, the rhetoric and symbols of a rich national history, the high drama and low comedy of democratic politics in action. . . .

THE CONVENTION AS SUBJECT: A CHANGING POLITICAL INSTITUTION

For most of its institutional history, the national party convention was practically centered on the creation of a delegate majority behind a major-party candidate for president of the United States. The nomination of such a candidate was the original—and really sole—reason for creating the convention; the presence of that nomination was what produced the accretion of most other convention activities. In the early 1950s, however, in response to a set of larger, external, social forces, the nomination effectively departed the convention. Elements of the nationalization of presidential politics were the fundamental cause of this informal departure, but a change in the strategic calculations of key actors—party officials at that time—was the more immediate cause. These officials discovered that preservation of their influence required attention to explicitly national rather than purely local events in presidential politics. This realization implied that candidate affiliations had to be cemented earlier, to the point where candidate majorities were reliably effected in advance of the convention. . . .

Without formal decision by anyone, then, the nomination left the convention, and it has remained outside, in the process of delegate selection, ever since. The Democratic and Republican conventions of 1952, the first without a candidate initially nominated before the end of the Second World War, were also the last to feature a nomination realized within the convention hall. Approximately a generation later, after the disastrous Democratic convention of 1968, many of the same continuing forces from the nationalization of politics combined with a much more focused reform movement to extract sweeping alterations in the process of delegate selection—and to lock the nomination, procedurally, outside the convention. An older order dominated by a mix of internal party institutions gave way to a new order based on presidential primary elections. The key actors in this new order changed simultaneously, with party officials giving way to rank-and-file participants, or at least to those who turned out for the burgeoning primaries and participatory conventions.

The calculations of these new key actors, however, were essentially unchanged in their practical impact. These calculations still centered on national developments; they still produced delegate majorities in advance—often well in advance—of the national convention. In fact, when compared to party officials, these newly central rank-and-file participants were less initially informed and less ideologically rooted, and hence even more easily moved by early developments in nominating politics. The resulting tendency for the "bandwagon" (by which a nominating majority was created) to roll earlier and earlier was reinforced by a similar recurring movement among financial contributors and campaign activists. It was reinforced again, most powerfully, by the concentration of the national media on the earliest contests. In response, the convention, once the central forum for this nominating politics, became a fallback mechanism for a set of unlikely circumstances, effectively the nominator of last resort.

A marked shift in the political identity of those who became delegates to these evolving conventions followed hard upon the interaction of reform in the institutions of delegate selection and evolution in the environment for nominating politics. . . . Directly, procedural reform devastated those institutional arrangements which created delegates through an official party structure, while it replaced them with arrangements which provided no certified place for the official party. Indirectly, procedural reform devalued the informal assets of party officials as well: a nominating politics which required multiple, independent, national campaigns made it very difficult to mobilize an extended party behind one candidate; candidates who needed early commitment and personal loyalty, above all, found party officials less useful even as individual participants.

The practical result was very close to the eclipse of the official party in the politics of presidential selection, and the diminution of party officials as national convention delegates. The major impact of this result on the convention, in turn, was to drive it further in the direction of the dominant ideology of its party—Democrats to the left, Republicans to the right. Party officials as a formal, organizational category were distinguished among political elites by their concern with presenting a broad party program, one capable of electing a wide array of party candidates, normally by moving both program and candidates toward the political center. When their influence at national conventions declined, and when even those party officials who did attend were less likely to offer this traditional orientation, the delegates as a collectivity were freed of that moderating restraint, and the convention as an institution moved off from the political center.

The withdrawal, constriction, or outright defeat of the official party, however, was only part of the change in delegate identities. Presidential aspirants could hardly hope to build the independent nominating campaigns required by a reformed politics out of individual pieces, so that the support of some existing framework remained an operational necessity. By the same token, organizational leaders outside the official party structure could hardly remain ignorant of this fact for long. The result was the rise of the organized interests, of interest groups and issue organizations, as the base for nominating campaigns. The result was also the coming of the interested partisans, of interest group representatives and independent issue activists, as the national convention delegates produced by these campaigns. In response, the convention changed additionally as an environment for internal politicking.

Not only did these interested partisans not face a broad range of constituencies to knit together for November, but they needed very specific—and noticeable—policy successes to satisfy their organizational membership at home. Not only did they not want to see the nominee move toward the political center in anticipation of the general election campaign, but they needed to use the convention to lock in their putative gains from the politics of nomination. The balance of ideologues over simple partisans thus continued to rise, to the point where those who were distressed by that balance began to look for ways to reintroduce the official party, through guaranteed formal representation if necessary. Their efforts, by then, were probably bootless, for they also confirmed the transformation of the political parties, from a collection of officeholders to an aggregation of activists in their organizational essence, and from partisans to ideologues as national convention delegates.

MORE ELEMENTS OF CHANGE IN THE CONVENTION

The disappearance of the nomination almost automatically promoted a second major activity as the political centerpiece of these postreform conventions, just as change in the identity of convention delegates almost automatically contributed a different set of internal conflicts around this newly
central activity. With the nomination gone but press attention continuing, many participants came to see the convention as a means to advance
various external campaigns. For the nominee and top officials, this meant
orchestrating the convention to set out the themes of—and effectively to
launch—the general election campaign. For many others, however, it meant
focusing the convention on some *other* concern, be that a future presidential
bid, a current legislative effort, or supportive publicity for a nascent cause,
group, or program.

Recurring lines of conflict followed this newly central activity. A division
between the nominee and his remaining challengers provided one such
line, and it was always the most serious when it surfaced. But a division
between the convention leadership and the delegate rank and file, and
thus often between the successful nominee and some minority of his own
supporters, was a second recurring line of conflict, more reliably present
and perhaps more diagnostic of the internal environment for postreform
convention politicking. The nominee reliably aspired to move toward the
political center and toward an identification with the general public. Many
delegates preferred to affirm his ideological distinctness and to secure his
group attachments from the nominating campaign.

Struggles over the focus of the convention were an obvious way to establish this balance. Moreover, indications were that these struggles still
mattered. A sizable minority of the general public claimed to reach a voting
decision during the convention, a claim which no candidate dared cava-
lierly dismiss. Beyond that, the convention was the last real opportunity for
many participants to secure something concrete from the nominating campaign, while the internal course of that convention inevitably determined
the extent to which the nominee could use it to set out his themes, even
as it relentlessly painted a picture of the candidate and his party, whether
their launching effort was successful or not.

The foci for these conflicts were those continuing activities which had
always been at the organizational heart of the national convention—the
mechanics for nominating a president, of course, but also the mechanics
for nominating a vice president, affirming delegate credentials, adopting
procedural rules, and proclaiming a party platform. Yet in an era when the
launching of external campaigns had become the central activity of the
convention, and when the reformed cast of participants was increasingly
drawn to presidential politics by a concern for specific issues and interests
rather than by simple partisanship and electoral calculation, the internal
politics of each of these arenas was naturally, perhaps inevitably, different

as well. The priority for these various theaters of conflict changed; the strategies of the participants within these theaters changed; eventually, the very organization of each arena—and hence the internal structure of the national party convention—began to change in response as well.

As between the two major nominations, the confirmation of a president dropped in priority, in an era when that nomination was effectively settled. At the same time, the selection of a vice president unequivocally rose—as a publicity device, a bargaining chip, or a symbolic reward. Among committees, Platform was up substantially, thanks to the promise of policy commitments, however ethereal these might be. Rules gained marginally, as the apparent source of regulations which might shape a nomination— perhaps still at this convention, definitely by the next. And Credentials dropped sharply, thanks to developments in both parties which made prior outcomes decisive. In strategic terms, dissident delegates sought policy demands which were sufficiently extreme to attract the attention of viewers at home. Nominees, from the other side, sought to compromise with these demands, even when they appeared to be politically indigestible, so as to get on with the business of orchestrating the convention. In the process, regardless of the outcome in any given convention, the resulting party programs became increasingly divergent. In the process, a new set of convention participants—perhaps the key intermediaries in American party politics— was initiated forcefully into these newly divergent views.

Implicit in this shift in the central activity of the convention (to the politics of launching one or another campaign) and in the effort by most participants to influence one or another of these launchings was the notion that *public impressions* were the principal measure of success. From there, it was but a small step to the perception that this reward came not through some official resolution but rather through a press portrait, to be gained indirectly from developments at the convention. As it happened, the departure of the nomination coincided precisely with the rise of television as the principal source of convention news—so that efforts to shape public impressions of the convention became conflicts over coverage by national television networks. The audience for television coverage soared instantaneously. Efforts to manipulate that coverage followed hard upon this trend.

In fact, the resulting conflict over press portraits of the convention quickly became a three-cornered affair. First were the historically dominant struggles, among candidates and delegates over the substance of the convention—but played out, in the television era, with continuing attention to their impact on a viewing audience. Second were some existing but newly augmented struggles, between partisan actors and network news officials, over priorities and perspectives for the televising of conventions. Third were the latest and least visible of these conflicts, within television news departments themselves, over what was initially a question of proper focus but ultimately became a question of the proper *amount* of coverage too. These struggles, like those around the traditional agenda, began to change the very structure of the convention, altering its physical appearance through the introduction of television equipment, its procedural pace through the generation of comprehensive scripts, and even its practical behavior through the banning of extended floor demonstrations.

The fact that television coverage via national network news was the central element in modern press portraits of the convention was almost immediately recognized by the active participants. Yet even they could be excused for concentrating on the details of that coverage during the period, from the early 1950s through the late 1970s, when its parameters remained essentially stable. Nevertheless, as the organizational and political environment for decisions about coverage changed, this gavel-to-gavel standard came under pressure. Organizationally, the networks saw their audience stagnate while operational and programming costs continued to rise. Politically, and more consequentially in the end, not only had the convention lost the nomination itself but additional events of obvious consequence—six months of presidential primaries on one side, the institutionalization of national debates on the other—began to chip away further at the importance of the convention.

In response, all three national networks reduced their coverage for 1980, cutbacks which they extended in 1984. The result was the unintended but effective creation of what might reasonably be called the bifurcated convention, with one convention on site and another (via television) at home, each powerfully different one from the other. . . .

The Making of the Delegates, 1968–1988

MARTIN PLISSNER AND WARREN J. MITOFSKY

One of the goals of the presidential nominating reforms was to make convention delegates more representative of rank-and-file party supporters. Martin Plissner and Warren J. Mitofsky indicate the extent to which this goal has been achieved by summarizing the results of the CBS News/New York Times surveys of delegates from 1968 through 1988. They find that there is better demographic representation, although income and education levels remain skewed in the direction of those in the higher brackets. The issues and ideological positions of the delegates, however, are more extreme, with Democratic delegates more liberal and Republican delegates more conservative than their parties as a whole.

This year's Republican convention in New Orleans was the first since 1968 at which Charles McC. (Mac) Mathias, the former senator from Maryland, was not a delegate. Mathias's departure left the Republican convention floor void of any members of Congress or any other major public officeholder who, when asked if he called himself liberal, moderate, or conservative, picked "liberal." Of the entire 2,277 delegates, less than one-half of one percent, nine to be exact, so identified themselves when asked to do so by CBS News. Of the nine, four were among the convention's relatively few blacks; one was Hispanic. The most prominent position held by any of them was mayor of East Washington, Pennsylvania. At Mac Mathias's last convention, four years ago, nearly three times as many (twenty-six) had acknowledged that they were liberals.

Starting in 1968 CBS News has tracked all delegates to national party conventions. The surveys typically reach in excess of 95 percent of the delegates, and there is no statistical error in the findings. They record a great variety of trends, like the near-extinction of the liberal wing of the Republican party. This article brings up to date an earlier review of the CBS News delegate surveys published after the 1980 conventions (*Public Opinion*, October/November 1980).

If liberals have all but vanished from Republican conventions, the Democratic conservative is almost as lonely at his party's conventions. Two decisive lickings in a row by Ronald Reagan and a fairly public effort to dissociate itself from the "L-word" did little to narrow the liberal/conservative ratio among the 4,212 delegates who nominated Michael Dukakis in Atlanta.

Source: *Public Opinion* (September/October 1988): 45–57. Reprinted with permission of the American Enterprise Institute for Public Research, Washington, D.C..

Forty-three percent called themselves liberals, the same as at the convention that nominated Walter Mondale. Barely 5 percent weighed in as conservatives. Just four of the seventy-six U.S. senators and governors at the convention were in this tiny minority that made up the Democratic party's right.

NIGHT AND DAY ON THE ISSUES

On specific issues posed in this year's surveys, not just on ideological tags, the delegates to each convention were like night and day. Left to their own judgments, before the Dukakis whips turned them around on a platform vote, Dukakis as well as Jackson supporters in Atlanta overwhelmingly favored higher taxes for people earning over $100,000 a year. Republican delegates, without being whipped, opposed such a tax increase by three to one.

Democratic delegates favored federal funding of abortion by five to two. Republican delegates opposed it by four to one. Democratic delegates favored a gay rights law by nearly four to one. Republicans opposed it by two to one. Asked if defense spending should be cut to permit more spending on social programs, Democrats opted for social programs by seven to one. Republicans stuck with defense by six to one.

Pick any constitutional amendment under discussion, and the delegates at the two conventions were on opposite sides. Democratic delegates favored the equal rights amendment by more than twenty to one; Republicans opposed it by five to three. Democratic delegates opposed a balanced budget amendment by five to four; Republicans favored it by six to one. Democrats opposed a school prayer amendment by three to one; Republicans supported it, five to three. Perhaps most typically, Democrats preferred by four to one a bigger government that would provide more services, to a smaller one that would do less. Republicans chose smaller government by twenty to one.

DELEGATES COMPARED TO VOTERS

The delegates surveyed in both parties thus continued the pattern—found in past surveys of both convention delegates and national committee members—of Democratic elites being decidedly more liberal and Republican elites more conservative than ordinary, garden-variety adherents of their respective parties.

In current CBS News/*New York Times* polls of Democratic voters nationally, self-identified conservatives are about as common as liberals. This contrasts sharply to the eight-to-one liberal Democratic delegates and ordinary Democratic voters do take similarly liberal sides on such issues as higher taxes for the rich, the equal rights amendment, spending on social

TABLE 1.   Views of the Delegates Voters—1988

	DELEGATE SURVEY		CBS/NYT POLL JULY 1988	
	Rep.	*Dem.*	*Reg. Rep.*	*Reg. Dem.*
Ideology				
—Liberal	0%	43%	11%	26%
—Moderate	36	43	44	42
—Conservative	59	5	40	28
Size of govt[a]				
—Small	81	14	59	33
—Big	4	56	30	56
Fedl. funding abortion				
—Favor	16	57	28	32
—Oppose	69	22	62	56
Gay rights law				
—Favor	26	65	28	43
—Oppose	58	18	57	40
Sympathy for Palestinians				
—More sympathy	28	50	22	26
—No more	46	22	53	49
Government spending				
—Defense	72	10	53	34
—Social programs	13	75	39	55
Death penalty				
—Favor	88	49	79	64
—Oppose	6	38	15	27
School prayer[b]				
—Favor	51	22	72	67
—Oppose	34	65	25	26
E.R.A.[b]				
—Favor	34	86	68	80
—Oppose	51	4	25	11
Bal. budget amendment[b]				
—Favor	77	38	80	77
—Oppose	13	47	11	9
Top tax rate				
—Increase	19	67	61	63
—No change	64	14	32	27

Note: [a] CBS/NYT poll May 1988.
      [b] CBS/NYT poll August 1988.

needs rather than defense, and bigger as opposed to smaller government. They do so, however, by generally narrower margins than convention delegates. The voters, moreover, part company with the delegates on federal funding of abortion, prayer in schools, and a balanced budget amendment to the Constitution. In each of these cases, Democratic delegates are well to the left of their party's voters.

If Democratic delegates veered to the left of their party's voters, Republican delegates on balance veered to the right. Liberals and moderates together outnumber conservatives by five to four among everyday Republicans; among delegates, conservatives led by five to three.

Rank-and-file Republicans went along with their more conservative delegates in opposing federal funds for abortion, in favoring smaller government and the school prayer and balanced budget amendments. But they parted company with the delegates by supporting the ERA and higher taxes for the rich.

The disparity between Republican convention delegates and almost any other definable group of voters is most striking if you compare the three-to-two margin against ERA in New Orleans with the July CBS News/*New York Times* national survey. American voters as a whole favor ERA by a margin of five to one. A solid majority of every one of the seventy-two voter subgroups support it, and in all but one case (Republicans who supported Bush's opponents in the primaries), they support it by margins of at least two to one. Those overwhelming supporters of ERA include not only Democrats who voted for Ronald Reagan in 1984 (four to one) but also Bush's own primary supporters (three to one), conservatives (five to two), and evangelicals (two to one). They do not, however, include the delegates to this year's Republican national convention.

WHO THEY ARE—THE DEMOCRATIC DELEGATES

It was the first CBS News Democratic delegate survey, in 1968, that ascertained that just 13 percent of that year's Democratic delegates were women and just 5 percent were black—far out of line with their share of the population and even more out of line with their share of votes they cast for Democratic candidates. It was these findings, specifically, that caught the eyes of the subsequent reform commission, headed by George McGovern, that radically reshaped party practice in selecting future delegates.

At the 1972 convention, the proportion of both blacks and women tripled, and in 1980 the party fixed the division between men and women at a flat fifty-fifty. The "goal" for black participation was set as the black share of the "Democratic electorate." If that share was measured by the portion of Walter Mondale's vote that was found to be black in the November 1984 CBS News/*New York Times* exit poll, it would be 19 percent.

TABLE 2. Who the Delegates Are

	1968		1972	
	Dem	*Rep*	*Dem*	*Rep*
Women	13%	16%	40%	29%
Black	5	2	15	4
Under Thirty	3	4	22	8
Lawyer	28	22	12	—
Teacher	8	2	11	—
Union member	—	—	16	—
Attending first convention	67	66	83	78
Protestant	—	—	42	—
Catholic	—	—	26	—
Jewish	—	—	9	—
Liberal	—	—	—	—
Moderate	—	—	—	—
Conservative	—	—	—	—
Median age	49	49	42	—

The 1988 convention easily met this standard. Twenty-three percent of the delegates were black, a record for conventions of either party. Eighty-five percent of the pledged black delegates were there as a result of Jesse Jackson's campaign. Twenty-one percent of Jackson's delegates were white, up from 6 percent in 1984, reflecting not too badly his share of the white primary and caucus vote in each of these years.

About half the Democratic delegates were Protestant, 30 percent were Catholic, and 7 percent Jewish. White Protestants were 30 percent of the total. The median income for all delegates was $52,000. The median age was 46.

About a third of the Democratic delegates held public office. Forty percent held party office. One out of four delegates were union members, one in ten were union officials (one in fourteen made their living at it). Forty-one percent of the Democratic delegates held graduate degrees. Eighty-eight percent had attended college. In expanding his delegate base this year, Jesse Jackson did not lower his academic sights a bit. In 1984 his delegates had more master's degrees and Ph.D.s per capita than any other camp. This year Jackson delegates led in these degrees again.

WHO THEY ARE—THE REPUBLICAN DELEGATES

"It will be surprising to some people," said House Republican Leader Bob Michel to the *Washington Post*'s Paul Taylor last May, "when they look at

TABLE 2.   *Continued*

1976		1980		1984		1988	
Dem	*Rep*	*Dem*	*Rep*	*Dem*	*Rep*	*Dem*	*Rep*
33%	31%	49%	29%	49%	44%	48%	33%
11	3	15	3	18	4	23	4
15	7	11	5	8	4	4	3
16	15	13	15	17	14	16	17
12	4	15	4	16	6	14	5
21	3	27	4	25	4	25	3
80	78	87	84	78	69	65	68
47	73	47	72	49	71	50	69
34	18	37	22	29	22	30	22
9	3	8	3	8	2	7	2
40	3	46	2	48	1	43	0
47	45	42	36	42	35	43	35
8	48	6	58	4	60	5	58
43	48	44	49	43	51	46	51

that Democratic convention out there and see one-third blacks." Michel was overstating things, the Democratic convention was little more than a fifth, not a third black.

But when Michel, as permanent chairman of the Republican convention, brought down his gavel in New Orleans, he was addressing far fewer black delegates. Only 4 percent of the Republican delegates were black, about a third of what they constitute in the voting population.

Women, too, made up a much smaller share of the delegates in New Orleans than they did in Atlanta. Half the Democratic delegates were women, only a third of the Republican delegates were.

This is an unusual case of an actual setback for women's participation. From 1972 through 1980 women consistently made up about 30 percent of the Republican convention delegates. In 1984, through a particular effort on the part of the Reagan campaign, the participation of women rose to 44 percent. In 1988 it fell back to 33 percent, close to the 1972–1980 norm.

Lee Atwater, who was deputy campaign manager for Reagan-Bush in 1984 and ran the Bush primary campaign in 1988, says that, with no primary contest in 1984, getting more women to the convention was a high priority for the national staff. In 1988 the top priority was getting Bush delegates elected. Gender was secondary.

If women and blacks were in relatively short supply, the Republican party's standing as the party of the WASP went unchallenged by the makeup of this year's convention. Sixty-five percent of the delegates were white Protestant, more than twice the percentage in Atlanta. Twenty-two percent were Catholic, 2 percent were Jewish, and 14 percent of the Protestant delegates called themselves Fundamentalists.

Even rarer in New Orleans than blacks, though not so rare as liberals, were union cards. Only 3 percent reported union membership, most of them as teachers or (like the former union chief who has led the party's most successful ticket) entertainers. No Republican delegate made a living working for a union. In Atlanta it was the sixth most prevalent occupation.

As usual Republican delegates were, on the whole, richer than their Democratic counterparts. Half the Republican delegates responding to the survey had annual family incomes over $72,000. The median income for the Democrats was $52,000. On average, Republican delegates were older; the median age in New Orleans was fifty-one, compared to forty-six in Atlanta.

What the great majority of the delegates to both conventions had in common, however, and what distinguished them from the great majority of delegates in 1968, is that their vote for president on the convention's only ballot had been dictated months earlier by the votes cast in primaries. At the 1968 Republican convention, Richard Nixon's majority hinged to a large degree on personal delegate commitments and, for a moment or two, seemed in danger of slipping away. Hubert Humphrey's nomination in Chicago that year was achieved without a single primary victory and could have been taken away in a flash by President Lyndon Johnson. This year's conventions of both parties, in contrast, only ratified the will of the primary voters. The delegates, whoever they might be and whatever their views, were there not to make a choice but to deliver a message.

Formality, Deviltry, and Love as the G.O.P. Starts Its Party

MAUREEN DOWD

Reporter Maureen Dowd provides a glimpse of the participants at the 1988 Republican convention. Her brief chronology of Day One depicts the candidates, politicians, and delegates amid the pomp and pageantry of these national, made-for-television events.

Bob Dole watched his wife, Elizabeth, with mock suspicion to make sure she was not campaigning harder than he was for the coveted Vice-Presidential spot. Ronald Reagan swept his wife up in his arms and told the world, in unabashed prose that made Nancy Reagan blush and mist, just how much he loves her. George Bush and his wife, Barbara, stayed out of sight and out of town and worked on the speeches that must explain who the Vice President is and what he wants to do with this country.

It seems safe to say, even at this tender hour, that the reputation of the 1924 Cleveland convention as the most boring in Republican history is intact. In the meeting that nominated "Silent Cal" Coolidge, the delegates had to deal with Prohibition, Cleveland in June and a popular drink concocted of raw eggs and fruit juice called a Keep-Cool with Coolidge highball. Will Rogers was so appalled at the stagnant scene, as Paul Boller recalls in his book, "Presidential Anecdotes," that he proposed that the city open up the churches to add some spice.

From Bourbon Street to the Louisiana Superdome, steamy New Orleans has enough spice for several conventions, and the Republicans began their first evening session by dancing in the aisles to Jimmy Maxwell's New Orleans Swing Band playing "In the Mood."

9:30 A.M. At times the scene of 14,000 members of the international press corps in full cry after a few shards of information is reminiscent of Oscar Wilde's observation about fox hunting, which he dismissed as "the unspeakable in pursuit of the inedible."

In a convention with very little suspense, George Bush's Vice-Presidential choice is the subject that drives reporters into a frenzy.

Jack Kemp is surely reminded of that as he arrives to face the press.

The New York Congressman, who is a contender for the Vice-Presidential nomination, tries to talk about his favorite subjects: free enterprise, free markets and something he calls "the failure of the fossil age of Socialism-Marxism." But the reporters are still hungry for running-mate tidbits. A foreign correspondent, speaking with a Hispanic accent and uncommon bluntness, pipes up to ask Mr. Kemp if Mr. Bush wants "somebody like you but not yourself?"

Taken aback for a moment, Mr. Kemp recovers deftly by adapting Jesse Jackson's answer after he was bypassed for the No. 2 spot on the Democratic ticket. "I'm too cool," Mr. Kemp said, slowing down his speech to imitate Mr. Jackson's deliberate tone, "I'm too collected and I'm too qualified to answer that question."

10 A.M. The Republican convention, naturally, convenes on the dot. Yakov Smirnoff, the Russian-born comedian, says the Pledge of Allegiance and makes no jokes. Shirley Temple Black, a California delegate, makes a resolution without even tapping her foot.

12:15 P.M. Mary Latham, a convention volunteer from Metairie, a suburb of New Orleans, lurks near the back of the arena, her autograph book in hand. She is waiting to pounce on Alexander Haig, who is slowly making his way up the aisle with his wife, Pat, after stunning the Republican Party by comparing the Democratic Party to a bat "up to its navel in guano" and calling the party's standard-bearer, Michael S. Dukakis, "a diminutive clerk from Massachusetts." The Haigs sign their names in the book beneath the Mayor of Maui, the former Governor of Nebraska and Shirley Temple Black. "If I didn't get anyone else at all," bubbles Mrs. Latham, a former passenger on the childhood star's Good Ship Lollipop, "I'd die if I didn't get her."

12:45 P.M. The convention floor has an anthropology all its own. Each state tribe has its own totems and customs and plumage. When Jennifer B. Dunn, the Republican state chairman from Washington comes to the platform to address the convention, the Washington delegation greets her and preens by opening green and white umbrellas and waving them over their heads. Florida delegates sizzle in bright orange vests with blue elephants emblazoned on the back. The Arizona delegates lope along in tan Western vests, with a rising sun stitched on the back. Tennessee delegates look down-home in white baseball caps and the Hawaiians luxuriate in the tropical splendor of red, white and blue flowered shirts. New Mexico delegates sport small yellow golf caps, which read, turned inside out, "Bush–Domenici." Senator Pete V. Domenici of New Mexico has been mentioned as possible Vice Presidential candidate.

And the Illinois delegates are wearing electric orange blazers that give them the appearance of produce clerks in a supermarket. All, that is, except Gov. James R. Thompson, a Vice Presidential dropout, who looks out of place in his tribe wearing a light gray, pinstriped suit. "I forgot mine," he explains. "Honest. It's in the closet. I promise to wear it tonight."

1:30 P.M. If Jimmy and Rosalynn Carter were the most ubiquitous and feted couple of the Democratic convention last month, then Bob and Elizabeth Dole earn those honors in New Orleans. As the handsome twosome enters the New Orleans Convention Center for a luncheon honoring Nancy

Reagan, they are stopped at every step by admiring fans with automatic cameras and curious reporters who want to know how they are handling their historically unique situation. What, Senator Dole is asked, do they say to each other behind closed doors about their competition for the Vice-Presidential spot?

"I was kidding her a lot but she doesn't like me to do it anymore," Mr. Dole said with a grin as his wife cast a dubious but smiling sidelong glance at him before she was pulled away by her own tide of Republican admirers. "I tell her I'm just fronting for her, spreading her name around."

Asked if she returns the compliment, the Senator says "Oh, no," and cranes his neck to see what his wife is doing. "She's probably over there somewhere campaigning right now," he says wryly.

3:15 P.M. The Massachusetts Governor may have warmed up his image by showing his passion for his wife, Kitty, but Ronald Reagan proves again this afternoon why he is the world champion of political romance. He surprised his wife, Nancy, at the end of the lunch by strolling onstage and wrapping her in a bear hug. It wasn't a complete surprise of course, since the hall was suddenly flooded with Secret Service agents and the Presidential seal was placed on the dais. But it was a sweet moment, and the President offered his First Lady a tribute worthy of a monologue in a Harlequin romance novel.

"I simply can't imagine the last eight years without Nancy," he told the 3,000 salmon-sated lunch guests. "The second-floor living quarters would have seemed a lonely spot without her there waiting for me."

He asked the audience, which was thrilled with the sentimental climax to a romance that has captivated the nation over the last eight years, "What can you say about someone who gives your life meaning?"

"You can say," he answered his own question, "that you love that person and treasure her."

"Every President," he concluded, as his First Lady ducked her head down in embarrassment and grew misty eyed, "should be so lucky."

7 P.M. The evening session is brought to order exactly on time, soon to be followed by a Mardi Gras parade with clowns, river boat captains, dance hall girls, Indians, high-stepping dancers doing a "second line" dance—one of New Orleans's indigenous, sinuous struts.

For Delegate Trackers, Timing Is Everything

ANDREW ROSENTHAL

The launching-pad goal of contemporary conventions requires that front-running candidates, who may be assured of the nomination, control the proceedings as well as the events that occur on and off the convention floor. Most of these candidates set up elaborate internal organizations that operate from a central command post and are linked to each state delegation through a telephone system. Andrew Rosenthal, a reporter covering the 1988 Democratic convention for The New York Times, *describes the Dukakis operation on the night that he was nominated. As Rosenthal's report attests, the people who tracked the Dukakis delegates left little to chance.*

It was an adroit bit of political legerdemain.

When the nominating vote was taken Wednesday night at the Democratic National Convention, the states were called in alphabetical order. Yet it was California, the fifth state in the rotation, that gave Michael S. Dukakis the last few votes he needed to go over the top.

The answer to this alphabetic anomaly could be found in a cramped trailer under the convention hall, where, on the third night of the convention, Tad Devine, chief delegate tracker for Mr. Dukakis, was running the nominating vote like a conductor in the computer age: with a radio headset instead of a baton.

"Be sure your whips know we want the states to be ready to vote when their turn comes up," he shouted to his assistants in the trailer. "No one passes unless we tell them to pass."

It was 8:30 P.M., nearly two hours before the nominating roll call was to begin, but Mr. Devine's 15 delegate trackers, all of whom are in their 20's, were running the vote by remote control.

There was no sense that this was a mere formality among the trackers, who, using radios, were directing an elaborate system of floor leaders and delegation coordinators, the whips. They were making sure that California, where Mr. Dukakis had clinched the nomination in its primary June 7, announced the vote that would officially put him over the top.

KEEPING DISCIPLINE

Every chant, every sign, every round of applause was run from the trailer, which was parked in a loading area under the Omni Coliseum. The task was to keep discipline.

At 8:40 P.M., 20 minutes before the networks switched on their coverage of Mr. Dukakis's crowning night, the trackers ordered whips to distribute more signs—both blue and red ones.

Later, Mr. Devine, who alternated commands to those in the trailer and, through a headset, to people on the floor, decided he did not like the way it looked on his television screen. "I want the red Dukakis signs down," he said. "Down, on the ground. Keep them there all night. Red down. Got it?"

The trackers ran to their phones, and the red signs went down.

ORDERING NOISE

Everything was smooth until a television broadcast reported that California would put Dukakis over the top. The campaign was now committed to the plan. "It's going to take a lot of cooperation out there," Mr. Devine said.

As the time approached for Gov. Bill Clinton of Arkansas to put Mr. Dukakis's name in nomination, Mr. Devine ordered: "When Clinton is introduced, I want to start turning the volume up. We should build it and build it. Anytime he says Dukakis, we want applause."

While Mr. Clinton was speaking, the order went out to start a chant, "We want the Duke," to be followed by "Duke, Duke, Duke."

The chants started as scheduled.

The 32-year-old Mr. Devine, spending his third convention in a candidate's "boiler room," was not satisfied. He ordered trackers to "turn the juice up."

At 10:05, a crisis: Puerto Rico did not want to pass. Phones were snatched up. "If they want to play, they've got to pass," a tracker warned the Dukakis whip in the Puerto Rico delegation.

When the voting started, Mr. Devine demanded quiet. The arithmetic was tricky and not everything went as planned. Arkansas, the fourth state, passed, which was not planned. "We'll go with the flow," Mr. Devine said.

Then California passed, as planned.

At 10:45, Massachusetts, the candidate's home state, passed.

"O.K.," Mr. Devine said with a smile. "Everyone thinks Massachusetts is going to put him over."

New York was not willing to pass. When Puerto Rico's turn came, though, the delegation passed. A few trackers applauded.

As the count got close to the 2,082 needed for the nomination, the campaign persuaded Texas to pass. When West Virginia passed, Mr. Devine shouted: "Tell Arkansas they can vote. California's doing it."

Susan Estrich, the campaign manager, went into the trailer to call in a "thank you" to the Tennessee delegation, which had given up its turn. Staff members passed out cigars with Mr. Dukakis's picture on the bands.

When the alphabetic rotation began again, Arkansas voted. When California capped Mr. Dukakis's victory, Mr. Devine permitted himself a smile. Then he embraced the nearest tracker and let out a whoop.

Behind Call to Quayle, a Calculation on Balancing Excitement and Risk

GERALD M. BOYD

The choice of the vice presidential nominee may be the most important choice the presidential candidate has to make, yet frequently the selection process has been shrouded in secrecy and the decision made quickly, without adequate information. In some cases, the chosen vice presidential candidate has subsequently been criticized as unqualified, or embarrassing and politically harmful to the presidential nominee. This happened to George McGovern in 1972, to Walter Mondale in 1984, and to George Bush in 1988. How are these choices made? Reporter Gerald M. Boyd, who covered George Bush's campaign for The New York Times, *reveals the advice and calculations that led the Republican nominee to pick Indiana's junior senator as his running mate.*

As Vice President Bush retired to the seclusion of his residence on the grounds of the Naval Observatory last weekend, several considerations about a running mate were swirling around in his mind and scrawled on a yellow legal pad.

With the intense three-week process of picking a Vice Presidential candidate nearing an end, aides said today, Mr. Bush had come to believe that any choice he made was a risk. He was convinced no potential candidate guaranteed victory nationally, regionally or in any of the swing states that the Bush campaign planned to target.

Mr. Bush also wanted to excite the voters with his ticket, with a Republican Vice-Presidential choice who could effectively take the battle to Michael S. Dukakis this fall.

SOMEONE TO RELISH THE ROLE

And he also felt strongly that his running mate should not merely relish the role of serving as Vice President, but should relish the role of serving as number two to George Bush.

In the end, Mr. Bush decided on Senator Dan Quayle of Indiana. When the first telephone call went out the junior Senator was strolling in the

French Quarter here and unreachable. On the second try, the Vice President reached Mr. Quayle and said:

"You are my choice, you are my first choice, you are my only choice."

But leading up to that simple declaration was a complicated process in which Mr. Bush called a dozen candidates before the Indiana Senator ever came under consideration.

Mr. Bush, acting alone, made the final decision in Mr. Quayle's favor early Tuesday morning as he left Washington to come here.

He wanted to pick someone who was seen as "and who was a rising star, both in the Senate and in the Republican Party," said Robert Teeter, Mr. Bush's chief poll taker and a key player in the selection process. "He wanted someone who was a leader of the future, of a different generation."

But Mr. Teeter added a disclaimer voiced by other senior Bush aides today: "In the last analysis, nobody ever knows exactly why someone picks someone."

According to aides involved in the selection process, Mr. Quayle was not under consideration at first. His name was raised by a senior Bush adviser at a staff meeting and his stock grew gradually over recent weeks, an aide said.

Although he lacked the national stature of several of the also rans other factors played to the Senator's advantage. Earlier in the summer, he had battled in the Senate to remove a provision from the trade bill requiring workers to receive 60-day notification of plant closings. His effort, strongly opposed by organized labor, ultimately failed and President Reagan, unhappy with the provision, vetoed the trade bill.

Mr. Bush, one aide said, had been impressed with Mr. Quayle's attempt to defuse the issue in the handling of the plant closing debate, which had posed a troubling political problem for the Vice President. Mr. Bush had hoped the President could avoid vetoing a bill with such strong support among workers.

In addition, at least two of Mr. Bush's top aides were quite familiar with Mr. Quayle's campaigning skills: Roger Ailes, the Vice President's chief media adviser, had handled advertising for Mr. Quayle's successful 1986 Senate re-election bid, and Mr. Teeter had conducted private polls for Mr. Quayle since Mr. Quayle's first Congressional campaign in 1976.

"Just from my knowledge of his Indiana campaigns, he ran very well among working class voters and I don't ever believe any of his campaigns had a gender gap," Mr. Teeter said.

BUSH SENSITIVE TO FEELINGS

Aides said that from the start, the selection process was designed to be thorough, but not necessarily easy. As one who had gone through a similar selection in 1980, Mr. Bush was sensitive to any appearance of demeaning those under consideration and thus decided not to conduct personal interviews which, as the center of press attention, could become public spectacles.

Instead his questions to the candidates were relayed to Mr. Teeter and Robert Kimmitt, a Washington attorney who was responsible for the background investigations of the candidates.

According to aides, Mr. Ailes pushed extremely hard for Mr. Quayle, while Mr. Teeter also supported him.

But Mr. Bush was also receiving other advice. The process devised by the Vice President asked for recommendations from a variety of sources: governors, members of Congress, and Frank J. Fahrenkopf Jr., the chairman of the Republican National Committee.

Repeatedly, one Bush aide said, the top choices of various advisers included Senator Bob Dole of Kansas and Representative Jack F. Kemp of New York, two of Mr. Bush's Republican primary opponents. In addition, several of his senior campaign aides also supported Mr. Dole, who was actively campaigning for the nomination.

For his part, Mr. Bush refused to show how he was leaning, although he asked questions and took notes when aides discussed the subject.

NO HINT OF LEANINGS

"I've played a lot of poker and this guy would just sit there stone-faced," said one participant in the meetings.

But if there was a turning point, Bush advisers say, it came when Mr. Teeter began polling to determine if any candidates helped the Vice President nationally or at least in a swing state the campaign was coveting, such as Pennsylvania, Illinois and California. "We did not find that there was someone from a state that we looked at that absolutely guaranteed their state," Mr. Teeter said.

Because of that finding doubts were raised about several of the candidates, including Richard Thornburgh, the former Governor of Pennsylvania and Governors James R. Thompson of Illinois and George Deukmajian of California.

With the lack of a compelling electoral college argument for selecting a particular candidate, Mr. Bush's aides began to promote other factors.

EMPHASIZING THE FUTURE

Mr. Bush had campaigned for Mr. Quayle in Congressional and Senate races since 1976 and thus knew him, although not as well as some others under consideration. He was told, however, that Mr. Quayle had run well among women voters, was an aggressive campaigner and was a strong vote getter in the Midwest, a region where Mr. Bush is weak.

Moreover, he could presumably communicate with his generation of "baby boom voters" more effectively than someone older and thus offered an appeal that other candidates lacked.

"I think you've got a group of voters who now have a candidate of their own generation—the first one—someone younger than most candidates for President and Vice President. That alone will make him an interesting pick for a large number of voters."

Moreover, by choosing Mr. Quayle, Mr. Bush was told that he could pursue a "future-oriented" campaign, a point made Tuesday by James A. Baker 3d, Mr. Bush's campaign manager.

Some aides had raised Mr. Quayle's association with Paula Parkinson, a lobbyist who said that she had had affairs with "fewer than a dozen" Republican Congressmen seven years ago. But, according to Mr. Teeter, Mr. Bush was assured by Mr. Kimmitt that he had looked into it "very carefully" and that there was "absolutely nothing" to it.

Mr. Quayle said today he had nothing to add to his previous denials of any impropriety.

According to Craig L. Fuller, the Vice President's chief of staff, Mr. Bush deliberated over the weekend, often referring to the notes on his yellow legal pad. By the time he reached New Orleans he had decided on Mr. Quayle.

Telling Mr. Reagan when he arrived of his decision, he then placed calls to those not selected before calling Mr. Quayle. Next, he called former Presidents Nixon and Ford, to inform them of his decision before his surprise announcement on the waterfront in New Orleans Tuesday afternoon.

Convention Coverage: Endangered Species?

JEREMY GERARD

Television coverage of the conventions has affected the way conventions are conducted. They have become more glitzy, more staged, and subsequently less interesting. But television coverage may be sowing the seeds of its own destruction. Reporter Jeremy Gerard suggests that gavel-to-gavel coverage of conventions is less likely in the future because, thanks to television, conventions have become more show than news.

In the television industry, the talk of the 1984 Democratic National Convention in San Francisco was the Rev. Jesse Jackson's speech, the dwindling audience and whether such conventions, in becoming irrelevant to the process of choosing candidates, had also become irrelevant as news events.

The talk of this year's Democratic National Convention in Atlanta was Mr. Jackson's speech, the dwindling audience, and the networks' eroding faith in the news value of conventions.

So it came as no great surprise when Roone Arledge, president of ABC News, suggested this week that the Democratic convention had been so boring that he was thinking about cutting back his network's coverage of the Republican National Convention next month in New Orleans. It was an echo of his own executive producer's comment in 1984, to the effect that television coverage of the conventions had become a "dinosaur."

Other network executives distanced themselves from Mr. Arledge's statement, saying any changes before 1992 would be premature and unfair to the Republicans. If the networks were going to curtail their convention coverage further, no one wanted the distinction of being the first to do it.

A NEED FOR MORE VIEWERS

Joseph Angotti, executive producer of election-year coverage for NBC News, said the problem for the networks was "getting more people to watch." But he added that he was worried about the suggestion by some network executives "that we sit down with the parties to discuss ways to make the conventions more interesting; that's a serious conflict of interest."

On Thursday, the last night of the Democratic convention, CBS began its coverage at 8 o'clock, an hour before NBC and ABC. The result, including interviews and other spontaneous events on the convention floor, was a surprise to those producers accustomed to having every moment choreographed by the political parties. "We controlled the hour instead of the party, which is what producers are supposed to do," Howard Stringer, the president of CBS News, said yesterday.

"When we're reduced to two hours the parties schedule the two hours," he added. "The parties might re-examine the methods by which they do that."

He noted that changes in the political process, with major decisions made long before the conventions start, had cut out much of the drama that might attract viewers.

For the network people who live by the numbers, it's hard to argue with the fact that on July 11, 60 percent of the nation's television households were tuned to network programming, while one week later, on the first night of the Democratic convention, the number was half that. Moreover, the cumulative average over the four nights of the convention had dropped to just over 20.

HARDER TO SELL ADVERTISERS

Not only are the conventions losing viewers, but their audience is spread among three networks and two cable broadcasts, making them even harder to sell to advertisers.

"We know there are certain things that just will not make a lot of money," said Larry Fried, the vice president for news and early morning advertising sales at ABC.

However, while the audience for news programs is smaller than the audience for entertainment, it is wealthier.

"Our advertisers have been realistic," said Diane Seaman, an NBC marketing vice president. "They sponsor this type of programming because they have a specific target audience—an upscale audience, professionals and office managers. The ratings are about 9 percent off 1984, but the upscale target audience is there."

This year, for the first time, the networks sold advertising to be broadcast during the conventions as part of a package that includes political events throughout the year.

PACKAGES SOLD TO SEVEN COMPANIES

"We sold our package starting with the December 1987 debate, through and including Inauguration Day 1989," said Ms. Seaman. "We sold packages of $1 million to $5 million to seven different advertisers."

Network officials said the companies buying those packages were mostly in the communications, automobile, insurance and banking businesses, and they have spread themselves fairly evenly. For example, the Chrysler Corporation bought political coverage time on ABC, the Ford Motor Company on NBC and the General Motors Corporation on CBS; Merrill Lynch & Company bought time on both CBS and Cable News Network.

"We decided to be represented whenever something happened politically this year, in order to be seen emerging from the crowd," said Werner Michel, senior vice president for corporate programming at Bozell, Jacobs, Kenyon & Eckhardt, who placed advertising for Merrill Lynch. "The demography is good, even if the households are low. Merrill Lynch should be associated with these kinds of programs. And I don't want to overstate it, but there's a public service overtone."

CNN SAYS IT'S A WINNER

NBC's coverage led the ratings on Monday, Tuesday and Thursday nights this week, pulling in an average of 7.3 percent of the nation's television households. But the Atlanta-based CNN, which covered the convention in its hometown from gavel to gavel, also declared itself a winner.

"From a dollars-and-cents standpoint, I know that we did a lot better than we did in 1984," David McCoy, the sales manager for special projects at CNN, said yesterday. "Our average rate for 30 seconds in prime time is $3,000 to $3,500. For the convention we got $5,000. We guaranteed 700,000 households and delivered over a million. On Monday and Tuesday we doubled our normal viewership."

However, CNN's ratings were minuscule by the standards of network broadcasting, and its advertising rates are about one-tenth those of the networks.

On Tuesday, the night Mr. Jackson made his speech, about 21 million American households were tuned into the convention. But that was less than one-fourth of the number possible.

Mr. Stringer, who will take over as president of the CBS Broadcast Group in August, said that was the public's loss, not the network's.

"Tuesday night was fascinating," Mr. Stringer said. "If I'd been sitting with a one-hour wrap-up special I would have been terribly frustrated. And Thursday night was full of surprises—the mood in the hall you could not have predicted. That was an American event. What happens four years from now will depend on where the networks will be four years from now. It was a great Tuesday and a great Thursday, and you couldn't have predicted that."

"This Is Ann Compton" —
Chasing Airtime

JONATHAN RAUCH

*With thousands of newspaper reporters and television correspondents covering
national conventions, it is difficult for a reporter to get news, let alone a
scoop. Most correspondents follow the predictable—the regularly scheduled
speeches, the votes, and the newsworthy people—trying to get an angle, reveal
a dimension, obtain an interview, or report an event before their competitors
do. Jonathan Rauch describes how one such reporter, Ann Compton of ABC
News, went about her task. It details her night covering Jesse Jackson and
trying, albeit unsuccessfully, to get on the air.*

The quarry is Jesse Jackson, and the hunt is on. It is Jackson's big night
at the convention: He is the news, and Ann Compton, an ABC News
correspondent, is after him. Like every other television reporter in and
around the Omni, she wants to get on the air. On this night, Jackson is
the ticket.

Getting on the air is not an easy thing to do these days, even for a
veteran member of a network news staff. Back when the networks covered
the conventions gavel-to-gavel, there was plenty of dead or dull time on
the podium and thus lots of time to cut to correspondents for on-the-spot
interviews, analyses, arresting scenes.

That is changing. Scheduled network coverage is down to two hours a
night, and more of that time is given over to the big speeches—like those
of Jackson, former President Carter, Ann W. Richards—that the networks
don't interrupt. More than ever, to get airtime you have to come up with
an exclusive, a clever angle or an eye-catching interview. (NBC won kudos
for creative thinking when it got commentary on Richards's keynote speech
from New York Gov. Mario M. Cuomo, whose keynote address at the 1984
Democratic convention is legendary.)

You have to come up with something good enough to grab the attention
of the producers who decide where the network spends its precious seconds.

Compton, who has been a network correspondent for 15 years, covered
the Carter White House and, in 1976, was the first woman to be a convention floor correspondent—which, after anchoring, is the top of the line for
prestige and visibility. At the Atlanta convention, however, she was roving
the perimeter rather than being one of ABC's four reporters on the floor.

On the night of Jackson's speech, she did not make it on the air. It was not, however, for lack of trying.

8:45 P.M. Compton and the producer who accompanies her, a weary 27-year-old named Ted Duvall, have taken up a position by the Elephant Door. This is a big roll-up door deep in the bowels of the Omni; it's where big-shots' cars arrive. If Jackson's car pulls in here, rather than taking him straight to his campaign trailer, Compton will try to nab him for a quick stand-up interview as he leaves his car. She calls that a hit and run.

"That's the game we play," she says. "It's the currency in which we do our business: who's got who first, fastest and preferably exclusively."

On the first night, she almost got on. She grabbed former Missouri Sen. Thomas F. Eagleton, whom George McGovern abandoned as running mate in 1972. The producers said they would come to her but never did.

She is asked whether she cares about getting on, and the answer is emphatic. "I care very much. I've been here since Friday, it's now Tuesday, and I haven't been on the air once. I don't come to these things for my health."

In this game, information is everything. Where is Jesse now? Where will he go when he gets here? The place is swarming with Secret Service agents, including top brass; a lot of them are people Compton knows well from her years around the White House. She pals around with them, and they give her what tips they can about the candidates' locations and plans.

Apparently, Jackson will arrive at the Omni more than an hour before he speaks. That ought to leave time for an interview. If this gambit doesn't work, she has a position ready near the elevator from which Jackson will emerge on his way to the podium.

Compton is wearing a crimson suit with a white blouse and comfortable canvas shoes. The other TV correspondents are mostly wearing sneakers. Compton is wired for sound: An earpiece connected to a box clipped under her jacket feeds her the newscast audio and, over it, any one of three control rooms giving instructions and information. (One takes care of the technical business, one controls Compton and one controls Peter Jennings, the anchor up in ABC's skybox.)

On Compton's end, the sound man and cameraman keep her mike and camera feeding to the booth, where at any moment, if things are dragging on the podium or she gets something hot, a producer can flick a switch and put her on live national TV.

9 P.M. Jennings has just opened the newscast. Compton isn't getting the audio; technical problems are never more than a loose cable or low battery away. To the sound man: "I have no program and I need program." Into the mike: "This is Ann Compton. I can hear you, I can hear you at Elephant Door." A new mike and some other adjustments do the trick.

9:10 P.M. The big door rolls up: Carter is arriving with his wife, Rosalyn, and his brother, Billy. Carter knows Compton, and as he steps out of his car he comes over to talk to her. Cameras and booms descend. But Sen.

Edward M. Kennedy of Massachusetts is speaking upstairs in the convention hall, and Compton knows that the booth won't interrupt him for Carter. "I don't let anybody walk by me without talking to me," Compton says. The brief interview with Carter, now on tape, might be useful later on.

Meanwhile, Compton has stationed Marianne Keeley, an off-camera reporter who has been assigned to Jackson full-time since January, right next to her. Jackson knows Keeley and will be likelier to come over to her.

9:25 P.M. No one knows where Jackson is. The Secret Service says he hasn't left the hotel, but an ABC producer says he is on his way. "We'll know when the doors open," someone says. Andrea Mitchell of NBC sets up in a space next to Compton. Whatever Compton gets, Mitchell also will probably get. Fair game, Compton says.

9:35 P.M. A producer announces, "He's in the car." The Secret Service confirms it. Someone asks, "Is it true he has Rosa Parks with him?" Everybody maneuvers behind a red rope for the all-important "good shot." Kennedy has stopped speaking. The big door rolls up.

9:45 P.M. Jackson's car pulls in. The candidate's sons emerge, followed by Jackson. He is indeed escorting Parks, the woman who catalyzed the civil rights movement by refusing to sit in the back of the bus. Compton and Keeley beckon to him, and sure enough, smiling tightly, he walks over. Compton asks him about Parks, then Mitchell about the vice presidency, and then he leaves for his trailer.

"They took it," Compton says, as Jackson disappears: The first question and answer, before Mitchell came in, went live.

This is only a small victory: Compton remained off camera, and Jackson didn't say anything very interesting. Compton says, "That was the product of an hour and 40 minutes of waiting here." But Compton says it without bitterness. "The hours that go into getting a little something on is the norm in the industry."

10:05 P.M. Jackson, without stopping, is escorted past again on his way to the podium. The Dukakis family arrives. Compton makes no move to talk to Kitty Dukakis: They talked twice yesterday for tape, and she knows that Mrs. Dukakis won't draw the control room away from other business tonight.

10:15 P.M. The producers have cleared Compton to move to a new camera position. She is freshening up in the ABC ready room, just off the convention floor. She is asked about the Jackson interview. "I feel marginally better than I did at 8:30," she says. Not, clearly, as good as she would feel if she had done an on-camera report.

10:30 P.M. Ever enterprising, Compton has moved to the space between the Jackson and Dukakis campaign trailers, where she is standing in front of Jackson workers who are rushing to put posters together. It is a pretty good shot, and she pitches it to the booth, saying, "They're putting posters together—this is the closest thing to a real demonstration that we're going to get."

While she waits, her camerawoman turns off the TV light, to save power, and the correspondent is cast into shadow. Compton objects: "If you turn it out, they're less likely to come to us." Light restored, she stands ready to go until 10:45, when the poster-making is finished. They didn't come. In the hall, Jackson is being introduced by his children.

10:55 P.M. Jackson begins his speech. The booth won't leave him, and so Compton watches on TV in the ready room. ABC cuts briefly to a delegate who is moved by the speech. A technician shouts: "Good tears! Good tears!"

11:55 P.M. The speech is over, and Compton is in motion. Upstairs, Jennings is signing off, but Compton remains at the ready with her crew while Jackson is in the hall. Good tape could come in handy for *Nightline* or the next day's *Good Morning America*.

At this point, the Democratic National Convention is passing the halfway mark and Compton has still not gotten on. Asked whether the constant scrambling and waiting and pouncing, all in search of an elusive minute or two on TV, doesn't get old, she says, "Never." The funny thing is, she seems to mean it. "I love the immediacy," Compton says. And in her business, the one thing that is for sure is that tomorrow will not be like today.

Covering the Convention Coverage

S. ROBERT LICHTER AND LINDA S. LICHTER

From the perspective of those who plan conventions and those who cover them for news organizations, the media can have a discernible impact on the perceptions and opinions of viewers and readers, perhaps ultimately influencing their vote on Election Day. Robert and Linda Lichter describe the content of television coverage in 1988. Using the Quayle nomination, they show how the orientation of the news media can influence the slant of the reporting and can lead to charges of bias by the politicians.

The political conventions are the first media events of the general election campaign. Once they were merely vehicles for selecting the nominees. In the age of media politics, however, conventions have become television pilots that introduce the fall season's cast of characters. They can mean the difference between good and bad early ratings. . . .

The three networks lavished nearly 60 hours of air time on the conventions. To be precise, they gave 29 hours and 16 minutes of precious prime-time coverage to the Democrats and 29 hours and 39 minutes to the Republicans. Barely half of that coverage (54 percent) was given over to party activities like speeches, films, and roll calls. That left plenty of time for the networks' own floor reports, film stories, interviews, commentaries, and general punditry.

Researchers at the Center for Media and Public Affairs viewed all prime-time coverage of both conventions and coded the topics of discussion and evaluations of the candidates. The coverage was broken up into self-contained segments, such as speeches, interviews, and round-table discussions. Within each segment, a speaker was coded only once in a given category. So Ted Kennedy wasn't credited with a new anti-Bush evaluation every time he asked where George was. We figured viewers got the point the first time.

THE DEMOCRATS

The Democratic confab was very much a two-man show, with Michael Dukakis and Jesse Jackson sharing the spotlight. As Table 1 shows, Jackson actually attracted more coverage than Dukakis over the four days. But both

Source: *Public Opinion*, (September/October 1988): 41–44. Reprinted with permission of the American Enterprise Institute for Public Policy Research, Washington, D.C..

TABLE 1.   Network Convention Coverage (Number of Segments Discussing Each Topic)

DEMOCRATS			REPUBLICANS		
Dukakis	79		Reagan	61	
Jackson	98		Bush	92	
Bentsen	26 ⎱ 47		Quayle	125 ⎱ 197	
V.P. Selection	21 ⎰		V.P. Selection	72 ⎰	
Policy Issues	79		Policy Issues	72	
Campaign Strategy	42		Campaign Strategy	68	

finished with highly attractive media profiles, as the evaluations in Table 2 demonstrate. Dukakis was praised by ninety-one speakers and criticized by only four; Jackson received praise from eighty-five sources and criticism from only one.

Vice presidential nominee Lloyd Bentsen finished a distant third in the coverage. He managed to garner twenty-nine statements of support without a single vote of opposition—not a bad start for a newly named second banana. But George Bush attracted nearly as much attention, most of it in the form of barbs and jibes. Bush was singled out for criticism by twenty-three speakers. His sole defender on camera was his own campaign manager, Lee Atwater, during an interview on ABC. In addition, the Reagan administration was lambasted by twenty speakers and praised by only three. So the Democrats succeeded in giving a big hand to their two stars and the back of their hand to the opposition.

The networks mostly reinforced the sentiments of the delegates. Naturally, clear evaluations of the candidates were less common among reporters. And their attention was focused more on presidential candidate Dukakis than runner-up Jackson. But the proportion of favorable comments was even higher in the network booths than on the convention floor. All

TABLE 2.   Network Evaluations of Candidates*

	ALL SOURCES		REPORTERS	
	Positive	*Negative*	*Positive*	*Negative*
Democratic Convention				
Dukakis	91	4	19	0
Jackson	85	1	11	0
Bentsen	29	0	0	0
Bush	1	23	0	0
Republican Convention				
Bush	114	5	16	0
Quayle	83	12	3	0
Dukakis	0	37	0	0

*Clearly positive or negative judgments.

nineteen assessments by reporters favored Dukakis, as did all eleven evaluations of Jackson. Bentsen received all the attention customarily accorded vice presidents—not a single clear evaluation.

Positive evaluations of Dukakis tended to be rather mild. Dan Rather, for example, praised him for orchestrating the convention "remarkably well," and David Brinkley noted that he was "in charge," having rallied behind him even those delegates "who, in the beginning, thought he was a Jimmy Carter without the peanuts." After Dukakis's emotional acceptance speech, however, the praise flowed somewhat more freely. Rather called it "dramatic" and noted that Dukakis "has made a career of exceeding expectation."

Journalistic praise of the runner-up was less frequent but more effusive. In Tom Brokaw's words, "The Reverend Jesse Jackson—a remarkable picture. . . . Here is a man who (as he often says) was born in the slum, but the slum was not born in him." And no speaker received a more enthusiastic introduction than Brokaw's: "Fasten your seatbelts! Jesse Jackson has arrived to deliver the most widely anticipated speech of the convention. . . . He is clearly the most gifted orator in the Democratic party today."

Nor did Jackson have trouble living up to such high expectations. ABC's Jim Wooten summarized the impact of his oratory on members of the party and press alike: "Press and convention officials . . . were rapt as well. I've never seen that happen. A lot of reporters stopped writing, stopped taking notes. A lot of convention officials actually listened to the speech. That's a real change." In a fitting tribute to a campaign that received by far the most favorable TV news coverage during the primaries, ABC's Jeff Greenfield dubbed Jackson the Democratic answer to Ronald Reagan: "He transcends conventional politics, conventional experience, conventional limits."

The Reverend Jackson also figured heavily in the major theme that characterized coverage of the convention itself—that the Democrats had succeeded in unifying their often fractious party. Jackson's positive effect on party unity was praised on twenty-nine separate occasions, and nineteen additional speakers pronounced that unity had been achieved. No speaker either called the party divided or portrayed Jackson as a divisive force. . . .

THE REPUBLICANS

To a degree that may seem surprising in light of the controversy surrounding Dan Quayle, the Republican ticket nearly matched the Democrats in positive convention coverage. Bush scored even higher than Dukakis, with 114 paeans of praise and only five dissenting voices. Even more striking, he nearly matched his opponent's good press from reporters, drawing sixteen positive statements without any negatives. The night after Bush announced Quayle's selection, for example, Walter Cronkite commented, "He did prove that he's his own man. He's strong, he picked a daring candidate. . . . " It was Bush's speech, however, that drew real kudos. David

Brinkley called it "poised and poetic." John Chancellor found it "a splendid piece of work," and Sam Donaldson pronounced it "a much better speech than Dukakis's." Tom Brokaw seemed to sum up his colleagues' sentiments: "George Bush came into this hall and accomplished all that he wanted to." Meanwhile, Republican speakers returned the Democrats' fire by attacking Michael Dukakis thirty-seven times without a single counterattack.

So far the show was going according to the GOP script. But what about the storm that descended on their vice presidential candidate? The damage can be measured less in terms of bad press than in the sheer amount of attention Quayle attracted (and thereby distracted from the head of the ticket). As Table 1 shows, Senator Quayle was the number one topic of discussion in the network coverage. He was mentioned more frequently than George Bush and twice as often as Ronald Reagan. Indeed, when all discussion of the vice presidency is added to Quayle's personal total, the second slot on the ticket drew more than twice as much attention as the party's presidential candidate and three times as much as the current president.

The Indiana senator was the subject of ninety-five clear evaluations, eighty-three positive and twelve negative. That's twelve more negatives than his counterpart on the Democratic ticket received and over twice as much criticism as Dukakis, Jackson, and Bentsen combined during their party's convention. In addition, six speakers asserted that Quayle would hurt the ticket's chances for victory, compared to only one who deprecated Bentsen's contribution. Nonetheless, his evaluations, like those of the other candidates, were predominantly positive. Further, Quayle received only three clear evaluations from reporters, and all were positive.

How can this be, in view of the flap over media coverage that led an angry crowd to hector reporters as they tried to question the candidate in his home state and gave rise to a memorable front-page headline in the conservative *Washington Times:* "Networks toss fairness to the wind, go for jugular"? The answer involves our understanding of good and bad press, in a way that illuminates contemporary journalistic practices as well as the special character of network convention coverage.

BAD NEWS OR BIAS?

Our coding system was designed to err on the side of caution by charting only clear, direct, and one-sided evaluations. Further, journalists' spoken evaluations of candidates were assigned to other sources if they were attributed, even through phrases such as, "questions have been raised about . . . " or "critics have charged. . . . "

These were precisely the kinds of qualifiers reporters used with virtually every quotation or assertion they aired about Quayle's military service.

Typical was CBS's lead story on the convention's final night. Dan Rather's lead-in described the situation in grim terms:

> Bush finds himself under a cloud, a cloud of controversy swirling over his running mate; how and why he chose Sen. Dan Quayle of Indiana, and Quayle's military service record. Questions are being raised over what influence, if any, was used to get Quayle into the Indiana State National Guard at the height of the Vietnam War. . . . That controversy has turned this convention upside down.

After sources were quoted to similar effect, Bruce Morton's summary repeated the main themes of the controversy in a manner that again suggested a crisis atmosphere without endorsing the charges:

> So the matter of Quayle's military service, of what effect family influence had on getting him into the National Guard, what effect *that* might have on the campaign; all of those things remain unresolved. Bush campaign officials have been insisting all day there is no question of dropping Quayle from the ticket.

This certainly sounds ominous, and it raised doubts about Bush's judgment, Quayle's honor, and the party's prospects without even asserting that the charges are true or the fallout deserved. So it is bad press, in one sense, without including any overtly negative judgments. Nor does it address whether the substance and magnitude of the controversy are justified by the facts.

Once such a controversy exists, it is news, and bad news at that. Once it has surfaced, therefore, it becomes self-perpetuating. How it came into existence is beside the point to the reporter but very much the point to the target of the report. That is one reason disputes over alleged media bias have become a regular and predictable feature of campaign news. What the journalists define as bad news, the politicians define as biased reporting.

Thus, network reporters seemed to follow a rule of speak no evil, unless you can quote someone. Tom Brokaw was willing to applaud Quayle's Thursday night speech: "He knocked it out of the park from that podium tonight. That's one of the best television speeches we've heard all week. . . . He is a modern media candidate." But when NBC's Ken Bode put the knock on Quayle, the criticism was always attributed to other sources:

> One former Republican National Committee official said, "Last night at dinner we were joking about Quayle. We trashed him!" A famous conservative said, "It makes Bush look like he wasn't strong enough to pick Kemp or Dole." And from Indiana today, one of Dan Quayle's home-state politicians said, "It can't be Quayle, can it really?"

This approach is partly a matter of journalistic style, but it seems particularly prevalent in convention coverage. Our study of the networks' 1988 primary coverage found that nearly half the one-sided assessments of candidates were negative; of these almost one in seven was delivered by a journalist without

TABLE 3.   The Quayle Watch

NETWORK	SEGMENTS MENTIONING QUAYLE	NEGATIVE EVALUATIONS OF QUAYLE*
ABC	22%	11%
CBS	36	50
NBC	42	39
	100%	100%
Number	125	17

* Includes criticism of his contribution to GOP ticket.

attribution. Even during convention week, the evening news seemed more pointed than the convention coverage itself. . . .

. . . The role of news judgment in pursuing a breaking story is illustrated by differences in the tone and emphasis the three networks gave the Quayle controversy. Specifically, ABC's reporting was far more restrained than that of CBS and NBC, as Table 3 illustrates. Quayle was the topic of twenty-eight segments of ABC's coverage, compared to forty-five on CBS and fifty-two on NBC. And ABC broadcast only two evaluations that were entirely negative (including assertions that he would hurt the ticket) compared to seven on NBC and none on CBS. ABC correspondent Jeff Greenfield even warned his colleagues on the air that many journalists had avoided Vietnam service just as they were accusing Quayle of doing.

So it was no lemming-like compulsion that created such intense pursuit of the Quayle controversy. It was the reaction of a press freed from captivity to a second week-long orgy of partisan self-congratulation. Political conventions are normally scripted by political consultants rather than network producers. A genuine news story can act like a wake-up call, startling a somnolent press corps into frantic activity. If there was a media "feeding frenzy" in New Orleans, it was partly in reaction to the starvation diet that preceded it.

6. Campaign Strategy and Tactics

Like campaigns of old, modern campaigns are run by organizations, guided by strategies, and use tactics to deliver their message. But the structure and the methods of conducting campaigns have changed significantly in the past three decades.

Today the organizations tend to be larger and more complex than they used to be. Composed of people with different political backgrounds and more finely honed technical skills, they are less party oriented and more candidate directed. They are also more transitory, frequently existing only for the election and disintegrating when it is over. Although the organizations are good reservoirs for recruitment, they are less useful as instruments for governing.

The people who run the campaigns have changed as well. Party regulars have been replaced by professional pollsters, fund-raisers, media consultants, grassroots organizers, lawyers, accountants, and others who specialize in election campaigns. Strategies are now based on "high tech," as are the tactics employed to implement them. Even the instruments of modern campaigns are different. Computers have replaced blackboards and typewriters; phone banks substitute for home visits; and video tapes convey the image of live speeches. In fact, contemporary candidates spend far more time in television studios recording their messages than at public rallies giving speeches and meeting voters. The science of electioneering has replaced the art of politics.

The magnitude of these changes has been the subject of dispute. The chapter begins with a historical account of the first media campaign. In it, Keith Melder describes the nineteenth-century "log cabin" campaign of William Henry Harrison and John Tyler, a campaign that had many of the ingredients of modern electioneering: image making, public rallies, songs, literature, and even attempts to manipulate the press.

The rest of the selections provide a more contemporary perspective. They focus on campaigns in 1988 and 1990, specifically on the organization, strategy, and tactics that we have come to associate with national campaigns in this mass media age. In doing so they address the so-called "high tech" issues: Have campaigns lost their personal touch? Are candidates programmed? Are strategic decisions driven by poll responses, marketing formulas, and highly polished public relations appeals? Are tactics geared primarily to how it will play on television?

The second reading concerns George Bush's staffing of his 1988 presidential campaign. It is an illustration of success, of what it takes to win a presidential election. The article by David Hoffman and Ann Devroy indicates the extraordinary detail that is necessary, the dynamic quality of campaign organizations, and the skills that must be assembled to carry out the mission. Nothing can be taken for granted.

The selection that follows takes the Bush example into the next stage of development, describing the political situation in which that campaign found itself in the summer of 1988 and the strategy that was designed to deal with it. Thomas Edsall describes the decision to emphasize the negative, a strategic decision that paid handsome dividends to George Bush although not necessarily to the American voters.

The next two readings illustrate the hows of implementing a campaign strategy: how to use the mails to convey a message and project an image, and how to target voters, ascertain their prospective voting decisions, and get likely supporters to the polls on election day.

The chapter then turns to congressional races. In recent decades one of the most persistent trends has been the success that members of Congress have had in being reelected. Incumbents have won well over 90 percent of the time in the 1980s (96 percent in the House and 97 percent in the Senate in 1990) despite large-scale public dissatisfaction with Congress. Why are members of Congress being reelected so easily? Tom Kenworthy indicates the principal reasons: their name recognition, their fund-raising skills, and their ability to service their constituents. Kenworthy notes these advantages and how incumbents maximize them during their term *in* office to ensure future terms *of* office.

The odds that challengers face are so great that many well-qualified individuals choose not to run. Those who do run are often frustrated by the effort. In the last reading, Mark Michaelsen describes what it is like to be a candidate and to lose. His lament points to a real problem in our democratic government, one that has produced pressure to limit congressional terms (a topic that we consider in chapter 9).

The Whistle Stop:
The First Media Campaign

KEITH MELDER

The first presidential campaign to resemble contemporary ones was conducted in 1840. A contest between the Whigs and Democrats, it featured rallies, parades, slogans, jingles, testimonials, and much party propaganda. Keith Melder, curator for political history in the National Museum of American History of the Smithsonian Institution, describes this campaign as the first to involve the candidates themselves, the first to make a grassroots appeal, and the first to use the mass media—at that time, newspapers—in this effort. Melder's article provides a historical perspective by which modern campaigns can be assessed.

Political buffs and collectors agree with historians that the great log-cabin and hard-cider campaign of 1840 was one of the most spectacular political events in American history. . . .

For both Democrats and Whigs, the campaign began with the election of 1836, won by Martin Van Buren over William Henry Harrison and three other regionalized Whig candidates. As the incumbent in 1840, President Van Buren naturally succeeded to the Democratic nomination. For the Whigs, who had not yet won a presidential election, the choice of a candidate was more complicated. Long-time politicians Henry Clay and Daniel Webster were both very much in contention for the nomination. As the most prominent of all Whigs, Clay was the man to beat, although he had made many enemies during his long years in politics. Harrison, the Whig front-runner in 1836, remained in the running between 1836 and 1839 by cultivating party leaders in the states. Another crucial fact of this period was the economic depression of 1837, which brought severe hardships to business and working people alike. Still felt in 1840, the effects of this depression threatened to have an impact on the election.

The very first Whig national nominating convention met in December 1839, setting several precedents. Thurlow Weed, Whig leader from New York state, and Thaddeus Stevens of Pennsylvania led in organizing this convention to defeat Clay, who—they believed—could not win the presidency. By rigging the rules so that each state delegation would cast its whole vote for a single nominee, the convention eliminated many votes for Clay and ensured a vigorous floor fight. Using modern procedures and

Source: *Campaign and Elections,* (Fall 1985): 62–68. Reprinted by permission of the author and *Campaigns and Elections.*

shrewd machinations, the Whig leadership united behind William Henry Harrison of Ohio. John Tyler was added to the ticket as vice-presidential nominee, almost as an afterthought, to balance the ticket with a Virginian. As a precaution the convention issued no Whig election platform; the party was not sufficiently united to risk taking a stand on basic issues. Instead, a colorful campaign would represent Harrison to the voters.

Before the convention's end, Whig leaders called for a winning campaign of exciting displays and mass participation. Through a remarkable coincidence, Harrison's principal campaign image was suggested by a Democratic newspaper, the Baltimore *Republican*. Sneering at "Old Granny" Harrison, the paper declared, "Give him [Harrison] a barrel of hard cider, and settle a pension of two thousand a year on him, and my word for it, he will sit the remainder of his days in his log cabin . . . ." The Whigs gleefully took this sarcastic estimate of their candidate and converted it into the central theme of their campaign. Harrison was far from having a log-cabin nativity, however. He was born on a great Virginia plantation, the son of Benjamin Harrison V, a signer of the Declaration of Independence. He belonged to the early American elite.

CREATING AN IMAGE

Political organizers designed Harrison's campaign around the log-cabin and hard-cider image. His own ample residence at North Bend, Ohio, was identified as a log cabin (the original structure had been built of logs) and the candidate was endowed with the rural simplicity and virtue of the frontier cabin-dweller and farmer. The "Farmer of North Bend" became one of his many identities. Campaign events and devices celebrated the log cabin endlessly. It was featured on thousands of novelties and devices such as ribbons, ceramics, sheet music, and banners. "Cabin raisings" took place in hundreds of communities where cabins were built to serve as local Whig party headquarters. Miniature cabins were carried in parades and full-sized cabins were constructed on campaign parade floats. Campaign organizers distributed draughts from actual barrels of hard cider carried on floats or located at their headquarters. Sign painters by the hundreds were recruited to paint banners associating the Hero of Tippecanoe with cabins, cider, and the simple, rustic life.

What followed can be likened to a series of explosions taking place around the country. First there were numerous ratification meetings in the states. Then came George Washington's Birthday, which Whigs in many places made into a great partisan celebration and the first major Harrison rally of the year. Some of the flavor of these occasions is picked up in a contemporary description of the Ohio State Convention, February 21–22, 1840:

> The grand procession on the 22nd surpassed in enthusiasm anything ever before or since in the history of Ohio. The people had been gathering . . .

and from all the counties of the State they had come together. From the banks of the Scioto... and every river and creek between Lake Erie and the Ohio, every log cabin seemed to have contributed its stalwart Buckeye boys to make the great crowd to set "the ball a rolling on for Tippecanoe and Tyler too." It was an army with banners moving through streets whose walls were hung with flags, streamers and decorations to honor a brave old patriot and pioneer... who had settled down in a log cabin to spend his days as a humble farmer at North Bend...

Similar scenes were enacted hundreds, perhaps thousands of times during the political season between February and November. Great leather "campaign balls" ten feet in diameter were rolled from place to place around the country.

MOBILIZING THE MEDIA

As he had done in the New York state campaign of 1838, Thurlow Weed hired Horace Greeley to edit the principal campaign newspaper. Even before "Old Tip's" nomination, Greeley began planning a network of Whig newspapers led by his own weekly, appropriately named the *Log Cabin*.

The *Cabin* reinforced all the campaign imagery depicted during rallies and processions. From May to November it carried endless sentimental stories of Tip's heroism, his kindness to the troops who fought under him, and his generosity to visitors at his North Bend cabin/mansion. Battle stories from the War of 1812 and Harrison's Indian fights endowed the Old General with a heroic, mythic, larger-than-life image similar to that assigned to Andrew Jackson in the campaign of 1828.

The *Log Cabin* featured texts of speeches by the great Whig orators— Clay, Webster, the Old Hero himself, and others. Although many of these orations were dull and pointless, some of them focused on real issues in the campaign, such as the economic hard times and abuses of executive power. Greeley also printed scurrilous attacks on the Democrats and their policies, especially those of President Van Buren. An infamous speech by Rep. Charles Ogle, and a favorite for reprinting by Greeley and other Whig editors, accused Van Buren of profligate waste of public funds in decorating the White House. It was one of the most offensive and effective of the Whig campaign smears.

Most *Log Cabins* included campaign music, poetry (generally dreadful doggerel), and advertisements for campaign gadgets and devices deemed "essential" for loyal Harrisonians. Reaching a circulation of 80,000 copies per week (Greeley believed it would have topped 100,000 had he been able to print that number), the *Log Cabin* was a vivid, highly effective promotional device for the campaign.

The campaign rollicked along through the spring and summer with huge regional Whig Convocations being held throughout the country. At Baltimore in May, on the day set for the Democratic nominating convention in that city, the Harrisonians staged a "Young Men's Whig National Convention" that completely eclipsed the gathering of their rivals. Typically, they convened "immense" delegations with bands, banners, and floats and paraded through Baltimore, much to the discomfort of the awed Democrats. In June the Whigs of Illinois and other Western states gathered for three days at Springfield for a rally attended by an estimated 20,000 souls, including old soliders of the Revolution and a young Whig named Abraham Lincoln. In August at Nashville, not far from Andrew Jackson's own plantation, Whigs of the great Southwest assembled for a regional celebration.

Probably more important in generating Whig enthusiasm were the local and state festivities that took place with great frequency, encouraging the participation of masses of local people heretofore uninterested in partisan politics. Every edition of the *Log Cabin* included lengthy descriptions of such rallies, "cabin raisings," and celebrations to illustrate the progress of the Whig cause, its popularity, and the general enthusiasm it aroused. Typical of these was an account of a New York state rally in August:

> This has been the proudest—brightest day of my life! Never—no never, have I before seen the People in their majesty! Never were the foundations of popular sentiment so broken up! The scene, from early dawn to sunset, has been one of continued, increasing, bewildering enthusiasm. The hearts of TWENTY-FIVE THOUSAND FREEMEN have been overflowing with gratitude and gladness and joy. It has been a day of Jubilee—an era of Deliverance for CENTRAL NEW-YORK. The people in Waves have poured in from the Valleys and rushed in torrents down from the Mountains. The City has been vocal with Eloquence, with Music, and with Acclamations. Demonstrations of strength and Emblems of Victory and harbingers of Prosperity are all around us, cheering and animating a People who are finally and effectively aroused.

Reading such descriptions, who could doubt the campaign's success? One novel feature of some Whig gatherings was the enlistment of women as participants in parades, makers of banners, and numerous members of the audience.

Democrats were baffled, dazzled, and dispirited by the contagious enthusiasm of the log-cabin and hard-cider campaign and the magnitude of the Whig organization. Again and again in writing to President Van Buren, Democratic politicians expressed skepticism and surprise at the hi-jinks and popularity of their opponents. They voiced contempt for such "silly devices" as log cabins and complained about the "zeal" and "fanaticism" of ciderite crusading. For months Democratic leaders could not believe they were being outmaneuvered. They tried to respond with tactics and devices of their own, but Democratic resources could not match those of the Whigs. The special party newspaper, the *Extra Globe*, edited by Amos Kendall, circulated nearly as widely as the *Log Cabin*, but it lacked the latter's spirit and imagination. Ultimately the Democrats had to admit they had been "out-fought, out-drunk and out-sung."

SELLING THE GOODS

This presidential election included many elements of a latter-day Madison Avenue advertising campaign. Slogans, jingles, and testimonials saturated the communications media. Throughout the campaign, the Whig leadership sought to create good feelings about Harrison through such devices as identifying his image with that of George Washington. Like Washington, Harrison was a Cincinnatus who left his plough to save his country, serving the people again and again; now he was prepared to make another sacrifice to preserve the nation.

Campaign rallies were positive, uplifting experiences for vast throngs of participants. Whig partisans staged events to make people feel good about themselves and confident about the future — if Harrison were elected. Whether they did it consciously or not, campaigners handled the intangible qualities of their work with extraordinary finesse. All of these factors combined to produce the first thorough presidential *image* campaign.

What else was new about this contest? Most tactics and devices were borrowed from other kinds of public celebrations. Processions and parades had served for centuries as expressions of public attachment to civic and religious institutions. Whig strategists appropriated many elements from Independence Day celebrations until the entire summer took on the character of a giant Fourth of July party. Whig partisans also adapted some of the populist tactics that had served so well in Andrew Jackson's 1828 campaign. Such campaign devices as ribbons, souvenirs, music, and broadsides were not new. But under Whig management and with ample funds raised by Whig leaders, they proliferated as never before. The degree to which they were used and literally saturated the country was unprecedented. Thurlow Weed and other Whig leaders had expanded and perfected their organization to an extent never before seen in a presidential election.

CHANGING THE PROCESS

Two significant "firsts" may be attributed to the Whigs in 1840. The log-cabin candidate was the first presidential aspirant to go out on the stump in his own behalf. At a time when candidates for the highest office were supposed to remain aloof from electioneering, Harrison made twenty-three speeches, all in his home state of Ohio. As unprecedented efforts to display the candidate to the electorate, they symbolized the democratization of American politics. The electorate was curious and apparently pleased to see and hear their hero in the flesh.

The election of 1840 also produced the first national mass-based advertising campaign of any kind, a circumstance not generally admitted by historians of advertising. For the first time a national "product" was marketed vigorously and imaginatively across the land. Whig managers used every available means of communication to display the Harrison image. People everywhere could visualize the candidate from portraits of Harrison depicted on cloth ribbons, printed ceramics, publications, medals, and other devices. The campaign's events—rallies, processions, conventions—were converted into mass media of communication. A political communications revolution had taken place.

The log-cabin and hard-cider campaign also deserves to be remembered for other reasons. It climaxed the formation of the second American party system. In 1840, for the first time, two nationally organized, nearly equal parties sponsored effective presidential campaigns: Party politics had come of age. The political extravaganza also served as a grand exhibition of popular culture and entertainment.

THE LOG CABIN LEGACY

The campaign of 1840 became the model for presidential contests since its time. It set standards for campaign achievement and established a sequence of campaign events that guided rituals of American politics from the mid-nineteenth century to the present. The campaign developed in a sequence of five distinct stages: first a preconvention period when rival candidates maneuvered for popularity, then the stage of the nominating convention, followed by a period of strategy planning and money raising. Then the campaign itself began with the "senseless mummery" of hundreds of mass rallies and celebrations. As the campaign drew to a close, a record number of voters went to the polls on different election days (the federal government would later set a single date for presidential voting).

Did it work? Was the log-cabin and hard-cider campaign successful? At a superficial level, it certainly had the appearance of success, for Harrison won the election, the first Whig candidate to succeed to the presidency. Actually, no observer can say with assurance that the spectacular campaign was Harrison's magic formula for victory, even though Van Buren himself observed he had been "washed out of office by a flood of apple juice!" It could be argued that economic conditions were more important than hard cider in making "Old Tip" president. The lingering economic hard times may have influenced more voters than the endless processions and often senseless electioneering.

At another level the great campaign was certainly successful. Political mass participation and showmanship resulted in the largest turnout of eligible voters in American presidential politics to that time. More than 2,400,000 citizens cast ballots, or nearly eighty percent of those eligible. Only the unprecedented barnstorming of William Jennings Bryan in 1896 produced a similar turnout in the years since; recent elections have seen the figures fall to barely half. Harrison received an electoral vote of 234 to 60 for Van Buren and a popular majority of nearly 150,000.

This important campaign lives on in the thousands of "hurrah" campaigns for the presidency and other offices that have taken place in the years since 1840. To some extent it still lives, even though recent campaigners have substituted new technologies of television, direct mail, and polling for the assembly of thousands of people to participate in campaign rallies. They mash their apples differently today, but the juice tastes the same. That old 1840 flavor seems here to stay.

REFERENCES

Chambers, William Nisbet. "Election of 1840," in *History of American Presidential Elections 1789–1968*, ed. Arthur Schlesinger, Jr. New York: Chelsea House, 1971.

Chambers, William Nisbet. "Party Development and the American Mainstream," *The American Party Systems: Stages of Political Development*, eds. William Nisbet Chambers and Walter Dean Burnham. 2nd. ed., New York: Oxford University Press, 1975.

Greeley, Horace. *Recollections of a Busy Life.* New York: J. B. Ford & Co., 1868.

Gronbeck, Bruce E. "Functional and Dramaturgical Theories of Presidential Campaigning," *Presidential Studies Quarterly*, vol. 14, Fall 1984, pp. 486–499.

Gunderson, Robert Gray. *The Log-Cabin Campaign.* Lexington: University of Kentucky Press, 1957.

Howe, Daniel Walker. *The Political Culture of the American Whigs.* Chicago: University of Chicago Press, 1979.

McCormick, Richard P. "Political Development and the Second Party System," in *The American Party Systems: Stages of Political Development*, eds. William Nisbet Chambers and Walter Dean Burnham. 2nd ed., New York: Oxford University Press, 1975.

Norton, A. B. *The Great Revolution of 1840: Reminiscences of the Log Cabin and Hard Cider Campaign.* Mt. Vernon, Ohio: A. B. Norton & Co., 1888.

Martin Van Buren Manuscripts, Library of Congress.

The Log Cabin, published simultaneously in New York and Albany, by H. Greeley & Co., May 2, 1840–November 20, 1840.

The Complex Machine behind Bush

DAVID HOFFMAN AND ANN DEVROY

Presidential campaigns are elaborately structured and scripted. Bush's 1988 campaign is a case in point. According to Washington Post *reporters David Hoffman and Ann Devroy, "an army of ants" carried the Bush banner throughout the year-long campaign, making millions of phone calls, mailing millions of letters, and mobilizing millions of supporters on election day. It was people, not ideas; experience, not innovation; and organization and planning, not dumb luck, that carried Bush to victory.*

George Bush's 40-state election victory ... was a triumph earned not by a crusade of ideas or a revolution like the one Ronald Reagan earned eight years ago. Rather, it was the culmination of effort by an immensely complex, largely hidden machine that was painstakingly assembled and set in motion long before Democrat Michael S. Dukakis received his party's nomination.

Bush's machine plodded steadily forward for years, absorbing people and lessons from the past, and adding the latest technology from the present. At the helm was a dogged but only occasionally inspiring candidate who, nonetheless, knew well the routines and his role. From beginning to end, the Bush campaign was based on the premise that it would prevail by dint of experience and calculation, not by inspiration or the power of ideas.

"We were an army of ants," recalled Mary Matalin, who for two years led various divisions in the army, including the early Michigan effort and the final nationwide get-out-the-vote drive.

The creed of this army was to leave nothing to chance. Almost everything that could be controlled, influenced or bargained in favor of Bush was attempted. For example, when he was being photographed outside his home in Kennebunkport, Maine, for the covers of news magazines just before the Republican convention, his aides insisted that photographers aim their lenses above the horizon, and not capture the craggy rocks of the shoreline. Rocks, the photographers were told, would be "elitist." Nearly all the photographers obeyed the rule—no rocks.

When Bush faced Pat Robertson in the "Super Tuesday" contests, his adviser Doug Wead stationed field operatives in several hundred evangelical churches across the South who reported weekly on the strength of the Robertson forces. Wead then arranged private meetings for Bush with evangelical church leaders; Bush told them "Jesus Christ is my personal savior." In time, the Robertson candidacy collapsed.

Source: *The Washington Post*, November 13, 1988:1 A1, A 16. Reprinted by permission of *The Washington Post*.

When Bush was trying to stave off Dukakis in the final weeks of the fall campaign, his strategists prepared—but never aired—some especially sharp-edged commercials in case Bush got into trouble. Some were sent to television stations for safekeeping in the event they needed to be broadcast immediately. In one that campaign aides called "Greatest Hits," the announcer repeated all the campaign's attacks on Dukakis—the prison furlough program, the Pledge of Allegiance, prayer in public schools—with ominous music in the background.

The ad was never used, but it was there, just in case.

The Bush victory in large measure reflected the two most potent themes in American politics: peace and prosperity. It was also due to the kind of campaign waged by Dukakis, who often shifted message and approach, while Bush pounded away on his rival as a liberal soft on crime and defense.

But the Bush campaign was also the product of thousands of small decisions and moments that kept it moving forward. At times, events spun wildly out of control, but there was always a counter-effort at damage control, recovery and preparation to fight again.

Bush had been part of every Republican national campaign since 1964 with the exception of the 1976 race when he was director of Central Intelligence, and he knew firsthand the essentials of what needed to be done. Even though he and Reagan were reelected by a landslide in 1984, Bush was enveloped in gloom over his poor performance that year. But gradually, he began looking ahead to his own try at the presidency in 1988. The quest began with the recruitment of Lee Atwater as his political operative and sometime later, Craig L. Fuller as chief of staff. Atwater said it was apparent from his first meeting on Dec. 19, 1984, with Bush that the vice president knew his task was to "separate himself from Ronald Reagan, demonstrate he was his own man, and set out a clear direction and goals." But, he added, Bush "intended to do it in his own way and on his own timetable."

In May 1985, a political action committee called the Fund for America's Future was set up to give Bush the vehicle to run. The committee, which offered scant help to other candidates, was simply a shadow Bush campaign organization. Later, Bush added media consultant Roger Ailes to his retinue and began meeting privately with him every other week. Along with pollster Robert Teeter and investment banker Nicholas Brady, the core group was in place, with Treasury Secretary James A. Baker III always a presence.

The furor that broke in November 1986 over the Iran-contra scandal dogged Bush for more than a year, but in the end, it was not a liability. Indeed, during a March 1987 campaign trip to Iowa, Bush was asked few questions about it by Iowans. Looking back, a senior Bush adviser concluded, "It got to the point where there were not any new answers. People really had made up their mind about Iran-contra. They didn't hold it against George Bush—they just wished he had performed better. We could deal with that." Bush promised to answer any and all questions submitted to him, but never did.

Nonetheless, the topic animated Bush. One frigid day early in the Iowa campaign, Bush held a combative impromptu news conference about his role in the Iran arms sales. As reporters' tape recorders slowed to a crawl in the freezing weather, press aide Bruce Zanca was on his hands and knees trying out of camera range to keep the press and candidate at reasonable distance. Zanca had one problem: Bush, intent on firing back at reporters, stepped on Zanca's hand and stayed on it unknowingly.

Bush also demonstrated that he could fight the trench warfare demanded in the long struggle over Michigan delegates. He worked the state precinct by precinct. "It was like being a Fuller brush man." Matalin recalled. "We went door to door." Bush's sales weapons were not ideas or visions about the country, but rather hundreds of telephone calls, personal notes, even "kid calls"—politicking by his sons George and Neil, as directed by field operatives, who true to the principles of the organization, submitted a form describing the prospect, the best message and so on.

A TRIP TO EUROPE

By the end of 1987, the Bush camp was choreographing the events that would propel the vice president into the campaign year. First, at taxpayer expense, Bush visited Poland, where he was greeted wildly by pro-American crowds, and then breezed through the Western European capitals. Bush denied the trip was political, and even in private was "extraordinarily sensitive" about the film crews Ailes had hired to go along in Western Europe, a senior Bush adviser said.

But, the adviser added, the trip was definitely political: photographs of Bush at Auschwitz, the Nazi concentration camp, and a videotape of Bush meeting British Prime Minister Margaret Thatcher were used in fall campaign advertising.

In his formal announcement of his presidential bid just after this trip, Bush found a voice for himself. He worked at length on the announcement speech with Peggy Noonan, Reagan's former speech writer. Unlike others who had written for Bush, Noonan spent hours with the candidate and drew him out. The technique seemed to work, producing a speech Bush was comfortable with and which remains a portrait of his reasons for running.

NEWSWEEK'S "WIMP" STORY

Then Newsweek published its cover story, "Fighting the 'Wimp Factor.'" Bush felt like the cover was a torpedo aimed at him and his family. "That hit him harder than anything else I've seen," a top aide said. "It took the wind out of the sails. It tore up the family."

Ever watchful, on the Friday before the issue was published, the Bush staff had been tipped about the "W word" on the cover. Bush, who had planned to pose for a cover photograph on his way to a State Department reception, stood up the Newsweek photographer at the last minute.

Caution and calculation remained the trademarks of the Bush effort as the Republican primary debates began. The first one, sponsored by William F. Buckley's "Firing Line" program, "was a big risk," a Bush aide recalled. "We were always looking for ways to minimize the risk." In this case, Bush took whole days out of his schedule to prepare with briefings, mock debates, videotapes, "pepper drills" and staff memos. He came out of the debate as the lone Republican defender of Reagan's proposed medium-range missile treaty with the Soviets, and he stuck with the issue after exploiting the summit last December between Reagan and Soviet leader Mikhail Gorbachev to best political advantage.

The first political contest of 1988 was the Iowa precinct caucuses. But long before the votes were cast, the Bush team knew they were in trouble in this critical state. As early as March 1987, Bush spent two days hopscotching around Iowa for his question-and-answer "Ask George Bush" events. Immediately afterwards, Atwater sat down in a Cedar Rapids motel with 25 voters who supported Bush in 1980 but no longer had much enthusiasm for him.

Atwater found out why: The Iowans disliked Reagan and wanted Bush to be someone other than Reagan's loyal vice president. Thus, Bush's very base was crumbling long before the first critical showdown of the election. "He was a man without a country," Atwater recalled.

"There wasn't a single thing about Iowa that indicated he could win," he added. "If you were a doctor examining the patient, you would say it had a bad heart."

To make matters worse, Bush had come in third in the important Ames, Iowa, GOP straw poll because the Bush team miscalculated Robertson's support. Prior to the straw poll, Atwater had assured the senior advisers that Bush would win. Afterwards, Rich Bond, the young architect of Bush's 1980 triumph, had the unpleasant task of returning full-time to fight a losing campaign. At one point, they suggested Bush pull out of Iowa. He refused.

For all his determination not to be out-hustled, Bush still longed to keep up his vice presidential duties. A senior adviser said it wasn't until the Iowa defeat that Bush realized he needed to give up his weekly luncheons with Reagan and his meetings with visiting foreign dignitaries and devote all his time to the campaign.

"He was pretty shellshocked," said a long-time friend who talked with Bush after the Iowa loss. "He knew he was going to lose, but not that badly. He seemed confused, tentative, unsure. He didn't understand how he had done so badly, how so many Republicans could vote against him in that place that gave him his start."

Even the "army of ants" had to scramble in the days after Iowa. Atwater said he told New Hampshire organizer Ron Kaufman to build a "fortress" in the state that could withstand an Iowa defeat. On the first day of campaigning, there were cracks in the fortress. Bush, having gone to a factory to greet workers, went to the wrong door and found few hands to shake. He was getting conflicting advice about what to say. This period was "very painful, really painful," recalled the vice president's oldest son, George.

But Bush fought back with the machine he had created. "Shouldn't anyone worry about George Bush's determination, or his friends," his son recalled. "That is where some of it paid off, in New Hampshire. You had 500 or 600 folks flooding that state. Friends from Florida with oranges, friends from everywhere. In a state that small, every bit of that can help."

Within four days, the machine had acted: A half-hour "Ask George Bush" taped commercial was broadcast on every Boston television station, blanketing New Hampshire; thousands of handbills went to undecided or leaning voters urging them to watch it; Gov. John H. Sununu, a Bush ally, persuaded the Manchester television station to open up a slot to broadcast the negative "Straddle" commercial against Sen. Robert J. Dole (R-Kan.); Bush brought speech writer Noonan to New Hampshire and sharpened his rhetorical fire at Dole as a creature of Congress; and Bush taped a five-minute television commercial opened by Barry Goldwater and shown only once, on the eve of the vote, in which Bush declared calmly, "I sense a rising tide."

TRUCKS, FORKLIFTS, DOG SLEDS

Bush also rushed around the state looking for impromptu campaign stops—posing in trucks, forklifts and at a dog sled race. Sununu proved invaluable in showing Bush where to go and when. Bush's victory had the unintended consequence of reinforcing the idea that all he had to do was show up at various places in a state to win. Thus, he was later campaigning at a rock quarry in North Carolina, at a southern-style food restaurant in South Carolina, at a construction site in Florida. "It became another dimension of chaos," one aide lamented. "He was told just go out and campaign. Issues and substance were less important."

Atwater had played a role in putting the South Carolina primary right before the "Super Tuesday" voting, and Bush pole-vaulted into the Republican nomination with big wins in both. But his "army" was suddenly disoriented: They had not planned on winning the nomination so soon.

Thus began a long period of drift for Bush. He burned money and time. Outside events rattled the campaign: Reagan's veto of a major civil rights bill; ethical questions about then-Attorney General Edwin Meese III; the disclosure of Nancy Reagan's use of astrology, and the possibility of a plea bargain for Panamanian military strongman Gen. Manuel Antonio Noriega. Where possible, the Bush team quietly tried damage control. Through intermediaries, for example, they secretly encouraged Meese to quit before the Republican convention.

Even as Bush drifted, some in his "army of ants" were preparing the next phase of the campaign. In the New York primary, Sen. Albert Gore Jr. (D-Tenn.) had used against Dukakis the case of William Horton Jr., who escaped from a Massachusetts prison furlough program and raped a Maryland woman and stabbed her boyfriend. Bush campaign research director Jim Pinkerton checked with Andy Card, a former Massachusetts Republican legislator. Card told Pinkerton, "If you think that's bad, let me tell you about the pledge."

"It was sort of like looking for penicillin, and discovering nylon instead," Pinkerton recalled later.

The research on these issues—the Horton case and Dukakis' veto of a Massachusetts legislative bill requiring teachers to lead their students in the Pledge of Allegiance—was used in two New Jersey voter focus groups in May. The results were so encouraging that Bush operatives decided to clobber Dukakis with them right after the California primary.

In meetings in Kennebunkport over the Memorial Day holiday, pollster Teeter stressed the importance of controlling the agenda and keeping it on Bush's issues. With help from Noonan, they wrote an attack speech for Bush at the June 9 Texas Republican Convention. As a precaution, they alerted Baker in case Bush balked at the material—but Bush dived right in. He, too, had seen the focus group tapes, according to Atwater.

While the Democrats ridiculed Bush in Atlanta, he and Baker vacationed in seclusion in Wyoming. On his return, Bush was shown clips of the Democratic convention speeches, the "Where Was George?" chanting and the "silver foot" analogy. An intimate of Bush said that while the vice president is "squeamish, really squeamish" about "bare-knuckles campaigning," he was primed to attack after he saw the convention tapes.

"This guy didn't need any lessons on how to run," Bush's son, George, said of him. He recalled a summer conversation in which his father told him, "The differences are going to come into focus. I have been out there before. I felt those klieg lights and he hasn't. That's why I'm not worried. We're going to be a better-run campaign than the other guy."

The Bush machine did not produce Sen. Dan Quayle (R-Ind.) as a running mate, but it helped him get through the campaign without a serious embarrassment after the initial controversy over his selection. Bush's son, George, said the choice diverted Dukakis into chasing Quayle instead of attacking his father. "He let dad run free," he said.

THE BIG SPEECH

Bush again found his voice at the Republican convention with the help of Noonan, Teeter, Richard G. Darman, a former Treasury and White House aide, and Robert B. Zoellick, campaign domestic policy aide. Noonan trailed Bush for two days, going everywhere. He wrote her a two-page memo of his thoughts on the role of government: he sent her a list of words he liked to use, such as "harmony" and "tolerance."

But the heart of the convention speech was a set of declarative sentences in which Bush differentiated his views from Dukakis. Several sources said this was Darman's inspiration. "Should public school teachers be required to lead our children in the Pledge of Allegiance? My opponent says 'no'—but I say 'yes,' " Bush declared.

For the fall, the Bush "army" exploited the lessons of the last 25 years about the importance of television. Every penny available was squeezed for deployment of the air war—the contest of television commercials. "I always view advertising as guerrilla warfare, not the Normandy invasion," said Ailes, who wrote a series of short memos about Dukakis, depicting him as out of the "mainstream" on values and issues and suggesting that, based on past performance, the governor would take the bait if Bush taunted him.

The taunts came: Bush attacked on the polluted Boston Harbor: on the Horton case and the pledge; on defense and foreign policy; on the Massachusetts economy. Going into the first debate, the Bush high command had two contingency plans; Go positive on economic prosperity if Bush did well, or go negative on crime issues if he did not. Television commercials on both topics were sent to all stations. After the debate, the crime ads went up.

There were also commercials the public never saw. One of the most controversial was the "Pledge" ad, which showed an all-American teacher in an all-American town, leading the class in the pledge. The narrator simply says that Bush believes that teachers should lead the children in the pledge while his opponent does not. Inside the campaign, there were long debates over whether to use it. Baker was wary, fearing that the issue had already attracted much attention and using the ad would only bring a backlash.

The Bush "army" also had a secret team known as the Rapid Response Group. Every week, they telephoned major television stations in 20 contested states to find out what commercials Dukakis had booked. The information was fed into a computer, along with reports on eight other big states. Each Friday, Bush campaign operative Janet Mullins got a report on where Dukakis was buying commercials. If there was a sudden change, she received a "red flag report." Three weeks before the election, a red flag came in: Dukakis had suddenly "gone dark" in Ohio, suggesting he was giving up in the state.

While Bush careered about the country, his high command supervised the "army" every morning at their 7:30 a.m. staff meeting, with Baker, deputy Margaret Tutwiler, Bond, Atwater, Ailes, Teeter and Paul Manafort, a Republican political consultant. At the end of the campaign, many in this group had been driven into a frenzy by the enormity of the effort and the uncertainty of the outcome. Dukakis was making gains; some Bush aides were getting physically ill waiting for the clock to strike midnight.

In the final days, the army went all-out. According to Matalin, the Bush campaign made 12.1 million telephone calls in the final three days before the election. It sent voters 52 million pieces of mail, many of them designed to answer specific concerns voters had expressed when they were called earlier by the campaign.

Bush, too, was paying attention to detail at the very end. A longtime Bush associate who stopped by the nominee's suite on election night found the next president on the telephone with a television network official. It may have been the climactic ending to a decade of campaigning for president, but George Bush was still talking exit poll numbers.

Why Bush Accentuates the Negative

THOMAS B. EDSALL

The most controversial aspect of the Bush campaign was the negative attack he launched against Michael Dukakis. Accentuating the negative was a key strategic decision of the Bush campaign. Thomas Edsall, a writer for the Washington Post, describes the architect of this strategy and the reasoning behind it, and indicates why it was successful.

George Bush's attempt to paint Michael Dukakis into a liberal corner during the presidential debate in Winston-Salem ... was part of a strategy that goes beyond victory in November. The barrage of negative attacks on Dukakis by Bush and, more harshly, by a host of GOP surrogates—attacks portraying the Democratic nominee as weak on defense, soft on crime, unpatriotic, in hock to black voters and in favor of expanded gay and lesbian rights—meshes with two long-range Republican objectives:

- To reinstate and soldify the image of the Democratic Party as a collection of reviled "liberal" special interests and to cripple Dukakis' initial success in resurrecting support for the Democratic Party and his candidacy. Poll data suggest that this part of the Republican strategy has been partially successful, at least so far.
- To convert the 1988 presidential campaign into a battleground with the Democratic Party on the defensive over a set of social issues designed to encourage, if not force, a broad-scale realignment of the presidential electorate in favor of the Republicans, strengthening the GOP gains of the Reagan years. The success of this part of the Republican strategy will not be determined until Nov. 8.

Lee Atwater, manager of the Bush campaign, argues: "One of the ongoing goals is to establish a Sun Belt political base that will serve every Republican candidate to the year 2000. If George Bush wins the South, that will be three consecutive back-to-back victories and I am convinced that the South will go Republican for the rest of this century. National defense and all the value issues that are being discussed—law and order, taxes—they are big in the South."

Atwater, Bush pollster Robert Teeter and other key figures in the campaign all say that as long as the polls show a close race between Bush

Source: *The Washington Post*, October 2, 1988: C1, 4. Reprinted by permission of *The Washington Post*.

and Dukakis, their first priority is the election of Bush, and broader partisan advancement will remain secondary unless Bush pulls out to a decisive lead.

But—in direct contrast to the Dukakis staff—the Bush organization is dominated from top to bottom with men and women with extensive experience not only in electing individual candidates, but in Republican party-building strategies. Many key Bush campaign staffers—such as Lanny Griffith, James Wray, Norman Cummings, Jay Morgan, Jim Shearer, Bill Lacy, Ron Kaufman and Haley Barbour—have professional backgrounds in Republican state parties or as regional operatives for the Republican National Committee.

The larger partisan goals underlying the broad-brush negative campaign against Dukakis grow out of more than two decades of increasing Republican expertise in winning elections, winning in part through the selection of issues that divide the once-dominant Democratic coalition. Bush's attempts to link Dukakis to ACLU opposition to certain anti-pornography laws and to prayer in the schools provide ideal "wedge issues" to encourage moderate-to-conservative Democrats to abandon their party, said Chris Henick, the RNC's southern political director.

Wedge issues fit easily into a negative campaign strategy. "When I first got into [politics]," Atwater said in a 1985 interview, well before the current presidential campaign had begun, "I just stumbled across the fact that candidates who went into an election with negatives higher than 30 or 40 points just inevitably lost." It was this discovery early in Atwater's career—running South Carolina campaigns during the years that the southern Democratic party was under siege by the GOP—that led to Atwater's specialty: "Driving up the opposition's negatives."

This year, the Democratic party has gone to great pains to disassociate itself from the left/activist legacy of the 1960s and 1970s, nominating in Dukakis a candidate who had pointedly adopted pro-business stands and who conveys a commitment to culturally conservative values in the conduct of his own life. The architects of the Bush campaign were initially confronted with an electorate in which a large segment appeared prepared, from early poll data, to restore its faith in the Democratic Party after 20 years of deep mistrust.

To counter this, the Bush campaign mounted a series of attacks designed to revive the liberal liabilities of both Dukakis and his party. Bush himself outlined a part of this strategy at a rally last week in Hampton, Ga., expanding on a theme he had used a week ago in the debate with Dukakis. Stressing that his opponent is running a party controlled by "national Democrats," Bush told the audience. "To wrap up that Democratic nomination, he had to stay where he's been in his entire political life, and that's on the left side of things."

In seeking to break moderate and conservative Democrats away from the "national" Democratic party, Bush said, "I'm from Texas, I know the Democratic Party of Texas, and it ain't way out in left field. I know

Democrats in Georgia, and I don't think of them as way out in left field." Bush's distinction between the local southern Democratic state parties and the national party was designed to buttress the Republican claim that forces in the Democratic presidential selection process have pushed the party far to the left of the general electorate.

This wedge-driving strategy coincides with an effort to push up the negatives of the Democratic nominee himself. This undertaking was immeasurably aided when rumors of unknown origin—later proven false—surfaced that Dukakis had received psychiatric help, rumors that reached the front pages when President Reagan referred to Dukakis as an "invalid." The brief controversy "generated the idea that there might be some risk to Dukakis before much of the public had any real idea of who he is," a Dukakis aide acknowledged.

At a time when the public is seeking a forceful leader equipped to address the deficit, the trade imbalance and a rapidly changing job marketplace, the Republican strategy has been to firmly place Dukakis in the lineage of a series of unsuccessful, and in many ways discredited, Democratic candidates including George S. McGovern, Jimmy Carter and Walter F. Mondale.

"Our goal is to Mondalize him, Carterize him and McGovernize him," one Republican southern operative said.

For the architects of the Bush campaign, the negative attacks on Dukakis have involved an extremely subtle ideological balancing act. In the main, Bush's criticisms have been launched from the political right: Dukakis "is opposed to every new weapons system since the slingshot," "He clearly wants to raise taxes," "he is a card-carrying member of the ACLU."

At the same time, however, a key element of the Bush campaign strategy has been an attempt to place Bush in a position where he has one foot firmly in the conservative camp on such issues as abortion, gun control, the death penalty and national defense, and the other planted in terrain more closely identified with traditional liberalism.

The overall effectiveness of this exceptional combination of styles, ideologies and strategies remains untested as the general election approaches, but the mix has been critically important to the holding together of an enlarged Republican core constituency that is far more diverse than it was as recently as 1980: To the base of traditional Republicans have been added Christian fundamentalists, a significant block of young voters, many white southerners who have completed their break with the Democratic Party and fluctuating percentages of northern white working class and ethnic voters.

Bush's move to the left on such issues as child care, the environment and the minimum wage is geared to maintaining the allegiance of those voters whose leanings toward the GOP are fragile. The appeal is encapsulated in Bush's call for a "gentler and kinder" government to follow up on the laissez-faire Reagan years.

GOP strategists consider this election crucial to their base-building strategy. "Among voters in their early and mid-twenties, there is now a substantial majority who have never voted for a Democratic president. If we can get them to vote Republican once again in 1988, we have the chance to turn them into voters who will instinctively look first to the Republican candidate," a Bush strategist said.

At the state level, particularly in the South but also in the West, there has been far less ideological ambiguity in the Republican attack on Dukakis, as the thrust has been overwhelmingly from the right. The state-level attacks also point toward the continued importance of race as a "wedge" issue dividing the Democratic coalition, and the hostility among many whites toward Jesse Jackson.

In Georgia, a GOP brochure contends that Dukakis "supports allowing homosexual couples to adopt children." (In fact, Dukakis angered leaders of the Massachusetts gay community by endorsing state regulations that effectively prevent homosexuals from becoming foster parents.)

A letter put out by the California Republican Party asks "why is it so urgent that you decide now?... Here are two [reasons]:" Two photographs are displayed, on the one side, Bush standing next to Reagan, on the other, Jesse Jackson towering over Dukakis. "If [Dukakis] is elected to the White House, Jesse Jackson is sure to be swept into power on his coattails." Displayed on the next page are "two more reasons" to support the GOP: photographs of Republican Gov. George Deukmejian as one and Willie Brown, the black speaker of the California Assembly as the alternative.

A "crime quiz" spot, first aired regionally and now nationally, shows a smirking, darkly-lit Dukakis while the voice-over suggests that he, unlike the smiling George Bush also portrayed, is soft on drugs and crime. The Bush campaign is expected to release other negative ads, already "in the can," as the election nears.

In the past months, Bush and his team of advisers have succeeded in driving up Dukakis' negatives into the range that Atwater considers likely to lead to Republican victory....

For Bush, the meshing of seemingly contradictory campaign images—one, the environmentalist who supports federal money for child care, expanded federal aid to education and a boosted minimum wage, the other, the flag-waving hawk leading supporters in the Pledge of Allegiance—has worked to improve his prospects significantly. The broad attack on Dukakis' patriotic values has been a major factor in the collapse of support for the Democratic nominee in the South, according to officials of both campaigns.

At the same time, according to Dukakis aides, Bush's highly publicized tour of the heavily polluted Boston Harbor and his proposal to establish a $1,000 child-care tax credit for lower-income families have both worked to weaken Dukakis' command over two traditionally Democratic issues.

While the earlier ideological attacks on Dukakis appear to have been effective, particularly in the South, most recently, both Bush and his running mate, Sen. Dan Quayle (R-Ind.) have shifted to a full-fledged assault on a centerpiece of the Dukakis campaign: the claim of the Massachusetts governor that his administration helped significantly to produce an economic "miracle" in his state. This approach will test whether a broad-brush attack that includes a number of inaccuracies and distortions—charges with respect to personal income, bankruptcies and state debt that appear to be in contradiction to official statistics—will be effective or, as Dukakis aides hope, will work to cast doubt on future Bush claims.

Even if this approach ultimately offends some voters, data from polls conducted over the past months suggest that the attacks have successfully weakened Dukakis' candidacy on a number of fronts.

Over the past five months, for example, Washington Post-ABC polls have found that the percentage of people who believe Dukakis would be better than Bush at holding taxes down has dropped from 39 to 31 percent, that those who believe he would provide stronger leadership has dropped from 48 to 40 percent, and that those who believe he would maintain higher ethical and moral standards has dropped from 49 to 40 percent, while Bush has gone up in each of these categories.

Less scientific, anecdotal evidence from Washington Post-sponsored focus groups and door-to-door interviews reinforce the case that the Bush campaign's strategy has been effective.

Despite the fact, for example, that the Reagan-Bush administration received extensive critical publicity on its environmental policies—particularly during the first term when enormous attention was focused on Interior Secretary James Watt and EPA Director Anne Burford, as well as the regulatory rollback efforts of a White House task force chaired by Bush—recent interviews with voters found much more environmental criticism of Dukakis. The voter criticism was based almost entirely on Bush's well-promoted charge that Dukakis is responsible for Boston Harbor's pollution.

The negative barrage has been only one part of the Bush drive in which the architects and planners of the vice president's bid have demonstrated exceptional talents in moving their candidate from a position far behind in the polls to an even position or perhaps a modest edge. This shift, in turn, suggested that the GOP has developed a cadre of professionals equipped to take a candidate—even one like Bush, who carried, as many of his own supporters acknowledge, a heavy burden of liability—and to use him to strengthen the drive toward Republican primacy.

Mudslinging through Political Mail

ANDREW ROSENTHAL

How does a presidential campaign make a personalized appeal to millions of voters? Knocking on doors and calling on the telephone require a huge number of well-trained volunteers to be successful. A direct mail campaign does not. New York Times reporter Andrew Rosenthal reveals how both Democrats and Republicans took advantage of modern technology, combining computerized lists of voters with slick political appeals to target a message to millions of people who they hoped would be potential supporters. His article indicates the magnitude of this effort, the gimmicks that were used, and the extent to which they were tailored to specific audiences.

A pamphlet distributed in Michigan put Senator Dan Quayle of Indiana into a sort of political rogues' gallery with Ayatollah Ruhollah Khomeini of Iran and Gen. Manuel Antonio Noriega of Panama.

The Republicans in Ohio countered with a political flier for voters of East European heritage that showed Vice President Bush shaking hands with Pope John Paul II and Lech Walesa, the Polish labor leader.

A leaflet from a labor organization showing an unflattering picture of Mr. Bush asked: "Would you want your sister to date this guy?"

And a letter on Vice-Presidential stationery, with Mr. Bush's signature, told voters that Gov. Michael S. Dukakis had "turned loose first-degree murderers on unsupervised weekend parole" even after one of them "terrorized a Maryland couple."

POLITICAL JUNK MAIL

In a Presidential campaign noted for its tough speeches, emotional appeals and negative television commercials, some of the harshest attacks and the most well-honed messages have been made through "direct mail," the political version of junk mail.

Specialists in direct mail say more of it than ever has been sent out this year. By Election Day next Tuesday the voters will have received tens of millions of letters and leaflets from candidates and from the opponents and supporters of ballot initiatives.

The bulk of these are fund-raising appeals. But political campaigns also use the mail to promote a candidate or a ballot referendum and, increasingly, to attack the opposition.

In practice, most political brochures are not created or paid for by the Presidential candidates. But both Mr. Bush and Mr. Dukakis have accused each other of encouraging mudslinging through the mail, and direct mail has been at the center of the argument over negative campaigning this year.

There is no dispute over the effectiveness of such mail, which Larry Sabato, the author of several books on modern campaign techniques, calls "the silent killer."

Both parties have raised tens of millions of dollars through the mail. By Election Day the Republicans alone plan to send political mail to 46 million households, with messages carefully tailored for recipients who are selected by computers sorting long mailing lists.

In Ohio, the Republican Party will have sent out four million pieces of mail by the end of this week; every Republican in the state can count on getting at least three different letters. For elderly people and members of certain ethnic groups, such as Polish or Latvian, the number could be as high as five or six. And that's just from the Republicans.

"There's a lot more mail this year than at any other time I can remember," said Richard Viguerie, a leading Republican mail consultant. "Direct mail is a sleeping giant in American politics, and each Presidential year it just stirs a bit. This time it's moving about."

A VARIETY OF GIMMICKS

Direct mailers use every conceivable gimmick to avoid having voters toss their literature unopened into the wastebasket. Political fliers have been disguised as jury summonses, utility bills and Social Security checks. For a California contest over no-fault insurance, voters got leaflets in envelopes that looked like renewal notices from their own insurance agents.

Mr. Viguerie says most political mail is positive and fair. But this year it has been the negative material that has got the attention.

Those who work in or study political mail agree that it is the most effective instrument for making an especially tough attack, as letters can be sent to audiences that will be the most receptive and not to those who might be offended.

The Maryland Republican Party, for example, sent letters to thousands of conservative married couples suggesting that rapists and murderers would invade American homes if Mr. Dukakis became President. And the South Dakota Democratic Party mailed a flier to sportsmen and hunters saying Mr. Bush was "blowing smoke" on gun control.

IT'S DIFFICULT TO DETECT

Mail is also less easily detected; the first complaints about the Maryland letter and the first news articles about it came six weeks after the flier was mailed.

Like other brochures not produced by the Presidential campaigns themselves, the Maryland letter had a line explaining who paid for it. It was signed by Daniel E. Fleming, the state Republican chairman.

But such disclaimers often are in small print, and some analysts suggest that voters do not always get the message.

"The distinction between a party or a candidate is not germane to most people," said Michael Traugott of the Gallup Organization. "A lot of this can't be linked directly to the candidate, but they certainly are collateral messages, just exaggerated or taken to extremes."

The Bush campaign has disavowed the Maryland letter, along with one like it in Illinois. The Dukakis campaign has said it does not control groups that produced brochures in which a picture of Mr. Bush's running mate, Senator Quayle, appears next to photographs of Ayatollah Khomeini and General Noriega and called them all the Vice President's friends.

Still, the literature springs from the themes the candidates themselves have been sounding.

Mr. Fleming said neither the Republican National Committee nor the Bush campaign helped him draft his letter, nor did they approve it. But he said he felt he was following the lead of the committee. He also used material from a videotape on the Massachusetts furlough system and a book on Mr. Dukakis's record that were distributed by the Republican National Committee.

Although the Bush campaign's television advertising never mentions the Horton case, Mr. Bush talks about Mr. Horton on the stump. The Vice President also included the murderer's name in a party fund-raising letter written on official stationery and sent to hundreds of thousands of homes in August.

Similarly, the Democrats have provided state parties with "fact sheets," position papers and other research that stress the Iran-contra scandal and the Reagan Administration's relationship with General Noriega as issues that can be used against the Republicans.

"I think it is probably technically correct when the campaigns say, "We didn't direct that, we didn't authorize that, we didn't know about that," said Douglas Bailey, a Republican consultant who is not affiliated with the Bush campaign.

"But there's a kind of communication that is quite clear on both sides as to what the major themes are," he continued. "When there are major efforts by the state parties, it is almost always their interpretation of what they believe they've been told to do directly or indirectly."

Democrats Adopt GOP "Ground War" Tactics

THOMAS B. EDSALL

Computer-based technology has affected the conduct of contemporary campaigns. Although the Republicans were the first party to employ this technology on a large scale, the Democrats have also begun to use it. Thomas Edsall describes how both parties employed these methods to their advantage in 1988, combining the techniques of modern campaigning with the know-how of past elections to identify potential supporters.

Strategists for both the Democrats and Republicans are quietly preparing for the 1980s version of old-fashioned ward and precinct politics.

It will be a trench warfare combination of traditional and high technology voter mobilization. Known as the "ground war," it promises to be at least as tough and negative as the media competition.

The GOP is gearing up to use increasingly sophisticated mechanisms to drive home a hard-line ideological message, and the Democratic Party, for the first time, has taken some of the steps required to do battle in the world of computerized voter lists, targeted direct mail and phone banks...

The ground-war campaign involves highly complex techniques to identify and turn out firm supporters, to mobilize volunteers, to locate swing voters and swing precincts. After the "targets" are identified, the organizations then conduct intensive "persuasion" efforts through mail, phone and personal contact. The campaign also will try to locate pools of potentially sympathetic unregistered voters.

The efforts will be run through state Republican and Democratic parties, although both the Bush and Dukakis campaigns have moved former staffers over to the RNC and DNC to oversee the drives. . . .

Some GOP tacticians are exploring innovative use of "negative" phone banks, a tactic the GOP learned about the hard way in 1986 when unions bombarded voters with phone calls portraying Republican candidates as anti-Social Security.

An example of how Republicans plan to put forward their ideological approach is a brochure the Georgia Republican Party plans to mail.

Entitled "The Platform They Don't Want You to See," the brochure has a picture of Sen. Edward M. Kennedy (D-Mass.) holding Dukakis' arm up in a victory sign, and contains a set of allegations of mixed accuracy. It correctly lists Dukakis' opposition to the death penalty and to a number of weapons systems. It also contains such [inaccurate] charges as: Dukakis "supports allowing homosexual couples to adopt children" and that he "opposed all attempts in 10 years to cut taxes in Massachusetts." . . .

The Republicans are considerably ahead of the Democrats in terms of technology and planning. Since 1980, the RNC and local Republican parties have been building well-defined voter-list data bases that have subcategories such as Democrats who voted for Reagan in 1984, citizens with surnames identifying Eastern European or Hispanic descent, voters in high-growth counties, potentially conservative voters in communities that cast high percentages of the vote for Sen. Albert Gore Jr. (D-Tenn.) on "Super Tuesday" March 8, and voters in states without partisan registration who participated in the Republican presidential primary.

This information permits the GOP to identify large blocs who can generally be relied upon to vote for Republican candidates in November and need encouragement only to get to the polls. In such nonparty registration states as Mississippi and Texas, for example, the 159,279 and 986,418 voters who cast ballots respectively in the two states' GOP primaries provide a core list of "automatics."

From other voter breakdowns, key target groups are first queried through phone banks to determine their leanings. Questions may touch on their views on such issues as gun control, judicial restraint and abortion.

Pinpointing target groups is far easier in urban areas—where it is relatively simple to eliminate heavily Democratic precincts, many of which are black and Hispanic—than in rural areas, where "you can't do things like pulling out the upper-middle income white precincts," one southern GOP strategist said. Republicans are targeting precincts that voted heavily for Gore because they are believed to contain conservative Democrats who "parked" their primary votes with Gore, but could be ready to vote for a Republican in November.

Many of these voters will first be surveyed through regional phone banks run by a New York firm called Campaign Technology. "Persuadables"—those who say they are undecided or, even if they lean to Dukakis, may hold opposing views to the candidate on an issue like gun control—will then receive four or more personalized mailings, and continuing phone calls, the frequency of which will vary according to different regional and state strategies.

While the GOP is far ahead on technology, the Democratic National Committee under Chairman Paul G. Kirk Jr. has taken a series of steps to catch up. The DNC has partially financed state efforts to build computerized voter lists and hired a network of Democratic consultants to go into 35 "battleground" states and put together detailed general election plans, using many of the identification, targeting and persuasion techniques employed by the GOP.

"We have a long way to go, but I have to say that I went into some of these states and was given the kind of basic information to start with that we didn't even come near to having at the end of the campaign [in 1984]," one of the Democratic consultants said. "There were places with Mondale that in the final three weeks of the campaign we were working out of phone books. The stuff they have now is light years from where we were." . . .

In addition, the DNC program has received extensive support from precinct-targeting techniques developed by the National Committee for an Effective Congress, which, like the RNC, is searching to find swing precincts and "Reagan Democrats"—those who backed Reagan in 1984 but supported Democrats for lower offices.

The emergence of Reagan Democrats—often concentrated in once firmly Democratic, white, blue-collar precincts—has been a major reason the Democratic Party has developed sophisticated voter identification, lists and persuasion techniques.

In the past, the Democratic Party has not felt the need to develop these techniques because it could simply target large blocs of voters for get-out-the-vote drives, secure in the belief that 60 percent or more of them would vote Democratic. The loss of some of the traditional elements of the Democratic coalition has, in effect, forced the Democrats to adopt strategies paralleling those used by the GOP, which since the 1930s has been forced to attempt to slice out segments of Democratic voting blocs to put together a majority.

Incumbency's Winning Ways

TOM KENWORTHY

An important instrument for a democratic society, elections provide a means for the people to decide who their public officials will be and to hold those officials accountable for their actions. For elections to fulfill this critical function, challengers must have a reasonable opportunity to defeat those in power. In recent years, this opportunity has not often been present. With a reelection rate exceeding 95 percent, members of the Congress seem almost invulnerable. Why is this? Washington Post reporter Tom Kenworthy reveals the advantages that incumbents have and how they utilize them to stay in office.

How does a first-term Democrat who won his House seat by 3,000 votes in a traditionally Republican district use his incumbency to assure his reelection? If you followed Rep. Peter Hoagland (D-Neb.) around his district during last month's congressional recess, you would count the ways.

Most of Hoagland's activities were "nonpolitical." Only two events on Hoagland's packed schedule for the week were obviously political gatherings. But during that week, Hoagland penetrated virtually every home in Nebraska's 2nd Congressional District with messages that have helped him achieve an enviably strong position at the outset of his first reelection year.

Hoagland was featured dozens of times on local television and radio news programs and in the pages of the Omaha World-Herald and smaller newspapers throughout his district. His name identification was reinforced with a blizzard of post cards, all sent at government expense to the vast majority of the 239,000 households in his district announcing a series of town meetings he held during his trip. And he cultivated powerful groups like the local banking community that will serve as a source of campaign funds in his reelection drive.

Hoagland, in short, spent the February congressional recess as many of his House colleagues did. In the course of representing his constituents, he also was harvesting the plentiful fruits of incumbency and reaping the benefits of an increasingly closed system that has grown largely impervious to outside challengers. In the last two election cycles, more than 98 percent of House incumbents who sought reelection have won. Hoagland, who ran for an open seat, faced no incumbent in his 1988 election.

Even before he took office, Hoagland knew he would be at the top of the GOP's list of targeted races in 1990, and Republican officials have gone to extraordinary lengths to insure he has a tough reelection battle.

Source: *The Washington Post*, March 12, 1990: A1 Reprinted by permission of *The Washington Post*.

Shortly after Hoagland returned to Washington from the February recess, National Republican Congressional Committee co-chairman Edward J. Rollins corralled a challenger he had been chasing for some time. Ron Staskiewicz, a Republican who serves as county prosecutor for Douglas County—which includes Omaha and covers 82 percent of the congressional district—agreed to run for the House instead of challenging Sen. J. James Exon (D-Neb.).

Officials at the Democratic Congressional Campaign Committee (DCCC) regard Staskiewicz as a more formidable opponent for Hoagland than Ally Midler, a former Senate aide who also is seeking the GOP nomination. But they also believe that Hoagland has provided a textbook example of how a freshman can use the many tools at his disposal to solidify his hold on a marginal district.

"He's done everything right," said one DCCC staffer.

Because members of Congress tend to be most vulnerable in their first reelection contest, the DCCC lavishes attention on the party's freshmen, including a series of special seminars on how to get reelected. The object is to insure that members tailor their legislative behavior to their political needs, that the political campaigns that got them to Washington essentially continue unabated through their first terms and that members make full use of the enormous resources provided by the taxpayers.

Hoagland has done all of those things about as well as the DCCC had hoped he would.

As a member of the banking committee, Hoagland spent much of his first year in Congress concentrating on one of the 101st Congress's most important issues: the massive bailout of the savings and loan industry. The legislation had great importance in Omaha, a regional financial center where several savings institutions have collapsed and where commercial banking interests have considerable political clout.

By getting an amendment to the savings and loan bill that toughens regulation of credit unions, Hoagland scored points with constituents affected by the fraud-driven collapse of a local credit union. In opposing the bill on final passage because it put much of the bailout's cost off budget, he enhanced his credentials as a fiscal conservative. And by insisting on stiff capital standards for thrifts, he boosted his relations with commercial bankers.

As he does on a regular basis, Hoagland had lunch during the February recess with several dozen bankers, including the president of the American Bankers Association, who is a Nebraskan. Though Hoagland is by no means an automatic vote for the banks, his accessibility and attention to their concerns is paying dividends: The bankers association already has contributed $10,000 to his reelection campaign, and Hoagland can count on many thousands more in contributions from other banking political action committees (PACs) and individual bankers.

"He's not 100 percent with our positions," said Nebraska Bankers Association President James F. Nissen, "but he's very fair and reasonable." In 1988, the bankers all but ignored Hoagland's candidacy.

If Hoagland has earned a reputation in Congress as a serious, diligent and effective legislator—"straight as an arrow and does his homework," said Banking, Finance and Urban Affairs Committee Chairman Henry B. Gonzalez (D-Tex.) in a profile in the trade publication American Banker— he has been equally assiduous in melding his official duties with the political requirements of a tough reelection battle.

It was no accident, for example, that Hoagland chose as his chief Washington aide an old friend who had served recently as a top field operative for the DCCC. Nor has much been left to chance with the three key elements to his reelection: media, money and mail.

All three came into play during Hoagland's February recess trip to his district, a visit that illustrated the often blurred lines between the work a House member does to represent his district and the ongoing effort to get reelected. As is often the case, good representation by Hoagland also translates into good politics.

Planning for Hoagland's trip began weeks in advance, as staffers set up a schedule to provide what one called a series of "news bursts"—a string of events that would keep Hoagland almost constantly in the media during his visit. It was a more intensive version of the media strategy he follows in Washington, where weekly long-distance news conferences with Omaha radio stations and satellite linkups with Omaha television network affiliates have insured he gets regular exposure.

On his second day in the district, for example, Hoagland traveled to the State Capitol in Lincoln, where he spent eight years in the legislature. As cosponsor of national legislation to set up boot camps for drug offenders, Hoagland testified on behalf of similar state legislation before the legislature's Judiciary Committee that he used to chair. He also appeared at a news conference with Sarah Brady touting legislation for a waiting period for handgun purchases. Both events got him on television and radio and into the newspapers.

During his week at home, Hoagland also held a series of 10 town meetings, a staple of congressional life and a model of good government. Hoagland's meetings were typical of the genre: free-wheeling discussions with hundreds of constituents on issues great and small during which voters can communicate directly with their congressman and the congressman, in turn, can take the pulse of his district.

Hoagland, who appears to genuinely enjoy these quarterly exchanges, said town meetings give constituents "a feeling I honestly care about their views and that I am willing to discuss the issues with them."

But if town meetings constitute representative government at its best, they also permit members of Congress to unleash one of the most powerful weapons in their arsenal: mail.

In the days before Hoagland arrived back in Omaha, nearly a quarter million postcards flooded his district inviting second district residents to the town meetings. The postcards were more than invitations; they linked Hoagland's name to the war on drugs, a critical issue in a city beset with drug-related gang violence where there were almost a dozen drive-by shootings in the 10 days before his visit.

The postcards make up one part of a larger mail strategy in which Hoagland has sent more than two million pieces of mail to his district since his election, much of it narrowly targeted to particular groups of voters such as senior citizens, all of it financed by the government through the franking privilege, which lets members send mail home for free.

Mail, said Hoagland, represents "the confluence of good politics and good government. The untold story of the franking issue is that people really like to be informed."

As for the good politics, Hoagland's approval rating in World-Herald polls has gone from 38 percent in the second month of his first term to 62 percent last December.

My Life as a Congressional Candidate

MARK G. MICHAELSEN

Challengers often face overwhelming odds when taking on an incumbent. Their experiences are frequently frustrating. One-time congressional candidate Mark Michaelsen describes the dreams he had and the nightmares he experienced in his quest for election to Congress. Michaelsen's engaging tale suggests why many qualified individuals do not run, and why the movement to limit the number of legislative terms of office has gained widespread backing.

It was quite late and I was in bed, just drifting off to sleep, when the telephone rang. The caller identified herself as working for the *New Republic*.

I snapped to attention. The *New Republic*! As the Republican candidate for Congress in Wisconsin's Seventh District in 1984, I was accustomed to late-night calls from journalists, usually wire-service reporters racing to meet a deadline. But never had I received a call from such an important publication.

I told her what a fine magazine I thought the *New Republic* was and how much I had enjoyed a recent article on Sandinista human rights abuses. At the same time, my mind raced ahead: How did I come to their attention? Was it my stand on family issues or defense? The quixotic campaign of a 26-year-old neophyte against an entrenched seven-term liberal incumbent Democrat? My skillful exploitation of the resentment of northern Wisconsin sportsmen toward an agreement to let American Indians ignore fish and game laws?

What would the article say, I wondered. Would it be favorable or unfavorable? It didn't really matter. Regardless of tone, a *New Republic* article mentioning my candidacy would surely unlock a torrent of political action committee contributions, instantly transforming my campaign from amateur shoestring effort to formidable, well-financed juggernaut. Big Mo was just around the corner; I could taste it.

What could I do for the caller, I asked.

"We've noticed we haven't received your subscription renewal," she said. "If this is just an oversight, we'll be happy to continue sending you the *New Republic* until we receive your check."

My dreams popped like a big soap bubble. This wasn't a reporter, it was a telephone solicitor!

On election night, 1984, I was blown out by incumbent Rep. David R. Obey, who received 61 percent of the vote. That same night, President Ronald Reagan trounced Walter Mondale in one of history's great landslides. In Wisconsin's Seventh Congressional District, Reagan beat Mondale 53 percent to 46 percent. So much for coattails.

The obvious question is *why*. Why would a 26-year-old kid with no name identification challenge the formidable 49-year-old chairman of the Joint Economic Committee, who had served in Congress since 1969, when former Rep. Melvin R. Laird vacated the seat to become Nixon's defense secretary?

The answer: almost by accident. I didn't mean to be the candidate. A native of central Wisconsin, I was working at Hillsdale College in Michigan in early 1984, when I learned that Wisconsin state senator Walter John Chilsen was mulling a run against Obey. Obey had edged the former senate majority leader in the 1969 special election to fill Laird's seat. There had been no rematch. I let Chilsen know that I was interested in helping him oust Obey. He put me in touch with his Washington consultant, who suggested I become campaign finance director.

I pored over district vote totals and read whatever I could find about district demographics, fund-raising, issues, Obey's voting record, and public speaking. It would be tough, but with a strong coattail effect from Reagan's re-election, a ton of money spent on advertising and mail, and a little bit of luck, Chilsen could win in November. I was excited by the possibilities.

When Chilsen opted not to vacate a safe seat in the state senate to challenge Obey, I was disappointed. Election after election, Seventh District Republicans had fielded token challengers with little financial support—retired vacuum cleaner salesmen, bankrupt mobile-home moguls, a fellow named Burger who campaigned wearing a chef's hat and a white apron, and so on. None had received more than 38 percent of the vote.

I stepped forward. I had the energy, the knowledge of national issues, the speaking skills, and the fund-raising prowess to be the candidate. I had a deep love for, and knowledge of, the towns and cities, forests and dairy farms of the Wisconsin Seventh District, which sprawls across all or part of eighteen of the state's central and northwest counties. I cared deeply about America's future and was a dedicated conservative. I had some connections in the conservative movement in Washington. Those were my strengths.

But I had weaknesses, too. Almost no one outside my hometown had ever heard of me. I didn't hold public office. I wasn't rich. I hadn't lived in Wisconsin for four years. And my name was really hard to pronounce, an alliterative tongue-twister which confounded broadcasters, statesmen, and voters.

I figured these weaknesses could be overcome with an advertising campaign which started with a spot where people mispronounced my name, perhaps ending with a tag line such as "It doesn't matter how you say it. Mark Michaelsen for Congress." With name identification established, spots clobbering the incumbent on issues would follow. The media campaign would end with warm, sentimental spots about shared values and dreams for a better future, loaded up with pretty Wisconsin pictures: "It's morning again in north-central Wisconsin."

With pride and gratitude, I accepted the unanimous endorsement of Seventh District Republicans. On the advice of Chilsen's consultant, I procured a promise from district Republican leaders to raise a hefty amount of startup cash. That money would be necessary to hire a talented campaign manager and finance director, and to get started raising big money and enlisting an army of volunteers for what would be the strongest challenge ever to Obey. I packed my belongings in a U-Haul trailer to head home for Wisconsin.

The months flew by, an endless stream of parades, speeches, fundraisers, and county fairs. Cows were admired, good deeds were praised, and hands were shaken.

"I'm Mark Michaelsen," I said, dratting the troublesome moniker, and offering a handshake. "I want to work for you in Washington."

"You've got an uphill road ahead of you," nodded the object of my greeting.

"I'm Mark Michaelsen," I said, extending my hand. "I want to be your congressman."

"Ah, you've got a tough row to hoe," observed my new acquaintance.

Maybe it was the Ogema Christman Tree Festival. Or the Spooner Rodeo. Or the Central Wisconsin State Fair.

"I'm Mark Michaelsen." I said, smiling and proffering my callused mitt. "I'm running against Dave Obey."

"You've got a tough, uphill road to hoe," said the voter.

Exactly! This unintentional mixed metaphor perfectly described my plight. Imagine a man using a garden implement to try to dislodge asphalt from a road running almost straight uphill, like one of Hercules's mythological labors. That was me.

The money trickled, not poured, in. The promised Republican cash never materialized. The PACs, seeing no "viability" (their word for a snowball's chance in hell) in my election, weren't about to invest in my race. I faced the American campaign Catch 22: I couldn't raise money until I showed momentum, I couldn't show momentum until I raised money.

Top consultants were hired, then fired. My campaign manager quit; he said he was homesick for Chicago. And, worst of all, my opponent ignored me—ignored my stinging press releases, critical of his votes on school prayer, national security, and federal spending; ignored my call for debates throughout the district; ignored my very existence as a candidate.

At least I had the van.

A small group of hometown supporters had purchased an aging Ford Econoline, painted it red, white, and blue, and outfitted it with a bed and desk. But most impressive was the public address system, which allowed me to blare Sousa marches at deafening volumes while I greeted voters along parade routes.

One day I was late for an interview at a television station in one of the district's remote cities and I couldn't find a place to park. Desperate, I left the van in a parking ramp near the studio. After the interview, I was leaving the ramp when I noticed how low the ceiling was getting. Suddenly I heard a sickening crunch. My roof-mounted loudspeakers crashed to the ground.

I retrieved them and continued my progress toward the exit. Headroom continued to shrink. Twenty feet from the exit the van's roof began to scrape on the concrete ceiling. I had to let nearly all the air out of the tires to finally escape. Behind me, a dozen cars were lined up, their egress blocked by my embarrassing plight.

What kind of idiot was causing their delay, I could feel them wondering. "Michaelsen for Congress," answered my van in eight-inch letters.

As the grand finale to a candidate training school sponsored by the National Republican Congressional Committee, would-be GOP congressmen were herded into the Gold Room of the White House to be photographed with the President and Vice President.

I was somewhat nervous and tongue-tied when I met the Leader of the Free World. I should have said, "Mr. President, dairy farmers of northern Wisconsin are concerned about your agriculture policy" or implored him to come campaign on my behalf. Instead, I mumbled something about having worked for Hillsdale, which he had visited and praised. President Reagan grinned genially, and we sat. He hadn't heard a word; I'd spoken in his bad ear.

As we sat in the ornate chairs by the fireplace, cameras whirring, he cocked his head and said, "Wisconsin. That's just north of my old stomping ground in Illinois." He leaned forward and put his hand on the arm of my chair. He was a nice man.

We shook hands and I left, to be replaced by another candidate. I was already kicking myself for being such a boob with President Reagan. I fared better with the Vice President.

I'd met George Bush twice before, during the 1980 Wisconsin presidential primary. I inquired about one of his sons whom I'd also met in 1980. He became quite animated. His son and daughter-in-law were expecting their first child any day.

Newcomers to my current office see my pictures with Ronald Reagan and George Bush and assume the photographs are clever forgeries purchased from an arcade.

Election night found me in a local watering hole, appropriately named The End of the Line, watching returns and swilling something strong with a few of my friends. As the returns came in it was clear that I had lost, and lost big. For most of my acquaintances from campaign school, the night would end similarly. That night only thirteen GOP candidates would unseat Democratic opponents despite the avalanche of support for President Reagan at the top of the ticket.

For me, it could have been even worse. Although Obey outspent me nearly five to one, my 92,507 votes were both the highest total and highest percentage of votes cast against Dave Obey since he was elected in 1969.

I won one northern county and lost another by only five votes. I won my hometown by a landslide, but lost my home county. My campaign treasury finished with a slight surplus; I owed no creditors. The worst possible result would have been to amass a huge debt, come very close, and lose; that might have tempted me to run again in 1986. At least now I would never have to wonder what I could have done differently to put me over the top.

7. Mass Media

Candidates need to communicate their messages; parties need to project their appeals and build support for their candidates. Traditionally, personal contact, public rallies, and political literature have been the principal means of reaching voters. In an age of mass media, dominated by television, those are not the only ways or even the most important ones for reaching voters. Today, most people see the campaign in their living rooms, not on the street or at large public gatherings. Candidates speak in a made-for-television language. Their remarks are conveyed in news clips and political advertisements that are carefully crafted to transmit limited information and targeted to achieve maximum effect. Parties also run advertisements to remind the electorate what they stand for and why their nominees should be supported and their opponents should not be.

This revolution in mass communication began with radio in the 1920s. The first national conventions were broadcast live in 1924, and four years later, candidates of both major parties used radio to reach national audiences and spent campaign funds on radio advertising. Franklin Roosevelt, a master of radio, employed it effectively in all his presidential campaigns.

After World War II a new electronic medium emerged. Television quickly became the *modus operandi* for reporting news events such as political campaigns. The number of homes with television sets rose dramatically in the 1950s; by the mid-1960s most Americans claimed to receive most of their news from television and to consider it more believable than any other medium. This revolution in the habits of the American public was not lost on those with messages to sell and appeals to be made—notably commercial advertisers and political candidates. Campaigns have not been the same since.

The changes that have occurred are many and varied. The candidates' personal qualities have become more important. Leadership style has been a primary concern of both those who convey the images and those report on them. In-depth discussions of policy issues have received less attention. Partisan considerations also seem to be less important to both the candidates and to the voters.

Media plans are now a critical component of any campaign strategy. Decisions about how themes are articulated, how events are staged, and what candidates say—and when and how they say it—are made with television in mind. Media consultants are in the inner circle of advisers, and much of the campaign budget goes to pay for production and to buy air time.

As candidates try to affect the coverage they receive, reporters and correspondents affect the campaigns they cover. The reporters' orientation and their news format, what they report and how they report it, influence the strategy and tactics of the candidates, the agenda and debate on the issues, and ultimately the impact of the campaign on the voters.

Most of the campaign coverage is done by commercial media who have a profit motive. Because of this, the people who report the news and those who print it or air it are concerned with the numbers of their readers and viewers. The kinds of stories and the styles of reporting that increase the size of the audience, such as who is winning the horserace or what unexpected event has occurred, are likely to be featured. Drama, conflict, and human interest tend to engage more people more quickly than do learned discussions of policy matters. Candidates know this. They know that their misstatement will be news but cannot be assured that their position paper or formal address will receive as much attention. To increase the likelihood that they will be heard, candidates try to include succinct and captivating language—"sound bites"—in their speeches.

All of this suggests that to some extent the media and the candidates are antagonists and that the campaign is waged between them. But those who cover the campaign are also dependent on information and access that only the candidates and their organizations can provide. In this sense, the media and the candidates are partners in providing information that is critical to a democratic society.

The readings in this chapter reflect the tension inherent in this adversial, yet symbiotic relationship. They show how candidates are using the media, how the media—primarily television—covers the candidates, and indirectly, how all of this affects the electorate.

The first two readings are about campaign advertising. They discuss the styles and content of television advertising, illustrating their discussion with examples from the 1988 presidential campaign. The initial goal for most candidates is name recognition. The early ads attempt to present a distinctive and attractive portrait. Later, candidates work to refine their portraits, while portraying their opponents negatively. The vehicle for doing this is a *spot,* a short advertisement as brief as thirty or sixty seconds or as long as five minutes, that makes a point by creating or reinforcing an image. Edwin Diamond and Adrian Marin describe the use of spots in the 1988 presidential campaign and evaluate the effectiveness of the Bush and Dukakis commercials.

The most effective spots feed on strong emotions, tapping into issues about which people care the most. Fear of crime has been one of those issues. A political action committee that supported George Bush ran an ad in 1988 that touched a responsive cord in many voters. Author

Martin Schram discusses this ad and explains its seemingly powerful effect on voters.

The 1988 presidential campaign was marked by a number of political commercials that accentuated the negative, concentrating on what was undesirable about a particular candidate. These ads left a sour taste in the mouths of many people, including Democrat Michael Dukakis, who was the object of some of them. Dukakis raised the issue of negative advertising in his own advertising, thereby helping to stimulate a debate on the subject. The "op-ed" pieces by journalist Charles Freund and Professor Kathleen Hall Jamieson take opposing sides in this debate, one that is likely to continue for some time.

In addition to conveying their messages and their images directly through advertising, candidates try to influence the kind of news coverage they receive. One of the ways they do this is by carefully staging events and by tailoring their speeches and responses to their audience. The next two readings illustrate some tactics the candidates used to make a point or reinforce an image. Both Michael Oreskes and Kiku Adatto describe the garb in which candidates must dress themselves for modern media campaigns and indicate why good appearances, good lines, and good acting are thought to be essential today.

Finally, Robert Lichter and his associates provide an analysis of the campaign that the public saw on the evening news in 1988. They refute some myths about the content and slant of election news, concluding that the television networks were relatively fair and balanced in their coverage. Moreover, they suggest that skillful media campaigns did make a difference in the coverage that the presidential candidates received.

Spots

EDWIN DIAMOND AND ADRIAN MARIN

Television advertising has changed the substance and style of campaign ap-
peals. The cost of such advertising, the need to keep the attention of viewers,
and the techniques of mass marketing have led campaign media consultants
to rely on short commercials, or spots, to convey an image, present a mes-
sage, or project an appeal. Professor Edwin Diamond, author of a book on
political spots, and his student, Adrian Marin, analyze the use of spots in
the 1988 presidential election. They argue that the Bush campaign effectively
coordinated them into a coherent whole, while the Dukakis campaign did not.

The value of political spots goes up and down from election to election. In
1984, Ronald Reagan and Walter Mondale together spent an estimated $50
million on television advertising in their presidential campaigns—without
changing the electoral balance a dime's worth. A majority of voters loved
Reagan as much in November as they had in January; the money might just
as well have gone to promote Burger King or Alpo.

Campaign '88 was radically different. Four years ago, Reagan's soft-focus
"It's Morning in America" ads—the camera lens supposedly was coated with
petroleum jelly—further lulled an electorate that saw itself as prosperous and
at peace. Mondale, meanwhile, attempted to look "presidential," seldom
raised his voice, and did not disturb the calm. In 1988, with no incumbent
up for reelection, what seemed like a wide-open race to the White House
began when a flurry of Bruce Babbitt ads appeared on Iowa TV in 1987—
so-called early media. Moreover, the spot makers took the coating off the
lens and cast around for new formats, sensing the voters' volatility amid
uncertain economic conditions.

In fact, while 1988 evolved in a different way, the end result was not
much different from that in 1984. The "incumbent," a proponent of peace
and prosperity, won. George Bush did so by conducting *both* campaigns, and
he succeeded in defining both himself (soft-focus, good guy) and Michael
Dukakis (hard-edged, liberal, and coddler of murderers, polluters, and flag
defilers). The measure of his image-engineering abilities was clear. In October 1987, *NEWSWEEK* magazine ran a cover picture of Bush with the title
"The Wimp Factor." In July 1988, Dukakis was leading by seventeen points
in the polls, and embarrassing subjects such as Noriega and Iran-Contra
were still being discussed. By October, *NEWSWEEK* was pondering the
question "Why Is Bush Winning?"

Source: *American Behavioral Scientist* (March/April 1989): 382–388. Copyright 1989 Sage Publications, Inc.. Reprinted by permission of Sage Publications, Inc..

There were three reasons why: The Bush campaign was well organized, its paid and free media were well coordinated, and the "issues"—peace and prosperity—worked for the Republicans. . . .

The campaign hard stuff normally comes only after the obligatory identification, or biography, ads that give the candidate's life story. These ads are the first of the now predictable stages of a political campaign, which we outlined in *The Spot*. This past year, in identifying their clients, the ad makers took a giant step backward to an earlier time: every candidate (and in particular Bush of Andover, Yale, and Kennebunkport, ME) appeared to have sprung from the heartland outfitted by Ralph Lauren.

Bush's true media advantage began with Roger Ailes, 48, a bearded, portly, profane child of the TV age. Ailes normally works out of Ailes Communications, Inc., in Manhattan. For all of 1988 he was Bush's shadow; when the candidate kept calling Ted Koppel "Dan" during a *Nightline* appearance, Ailes popped up just off camera holding the hand-lettered sign "TED." Twenty-one years ago, a slim, clean-shaven Ailes was executive producer of *The Mike Douglas Show*. Richard Nixon, getting ready to run again for president, was a guest on the show; within a year, Ailes was helping produce political television for the "new" Nixon. Ailes has since prospered as a media consultant. In 1984, he worked on the spots produced by Reagan's "Tuesday team."

The Dukakis cast included several acknowledged Madison Avenue stars. One, Scott Miller, 43, did some of the classic work for Coca-Cola when he was with McCann-Erickson in the seventies; another Dukakis media man, Dan Payne, 44, did the single most effective Dukakis ad of the primaries; the flip-flop spot featuring an acrobatic look-alike of Representative Richard Gephardt, then a Democratic front-runner. ("Gephardt" was made to somersault dizzyingly, with the aid of videotape fast-forward and rewind, on both sides of every issue.) The Dukakis people, in turn, reported to a hydra-headed operation that included most of the campaign's various advisers, pollsters, and managers.

The contrasting results of the Bush and Dukakis media efforts were predictable. In the identifying phase of political advertising, the spots tend to be straightforward and positive—"the kind of stuff you can show your mother," as Payne puts it. Both campaigns took the high road in their first spots. Both harvested footage from the candidates' convention speeches. Both featured waving flags, rapt faces, balloon drops, and the candidates' best lines, such as Bush's "I . . . am . . . that . . . man . . . " Both sets of ID spots also showed the candidate close up and well lighted. In particular, the picture selection in the Bush spots was intended to stand in for the human eye and connect the candidate to the home audience: You are there. All of this is standard now; it was revolutionary when Ailes first did it in 1968, the Paleolithic age of political ads.

For all the traditional features, the feel of the Bush and Dukakis productions was decidedly different. The Bush spot by Ailes called "The Future" begins with a close-up of one of Bush's granddaughters running across a field. Of course, we've seen this affecting icon before; children are a favored device of spot makers, a screen on which viewers' feelings about hope, innocence, and vulnerability can be projected. In 1964 Lyndon Johnson's media experts at Doyle Dane Bernbach used a little girl picking daisies to stoke fears of Barry Goldwater's supposed nuclear adventurism. Ken Swope, who worked for Dukakis in the primaries, made a vivid spot with a wide-eyed Latino child to energize George McGovern's short-lived 1984 primary campaign (McGovern was running against U.S. policy in Central America).

In "The Future," the granddaughter runs toward the candidate. Cut to the convention; cut to family scenes; cut to a Bush close-up. "I want a kinder and gentler nation," Bush says. "I hear the quiet people others don't: the ones who raise the families, pay the taxes..." Cut to the granddaughter as she reaches her grandfather and is swept high in his arms. Freeze frame. Graphic on screen: EXPERIENCED LEADERSHIP FOR AMERICA'S FUTURE.

Ailes's ID strategy was open for all to see. He long ago concluded that "people watch TV emotionally." Thus in another Bush spot, poetically titled "The Mission," Ailes seeks to make more humane a man perceived as remote and prissy, and to show a more caring face of Reaganomics (the genial actor didn't always listen, but Bush will...).

The Dukakis campaign, more prosaically, gave its spots such titles as "Results" and "Taking Charge." The ads were businesslike, much in the manner of the candidate himself. "Results" and "Taking Charge" featured graphs and bar charts. The announcer intoned, "In the last four years, Michael Dukakis put 20 percent more cops on the street, five times as many drug offenders behind bars." On screen, the graphic repeats the voice-over: 20 PERCENT MORE COPS. One or two Dukakis spots rose above the flip-chart style of a governor's briefing. "Jimmy" has some of the haunting quality of an Edward Hopper painting. A young man is photographed through the window of a pizza parlor. It's nighttime; the camera looks in as the youth flips a pie. The announcer's voice-over explains that Jimmy "got accepted to college, but his family couldn't afford tuition." Dukakis appears on-screen. Voice-over: "Mike Dukakis wants to help... If a kid like Jimmy has the grades for college, America should find a way to send him..." The spot was supposed to receive major air time on NBC during the Olympics; it didn't. The leadership vacuum and the bureaucratic folly of the Dukakis advertising effort all but guaranteed such mistakes. A well-organized and well-thought-out effort might have helped.

The Dukakis spots were individually "competent," but they didn't add up to a coherent whole. They were isolated, unrelated to what the candidate was saying at his news events. As one of Dukakis's own media people acknowledged, "There's no breakthrough here. We can only work with the organization and themes we're given." Not surprisingly, Dukakis's phase-one advertising did little to stop the candidate's post-convention slide, much less move him forward.

Yet it was still close between Bush and Dukakis in the engagement phase of the campaign. These phase-two ads have to carry some weight; balloons are no longer enough. Studies of voter attitudes confirm the expected about such TV spots: nasty stuff is more memorable than reasoned discourse. Most viewers, to take the most vivid examples, can recall Bush's zinger lines "Read my lips . . . no new taxes," "card-carrying member of the ACLU," and "out of the mainstream." But just as obviously, negative advertising can hurt the attacker as well. Many voters have a sense of fair play and notions of public dignity. They especially do not like to see presidential candidates take the low road. "When the negative stuff begins, the number of undecideds usually goes up," Dan Payne explained to us in September—and he was proved right in October. After Bush's negative ads appeared—for example, the misleading spot about "polluted" Boston Harbor—polls showed voters expressing dislike of both candidates.

The Bush campaign was smart enough to distance itself from the most blatant of the Willie Horton materials. One vehicle that permitted this was the "independence committee." An attack spot on the "crime issue" shows side-by-side photos of a matinee-handsome Bush and a venal-looking Dukakis and says of the Democrat, "He allowed first-degree murderers to have weekend passes from prison." The line meshed with a major Bush theme—Dukakis's "liberalism"—but the nominal sponsor of the spot was a group called Americans for Bush. Under federal campaign law, Americans for Bush was considered separate from the main campaign because its expenditures were made independently. Technically, the main campaign continued to have clean hands. By the end of the campaign the tactic had worked; one in every four voters was able to identify Willie Horton as a black convict who raped a white woman while on a weekend furlough from a Massachusetts prison. Moreover, a *New York Times*/CBS News poll showed that 36 percent of those polled in July thought Dukakis was soft on crime; in October, the figure was 49 percent.

Just as the three phases of TV-spot campaigns tend to be predictable from election to election, so too do the complaints about political advertising. The first concern is that television campaigns have driven up the cost of running for office. Exact figures are hard to come by; clearly though, campaign spending has risen sharply, and television advertising has contributed to that rise. From 1912 to 1952, each national party spent about the same amount of money per vote cast in national elections. Then, with the introduction of television, campaign expenditures skyrocketed. By 1968, the Republican and Democratic committees were spending three times as much per vote as they had sixteen years earlier. Moreover, the share of spending going to television has increased at an even faster rate—and at the expense of other campaign methods. Total political spending (adjusted for inflation) has tripled since 1952, while the amount spent on TV has increased at least fivefold. . . .

A second question concerns the informational value of spots and whether the free media—the coverage in newspapers and magazines and on TV and radio news programs—give enough attention to the campaign. A lot of that free media coverage focuses on who's up and who's down rather than on the issues. When the media do cover substantial matters, they tend to select an issue that is clear-cut, controversial and newsy: Is the candidate for or against Contras, AIDS testing, abortion? On the other hand, the candidates, on their paid media, prefer what Thomas Patterson of Syracuse University calls "diffuse issues": a strong defense or more jobs for the American worker, for example. Still, even a candidate's choice of diffuse issues for ads tells us something about his or her priorities.

Most of all, there is the fear that the "values" of television in general and of the consultants in particular are taking over the political process. Media consultant Tony Schwartz (co-creator of Lyndon Johnson's infamous "Daisy" spot in 1964) remembers when there were "just fifteen or twenty of us." Today, according to John Phillips of Campaign Industry News, perhaps five thousand full-time specialists "make a buck off of campaigns," while another thirty thousand part-timers come in during the "high season." They are working on paid media as well as on the speeches, debates, rallies, and other campaign events that attract free media, because TV is where the voters can be found—ninety-five million Americans watch TV at prime time on any given winter night.

The Making of Willie Horton

MARTIN SCHRAM

*By far the most controversial spot in 1988 was the Willie Horton ad. Focusing
on fear of crime, it contained racial overtones that appealed to the fears and
biases of some white voters. A political action committee supporting Bush, not
the Bush campaign, produced and aired this advertisement. However, Bush
benefited from it. Writer Martin Schram tells the story of this controversial
political commercial: how it was developed and how it was utilized by the
Bush campaign.*

Larry McCarthy, a maker of TV ads and political images, sat in his editing
room, staring at three mug shots that had just come in the overnight mail.
God, this guy's ugly, he thought. Mean-looking, downright menacing. "This
is every suburban mother's greatest fear," McCarthy says now, recalling his
thoughts of that day late in the summer of 1988 as he wondered whether
he dared use in his new campaign ad that photo of—you guessed it—Willie
Horton.

That decision by the relatively unknown McCarthy set off repercussions
that Republicans have been trying to explain away ever since. Yes, it helped
make George Bush what he is today. But it also fueled the now widespread
public perception that Bush, Lee Atwater, and their Republican media-
meister Roger Ailes used Horton's photo to exploit racism during the 1988
campaign.

The making of Willie Horton as a symbol that outlived the campaign
and its promises is one of the more telling tales about the way our presidential politics really works. It was a visual symbol designed by McCarthy,
who actually is a moderate and most unprejudiced Republican. And it was
disseminated nationally mainly because McCarthy managed to con the television networks—not once, but twice.

Follow along: Larry McCarthy did not work for the Bush campaign. He
worked for something called Americans for Bush, an independent group
that was part of the hawkish National Security Political Action Committee,
headed by retired Admiral Thomas Moorer, a former chairman of the Joint
Chiefs of Staff. The Bush campaign, where Atwater was campaign manager
and Ailes was the message strategist, had no official connection with—and
publicly disavowed—Americans for Bush, which was raising its own money
and running its own ads. In fact, the Bush campaign was barred by law
from contact or coordination with this group.

But there were past ties. McCarthy used to be senior vice president of

Source: Martin Schram: *The New Republic* (May 28, 1990): 17–19. Reprinted by permission of
The New Republic © 1990, The New Republic, Inc..

Source: A/P Wide World

Ailes Communications. So he figured he could design a media ad campaign that would dovetail nicely with the one Ailes was planning for Bush—without consulting with his old boss. "I know Roger very well," said McCarthy. "I just tried to run it as if I were Roger. I tried to spare him from doing some of these things. I figured they'll go negative [and begin attacking Michael Dukakis in their ads] by mid-September. So I said, I'm going to lead them by about a week or two."

The Bush team had already used the Horton case in its campaign to illustrate how Dukakis was soft on crime—but McCarthy knew the Bush advisers had never used Horton's photo in making their case. Focusing on the Horton case was, surely, fair game. The case was so outrageous that it remains a mystery why any politician could fail to understand that Americans of all races would find it abhorrent. (Horton stabbed a teenage boy to death, dismembered the body, and stuck the penis in the cadaver's mouth. Horton was released on furlough ten times: on the eleventh, he fled, kidnapped a couple, raped the woman, and beat up the man.)

Now, about that photo: late in the summer of '88, as McCarthy looked at the close-up mug shots of Horton, he says he debated with himself. "I debated whether I could get this by the cable television network officials and on the air," McCarthy recalls. "This guy looked like an animal. . . . And frankly, because he was black, I thought longer and harder about putting him in there." McCarthy says he considered whether network officials would view the use of that photo as a racial appeal.

Then, he says, he began to think of reasons for using or not using a murderer's photo in an ad, reasons that he said had nothing to do with race but everything to do with whether the murderer looked menacing or mild-mannered. "If he looked like Ted Bundy [the serial murderer executed in Florida], I probably wouldn't have used his picture, because he looks perfectly normal—like a YR [Young Republican]," McCarthy explains. "But then I said, as an advertising guy, I should have been shot if I didn't use Horton's picture, because the picture says it all. It says this is a bad guy and Dukakis let him out. If it was a picture of a guy who looked like a crazy—an animal—but was white or Hispanic or Oriental, you'd use it. So I decided to put a criminal's picture on the screen."

Con Number One: Actually, McCarthy decided to make two ads. One omitted Horton's photo—that's the one he first sent to the cable networks: Cable News Network, Christian Broadcasting Network, Lifetime, and Arts & Entertainment. "I know they always look at the first spot hard," he says. A few days later he sent the second ad—the one with Horton's mug shot— as a replacement, figuring it would get less intense scrutiny. Each network routinely made the substitution as requested.

Con Number Two: McCarthy didn't have enough money to buy time for the Horton ad on the major broadcast networks. But he found a way to get more free airtime on commercial TV than he could ever buy. He slipped a videotape of his ad featuring the Horton mug shot to the producers of "The McLaughlin Group." They aired the ad on the next show, and the panelists discussed it. So now it was "news." Then the major network news shows aired it too—again, for free—by using it in stories about the ad.

The message was out. The commercial TV news and talk shows did McCarthy's work for him, for free. They carried the pictures that were his message. McCarthy knew that the TV news producers are always ripe for exploitation because they can't resist using any new videotape to wallpaper their news stories. Too many TV producers simply lack the discipline or the guts to just say no.

McCarthy believes it was smart to take his ads to cable networks first because they were less likely to balk at airing that photo of Horton. "The funny thing is, I don't think we could have cleared that spot with the commercial networks if we'd had the money to buy ad time with them," he says, contending the commercial network screening process is tougher. (A Turner Broadcasting System spokesperson says that's not the case with CNN, adding that Turner's vice president for sales, who screens all political and advocacy ads for CNN, has rejected ads that have appeared on the broadcast networks.)

A couple of weeks later Ailes aired his own Bush campaign classic: the revolving jailhouse door. Not only did the Bush campaign's ad not show Horton's photo, it never even mentioned his name. "We very carefully elected not to show him or mention him because we knew we'd be hit with racism," says Ailes. "Well, we still get hit with it. And the press still says I put Willie Horton's picture all over TV. They can't get it right."

Back when McCarthy's TV ad was spreading Horton's mug shot coast to coast, the Bush campaign protested loudly and publicly—with all the anguish of a pro wrestler pounding the mat in feigned pain. The independent Americans for Bush quickly announced it would be happy to yank its ad off the air if Bush campaign chairman James A. Baker III formally requested it.

And lo, Baker did just that—after the Willie Horton mug-shot commercial had run for twenty-five days and had just three days to go before its scheduled expiration.

Epilogue: In politics, as in basketball, some refs permit incidental contact, and others don't. McCarthy says he heard from his former boss once during the campaign. This incidental contact occurred just after McCarthy had begun working for Americans for Bush. "He called me up and he said— too bad, he wanted to hire me [for the Bush campaign] to do negative spots," says McCarthy, "but he couldn't now." Today Ailes says he doesn't remember making the call but doesn't dispute McCarthy's recollection.

Sticklers could argue that Ailes's comment was just the hint McCarthy needed to get the notion that he could help Ailes and Bush by making his own negative ads. Indeed, someone could have asked the Federal Election Commission sharpshooters to make a federal case out of that one phone call. But no one did.

Source: Steve Kelley ©1988

What's New? Mud-Slinging Is an American Tradition

CHARLES PAUL FREUND

Because of the Willie Horton advertisement and other commercials attacking candidates, negative advertising was raised to an issue in the 1988 campaign. In the readings that follow Charles Paul Freund, editor of the Outlook section of The Washington Post, *and Kathleen Hall Jamieson, Dean of the Annenberg School of Communications of the University of Pennsylvania, debate the use of such advertising within the American electoral tradition. They disagree on whether the attacks in 1988 were more vicious, deceitful, and scurrilous than in previous presidential elections. They agree, however, that such a campaign does little to enhance the democratic process; it does not educate and inform the voters. Freund blames the electorate for tolerating such mindless appeals; Jamieson chides the candidates for making and tolerating them and the media for not revealing their inaccuracies and omissions.*

You think the presidential campaign's been nasty so far? Well, wait 'til you hear this: One of the guys in the '88 presidential race used to *beat his wife*. Oh sure, the poor woman publicly denied it, but the brute probably thrashed the denial out of her. You know she's half his age, and he's said to make the most astounding, um, "demands" on her. What can you expect from a man who's had an illegitimate son, and who sat out his generation's war because he had money?

You are, of course, slavering to know who it is. Well, it's Grover Cleveland (sorry), who, according to one account, lost the presidency in 1888 in part because he couldn't squelch the rumor—spread by Republican clergymen—that he spent his evenings abusing Mrs. Cleveland. Cleveland did have an illegitimate son, and he paid someone to take his place in the Civil War. The wife-beating was a baseless rumor, ugly, noxious and vile. But many candidates, before and since, have probably wished that wife-beating was the worst that had been whispered about them.

This year's campaign is established in the public eye as an unprecedented farce: bereft of substance, a circus of trivialities, bite-sized negativism and character assassination. That judgment is correct, except in one detail: There's nothing unprecedented about this. Our elections have often been exercises in slander; the great issues of the day have often been beside the point. Odious campaigns are a national tradition, and so is complaining bitterly about them.

Source: *The Washington Post*, October 30, 1988: C1, 2. Reprinted by permission of *The Washington Post*.

Every four years we rediscover that our elections are stupid, and every four years we trot out the usual suspects and accuse them: Our candidates are mediocre; their handlers and ad men are cynical and manipulative; the press is cowardly and acquiescent: But somebody's missing from this line-up of rogues. Politics do not take place apart from a culture's other activities; especially in a mass democracy, they are a reflection of that culture. The question is, are our awful politics really imposed on us, or are we getting the kind of politics we have invited?

Look at this campaign. Never mind the distorting TV ads. The word-of-mouth and even printed slander we've seen this year have been colorful enough. One candidate faced a withering examination of his military record. Another candidate saw his wife's patriotism attacked by a false allegation that she burned a flag. Even nastier rumors about the candidates—questioning their sexual fidelity and mental stability—have been whispered about but generally not printed in the papers.

Base charges such as these are not fresh or original to this campaign. The debate's been here before. In fact, we might just as well be relieved that there are no great issues in the campaign. The greater the issues believed to be at stake, the more horrifying our campaigns have sometimes been; some of the juiciest stories have attached themselves to the biggest names.

Andrew Jackson, for example, had a rough campaign season. His mother was called a prostitute, his father, in an exploitation of the day's overt racial hatred, was identified as a mulatto, and his wife as "a profligate woman." All this was printed in the newspapers. When Mrs. Jackson read that she was a bigamist (which was technically true), she took to bed and died.

Abraham Lincoln was derided as illegitimate; the name of his "real" father was widely known (Abe Enlow, if you must know). Lincoln too was black, his wife was traitorous and his 20-year-old son was a millionaire war profiteer. All this was in the press. Carl Sandburg speculated that Booth could have been driven to kill Lincoln by reading the New York and Chicago papers, which all but demanded his murder. As for Lincoln's famous opponent, Stephen Douglas, he was harmed by a report that he had once kissed the pope's foot.

Theodore Roosevelt was a drunkard and a drug fiend; the combination had driven him mad. Woodrow Wilson couldn't keep his hands off women and by the end of his presidency was hopelessly insane, probably from advanced syphilis. Franklin Roosevelt was a lecher, a secret Jew whose real name was Rosenfeldt and a hopeless lunatic besides. During his press conferences, he laughed hysterically for no apparent reason. There were bars on the White House windows to prevent the president from flinging himself from the second floor.

More? Herbert Hoover was a German sympathizer in World War I; those who knew the truth about him had been executed. The crick in James Buchanan's neck was easily explained: In his youth he had tried to hang himself. Buchanan's opponent, John Fremont, was really Jewish. Martin

Van Buren dressed in women's corsets and doused himself with cologne (accusations levied by Davy Crockett in an election-year pamphlet). As for Buchanan's opponent, he was really black. Warren Harding was really black, too. Barry Goldwater was allied with Bavarian fascists. Grover Cleveland's opponent, James G. Blaine, was simultaneously a hater of Catholics and a Catholic himself, a triumph of rumor-mongering.

Not enough? George Washington was a dolt, a thief and a philanderer who offered his beautiful slave women to Mount Vernon's visitors. Washington was deeply embittered by these stories and is believed by some to have given up public life because of them. But American politics were young then. By the time Thomas Jefferson moved into the White House, the pattern was established. "I am the target of every man's dirt," he wrote, understating the situation. Jefferson was denounced from the nation's pulpits as the Antichrist himself; the name of his reported slave paramour (oh, all right: Sally Hemmings) is still well-known.

Where was the press—the TV of its day—in all this? Discreetly avoiding the mud until it had nailed down the stories as true or false? That's a good one. The press used to make up many of these lies itself. False "news" stories were so common, according to David J. Jacobson's account of campaign infamy, that they had a name: "roorbacks," derived from an 1844 press hoax in which a nonexistent Mr. Roorback reported his discovery of 42 nonexistent slaves branded with the initials of candidate James K. Polk.

What changes about American campaigns is not their mud-slinging; what changes is the direction in which the mud is thrown. As historian James Truslow Adams suggested in 1932, "So long as our politics are primarily concerned with men rather than measures, it will be men who will be attacked; characters, not ideas." These attacks, wrote Adams, will be always be based on "the dominant prejudices or standards of the voters to be influenced."

But why don't candidates choose to debate "measures," or, if you prefer, "issues" more? There are three reasons.

The first is because nobody else does. We are not a politicized people. We don't, by and large, define ourselves primarily as members of a social, economic, lingual, ethnic, religious or any other group with a political agenda. We are not polarized "workers" or "landowners" or Quebeckers or Maronites; we're mostly somewhere in the middle, and usually we're quite proud of that. But the result is that our major political parties cluster in the political center where we are, at least most of the time, and therefore stand for very mushy things. Frequently, the difference between their candidates really is personal, and that is where the debate finds its level.

Several recent elections, especially those from 1964 to 1972, featured spirited national exchanges on broad and important issues: civil rights, Vietnam, the morality of our foreign policy, nuclear arms, the fate of the environment, etc. But these debates did not take place because a bell rang after Labor Day every four years calling everyone to order; they took place because these issues were already under discussion when election time rolled around. Campaigns absorb ongoing debates about issues, they don't create them. Is someone under the impression that a spirited debate has been raging about anything during Ronald Reagan's second term.

A second reason why candidates may not be discussing pressing issues in meaningful detail is that few people might understand what they are talking about. There are reports all over the place detailing the staggering ignorance of Americans. If these reports are accurate, many Americans cannot find their own country on a world map, know nothing whatsoever about their own country's history or anybody else's, are totally ignorant of all scientific and technological matters and have only the foggiest idea—if that—of what is going on elsewhere in the world. Perhaps, as educator Diane Ravitch has argued, the electorate at large is not demanding more discussion of the issues because it isn't sure what they are.

The third reason that our campaigns are often bereft of issues is that whenever a candidate actually structures his campaign on them, he loses.

There are two kinds of campaigns. There are "issues campaigns," in which a candidate identifies problems and offers solutions, and there are "values campaigns," in which a candidate stands four-square for those things which have made our country great, and positions the other guy as an interloper. When these two kinds of campaigns face each other, guess which one always wins. Always. Sometimes the great American middle shifts. In 1964 it was "conservative extremism" that was the rejected interloper; this year liberals are under attack.

Michael Dukakis announced at the outset of this dismal campaign that the election was not about ideology. That amounted to throwing his intellect out the window on purpose, though in fact it was the politically astute thing to do. His people saw clearly that the operative issue in our politics is the personal one. But that's the only thing they saw clearly this year. Bush draped himself in the flag and stood for our great values. Using a campaign of innuendo, he positioned Dukakis as an outsider and is running off with the polls. In the closing days of the campaign, the electorate seems more interested in the fate of two icebound whales than in the fate of the two candidates.

So whose fault is all this? Why are our candidates so often mediocre, our campaigns so often mindless, our voter-turnout so often embarrassingly low? All these questions point to one villain.

It's not the press. The charge of press culpability is mystifying. "The press" is not the evening network news. If that's all most people watch, why pillory the networks? Never mind that the print press flourishes in gaudy profusion, and has immeasurably more integrity today than in its partisan days. Even the networks schedule many programs which address "issues" seriously. But if they ran those programs in prime time, who'd watch? PBS has precisely such a show; its nightly audience is minuscule.

The villain is not the candidates, either: We now choose them popularly through primaries and caucuses in every state. The political ad men then? To charge them is ludicrous. Even assuming that the level of political television is deteriorating, its manipulators can only dream of slinging the kind of mud available to the newspapers, pamphleteers, clergymen and rumor-mongers of the past. Anyway, the height or depth to which political advertising rises and falls isn't set by its creators. In the end it is in competition with numerous other purveyors of political information, and it falls to the level at which its consumers accept it. If anything stands out about the TV campaign this year, it's that only one of the candidates has had one.

Everybody on the selling end of campaigns takes the electorate as they find it. They're desperate to sell us something, and they'll sell that something any way they can.

You see the way this campaign is going? This is how they can sell us that something; they've had two centuries of experience to learn what works. If we're impulse buyers in the presidential marketplace, whose fault is it?

For Televised Mendacity, This Year Is the Worst Ever

KATHLEEN HALL JAMIESON

Never before in a presidential campaign have televised ads sponsored by a major party candidate lied so blatantly as in the campaign of '88.

Television ads of previous presidential contenders have, to be sure, seized upon votes cast by the opposition candidate and sundered them from context, resurrected political positions from the distant past and interpreted legislative moves as sweeping endorsements of unpopular positions. And, in eras gone by, the penny press, which didn't even feign political neutrality, published scurrilous assaults on would-be presidents, albeit to far more limited audiences than those reached by televised broadcasts. But in the era of mass visual communication, major party candidates have, until this year, assumed that outright lying in an ad would create an outcry from the press, a devastating counter-assault from the other side and a discrediting backlash from an incensed electorate.

That assumption no longer governs. Take, for example, this ad from the Bush campaign: The picture shows a pool of sludge and pollutants near a sign reading, "Danger/Radiation Hazard/No Swimming." The text indicts Dukakis for failing to clean up Boston Harbor. But the sign shown has, in fact, nothing to do with the Massachusetts governor or his record. Instead, it warns Navy personnel not to swim in waters that had once harbored nuclear submarines under repair.

Here's another from the Bush image mill: A procession of convicts circles through a revolving gate and marches toward the nation's living rooms. The ad invites the inference—false—that 268 first-degree murderers were furloughed by Dukakis to rape and kidnap. In fact only one first-degree murderer, Willie Horton, escaped furlough in Massachusetts and committed a violent crime—although others have done so under other furlough programs, including those run by the federal government and by California under the stewardship of Ronald Reagan.

There is only one precedent for such visual demagoguery in the history of electronic presidential campaigning. In 1968 during the Richard Nixon-Hubert Humphrey contest, the Republicans aired a wordless sequence of images as "Hot Time in the Old Town" played in the background. The images: Humphrey smiling; carnage in Vietnam. Humphrey smiling; Appalachian poverty. Humphrey smiling; bloodshed outside the Democratic

Source: Kathleen Hall Jamieson is professor of communications and dean of the Annenberg School for Communications of the University of Pennsylvania and author of *Packaging the Presidency* (Oxford, 1984, 1988, 1991) and *Eloquence in an Electronic Age* (Oxford, 1988).

convention. The inference invited was that Humphrey either approved or was responsible for the unsettling images juxtaposed with his own jovial one.

But when the 1968 ad sparked protests, the Republicans quickly withdrew it. No such protests greeted either the Boston Harbor or furlough spots. An electorate numbed by the negative campaigns of 1986—and a press corps preoccupied more with ad strategy than content—simply took the visual demagoguery in stride.

Thus encouraged, the campaigns moved beyond false implications to direct distortion. The Dukakis campaign joined in with an ad claiming that Bush cast "the tie-breaking Senate vote to cut Social Security benefits," when, instead, Bush had voted to eliminate a cost-of-living adjustment in benefits, thus eroding purchasing power but not diminishing the actual level of the checks.

From the Republicans came a portrait of the Democratic candidate looking somewhat silly as he rides in a tank and thus attempts to dramatize his support for a strong defense. "Michael Dukakis has opposed virtually every defense system we have developed," says the ad. Untrue. The Democrat favors the Trident II submarine and the D5 missile and the SSN21 Seawolf attack submarine among others. "He opposed the Stealth bomber . . . ," says the ad. Another falsehood. Dukakis supports Stealth.

Has the electorate lost its sense of fair play? Certainly earlier candidates of the electronic era feared that they might forfeit the election if they offended voters' notions of fairness and honesty. Even in 1964, which witnessed the most negative electronic campaign prior to 1988, caution pervaded the politicking. A 1964 Democratic ad highlighting the Ku Klux Klan's endorsement of Barry Goldwater was shelved, unaired, when Goldwater rejected the Klan's embrace. To document Goldwater's position on Social Security, one ad showed five corroborating sources.

Ads dramatizing Goldwater's stands repeated words actually uttered by the candidate. Goldwater had, in fact, said that he wouldn't mind if the "Eastern seaboard were sawed off" and that the nuclear bomb was "merely another weapon." The famous "daisy" commercial certainly played on voters' fears of a Goldwater presidency, but the ad didn't even need to mention his name; the electorate's disposition to believe that the candidate was trigger-happy had been well-fanned by his Republican opponents as they vied for the GOP nomination in the spring.

Comforted by such examples from recent decades, I concluded a survey of presidential advertising in a recent book on presidential campaigns with the assurance that the public had little to fear from distortions in TV and other ads. I was wrong.

Just as the Battle of Agincourt demonstrated the vulnerability of French armor to the British longbow, the 1988 campaign showed the deceptive power of visual association and the weaknesses of the protection provided by debates, news broadcasts, counteracting advertising and press coverage.

Part of the fault lies with the Dukakis campaign which ignored the Bush attacks until they had so pervaded the attitudes of the electorate that Dukakis had plummeted from front-runner to also-ran. Part of the fault resides with reporters more disposed to discussing advertising strategy than substance or accuracy. Part of the fault resides with a public more inclined to gather political information from inadvertent exposure to ads than from news accounts, attention to candidates' speeches or position papers.

Only in the last half of October did Democratic ads attempt to clean up a campaign environment so awash in distortions that Bush's portrayal of Boston Harbor seemed clean by comparison. Without counter-advertising by Dukakis, or clarification in news or debates, the electorate had no reason to doubt the inference invited by the Bush furlough ad.

Only those who had closely followed campaign speeches and position papers, as well as broadcast and print news accounts, would know that the facts provide absolutely no support for the implication that a President Dukakis would usurp the rights of the states and furlough first degree murderers to mug or murder Reagan Democrats. Among those little-known facts are that: only one first-degree murderer furloughed by the Massachusetts program, Willie Horton, had committed a violent crime; that the typical furlough jumper was an unarmed robber, not a murderer; that 72 of the escapees hadn't escaped at all—they had simply returned more than two hours late; that a comparable federal program continues, and that programs comparable to Dukakis' existed in other states (including under the Reagan administration in California) and that both the crime rate and the murder rate in Massachusetts were low for an industrial state.

So Dukakis could have knocked the GOP ad for a loop. But by refusing in the debates to rebut the distortions, and by waiting until October to respond in ads, Dukakis squandered two of the three means available to protect the public from deception in political ads.

For its part, the press, the third potential safeguard, spent much of this time focused on revealing the strategy rather than the inaccuracy of the ads. Only when the Bush "tank" ad rumbled into the World Series did its obvious distortion of Dukakis' defense posture prompt ABC, and then the other networks, The Washington Post and the other major papers to set the record straight.

But even if the news outlets had been more vigilant, news alone can't adequately protect the public from deception. Single news segments cannot erase dozens of exposures to a sludge-clotted Boston Harbor or the seemingly endless procession of scot-free murderers. Besides, most viewers in key states will have seen the ads repeatedly, whereas a far smaller number will see the single correction in network news stories. A smaller number still will thumb back from the comics and sports pages to the articles unmasking the distortions.

Nor can the networks be called upon to screen out deceptive political advertising. Were the product a Plymouth and not a president, Bush's claim to leadership on the INF treaty, his assertion that Dukakis opposed the Stealth bomber and the implication that Dukakis freed 268 Willie Hortons would not have aired. Nor would Dukakis' claim that Bush voted to cut Social Security. Whereas the networks protect the consumer from distortions in product ads, the need to protect a candidate's right to free speech means that stations and networks can't reject deceptive presidential ads.

How then can the electorate be protected? The best available defense seems to be the vigilance of the opposing candidate and party. But, as this campaign has shown, a candidate's access to news, counter-advertising and debates protects the public only if the attacked candidate moves quickly and strategically. Moreover, the protections of news and debates presuppose that the attacked candidate is comfortable with personally rebutting untruths and counter attacking. Neither seems to come naturally to Michael Dukakis.

There is also the real risk that a counter-attack may simply legitimize false claims and magnify their impact. It can also reduce the campaign to a shouting match in which each candidate calls the other a liar, leaving the electorate disillusioned and confused. That seems to be where the campaign of '88 is winding up. It's also where future campaigns are likely to be headed—unless this country can discover among the ranks of its politicians a pair of candidates self-assured enough to campaign on the facts.

Eye Bounce? Tactical Smile?
Some Pointers for Debates

MICHAEL ORESKES

Televised presidential debates have become an integral part of the quest for office. Candidates avoid them at their peril, but they also prepare for them elaborately. To avoid the kind of negative response Richard Nixon received in 1960, when he looked tired and acted fidgety in his first debate with John Kennedy, candidates are now briefed, dressed, and rehearsed by their media advisers. Journalist Michael Oreskes, who covered the media for The New York Times *in the 1988 campaign, reveals the kind of tips the candidates are likely to receive from their handlers before they face their opponent. He distills the experiences of previous debates and provides hints for candidates on how to avoid the kind of blows that their predecessors suffered and how to win the bout.*

To:

Vice President Bush and Gov. Michael S. Dukakis.

Re: Debates.

Next Sunday night America will finally tune in to your 1988 Presidential race. Millions of voters will be watching, certainly millions more than will see any other single event of this campaign. Live and on stage, the two of you will confront each other, or maybe not, in the first of two televised debates.

You don't want to blow any chance to send a message, be it subliminal or sock-in-the-kisser. So you and your handlers are laying tactics and making plans. Guard those plans closely. There's no point in tipping the opposition, although a few bits of carefully floated misinformation might throw the other guy off.

HOWITZERS AND BOUQUETS

But some of the moves you must make are no secret, at least to debate coaches and media advisers. Have you mastered the eye bounce? How will you address your opponent? Should the tactical smile be deployed? And why not toss a bouquet?

Many Americans will turn on their sets to see the Olympics, only to find that NBC has decided to bring them your debate instead of live coverage

Source: *The New York Times*, September 19, 1988, pp. A1,16. Copyright © 1988 by The New York Times Company. Reprinted by permission.

of the preliminaries of men's platform diving. Many will overcome their disappointment and stay tuned to the debate. That will do far more to expand your audience than anything either of you could do (although a nice Olympic reference during the debate will show you're in touch with what the rest of America is talking about these days).

Perhaps the debate will not be as thrilling as a back one-and-a-half dive with two-and-a-half twists (2.8 degree of difficulty). But by the time you step out on stage you better have thought out your moves as carefully as that diver at the edge of the board. But strive to make the calculated look natural.

This year is the 40th anniversary of broadcast Presidential debates. Gov. Thomas E. Dewey and former Gov. Harold E. Stassen did it first, on the radio, just before the Oregon Republican primary on May 17, 1948. That debate was also the last time a Presidential debate was limited to a single question: Should the Communist Party be outlawed? (Stassen said yes, Dewey no.)

Debates since then, including the first general election televised debate between John F. Kennedy and Richard M. Nixon in 1960, have never pursued a single subject in much depth. This year's debates will be ninety minutes long. That will probably be enough time for about twenty questions from the panel of three reporters.

Try to anticipate all the possible questions, and likely answers. Answers will be limited to two minutes, and rebuttals to one, so each of you will have about half an hour at the mike, in all. That means you can memorize the gist, if not the text, of answers (or waffles) to plenty of expected questions.

SNEAKY ONE-LINERS

Now, it's not fair, as some naysayers would have it, to contend that these debates have nothing to do with the job of being President. "Presidents," sniffed former Senator Eugene J. McCarthy, "don't debate." Maybe not, but the preparation for debate is much like that for a Presidential news conference. Sometimes the pressure of deciding what to say forces policy decisions, which is what Presidents, and even candidates, are supposed to do.

You and your staff are already studying in detail what your opponent has been saying and planning your responses. But you can also be sure he'll try to come up with one or two new lines, carefully plotted to grab attention and throw you off.

But watch out for the reporters. They are a tricky lot. Most of the time, they will ask about familiar "issues." But they may try to throw you off with something unexpected that might provoke a real insight into how you think on the spot. Ronald Reagan was surprised during the 1984 debate when he was asked by a reporter why he did not go to church. He said that his presence might endanger the congregation.

Special Tips

The debate is no place for brainstorms. If a bright thought suddenly pops into your head as you stare into your opponent's eyes, squelch it. "You can't afford instant wisdom," said Eddie Mahe, a Republican political consultant. "You don't try any line or any thought or any theme that hasn't been pre-tested. The thing you have to avoid is the snap response that becomes a disaster. If you haven't said it before, don't say it now."

Just the other day you noted, Mr. Bush, that your staff gets nervous when you speak unattended. Face it, you're gaffe-prone, misstating, for example, the date the United States was "hit hard" at Pearl Harbor. That tendency conjures up dreadful images of a date that will live in debate infamy, Oct. 6, 1976. That was when Gerald Ford said in his second debate with Jimmy Carter, "There is no Soviet domination of Eastern Europe." That misstatement, combined with the stubborn, clumsy way he handled its aftermath, may have cost Mr. Ford the election.

Now, fear of a mistake can be carried to paralyzing excess. Mr. Ford and Mr. Carter remained stock still for 27 minutes when the sound suddenly went out near the end of their first 1976 debate. Surely, one of them could have broken the ice, suggesting that they sit down, or perhaps even send out for a pizza. But they both feared that the danger of saying or doing the wrong thing was greater than saying or doing nothing.

But Mr. Dukakis, don't count on a gaffe by Mr. Bush. Focus on your own weaknesses. You tend to come across as a bit stern and, yes, arrogant. So loosen up or, if you want to relate to those baby boomers, chill out. Don't cut off questions before they're asked, as you did in the primaries. Figure out what you're going to say about the Pledge of Allegiance and stop pointing your finger. You're not on the lecture circuit, yet.

Anticipate the Spin

What gets said about the debate is often more important than what gets said at the debate. There is compelling evidence that voters form their opinions about the debate by what they hear afterward on television and read in the newspapers.

In one study voters watched the second Ford-Carter debate while taped to electronic monitoring devices. There wasn't even a blip when Mr. Ford liberated Poland. But within hours, America's blood pressure was raised by all the reporters chattering about the blunder, to say nothing of the Democratic National Committee's concentrated effort to get Democrats of East European descent to complain all over the country. Within days the nation agreed that Mr. Ford had lost the debate.

You, and your opponent, will be searching for pithy jabs and ripostes that you hope will define the debate and be picked up and repeated over and over on television news and in the newspapers. Who can forget Ronald

Reagan's "there you go again" putdown of Jimmy Carter or Walter Mondale's "where's the beef?" demand of Gary Hart.

It's a perfect opportunity to try to deal with troubling issues. President Reagan countered the impression fostered by his own meandering performance in his 1984 debate with Walter Mondale by arriving at the second debate ready to brush aside the age issue.

"I'm not going to exploit for political purposes my opponent's youth and inexperience," Mr. Reagan declared.

Visual Cues and Miscues

Sure, sure, substance is what counts. But people often form their impressions based on a whole host of visual cues. One of your main goals is to demonstrate that you have the character to be President. Your gestures and style must speak as loudly as your words that you are honest, steady and caring.

Richard Nixon looked "shifty-eyed" in his first 1960 debate against John F. Kennedy. The reason: he kept shifting his gaze to an off-camera clock. The same effect can occur if you look from one person to another on stage while the camera is focused tightly on you. To prevent this, consultants recommend the "eye bounce." Never move your eyes side to side. Always look down and then over.

Handled properly, a smile can be your most potent weapon. But use it carefully. "The smile, as most any tactic, has its risks," wrote Myles Martel, who helped coach Ronald Reagan for his 1980 debates. "It must not appear foolish or project ridicule; nor should it look like an arrogant smirk."

Careful staging is important, too. Mr. Ford's handlers, concerned about his clumsy image, had the water glasses braced to the lectern so he could not knock his over. Mr. Carter, shorter than Mr. Ford, arranged to have their lectern at different heights (the "belt-buckle agreement" because the lectern was set at the level of each candidate's belt buckle.)

How you attack will be a crucial decision. You've been blasting each other transcontinentally for weeks. But standing this close, the mud might splash back. If this all gets too ugly, toss your opponent a bouquet. Praise his devotion to family or even find one small praiseworthy element in his political career, the longer ago, the better. It will make you look more thoughtful, less combative. And, considering how the campaign has been going, it might leave your rival speechless.

The first televised debate between Richard Nixon and John Kennedy offered a vivid contrast in appearance and style. Nixon looked tired: deep shadows under his eyes were highlighted by the television lights and his face was darkened by a five o'clock shadow. He wore little makeup. Throughout the debate his eyes darted toward Kennedy, and he had a tendency to wet his lips with his tongue, reminding some viewers of a serpent. Kennedy looked more composed and relaxed. He talked quickly and confidently, providing statistics to give the impression of considerable knowledge. For those who saw the debate on television, Kennedy was judged the winner; For those who heard it on radio, Nixon won.

Source: Library of Congress

Source: Library of Congress

The Incredible Shrinking Sound Bite

KIKU ADATTO

One of the most persistent criticisms of the age of the televised campaign is the decreasing amount of news coverage given to the candidates themselves. Speeches are now written with "sound bites" in mind because media advisers know that only a minute portion of what the candidates actually say will be broadcast. Kiku Adatto contrasts network news coverage of the campaigns of 1968 with that of 1988 and finds that the number of words quoted directly from the candidates have shrunk, but the frequency with which their verbal slips have been reported has increased. Adatto also finds greater interpretation of the candidates' statements and actions by the news media. Candidates and their media consultants have responded to this type of coverage with more political advertising and more staged and scripted events.

Standing before a campaign rally in Pennsylvania, the 1968 Democratic vice presidential candidate, Edmund Muskie, tried to speak, but a group of anti-war protesters drowned him out. Muskie offered the hecklers a deal. He would give the platform to one of their representatives if he could then speak without interruption. Rick Brody, the students' choice, rose to the microphone where, to cheers from the crowd, he denounced the candidates that the 1968 presidential campaign had to offer. "Wallace is no answer. Nixon's no answer. And Humphrey's no answer. Sit out this election!" When Brody finished, Muskie made his case for the Democratic ticket. That night Muskie's confrontation with the demonstrators played prominently on the network news. NBC showed fifty-seven seconds of Brody's speech, and more than a minute of Muskie's.

Twenty years later, things had changed. Throughout the entire 1988 campaign, no network allowed either presidential candidate to speak uninterrupted on the evening news for as long as Rick Brody spoke. By 1988 television's tolerance for the languid pace of political discourse, never great, had all but vanished. An analysis of all weekday evening network newscasts (over 280) from Labor Day to Election Day in 1968 and 1988 reveals that the average "sound bite" fell from 42.3 seconds in 1968 to only 9.8 seconds in 1988. Meanwhile the time the networks devoted to visuals of the candidates, unaccompanied by their words, increased by more than 300 percent.

Since the Kennedy-Nixon debates of 1960, television has played a pivotal role in presidential politics. The Nixon campaign of 1968 was the first to be managed and orchestrated to play on the evening news. With the decline of

Source: *The New Republic* (May 28, 1990): 20–23. Reprinted by permission of *The New Republic*, ©1990, The New Republic, Inc..

political parties and the direct appeal to voters in the primaries, presidential campaigns became more adept at conveying their messages through visual images, not only in political commercials but also in elaborately staged media events. By the time of Ronald Reagan, the actor turned president, Michael Deaver had perfected the techniques of the video presidency.

For television news, the politicians' mastery of television imagery posed a temptation and a challenge. The temptation was to show the pictures. What network producer could resist the footage of Reagan at Normandy Beach, or of Bush in Boston Harbor? The challenge was to avoid being entangled in the artifice and imagery that the campaigns dispensed. In 1988 the networks tried to have it both ways—to meet the challenge even as they succumbed to the temptation. They showed the images that the campaigns produced—their commercials as well as their media events. But they also sought to retain their objectivity by exposing the artifice of the images, by calling constant attention to their self-conscious design.

The language of political reporting was filled with accounts of staging and backdrops, camera angles and scripts, sound bites and spin control, photo opportunities and media gurus. So attentive was television news to the way the campaigns constructed images for television that political reporters began to sound like theater critics, reporting more on the stagecraft than the substance of politics.

When Bush kicked off his campaign with a Labor Day appearance at Disneyland, the networks covered the event as a performance for television. "In the war of the Labor Day visuals," CBS's Bob Schieffer reported, "George Bush pulled out the heavy artillery. A Disneyland backdrop and lots of pictures with the Disney gang." When Bruce Morton covered Dukakis riding in a tank, the story was the image. "In the trade of politics, it's called a visual," said Morton. "The idea is pictures are symbols that tell the voter important things about the candidate. If your candidate is seen in the polls as weak on defense, put him in a tank."

And when Bush showed up at a military base to observe the destruction of a missile under an arms control treaty, ABC's Brit Hume began his report by telling his viewers that they were watching a media event. "Now, here was a photo opportunity, the vice president watching a Pershing missile burn off its fuel." He went on to describe how the event was staged for television. Standing in front of an open field, Hume reported, "The Army had even gone so far as to bulldoze acres of trees to make sure the vice president and the news media had a clear view."

So familiar is the turn to theater criticism that it is difficult to recall the transformation it represents. Even as they conveyed the first presidential campaign "made for television," TV reporters in 1968 continued to reflect the print journalist tradition from which they had descended. In the marriage of theater and politics, politics remained the focus of reporting. The media events of the day—mostly rallies and press conferences—were covered as political events, not as exercises in impression management.

By 1988 television displaced politics as the focus of coverage. Like a gestalt shift, the images that once formed the background to political events—the setting and the stagecraft—now occupied the foreground. (Only 6 percent of reports in 1968 were devoted to theater criticism, compared with 52 percent in 1988.) And yet, for all their image-conscious coverage in 1988, reporters did not escape their entanglement. They showed the potent visuals even as they attempted to avoid the manipulation by "deconstructing" the imagery and revealing its artifice.

To be sure, theater criticism was not the only kind of political reporting on network newscasts in 1988. Some notable "fact correction" pieces offered admirable exceptions. For example, after each presidential debate, ABC's Jim Wooten compared the candidates' claims with the facts. Not content with the canned images of the politicians, Wooten used television images to document discrepancies between the candidates' rhetoric and their records.

Most coverage simply exposed the contrivances of image-making. But alerting the viewer to the construction of television images proved no substitute for fact correction. A superficial "balance" replaced objectivity as the measure of fairness, a balance consisting of equal time for media events, equal time for commercials. But this created a false symmetry, leaving both the press and the public hostage to the play of perceptions the campaigns dispensed.

Even the most critical versions of image-conscious coverage could fail to puncture the pictures they showed. When Bush visited a flag factory in hopes of making patriotism a campaign issue, ABC's Hume reported that Bush was wrapping himself in the flag. "This campaign strives to match its pictures with its points. Today and for much of the past week, the pictures have been of George Bush with the American flag. If the point wasn't to make an issue of patriotism, then the question arises, what was it?" Yet only three days later, in an ABC report on independent voters in New Jersey, the media event that Hume reported with derision was transformed into an innocent visual of Bush. The criticism forgotten, the image played on.

Another striking contrast between the coverage of the 1968 and 1988 campaigns is the increased coverage of political commercials. Although political ads played a prominent role in the 1968 campaign, the networks rarely showed excerpts on the news. During the entire 1968 general election campaign, the evening news programs broadcast only two excerpts from candidates' commercials. By 1988 the number had jumped to 125. In 1968 the only time a negative ad was mentioned on the evening news was when CBS's Walter Cronkite and NBC's Chet Huntley reported that a Nixon campaign ad—showing a smiling Hubert Humphrey superimposed on scenes of war and riot—was withdrawn after the Democrats cried foul. Neither network showed the ad itself.

The networks might argue that in 1988 political ads loomed larger in the campaign, and so required more coverage. But as with their focus on media events, reporters ran the risk of becoming conduits of the television images the campaigns dispensed. Even with a critical narrative, showing commercials on the news gives free time to paid media. And most of the time the narrative was not critical. The networks rarely bothered to correct the distortions or misstatements that the ads contained. Of the 125 excerpts shown on the evening news in 1988, the reporter addressed the veracity of the commercials' claims less than 8 percent of the time. The networks became, in effect, electronic billboards for the candidates, showing political commercials not only as breaking news but as stand-ins for the candidates, and file footage aired interchangeably with news footage of the candidates.

The few cases where reporters corrected the facts illustrate how the networks might have covered political commercials. ABC's Richard Threlkeld ran excerpts from a Bush ad attacking Dukakis's defense stand by freezing the frame and correcting each mistaken or distorted claim. He also pointed out the exaggeration in a Dukakis ad attacking Bush's record on Social Security. CBS's Leslie Stahl corrected a deceptive statistic in Bush's revolving-door furlough ad, noting: "Part of the ad is false. . . . Two hundred sixty-eight murderers did not escape. . . . [T]he truth is only four first-degree murderers escaped while on parole."

Stahl concluded her report by observing, "Dukakis left the Bush attack ads unanswered for six weeks. Today campaign aides are engaged in a round of finger-pointing at who is to blame." But the networks also let the Bush furlough commercial run without challenge or correction. Before and even after her report, CBS ran excerpts of the ad without correction. In all, network newscasts ran excerpts from the revolving-door furlough ad ten times throughout the campaign, only once correcting the deceptive statistic.

It might be argued that it is up to the candidate to reply to his opponent's charges, not the press. But the networks' frequent use of political ads on the evening news created a strong disincentive for a candidate to challenge his opponent's ads. As Dukakis found, to attack a television ad as unfair or untrue is to invite the networks to run it again. In the final weeks before the election, the Dukakis campaign accused the Republicans of lying about his record on defense, and of using racist tactics in ads featuring Willie Horton, a black convict who raped and killed while on furlough from a Massachusetts prison. (See "The Making of Willie Horton" by Martin Schram.) In reporting Dukakis's complaint, all three networks ran excerpts of the ads in question, including the highly charged pictures of Horton and the revolving door of convicts. Dukakis's response thus gave Bush's potent visuals another free run on the evening news. . . .

Along with the attention to commercials and stagecraft in 1988 came an unprecedented focus on the stage managers themselves, the "media gurus," "handlers," and "spin-control artists." Only three reports featured media advisers in 1968, compared with twenty-six in 1988. And the numbers tell only part of the story.

The stance reporters have taken toward media advisers has changed dramatically over the past twenty years. In *The Selling of the President* (1969),

Joe McGinniss exposed the growing role of media advisers with a sense of disillusion and outrage. By 1988 television reporters covered image-makers with deference, even admiration. In place of independent fact correction, reporters sought out media advisers as authorities in their own right to analyze the effectiveness and even defend the truthfulness of campaign commercials. They became "media gurus" not only for the candidates but for the networks as well.

For example, in an exchange with CBS anchor Dan Rather on Bush's debate performance, Stahl lavished admiration on the techniques of Bush's media advisers.

> STAHL: "They told him not to look into the camera. [She gestures toward the camera as she speaks.] You know when you look directly into a camera you are cold, apparently they have determined."
> RATHER: [laughing] "Bad news for anchormen I'd say."
> STAHL: "We have a lot to learn from this. Michael Dukakis kept talking right into the camera. [Stahl talks directly into her own camera to demonstrate.] And according to the Bush people that makes you look programmed, Dan [Stahl laughs]. And they're very adept at these television symbols and television imagery. And according to our poll it worked."
> RATHER: "Do you believe it?"
> STAHL: "Yes, I think I do, actually."

So hypersensitive were the networks to television image-making in 1988 that minor mishaps—gaffes, slips of the tongue, even faulty microphones—became big news. Politicians were hardly without mishaps in 1968, but these did not count as news. Only once in 1968 did a network even take note of a minor incident unrelated to the content of the campaign. In 1988 some twenty-nine reports highlighted trivial slips.

The emphasis on "failed images" reflected a kind of guerrilla warfare between the networks and the campaigns. The more the campaigns sought to control the images that appeared on the nightly news, the more the reporters tried to beat them at their own game, magnifying a minor mishap into a central feature of the media event.

Early in the 1988 campaign, for example, George Bush delivered a speech to a sympathetic audience of the American Legion, attacking his opponent's defense policies. In a slip, he declared that September 7, rather than December 7, was the anniversary of Pearl Harbor. Murmurs and chuckles from the audience alerted him to his error, and he quickly corrected himself.

The audience was forgiving, but the networks were not. All three network anchors highlighted the slip on the evening news. Dan Rather introduced CBS's report on Bush by declaring solemnly, "Bush's talk to audiences in Louisville was overshadowed by a strange happening." On NBC Tom Brokaw reported, "He departed from his prepared script and left his listeners mystified." Peter Jennings introduced ABC's report by mentioning Bush's attack on Dukakis, adding, "What's more likely to be remembered about today's speech is a slip of the tongue."

Some of the slips the networks highlighted in 1988 were not even verbal gaffes or misstatements, but simply failures on the part of candidates to cater to the cameras. In a report on the travails of the Dukakis campaign, Sam Donaldson seized on Dukakis's failure to play to ABC's television camera as evidence of his campaign's ineffectiveness. Showing Dukakis playing a trumpet with a local marching band, Donaldson chided, "He played the trumpet with his back to the camera." As Dukakis played "Happy Days Are Here Again," Donaldson's voice was heard from off-camera calling, "We're over here, governor.". . .

The assumption that the creation of appearances is the essence of political reality pervaded not only the reporting but the candidates' self-understanding and conduct with the press. When Dan Quayle sought to escape his image as a highly managed candidate, he resolved publicly to become his own handler, his own "spin doctor." "The so-called handlers story, part of it's true," he confessed to network reporters. "But there will be no more handlers stories, because I'm the handler and I'll do the spinning." Surrounded by a group of reporters on his campaign plane, Quayle announced, "I'm Doctor Spin, and I want you all to report that."

It may seem a strange way for a politician to talk, but not so strange in a media-conscious environment in which authenticity means being master of your own artificiality. Dukakis too sought to reverse his political fortunes by seeking to be master of his own image. This attempt was best captured in a commercial shown on network news in which Dukakis stood beside a television set and snapped off a Bush commercial attacking his stand on defense. "I'm fed up with it," Dukakis declared. "Never seen anything like it in twenty-five years of public life. George Bush's negative television ads, distorting my record, full of lies, and he knows it." The commercial itself shows an image of an image—a Bush television commercial showing (and ridiculing) the media event where Dukakis rode in a tank. In his commercial, Dukakis complains that Bush's commercial showing the tank ride misstates Dukakis's position on defense.

As it appeared in excerpts on the evening news, Dukakis's commercial displayed a quintessentially modernist image of artifice upon artifice upon artifice: television news covering a Dukakis commercial containing a Bush commercial containing a Dukakis media event. In a political world governed by images of images, it seemed almost natural that the authority of the candidate be depicted by his ability to turn off the television set. . . .

In a moment of reflection in 1988, CBS's political correspondents expressed their frustration with image-driven campaigns. "It may seem frivolous, even silly at times," said Schieffer. "But setting up pictures that drive home a message has become the No. 1 priority of the modern-day campaign. The problem, of course, is while it is often entertaining, it is seldom enlightening."

Rather shared his colleague's discomfort. But what troubled him about modern campaigns is equally troubling about television's campaign coverage. "With all this emphasis on the image," he asked, "what happens to the issues? What happens to the substance?"

Media Coverage

S. ROBERT LICHTER, DANIEL AMUNDSON,
AND RICHARD E. NOYES

*In the final reading of this chapter, Dr. Robert Lichter and his associates at
the Center for Media and Public Affairs assess network news coverage. Their
analysis suggests that, contrary to popular belief, the coverage in 1988 was
balanced and tough, that it paid attention to issues, and that it was equally
critical of both candidates. Bush's advantage did not come from the coverage
he received but from the campaign he waged and the issues he raised.*

If George Bush won the election, it must be the media's fault. That's the
conventional wisdom that has poured forth from op-ed pieces, news talk
shows, and "news analysis" articles ever since Election Day. TV news, we
are told, was seduced by Bush speechwriter Peggy Noonan's sound bites,
manipulated by media strategist Roger Ailes's photo-ops and attack ads,
and shunted away from serious reporting by its own fascination with the
horse race. Ever since the polls closed, the campaign has been depicted
as a shallow and superficial process that manipulated, misinformed, and
misled the electorate, an affair as nasty and brutish as life in Hobbes's state
of nature (though not, alas, as short). . . .

These postmortems seem to be dissecting a different campaign from the
one monitored by the Center for Media and Public Affairs this year. After
analyzing all 735 general election stories that appeared on the ABC, CBS,
and NBC evening news from August 19 through November 7, we found
that the networks' coverage was notable for its balance, toughness, and
focus on the issues—precisely the opposite of the critics' charges.

The charge of "horse racism" is a hardy perennial, but its bloom may
finally be fading. In their study of television's 1984 general election coverage, Maura Clancey and Michael Robinson noted a shift away from the
usual prevalence of horse-race stories. The new beneficiary of media attention was not policy issues ("enduring disputes about how *government* should
behave") but campaign issues ("short-term concerns about how *candidates*
or their *campaigns* should behave").[1] As Table 1 shows, 1988 coverage was
cast in the same mold. Campaign issues like disputes over Dan Quayle's
National Guard service, negative ads, and mudslinging barely edged out
discussions of strategy and tactics as the most frequent topic of campaign news. Policy issues came in third, and horse-race news ran a distant
fourth.

Source: *Public Opinion* (January/February 1989): 18–19, 52. Reprinted with the permission of
the American Enterprise Institute for Public Policy Research, Washington, D.C..

TABLE 1.   Top Ten Story Topics

			NUMBER OF STORIES
Campaign issues	339	The debates	103
Strategy and tactics	338	Vice presidential choices	23
Policy issues	282	Media coverage	22
Horse race	168	Past campaigns	20
The electorate	108	Reagan's role	18

In fact the general election witnessed a dramatic reversal of the primary season in this regard. Throughout the primary campaign, over twice as many stories focused on the candidates' positioning for the nomination as their issue positions. This fall that ratio was nearly reversed, with 282 stories on policy issues and only 168 on the horse race. As Table 2 indicates, crime, defense, and the economy were each covered in over 100 stories. Between forty and eighty stories apiece dealt with unemployment, drugs, taxes, the environment, education, and the budget deficit. (Many stores covered more than one issue.)

Critics of this year's horse-race coverage usually focus on the profusion of poll reports, many of them commissioned by the networks themselves. The real issue here is the propriety of such coverage, not its preponderance. The horse-race coverage was heavily poll driven, but the polls didn't drive the issues off the air.

A SUPINE PRESS?

The other major complaint is that the networks let Bush and his image makers make patsies out of them. This passivity in the face of Republican skills at media manipulation allegedly gave Bush free rein to get his chosen message out each day. Thus, Kalb bitingly termed Roger Ailes a "de facto producer of the evening news," and *Newsweek* called for a return to "the days when reporters and editors picked the sound bites."

TABLE 2.   Top Ten Policy Issues

			NUMBER OF STORIES
Crime	142	Taxes	70
Defense	121	Environment	54
The economy	121	Education	46
Unemployment	77	Budget deficit	45
Drugs	74		

Once again, it is hard to square this portrayal with the data presented in Table 3. This fall 1,137 judgments from all sources were aired on the personal character, public records, campaign styles, issue stands, or other attributes of George Bush and Michael Dukakis. The result was mainly bad news for both men. Negative judgments outweighed positive ones by the same two-to-one margin (66 to 34 percent) for both candidates. Even the number of evaluations was virtually identical—564 for Bush and 573 for Dukakis.

Media criticism outweighed praise by roughly the same two-to-one margin among both partisan sources (the candidates and their supporters) and non-partisan ones (reporters, pundits, and ordinary voters) on all three networks, and on the major dimensions along which the candidates were evaluated—their issue stands, records in office, and performance on the campaign trail.

So Bush was *not* allowed to deliver his sound bites without challenge. On November 4, for example, he attacked Dukakis for financial misman-agement, while holding up a *Boston Herald* headline that read, "What a Mess!" CBS's Eric Engberg identified the *Herald* as a "pro-Bush Boston tabloid" and commented tartly, "Bush, without taking note of the fact that the federal deficit is now $155 billion, *acted* like an outraged prosecutor." Engberg closed by noting that the Bush campaign had "trotted out" some Massachusetts Republicans who said "with straight faces" that the vice pres-ident was surprised at this state of affairs.

TABLE 3.   Good Press

	BUSH	DUKAKIS	NUMBER OF SOURCES
Source			
All sources	34	34	1137
Partisans	32	35	795
Nonpartisans	38	31	342
Networks			
ABC	34	36	372
CBS	30	33	414
NBC	37	32	345
Topic			
Issues	31	27	221
Job performance	22	32	168
Candidate performance	34	36	418
Character	43	45	18
Time period			
Post convention (8/19–8/28)	75	26	78
Pre first debate (8/29–9/25)	23	28	288
Between debates (9/26–10/13)	28	31	216
Post second debate (10/14–11/7)	36	40	555

Note: Data based on clearly positive or negative source evaluations on ABC, CBS, and NBC nightly news-casts 8/19–11/7/88.

Bush may have gotten the sound bite he wanted that night, but the *story* was about the act he was putting on, and the tone was one of unmistakable sarcasm. Similarly, in his September 15 report about an earlier Bush attack on the "Massachusetts miracle," ABC's Brit Hume commented acidly, "Bush says he wants a kinder, gentler America, but there's nothing kind or gentle about the way he's campaigning."

CBS's reporting was even more aggressive on September 16. After Bush claimed that Massachusetts had lost thousands of jobs, Engberg stated flatly, "Wrong!" He then rebutted Bush point by point. On October 19, ABC's Richard Threlkeld performed a similar vivisection on Bush's notorious "tank" ad that painted Dukakis as dovish on defense. Such stories could hardly have done more to inoculate viewers against the candidate's intended message.

Of course Dukakis didn't fare any better. The airwaves were increasingly filled with complaints about his dullness, arrogance, and disorganized campaign techniques. For every story that protested Bush's new-found pugnacity, another ripped Dukakis's ineptitude as a counterpuncher. On November 6, NBC's Tom Pettit summed up one line of criticism: "While Bush was burning up the campaign trail, Dukakis was fiddling with state functions." After a shot of Dukakis posing with children (and looking distinctly unpresidential), Pettit noted sarcastically, "Remember, this is the Democratic candidate for president." He then ridiculed the Massachusetts governor for "displaying keen knowledge of gardening" at an agricultural event where he talked about compost piles. Pettit concluded, "This is what you call a turning point. Dukakis discussing composting, while George Bush was out being ferocious."

If the coverage was anything but fluff and puffery, why the flurry of assertions to the contrary? First, there's the frustration factor. Part of the battle for the presidency is the struggle for control of the battlefield—the media agenda. The combatants are the candidates on one side, and the journalists on the other. Both sides win some and lose some, and journalists always come away licking some wounds.

Remember 1984, which saw practically none of this year's notorious negative campaigning? It was derided as an issueless exercise in feel-good politics. On election eve NBC correspondent Chris Wallace complained that Reagan had waged "a campaign long on glitz and short on substance . . . a cynical campaign, manipulative . . . (that) offered pomp and platitudes. . . . " Since 1972, television has set the rules for presidential politics. Journalists disdain those who play the game poorly and resent those who play it well.

The complaints, however, do have some basis in reality. Bush ran a better media campaign than Dukakis, which is not the same as fooling the media or getting good press. The issues mentioned most often on TV news—crime and defense—were Bush's key issues. And Dukakis was called a liberal on the evening news sixty-five times this fall, compared to only fourteen times during fourteen months of primary campaigning. The proportion of the public who found him "too liberal" nearly doubled from May to October. But it's not television's fault that the Democrats lacked a coherent media strategy or that Dukakis proved a poor pugilist.

The one time that Bush clearly benefited from good press was during and just after the Republic convention. His coverage in late August fulfilled all the conditions for the type of media breakthrough enjoyed by Jimmy Carter in 1972, Gary Hart in 1984, and Jesse Jackson earlier this year. By exceeding expectations he briefly dominated the field as a highly visible, viable, and desirable candidate. Why the sudden shift? The traditional convention honeymoon coverage was magnified by journalistic amazement that the 97-pound weakling of American politics had turned into a muscle-bound macho man. His media image and poll ratings soared in tandem as he kicked sand into his rival's face. It was a textbook demonstration of the power of positive viewing.

So, did television give Bush an unfair boost after all? We think not, unless the canons of media fairness are interpreted to require balanced coverage during every week of the campaign. Bush's good press plummeted even before Labor Day and ran behind Dukakis's the rest of the fall. At the time, moreover, notions of a media boost for Bush seemed absurd. The question being raised in late August was whether the media had done in the Bush campaign by its aggressive coverage of the Quayle controversy.

During the twelve days after his selection on August 16, Quayle was the subject of ninety-three stories on the evening news—more coverage than any presidential candidate but Bush had received throughout the entire primary campaign. Quayle's 21 percent positive rating from nonpartisan sources at the height of the controversy was nearly as low as we logged for Gary Hart during the Donna Rice scandal in May 1987.[2] (Quayle's image never recovered. His nonpartisan good press score rose to only 31 percent, compared to an unbeatable 100 percent for Lloyd Bentsen.)

Ironically, the Quayle affair worked to Bush's advantage by keeping him on-screen every night defending his running mate in a decisive, resolute manner that reinforced his new take-charge image. In addition it moved up the kick-off of the fall campaign. Bush roared out of the gate like an Oklahoma "Sooner," while Dukakis was still awaiting the traditional Labor Day starter's gun. In fact some of Bush's edge in good press derived from criticism of his opponent on precisely this point. As ABC's Jim Wooten noted on August 29, "The governor may remember in November what he didn't do in August."

VOTER PERCEPTIONS

Finally, the media's role must be understood within the broader dynamics of how voters decide. The playing field was tilted in Bush's direction this year by the combination of peace, prosperity, and a still-popular president.

And voters' perceptions are formed not only by the campaign drama but by the stage on which it is played out. Bush needed only to actualize this potential advantage by convincing voters that he was not a bumbling effete snob out of touch with their concerns. He accomplished this by focusing attention on his opponent's flaws rather than his own virtues.

George Bush has always had a media problem. Previous studies found that he attracted mostly negative press during the 1980 and 1984 campaigns, as well as the 1988 primary season.[3] He didn't convert many reporters to his cause this year, and his coverage showed it. Nonetheless, 1988 will be remembered as the year Bush succeeded in turning his media image from a threat into an opportunity.

NOTES

[1]Michael J. Robinson and Maura Clancey, "General Election Coverage: Part 1," *Public Opinion*, December/January 1985, pages 49–54 and 59.

[2]"Quayle Hunt," *Media Monitor*, September 1988.

[3]Robinson, "General Election Coverage, Part 1." Michael J. Robinson and Margaret Sheehan, *Over the Wire and on TV*, New York: Russell Sage, 1983. S. Robert Lichter, "How the Press Covered the Primaries," *Public Opinion*, July/August 1988, pages 45–49.

8. The Vote and Its Meaning

Political scientists generally focus on three sets of attitudes that influence vote choice: attitudes toward parties, issues, and candidates. Early studies found that partisanship was the most important determinant of vote, and although its role has declined over the past three decades, party identification remains a good predictor of vote choice. As increasing numbers of Americans identify themselves as independents or vote for Democrats *and* Republicans, however, other attitudes have become more important. More than ever, presidential campaigns are directed at television audiences, allowing potential voters to form firm impressions of the candidates. These candidate evaluations are now as important as partisanship; in some elections they are critical determinants of vote choice. For example, polls of voters exiting their voting stations in 1980 revealed that most Reagan voters supported him not because of his issue positions, but because they felt that Carter was not up to the job.

How voters' attitudes toward the issues of the campaign influence their vote choice varies. The presidential candidates in 1988 debated the proper level of defense spending, and the best way to deal with the problems of childcare, the homeless, and health insurance for the poor. Voters' attitudes toward issues are more important in those elections in which candidates take widely divergent policy positions (such as Goldwater and Johnson in 1964, or Nixon and McGovern in 1972), and less so when the parties nominate two mainstream, moderate candidates (such as Ford and Carter in 1976, or Bush and Dukakis in 1988). In most elections, only a minority of the public follows the campaign debate closely enough to be swayed by any but the most basic issues.

Although elections are an important mechanism for translating public opinion into public policy, the vote is an extremely blunt instrument. For example, in the 1984 presidential election, most voters were closer to Walter Mondale on most issues than they were to Ronald Reagan, but they also wanted to reward Reagan for what they saw as his role in the economic recovery of 1984. With only one vote to cast, they rewarded Reagan for his performance without endorsing his policy positions. Voters often face a difficult choice between two candidates with which they agree on some but not all issues. Many voters in 1988 felt closer to Dukakis on some issues and to Bush on others, but they could vote for only one candidate.

The bluntness of the ballot makes it extremely difficult to find a single message in any election. Nonetheless, presidents generally try to persuade others that their victory was a mandate for their entire policy program. Although the exit polls in 1980 showed that most voters cast ballots *against* Carter rather than *for* Reagan, the Reagan White House succeeded in convincing many Southern Democrats in Congress of a Reagan election mandate for increased defense spending and cuts in taxes.

Winners are not alone in attempting to build political interpretations for their victories. In recent years, Democrats have debated vigorously the meaning of their continued losses in presidential elections and their continued dominance of Congress. Some moderate and conservative Democrats argue that their party must move to the center to win more votes, while others suggest that their defeats are due to a series of special circumstances—the Iran-hostage crisis, the popularity of Reagan, and the ineffective campaign of Michael Dukakis—and potentially in 1992, the Persian Gulf war.

In the first reading in this chapter, Robert Dahl suggests that the concept of a presidential mandate is a myth created by presidents to generate support for their programs. He concludes that an election inherently has many meanings that no elected leader is uniquely situated to interpret.

William Schneider provides one interpretation of the 1988 presidential election. During the campaign, Bush both castigated and defined Dukakis's liberalism. After the Republican convention, Bush told the voters that liberals favored a number of expensive or unpopular programs, and that Dukakis was a liberal. Although Dukakis attempted in late October to put a more positive shine on the liberal label, by then it was too late. Schneider suggests that Democrats need not repudiate liberalism to win; rather they need to put forward a different thematic message and a different kind of candidate. Liberals can win only if they are perceived as tough.

Next, James Barnes discusses one difficulty facing Democratic candidates: the Electoral College is increasingly stacked against them. Republicans seem to routinely carry the mountain West and the deep South, as well as several states in the Midwest and Northeast. Their base gives them a very comfortable lead and more flexibility in allocating the resources of their campaign. That base will actually increase after the redistricting in 1992. To win, Democrats must carry nearly all of the industrial heartland of America, as well as most of the West coast. Since most of these states are very competitive, the tilt of the Electoral College puts the Republicans in the driver's seat.

Finally, Bob Biersack provides an interpretation of the congressional election of 1990. Despite widespread talk of voter rebellion against incumbents in 1990, most incumbents won easily. Biersack suggests that voter dissatisfaction developed relatively late in the election cycle, after challengers had been recruited. Since most challengers lacked the political experience to mount serious campaigns, they were unable to take advantage of the mood of the electorate. Moreover, many of them lacked the resources to do so. Biersack notes, however, that several poorly funded challenges won in 1990, and that many incumbents won by smaller margins than in previous years. The 1992 House elections will be especially interesting, for redistricting will create many open seats, and redrawn boundaries may weaken many incumbents.

Myth of the Presidential Mandate

ROBERT A. DAHL

During the 1980s, conservatives and liberals debated the proper interpretation of Reagan's elections. Conservatives argued that the voters had awarded Reagan a broad mandate to reduce federal spending, cut taxes, and strengthen the nation's military, but liberals countered that opinion polls did not show support for many of these policies. Political scientist Robert Dahl has written many books and articles on the American political system. Here he argues that the concept of a Presidential mandate is a myth created by presidents to marshal support for their policies.

On election night in 1980 the vice president elect enthusiastically informed the country that Ronald Reagan's triumph was

> ... not simply a mandate for a change but a mandate for peace and freedom; a mandate for prosperity; a mandate for opportunity for all Americans regardless of race, sex, or creed; a mandate for leadership that is both strong and compassionate ... a mandate to make government the servant of the people in the way our founding fathers intended; a mandate for hope; a mandate for hope for the fulfillment of the great dream that President-elect Reagan has worked for all his life.[1]

I suppose there are no limits to permissible exaggeration in the elation of victory, especially by a vice president elect. He may therefore be excused, I imagine, for failing to note, as did many others who made comments in a similar vein in the weeks and months that followed, that Reagan's lofty mandate was provided by 50.9 percent of the voters. A decade it is much more evident, as it should have been then, that what was widely interpreted as Reagan's mandate, not only by supporters but by opponents, was more myth than reality.

In claiming that the outcome of the election provided a mandate to the president from the American people to bring about the policies, programs, emphases, and new directions uttered during the campaign by the winning candidate and his supporters, the vice president elect was like other commentators echoing a familiar theory.

---

[1]Stanley Kelley, Jr., *Interpreting Elections* (Princeton, N.J.: Princeton University Press, 1983), 217.

Source: Reprinted with permission from *Political Science Quarterly*, 105 (Fall 1990): pp. 355–366.

ORIGIN AND DEVELOPMENT

A history of the theory of the presidential mandate has not been written, and I have no intention of supplying one here. However, if anyone could be said to have created the myth of the presidential mandate, surely it would be Andrew Jackson. Although he never used the word mandate, so far as I know, he was the first American president to claim not only that the president is uniquely representative of all the people, but that his election confers on him a mandate from the people in support of his policy. Jackson's claim was a fateful step in the democratization of the constitutional system of the United States—or rather what I prefer to call the pseudodemocratization of the presidency.

As Leonard White observed, it was Jackson's "settled conviction" that "the President was an immediate and direct representative of the people." Presumably as a result of his defeat in 1824 in both the electoral college and the House of Representatives, in his first presidential message to Congress, in order that "as few impediments as possible should exist to the free operation of the public will," he proposed that the Constitution be amended to provide for the direct election of the president.[2]

> "To the people", he said, "belongs the right of electing their Chief Magistrate: it was never designed that their choice should, in any case, be defeated, either by the intervention of electoral colleges or by... the House of Representatives."[3]

His great issue of policy was the Bank of the United States, which he unwaveringly believed was harmful to the general good. Acting on this conviction, in 1832 he vetoed the bill to renew the bank's charter. Like his predecessors, he justified the veto as a protection against unconstitutional legislation; but unlike his predecessors in their comparatively infrequent use of the veto he also justified it as a defense of his or his party's policies.

Following his veto of the bank's charter, the bank became the main issue in the presidential election of 1832. As a consequence, Jackson's reelection was widely regarded, even among his opponents (in private, at least), as amounting to "something like a popular ratification" of his policy.[4] When in order to speed the demise of the bank Jackson found it necessary to fire his treasury secretary, he justified his action on the ground, among others, that "The President is the direct representative of the American people, but the Secretaries are not."[5]

Innovative though it was, Jackson's theory of the presidential mandate was less robust than it was to become in the hands of his successors. In

---

[2]Quoted in Leonard D. White, *The Jacksonians: A Study in Administrative History, 1829–1861* (New York: Free Press, 1954), 23.

[3]Cited in James W. Ceaser, *Presidential Selection: Theory and Development* (Princeton, N.J.: Princeton University Press, 1979), 160, fn. 58.

[4]White, *Jacksonians*, 23.

[5]Ibid., 23.

1848 James Polk explicitly formulated the claim, in a defense of his use of the veto on matters of policy, that as a representative of the people the president was, if not more representative than the Congress, at any rate equally so.

> "The people, by the constitution, have commanded the President, as much as they have commanded the legislative branch of the Government, to execute their will. . . . The President represents in the executive department the whole people of the United States, as each member of the legislative department represents portions of them. . . . " The President is responsible "not only to an enlightened public opinion, but to the people of the whole Union, who elected him, as the representatives in the legislative branches . . . are responsible to the people of particular States or districts. . . . "[6]

Notice that in Jackson's and Polk's views, the president, both constitutionally and as representative of the people, is on a par with Congress. They did not claim that in either respect the president is superior to Congress. It was Woodrow Wilson who took the further step in the evolution of the theory by asserting that in representing the people the president is not merely equal to Congress but actually superior to it.

Earlier Views

Because the theory of the presidential mandate espoused by Jackson and Polk has become an integral part of our present-day conception of the presidency, it may be hard for us to grasp how sharply that notion veered off from the views of the earlier presidents.

As James Ceaser has shown, the Framers designed the presidential election process as a means of improving the chances of electing a *national* figure who would enjoy majority support. They hoped their contrivance would avoid not only the populistic competition among candidates dependent on "the popular arts," which they rightly believed would occur if the president were elected by the people, but also what they believed would necessarily be a factional choice if the president were chosen by the Congress, particularly by the House.

In adopting the solution of an electoral college, however, the Framers seriously underestimated the extent to which the strong impulse toward democratization that was already clearly evident among Americans—particularly among their opponents, the anti-Federalists—would subvert and alter their carefully contrived constitutional structure. Since this is a theme I shall pick up later, I want now to mention only two such failures that bear closely on the theory of the presidential mandate. First, the Founders did not foresee the development of political parties nor comprehend how a two-party system might achieve their goal of insuring the election of a figure of national

[6]Ibid., 24.

rather than merely local renown. Second, as Ceaser remarks, although the Founders recognized "the need for a popular judgment of the performance of an incumbent" and designed a method for selecting the president that would, as they thought, provide that opportunity, they "did not see elections as performing the role of instituting decisive changes in policy in response to popular demands." In short, theory of the presidential mandate not only cannot be found in the Framers' conception of the Constitution; almost certainly it violates that conception.

No president prior to Jackson challenged the view that Congress was the legitimate representative of the people. Even Thomas Jefferson, who adeptly employed the emerging role of party leader to gain congressional support for his policies and decisions

> was more Whig than . . . the British Whigs themselves in subordinating [the executive power] to "the supreme legislative power". . . . The tone of his messages is uniformly deferential to Congress. His first one closes with these words: "Nothing shall be wanting on my part to inform, as far as in my power, the legislative judgment, nor to carry that judgment into faithful execution."[7]

James Madison, demonstrating that a great constitutional theorist and an adept leader in Congress could be decidedly less than a great president, deferred so greatly to Congress that in his communications to that body his extreme caution rendered him "almost unintelligible"[8]—a quality one would hardly expect from one who had been a master of lucid exposition at the Constitutional Convention. His successor, James Monroe, was so convinced that Congress should decide domestic issues without presidential influence that throughout the debates in Congress on "the greatest political issue of his day . . . the admission of Missouri and the status of slavery in Louisiana Territory," he remained utterly silent.[9]

Madison and Monroe serve not as examples of how presidents should behave but as evidence of how early presidents thought they should behave. Considering the constitutional views and the behavior of Jackson's predecessors, it is not hard to see why his opponents called themselves Whigs in order to emphasize his dereliction from the earlier and presumably constitutionally correct view of the presidency.

Woodrow Wilson

The long and almost unbroken success of mediocrities who succeeded to the presidency between Polk and Wilson for the most part subscribed to the

---

[7]Edward S. Corwin, *The President: Offices and Powers, 1789–1948*, 3rd ed. (New York: New York University Press, 1948), 20.

[8]Wilfred E. Binkley, *President and Congress* (New York: Alfred A. Knopf, 1947), 56.

[9]Leonard D. White, *The Jeffersonians: A Study in Administrative History, 1801–1829* (New York: Free Press, 1951), 31.

Whig view of the office and seem to have laid no claim to a popular mandate for their policies—when they had any. Even Abraham Lincoln, in justifying the unprecedented scope of presidential power he believed he needed in order to meet secession and civil war, rested his case on constitutional grounds, and not as a mandate from the people. Indeed, since he distinctly failed to gain a majority of votes in the election of 1860, any claim to a popular mandate would have been dubious at best. Like Lincoln, Theodore Roosevelt also had a rather unrestricted view of presidential power; he expressed the view then emerging among Progressives that chief executives were also representatives of the people. Yet the stewardship he claimed for the presidency was ostensibly drawn—rather freely drawn, I must say—from the Constitution, not from the mystique of the mandate.

Woodrow Wilson, more as political scientist than as president, brought the mandate theory to what now appears to be its canonical form. His formulation was influenced by his admiration for the British system of cabinet government. In 1879, while still a senior at Princeton, he published an essay recommending the adoption of cabinet government in the United States. He provided little indication as to how this change was to be brought about, however, and soon abandoned the idea without yet having found an alternative solution. Nevertheless, he continued to contrast the American system of congressional government, in which Congress was all-powerful but lacked executive leadership, with British cabinet government, in which parliament, though all powerful, was firmly led by the prime minister and his cabinet. Since Americans were not likely to adopt the British cabinet system, however, he began to consider the alternative of more powerful presidential leadership. In his *Congressional Government*, published in 1885, he acknowledged that "the representatives of the people are the proper ultimate authority in all matters of government, and that administration is merely the clerical part of government." Congress is "unquestionably, the predominant and controlling force, the center and source of all motive and of all regulative power." Yet a discussion of policy that goes beyond "special pleas for special privilege" is simply impossible in the House, "a disintegrate mass of jarring elements," while the Senate is no more than "a small, select, and leisurely House of Representatives."

By 1908, when *Constitutional Government in the United States* was published, Wilson had arrived at strong presidential leadership as a feasible solution. He faulted the earlier presidents who had adopted the Whig theory of the Constitution.

> . . . (T)he makers of the Constitution were not enacting Whig theory. . . . The President is at liberty, both in law and conscience, to be as big a man as he can. His capacity will set the limit; and if Congress be overborne by him, it will be no fault of the makers of the Constitution,—it will be from no lack of constitutional powers on its part, but only because the President has the nation behind him, and Congress has not. He has no means of compelling Congress except through public opinion. . . . (T)he

early Whig theory of political dynamics . . . is far from being a democratic theory. . . . It is particularly intended to prevent the will of the people as a whole from having at any moment an unobstructed sweep and ascendancy.

And he contrasted the president with Congress in terms that would become commonplace among later generations of commentators, including political scientists:

> Members of the House and Senate are representatives of localities, are voted for only by sections of voters, or by local bodies of electors like the members of the state legislatures. There is no national party choice except that of President. No one else represents the people as a whole, exercising a national choice. . . . The nation as a whole has chosen him, and is conscious that it has no other political spokesman. His is the only national voice in affairs. . . . He is the representative of no constituency, but of the whole people. When he speaks in his true character, he speaks for no special interest. . . . (T)here is but one national voice in the country, and that is the voice of the President.[10]

Since Wilson, it has become commonplace for presidents and commentators alike to argue that by virtue of his election the president has received a mandate for his aims and policies from the people of the United States. The myth of the mandate is now a standard weapon in the arsenal of persuasive symbols all presidents exploit. For example, as the Watergate scandals emerged in mid-1973, Patrick Buchanan, then an aide in the Nixon White House, suggested that the president should accuse his accusers of "seeking to destroy the democratic mandate of 1972." Three weeks later in an address to the country Nixon said:

> Last November, the American people were given the clearest choice of this century. Your votes were a mandate, which I accepted, to complete the initiatives we began in my first term and to fulfill the promises I made for my second term.[11]

If the spurious nature of Nixon's claim now seems self-evident, the dubious grounds for virtually all such pretensions are perhaps less obvious.

CRITIQUE OF THE THEORY

What does a president's claim to a mandate amount to? The meaning of the term itself is not altogether clear. Fortunately, however, in his excellent book *Interpreting Elections*, Stanley Kelley has "piece[d] together a coherent statement of the theory."

---

[10] Woodrow Wilson, *Constitutional Government in the United States* (New York: Columbia University Press, 1908), 67–68, 70, 202–203.

[11] Kelley, *Interpreting Elections*, 99.

Its first element is the belief that elections carry messages about problems, policies, and programs—messages plain to all and specific enough to be directive. . . . Second, the theory holds that certain of these messages must be treated as authoritative commands . . . either to the victorious candidate or to the candidate and his party. . . . To qualify as mandates, messages about policies and programs must reflect the *stable* views both of individual voters and of the electorate. . . . In the electorate as a whole, the numbers of those for or against a policy or program matter. To suggest that a mandate exists for a particular policy is to suggest that more than a bare majority of those voting are agreed upon it. The common view holds that landslide victories are more likely to involve mandates than are narrow ones. . . . The final element of the theory is a negative imperative: Governments should not undertake major innovations in policy or procedure, except in emergencies, unless the electorate has had an opportunity to consider them in an election and thus to express its views.

To bring out the central problems more clearly, let me extract what might be called the primitive theory of the popular presidential mandate. According to this theory, a presidential election can accomplish four things. First, it confers constitutional and legal authority on the victor. Second, at the same time, it also conveys information. At a minimum it reveals the first preferences for president of a plurality of votes. Third, according to the primitive theory, the election, at least under the conditions Kelley describes, conveys further information: namely that a clear majority of voters prefer the winner because they prefer his policies and wish him to pursue his policies. Finally, because the president's policies reflect the wishes of a majority of voters, when conflicts over policy arise between president and Congress, the president's policies ought to prevail.

While we can readily accept the first two propositions, the third, which is pivotal to the theory, might be false. But if the third is false, then so is the fourth. So the question arises: Beyond revealing the first preferences of a plurality of voters, do presidential elections also reveal the additional information that a plurality (or a majority) of voters prefer the policies of the winner and wish the winner to pursue those policies?

In appraising the theory I want to distinguish between two different kinds of criticisms. First, some critics contend that even when the wishes of constituents can be known, they should not be regarded as in any way binding on a legislator. I have in mind, for example, Edmund Burke's famous argument that he would not sacrifice to public opinion his independent judgment of how well a policy would serve his constituents' interests, and the argument suggested by Hanna Pitkin that representatives bound by instructions would be prevented from entering into the compromises that legislation usually requires.

Second, some critics, on the other hand, may hold that when the wishes of constituents on matters of policy can be clearly discerned, they ought to be given great and perhaps even decisive weight. But, these critics contend, constituents' wishes usually cannot be known, at least when the constituency is large and diverse, as in presidential elections. In expressing his doubts on the matter in 1913, A. Lawrence Lowell quoted Sir Henry Maine: "The devotee of democracy is much in the same position as the Greeks with their oracles. All agreed that the voice of an oracle was the voice of god, but everybody allowed that when he spoke he was not as intelligible as might be desired."

It is exclusively the second kind of criticism that I want now to consider. Here again I am indebted to Stanley Kelley for his succinct summary of the main criticisms.

> Critics allege that 1) some particular claim of a mandate is unsupported by adequate evidence; 2) most claims of mandates are unsupported by adequate evidence; 3) most claims of mandates are politically self-serving; or 4) it is not possible in principle to make a valid claim of a mandate, since it is impossible to sort out voters' intentions.

Kelley goes on to say that while the first three criticisms may well be valid, the fourth has been outdated by the sample survey, which "has again given us the ability to discover the grounds of voters' choices." In effect, then, Kelley rejects the primitive theory and advances the possibility of a more sophisticated mandate theory according to which the information about policies is conveyed not by the election outcome but instead by opinion surveys. Thus the two functions are cleanly split: presidential elections are for electing a president, opinion surveys provide information about the opinions, attitudes, and judgments that account for the outcome.

However, I would propose a fifth proposition, which I believe is also implicit in Kelley's analysis:

> 5) While it may not be strictly impossible *in principle* to make a reasoned and well-grounded claim to a presidential mandate, to do so *in practice* requires a complex analysis that in the end may not yield much support for presidential claims.

But if we reject the primitive theory of the mandate and adopt the more sophisticated theory, then it follows that prior to the introduction of scientific sample surveys, no president could reasonably have defended his claim to a mandate. To put a precise date on the proposition, let me remind you that the first presidential election in which scientific surveys formed the basis of an extended and systematic analysis was 1940.[12]

I do not mean to say that no election before 1940 now permits us to draw the conclusion that a president's major policies were supported by a substantial majority of the electorate. But I do mean that for most presidential elections before 1940 a valid reconstruction of the policy views of the electorate is impossible or enormously difficult, even with the aid of aggre-

---

[12]Paul F. Lazarsfeld, Bernard Berelson, and Hazel Gaudet, *The People's Choice* (New York: Columbia University Press, 1948).

gate data and other indirect indicators of voters' views. When we consider that presidents ordinarily asserted their claims soon after their elections, well before historians and social scientists could have sifted through reams of indirect evidence, then we must conclude that before 1940 no contemporary claim to a presidential mandate could have been supported by the evidence available at the time.

While the absence of surveys undermines presidential claims to a mandate before 1940, the existence of surveys since then would not necessarily have supported such claims. Ignoring all other shortcomings of the early election studies, the analysis of the 1940 election I just mentioned was not published until 1948. While that interval between the election and the analysis may have set a record, the systematic analysis of survey evidence that is necessary (though perhaps not sufficient) to interpret what a presidential election means always comes well after presidents and commentators have already told the world, on wholly inadequate evidence, what the election means.[13] Perhaps the most famous voting study to date, *The American Voter*, which drew primarily on interviews conducted in 1952 and 1956, appeared in 1960.[14] The book by Stanley Kelley that I have drawn on so freely here, which interprets the elections of 1964, 1972, and 1980, appeared in 1983.

A backward glance quickly reveals how empty the claims to a presidential mandate have been in recent elections. Take 1960. If more than a bare majority is essential to a mandate, then surely Kennedy could have received no mandate, since he gained less than 50 percent of the total popular vote by the official count—just how much less by the unofficial count varies with the counter. Yet "on the day after election, and every day thereafter," Theodore Sorenson tells us, "he rejected the argument that the country had given him no mandate. Every election has a winner and a loser, he said in effect. There may be difficulties with the Congress, but a margin of only one vote would still be a mandate."

By contrast, 1964 was a landslide election, as was 1972. From his analysis, however, Kelley concludes that "Johnson's and Nixon's specific claims of meaningful mandates do not stand up well when confronted by evidence." To be sure, in both elections some of the major policies of the winners were supported by large majorities among those to whom these issues were salient. Yet "none of these policies was cited by more than 21 percent of respondents as a reason to like Johnson, Nixon, or their parties."

In 1968, Nixon gained office with only 43 percent of the popular vote. No mandate there. Likewise in 1976, Carter won with a bare 50.1 percent. Once again, no mandate there.

When Reagan won in 1980, thanks to the much higher quality of surveys undertaken by the media, a more sophisticated understanding of what

[13]The early election studies are summarized in Bernard R. Berelson and Paul F. Lazarsfeld, *Voting* (Chicago: University of Chicago Press, 1954), 331ff.

[14]Angus Campbell et al, *The American Voter* (New York: Wiley, 1960).

that election meant no longer had to depend on the academic analyses that would only follow some years later. Nonetheless, many commentators, bemused as they so often are by the arithmetical peculiarities of the electoral college, immediately proclaimed both a landslide and a mandate for Reagan's policies. What they often failed to note was that Reagan gained just under 51 percent of the popular vote. Despite the claims of the vice president elect, surely we can find no mandate there. Our doubts are strengthened by the fact that in the elections to the House, Democratic candidates won just over 50 percent of the popular vote and a majority of seats. However, they lost control of the Senate. No Democratic mandate there, either.

These clear and immediate signs that the elections of 1980 failed to confer a mandate on the president or his Democratic opponents were, however, largely ignored. For it was so widely asserted as to be commonplace that Reagan's election reflected a profound shift of opinion away from New Deal programs and toward the new conservatism. However, from this analysis of the survey evidence, Kelley concludes that the commitment of voters to candidates was weak; a substantial proportion of Reagan voters were more interested in voting against Carter than for Reagan; and despite claims by journalists and others, the New Deal coalition did not really collapse. Nor was there any profound shift toward conservatism. "The evidence from press surveys. . . . contradicts the claims that voters shifted toward conservatism and that this ideological shift elected Reagan." In any case, the relation between ideological location and policy preferences was "of a relatively modest magnitude."

In winning by a landslide of popular votes in 1984, Reagan achieved one prerequisite to a mandate. Yet in that same election, Democratic candidates for the House won 52 percent of the popular votes. Two years earlier, they had won 55 percent of the votes. On the face of it, surely the 1984 elections gave no mandate to Reagan.

Before the end of 1986, when the Democrats had once again won a majority of popular votes in elections to the House and had also regained a majority of seats in the Senate, it should have been clear and it should be even clearer now that the major social and economic policies for which Reagan and his supporters had claimed a mandate have persistently failed to gain majority support. Indeed, the major domestic policies and programs established during the thirty years preceding Reagan in the White House have not been overturned in the grand revolution of policy that his election was supposed to have ushered in. For eight years, what Reagan and his supporters claimed as a mandate to reverse those policies was regularly rejected by means of the only legitimate and constitutional processes we Americans have for determining what the policies of the United States government should be.

What are we to make of this long history of unsupported claims to a presidential mandate? The myth of the mandate would be less important if it were not one element in the larger process of the pseudodemocratization of the presidency—the creation of a type of chief executive that in my view should have no proper place in a democratic republic.

Yet even if we consider it in isolation from the larger development of the presidency, the myth is harmful to American political life. By portraying the president as the only representative of the whole people and Congress as merely representing narrow, special, and parochial interests, the myth of the mandate elevates the president to an exalted position in our constitutional system at the expense of Congress. The myth of the mandate fosters the belief that the particular interests of the diverse human beings who form the citizen body in a large, complex, and pluralistic country like ours constitute no legitimate element in the general good. The myth confers on the aims of the groups who benefit from presidential policies an aura of national interest and public good to which they are no more entitled than the groups whose interests are reflected in the policies that gain support by congressional majorities. Because the myth is almost always employed to support deceptive, misleading, and manipulative interpretations, it is harmful to the political understanding of citizens.

It is, I imagine, now too deeply rooted in American political life and too useful a part of the political arsenal of presidents to be abandoned. Perhaps the most we can hope for is that commentators on public affairs in the media and in academic pursuits will dismiss claims to a presidential mandate with the scorn they usually deserve.

But if a presidential election does not confer a mandate on the victor, what does a presidential election mean, if anything at all? While a presidential election does not confer a popular mandate on the president—nor, for that matter, on congressional majorities—it confers the legitimate authority, right, and opportunity on a president to try to gain the adoption by constitutional means of the policies the president supports. In the same way, elections to Congress confer on a member the authority, right, and opportunity to try to gain the adoption by constitutional means of the policies he or she supports. Each may reasonably contend that a particular policy is in the public good or public interest and, moreover, is supported by a majority of citizens.

I do not say that whatever policy is finally adopted following discussion, debate, and constitutional processes necessarily reflects what a majority of citizens would prefer, or what would be in their interests, or what would be in the public good in any other sense. What I do say is that no elected leader, including the president, is uniquely privileged to say what an election means—nor to claim that the election has conferred on the president a mandate to enact the particular policies the president supports. . . .

Tough Liberals Win, Weak Liberals Lose

WILLIAM SCHNEIDER

In the aftermath of the 1988 election, commentators referred to the label liberal as "the dreaded L word," suggesting that Bush had succeeded in making liberalism seem distasteful to the American public. Political analyst William Schneider does not see liberalism as the death knell of the Democratic party. Rather, Schneider argues that Democrats can still embrace liberalism, but they need to articulate a consistent message and nominate candidates perceived to be tough.

It could have been a lot worse, say Democrats. Michael Dukakis got 112 electoral votes. That's a 750 percent improvement over Walter Mondale! Dukakis's 46 percent of the popular vote is the highest losing percentage the Democrats have gotten since 1964. Not only that, but the Democrats gained Senate seats, House seats, state legislative seats, and a governorship. That is a rare achievement for a losing party in a presidential race. "Coattails?" observed Representative Patricia Schroeder. "Bush got elected in a bikini."

On the other hand, think of it this way: the Democrats lost to George Bush and Dan Quayle. Last year a Democratic senator quipped, "If we can't beat George Bush, we'd better find another country." Well, they didn't beat George Bush. But there's an election in Canada later this month.

How's this for an irony? Democrats used to wear buttons saying, "The gender gap will get you." The gender gap turned out to be slightly wider this year than it was in 1980 and 1984. In the last two elections, however, it didn't make any difference. Both men and women voted for Ronald Reagan. This year it made a difference. According to the exit polls, women were either evenly split or gave a slight edge to Dukakis. Men voted for Bush by a wide margin. In other words, men elected Bush. The gender gap got the Democrats.

Here are three explanations for what happened to the Democrats this year: (a) Dukakis lost because he ran a lousy campaign. Implication: If Dukakis had run a better campaign, or if the party had put up a better candidate, the Democrats would have won. Not to worry. (b) Dukakis lost because of peace and prosperity. Implication: The Democrats lose because they always seem to run at the wrong time (like every four years). Just wait for things to get really bad under the Bush administration. Not to worry. (c)

Source: *The New Republic*, December 5, 1988. Reprinted by permission of *The New Republic*, © 1988, The New Republic, Inc.

Dukakis lost because the country doesn't want to buy what the Democrats have to sell. You just can't market liberalism these days. Implication: The Democrats can't win for the foreseeable future. Start worrying.

The correct answer is all three. The Dukakis campaign really didn't have anything to sell the voters. So it was forced to sell off Dukakis as a liberal. He was the first remaindered candidate in the history of American politics.

The Republicans knew from the outset that if the election were a referendum on Bush, they would lose. Bush just had too many negatives: the wimp image, his upper-class origins, his repeated lapses of judgment (Marcos, Noriega, Iran-*contra*, Quayle), and the normal desire for change after eight years. So the Republicans turned the election into a referendum on Dukakis. The central issue in the campaign became Dukakis's values instead of Bush's judgment. Bush called Dukakis a Massachusetts liberal. Dukakis had a hard time denying it. He *is* a Massachusetts liberal. It just wasn't anything he planned on talking about during the campaign.

The fact is, Michael Dukakis never had to defend his values before this year. Liberal values are not controversial in the Democratic Party. And they are no big deal in the Commonwealth of Massachusetts, where the Republican Party is a joke. Suddenly last summer, Dukakis came face to face with real Republicans. And like Sebastian Venable, he got eaten alive.

Bush used the Pledge of Allegiance and the "tank commercial" to convey the idea that Dukakis was weak on defense (with, perhaps, the subliminal message that a son of Greek immigrants was not a real American). Bush used the ACLU issue and the furlough ad to portray Dukakis as soft on crime (with, perhaps, a subliminal appeal to white racism). Dukakis's chosen theme of competence got sunk in Boston Harbor. How did Dukakis respond? By doing nothing. Which confirmed what Bush was saying: "I'm not the wimp. *He's* the wimp."

Dukakis thought he could win the presidency the same way he won the Democratic nomination—by being the "remainderman." During the primaries, he watched the other candidates either self-destruct (Hart, Biden) or destroy one another (Gephardt, Gore, Jackson). Dukakis just picked up the pieces and walked away with the nomination. He thought he could summer in the Berkshires and wait for George Bush to destroy himself.

In March, a week after Super Tuesday, when Dukakis won Florida and Texas, he came in an embarrassing third in Illinois. The next week Jesse Jackson beat him in Michigan. Everyone starting screaming advice at Dukakis, but the governor refused to panic. He knew that if he stayed cool, he wasn't going to lose to Jesse Jackson. That's exactly how Dukakis responded when the same thing happened to him in August. After Bush went negative on Dukakis, Democrats started pressuring him to fight back. Dukakis remained cool. He had heard it all before. No one would believe those preposterous commercials anyway. "We used to read this stuff and laugh and say, 'How can this be? Why would people take this seriously?' " his chief secretary recalled to the *New York Times*.

If Dukakis refused to take Bush seriously enough, Bush took Dukakis far too seriously. His anti-Dukakis commercials had an ominous, threatening quality. Bush depicted the governor of Massachusetts as a menace to the republic. Over *Jaws*-like theme music, the ads closed with the line, "America can't afford that risk." It worked. Dukakis's unfavorable ratings doubled from 25 percent in July to 50 percent in October, according to the NBC News-*Wall Street Journal* poll. The view that Dukakis would do a better job than Bush of maintaining a strong national defense dropped by ten points. In July, Dukakis beat Bush, 40 percent to 24 percent, as the candidate who would be tougher on crime. By October, Bush was ahead, 56 percent to 27 percent. In June, 30 percent of the public labeled Dukakis a liberal. In October, the figure reached 51 percent.

Dukakis's great weakness was his total inability to sustain a theme. He started out with competence, until his campaign proved otherwise. Then he told people that the 17 million added jobs under Reagan were not "good jobs at good wages." How many people like to be told that their jobs stink? He ran television commercials talking about the nation's "sham prosperity." But to most people, sham prosperity is a lot better than what they had under Jimmy Carter.

Dukakis spent a week or so on the "middle-class squeeze," during which he came up with approximately one new program a day. In the second debate with Bush, he hit upon the worst theme of all. "Tough choices will be required," he told the nation, "choices I am prepared to make and Mr. Bush is not prepared to make." Bush said, "I am optimistic and I think we can keep this long expansion going." The American people were asked to choose between a candidate whose theme was "We're all right, Jack," and a candidate who said, "Eat your broccoli."

Finally, Mr. Competence became Mr. "On-Your-Side." We got a dash of Gephardt nationalism and some warmed-over Mondale populism. The Dukakis campaign could never decide what it wanted to sell. So the Republicans took over the marketing. "Even though [Dukakis] avoided the interest group endorsements," a GOP strategist told the *Los Angeles Times*, "we were able to define him as a liberal because he did not have any overall theme or identity of his own."

Why has liberalism become such a scare word? The reason is that Reagan has changed the shape of American politics. He has created a powerful political coalition that brings together a variety of interests united by one thing—a distaste for big government. The key constituency in the Reagan coalition is middle-class voters who want low taxes. Thirty years ago, these voters thought of themselves as beneficiaries of government services. Now they think of themselves as taxpayers. Three things happened to change their view of government. In the 1960s the War on Poverty ended up in controversy and failure. As a result, social welfare programs began to lose their middle-class constituency. In the 1970s the inflation crisis gave rise to a tax revolt. The wrath of the middle class was aimed at big government, which was seen as poisoning the nation's economy. And in the 1980s Reagan's anti-government program produced, or at least coincided with, a six-year economic recovery.

Look at how Dukakis and Bush approached middle-class voters. When Dukakis talked about "the middle-class squeeze," he was dealing with middle-class voters the same way Democrats have always dealt with constituencies: "You've got a problem. We've got a program." He had a program to help with college tuition expenses, a program to meet child-care needs, a program to provide health insurance for all employees, and a program to encourage affordable home mortgages. These programs were all ingeniously designed to be "self-financing." Middle-class voters tend to be suspicious of government programs. They are afraid that the programs are going to end up costing them money and helping other people. Bush addressed middle-class voters quite differently. He said, "You're in a financial squeeze? Here's what we're going to do for you. We're going to keep the recovery going." The solution middle-class voters want isn't programs. It's prosperity. And that is exactly Bush's mandate—to keep the recovery going. If he does that, he will be a fine president. If he doesn't, he will be in deep doo-doo.

The Reagan coalition also includes business interests that favor a deregulated business environment. It includes religious conservatives who oppose judicial activism. It includes neoconservatives who want a more aggressive foreign policy. And it includes white voters motivated by racial fear and resentment. The two constituencies in which the Democrats have lost the most support over the last 25 years are Southern whites and Northern urban ethnics (formerly called the Archie Bunker vote, now the Morton Downey Jr. vote). These voters see the federal government as the protector of black interests and the promoter of the civil rights agenda.

FDR brought together a coalition of interests who wanted something from government. The Reagan coalition is its mirror image—groups that want less from government. To the amazement of many observers, the coalition held together this year for George Bush. What keeps it together is the perception of a common threat, namely, liberalism. Reagan voters fear that liberals will regain control of the federal government and use it, as they did in the past, to carry out an agenda that includes taxes, regulations, social reforms, and anti-military policies. Bush kept the coalition together because he succeeded in dramatizing the liberal threat.

At the very end of the campaign, Dukakis used economic populism to rally the Democratic Party base. It worked. No Republican since 1952 has done as badly among Democrats as George Bush did this year. In the end, Dukakis pulled the Democratic Party together better than either Carter in 1980 or Mondale in 1984. Then why didn't he win?

Because the Democratic base has shrunk. You can't win elections any more just by holding the Democratic party together. Exit polls show Democrats and Republicans evenly balanced among 1988 voters. In fact, Dukakis reclaimed a majority of Reagan Democrats. But they comprised less than ten percent of the electorate. Former Democrats who voted for Reagan are still around, of course. It's just that a lot of them no longer call themselves Democrats.

The class-warfare strategy worked for Harry Truman in 1948. It almost worked for Hubert Humphrey in 1968. But it didn't work for Michael Dukakis in 1988. Like Nixon and Reagan before him, Bush used social populism to undercut the Democrats' economic populism. Bush countered Dukakis's claim "I'm on your side" by asserting, "Values are the thing the working man is going to decide on. I've got those values on our side."

National Journal has produced a map of county-by-county results for the 1988 presidential election. Dukakis carried the black belt counties of the South. He carried the liberal belt along the Northern tier—New England, New York, the upper Midwest, and the Pacific Coast from Seattle to San Francisco. He carried the Hispanic belt in south Texas and New Mexico. He carried Hawaii, which is an Asian archipelago. He carried a scattering of farm belt counties in Missouri, Illinois, and Iowa. And he carried Appalachia, where there are a lot of poor whites but few blacks.

In presidential voting, the Democratic Party is now close to becoming a party of blacks and white liberals. In other words, the Jackson constituency and the Dukakis constituency. The two together are far from a national majority. And they don't even get along with each other.

Then why do the Democrats still do so well below the presidential level? Because races below the presidential level are rarely ideological. Challengers, who are often unknown to the voters, find it hard to engage incumbents on the issues. Since most incumbents are Democrats, the Democratic Party has a continuing advantage—so long as it can keep ideology from seeping into state and local voting.

There are two ways Democrats try to keep this from happening. One is to run on competence. Democrats are generally rated better at providing the kinds of benefits and services people want from government. The other is to exploit the advantages of incumbency. This means maintaining a good, and well-publicized, record of constituency service. "We do better the closer we get to people's garbage," one Democratic consultant told the *Washington Post.* Dukakis ran for president on competence—as if he were running for governor. Only it didn't work. You can't exclude values from a presidential election.

Democrats have been engaged in "rethinking" what their party stands for ever since the shock of 1980, and what have they come up with? Pragmatism. 1988 proves that pragmatism is not enough.

Dukakis, of course, is the ultimate pragmatist. He represents the post-ideological generation of Democrats, those who grew up with the civil rights and anti-war movements and remain loyal to those values, but have mastered a new technocratic style of politics. By putting Lloyd Bentsen on the ticket, Dukakis forged the ultimate pragmatic coalition. Bentsen is a Tory Democrat, a remnant of the *pre*-ideological tradition of the Democratic Party. Like Dukakis, Bentsen sees the Democrats as a governing party, not as a party of activists. With Dukakis and Bentsen on the ticket, the pre-ideological and post-ideological traditions joined forces. And it made a lot of liberals nervous.

Jesse Jackson, for one. Jackson went along with the ticket, but he never quite concealed his reservations about it. How could the Democrats win if they didn't *say* anything? In agreeing to support the ticket, Jackson said, in essence, "Go ahead. Do it your way. I'll do what I can to help." But there was another message: "This had better work." It didn't. When a party loses over and over again, as the Democrats have now done in five out of the last six presidential elections, it faces the likelihood of a fundamentalist revolt. At every Democratic convention, someone delivers the party's re-vival speech. Jackson gave the speech this year, just as Edward Kennedy did in 1980 and Mario Cuomo did in 1984. Each of them defined the party's traditions, ideals, and values. The delegates cried and cheered. Their souls were saved. The party then compromised its traditions, ideals, and values by nominating someone else. Now Jackson is saying that the "centrists" have had their chance. They got Super Tuesday, superdelegates, Dukakis, Bentsen, a meaningless platform, and a timid campaign. Enough compro-mises, says the left. Next time we want a real Democrat. The moderates have had their chance, and they failed.

The moderate position—pragmatism—has collapsed. So there is nothing between those who want to reaffirm the party's old-time religion and those who want to turn to the right. The problem is that both positions are unrealistic. By moving to the left, the Democrats are only going to make things worse for themselves. Whenever they put up a liberal ticket, the Democrats get locked out of the South. It wasn't supposed to happen this year, not with Bentsen on the ticket and Dukakis running on competence rather than ideology. But the minute Dukakis was exposed as a liberal, the lock closed. The South was lost. It was not quite as bad as in previous years, however. Forty-six percent is better than 40 percent.

It is equally unrealistic to argue that the Democrats should abandon liber-alism. The Democratic Party is a liberal party. That is not likely to change, nor should it. The country does not need two Republican parties, even if liberalism is currently out of fashion. After all, conservatives nurtured their anti-government doctrines for 50 years until the Great Inflation of the 1970s finally brought them to ascendancy.

In any case, the nominating process will not allow for much backsliding. No matter how many superdelegates there are, primary voters and caucus participants still control the outcome. And Democrats who choose to par-ticipate in those activities are strongly tilted to the left. This does not mean that the most liberal candidate will necessarily win the nomination. It means that the Democratic nominee must be acceptable to liberals, just as the Republican nominee must be acceptable to conservatives.

Jimmy Carter, for instance, was widely distrusted by liberals. But he was legitimized by the civil rights issue. No Democrat who got all those black votes could be considered outside the tent. When Lloyd Bentsen ran for president in 1976, he was very far outside the tent; he ended up with just 4,000 votes. Today there is good reason to believe that Bentsen would be acceptable to liberals. He has done his service for the cause.

The lesson of 1988 is that the Democrats have to run a thematic campaign. But the theme cannot be liberalism. There are plenty of themes a good Democrat can run on without repudiating liberalism. Paul Kirk is right when he says, "I don't think we need to go back and try to rediscover the soul of the Democratic Party." The Democrats need three things to regain the White House—the right opportunity, the right campaign, and the right candidate.

The right opportunity comes when there is a strong desire for change. Watergate created a powerful market for change in 1976, for instance, as did inflation and the hostage crisis in 1980. A lot of Democrats thought the Iran *contra* scandal and the stock market crash would do the same thing this year. But peace and prosperity prevailed, and the tide for change receded as the campaign went on.

The right campaign means finding out what the voters want that they are not getting. And then selling it to them. After eight years of Eisenhower, youth, dynamism, and vigor sold very well. In 1968, when the country was being torn to pieces, the voters desperately wanted order. After Watergate, 1976 saw a big market for morality. And in 1980, after Jimmy Carter, people were looking for leadership. None of these themes was ideological. They were based on a shrewd assessment of the times. The right theme for 1988 might have been competence, given Reagan's failings as a manager. But it never really sold. When things are going well, who worries about competence?

The right candidate is the biggest problem of all. What the Democrats need is a tough liberal. That is not an oxymoron. It is what Dukakis meant when he said, "I'm liberal in the tradition of Franklin Roosevelt and Harry Truman and John Kennedy." It is also what Bush meant when he said, "No, you're not. You're a liberal in the tradition of George McGovern and Jimmy Carter and Walter Mondale."

What's the difference between FDR, Truman, and Kennedy on the one hand, and McGovern, Carter, and Mondale on the other? To begin with, the first three aren't around anymore. Ben Wattenberg calls this the "dead liberal" syndrome. Dead liberals are good. Living liberals are bad. But there is another difference. Roosevelt, Truman, and Kennedy (as well as LBJ) were all tough guys. They couldn't be pushed around by the Russians or by the special interests in Washington. McGovern, Carter, and Mondale (and, for that matter, Adlai Stevenson and Hubert Humphrey) had the image of weak liberals. All of them were respected for their integrity. But none was considered tough enough for the job.

Tough liberals win. Weak liberals lose. What happened to Dukakis this year is that his image changed. He started out looking tough when he took on the Democratic field and went the distance with Jesse Jackson. But the Republican campaign turned him into a wimp. His support dropped to 40 percent—about the same as where McGovern, Carter, and Mondale ended up. Only when he came back swinging did Dukakis begin to rise again in the polls.

Ideology is a problem, but one that can easily be overcome. Just find the right theme. That's what Reagan did in 1980. The polls showed that his right-wing views frightened most voters. They were afraid he would start a war or throw old people out in the snow. Reagan was elected in spite of, not because of, his ideology. He offered people something they wanted— leadership. No Democrat is going to win the presidency these days *because* he is a liberal. But with the right campaign, he can win *despite* being a liberal.

Republican Tilt

JAMES A. BARNES

Ultimately, U.S. presidential elections are won in the Electoral College. Over the past two decades, Republicans have consistently won in a large number of western and southern states, and the electoral votes from these states constitute a base that is close to a majority. Writer James Barnes examines the idea that the Republicans have a "lock" on the Electoral College.

The last time Democrats lost five out of six Presidential elections, the party was suffering from the aftereffects of the Civil War. And those races were more competitive than the elections of 1968–88.

In terms of both the popular vote and the Electoral College count, Democratic presidential nominee Michael S. Dukakis posted the party's best performance in the past three presidential elections. But the state-by-state returns can't inspire much Democratic confidence about retaking the White House any time soon.

And after the decennial reapportionment, the Electoral College, swept by President-elect George Bush, 426–112, will tilt even more heavily in the GOP's favor. Based on current Census Bureau estimates, states located mostly in the East and Midwest will lose 18 House seats to the South and West. That's the equivalent of dropping Michigan into the Sunbelt. Half the states that Dukakis won on Nov. 8 will be losing a total of seven House seats. With the exception of California, which may pick up five seats — and, therefore, five electoral votes — 13 seats will shift to states that Bush carried by at least his national average of 54 percent.

Nowhere can the presidential tally be more disheartening for the Democrats than in Dixie. The party's prospects in the South this year were supposed to be brighter for a number of reasons: Conservative Texas Sen. Lloyd Bentsen was the Democratic vice presidential nominee in place of the 1984 running mate, liberal former New York City House Member Geraldine A. Ferraro; Bush did not seem to be as formidable an opponent as Ronald Reagan; and Democratic hopes for a presidential resurgence in the South appeared to be buoyed after they defeated four southern Republican Senators just two years ago.

But if there is any region where Republicans have solidified their presidential coalition, it is the South. For the second consecutive election, the Democrats were shut out in the states of the old Confederacy. In nine of those states—Alabama, Arkansas, Florida, Georgia, Mississippi, North Carolina, South Carolina, Tennessee and Virginia—with 99 electoral votes (105 after the 1990 reapportionment), Dukakis could muster no better than 43 percent of the unofficial vote; in each of them, he also fell below the party's average share of the vote for the previous seven elections.

"We have been talking about an emerging Republican majority in the South since 1968, and what we've seen is it is still there without Reagan at the top of the ticket," said Fred Steeper, a senior vice president of Market Opinion Research, a Detroit polling firm that worked for the Bush presidential effort. Critical to Bush's success in the region, Steeper said, was the Vice President's early decision to campaign as a conservative and Reagan loyalist and to avoid calls for expansion of the civil rights laws or domestic spending programs. "If Bush had run as a moderate, it would have made the race much more difficult," he said. "That would have sent mixed signals to the South" at a time when Dukakis was attempting to run as a fiscal conservative and there was still some disposition in the region to vote Democratic. "We could never have pointed out the sharp differences if Bush had done that," Steeper said.

Hometown regionalism didn't give Dukakis much of a life, either. The Massachusetts governor and the Republican nominee, who was also born in the Bay State and has a summer home in Maine, divided the electoral pie in New England. Dukakis carried Massachusetts and next-door Rhode Island, both of which have gone Democratic in six of the past eight presidential elections, for a total of 17 electoral votes. Bush carried Connecticut, Maine, New Hampshire and Vermont, none of which has been won by a Democratic presidential candidate since 1968.

The six mid-Atlantic states of Delaware, Maryland, New Jersey, New York, Pennsylvania and West Virginia (and the District of Columbia) appeared to develop a split identity in this election. For the first time since 1932, Pennsylvania and New York, the region's two most populous states, went in opposite directions. Bush carried the Keystone State, albeit narrowly, and Dukakis held on to New York. Swept into the Republican column were Delaware, Maryland and New Jersey.

THE DUKAKIS LAG

Although Pennsylvania's economic recovery has not been spread evenly, the suburban counties around Philadelphia that are experiencing substantial population growth are also doing well economically. When Democratic presidential candidates carried Pennsylvania in 1968 and 1976, they did it by less than overwhelming margins. Some of the Democratic voters in the western part of the state who contributed to Jimmy Carter's 123,073-vote edge in 1976 may have since left Pennsylvania for jobs in the Sunbelt. Though Bush did not spend a great deal of time campaigning in the

TABLE 1. State-by-State Results
(number of times from 1960–1984 each state was carried by Democratic ticket)

STATE	BUSH Popular	%	Electoral	DUKAKIS Popular	%	Electoral
Ala. (2)	809,361	60%	9	546,428	40%	—
Alaska (1)	102,381	62	3	62,205	38	—
Ariz. (0)	692,139	61	7	446,261	39	—
Ark. (3)	461,450	57	6	344,544	43	—
Calif. (1)	4,711,842	52	47	4,423,384	48	—
Colo. (1)	727,633	54	8	621,094	46	—
Conn. (3)	747,082	53	8	674,873	47	—
Del. (3)	130,581	57	3	99,479	43	—
D.C. (6)	25,732	14	—	153,100	86	3
Fla. (2)	2,500,627	61	21	1,615,581	39	—
Ga. (3)	1,066,048	60	12	713,054	40	—
Hawaii (5)	158,625	45	—	192,364	55	4
Idaho (1)	253,461	63	4	147,384	37	—
Ill. (2)	2,294,154	51	24	2,176,336	49	—
Ind. (1)	1,282,186	60	12	848,942	40	—
Iowa (1)	541,936	45	—	666,668	55	8
Kan. (1)	552,611	57	7	422,540	43	—
Ky. (2)	731,290	56	9	578,941	44	—
La. (2)	880,830	55	10	715,612	45	—
Maine (2)	299,703	56	4	237,782	44	—
Md. (5)	834,202	51	10	793,939	49	—
Mass. (5)	1,151,457	46	—	1,339,561	54	13
Mich. (3)	1,819,147	54	20	1,580,561	46	—
Minn. (6)	957,351	46	—	1,105,685	54	10
Miss. (1)	551,954	60	7	361,443	40	—
Mo. (3)	1,077,101	52	11	1,001,920	48	—

state, his frequent forays into New Jersey received extensive coverage in the Philadelphia media market.

The Garden State was never a safe bet for Dukakis, even though New Jersey's ethnic identity and a late-May Newark *Star Ledger* poll showing the Democrat leading by 54–40 percent suggested that he might have done well there. But the Democrats have not carried New Jersey since 1964, and Bush's 57–43 percent victory was only 3 points short of Reagan's in 1984.

The National Committee for an Effective Congress (NCEC), a Washington-based political action committee that supports moderate and liberal Democratic candidates by supplying their campaigns with in-kind contributions in the form of voter targeting data, did a composite of Democratic voting strength in state, local and federal races, including recent presidential results. The data suggest that Bush's strength in middle-class areas of New Jersey was strictly presidential.

In middle-class Middlesex County, the average NCEC Democratic vote is 51.4 percent. Bush captured 56 percent here and about 58 percent in

STATE	BUSH			DUKAKIS		
	Popular	*%*	*Electoral*	*Popular*	*%*	*Electoral*
Mont. (1)	189,598	53	4	168,120	47	—
Neb. (1)	389,394	60	5	254,426	40	—
Nev. (2)	205,837	60	4	132,555	38	—
N.H. (1)	279,818	63	4	162,330	37	—
N.J. (2)	1,697,327	57	16	1,268,413	43	—
N.M. (2)	260,792	52	5	236,577	48	—
N.Y. (4)	2,974,190	48	—	3,227,518	52	36
N.C. (3)	1,232,505	58	13	889,209	42	—
N.D. (1)	162,922	57	3	125,342	43	—
Ohio (2)	2,411,855	55	23	1,934,890	45	—
Okla. (1)	678,054	58	8	483,373	42	—
Ore. (1)	512,582	47	—	567,944	53	7
Pa. (4)	2,291,266	51	25	2,183,283	49	—
R.I. (5)	169,571	44	—	216,281	56	4
S.C. (2)	596,696	62	8	365,865	38	—
S.D. (1)	165,516	53	3	145,632	47	—
Tenn. (2)	937,966	58	11	676,239	42	—
Texas (4)	2,995,656	56	29	2,322,688	44	—
Utah (1)	426,289	67	5	206,642	33	—
Vt. (1)	123,166	51	3	116,419	49	—
Va. (1)	1,294,717	60	12	852,435	40	—
Wash. (2)	800,182	49	—	844,554	51	10
W. Va. (5)	309,459	48	—	340,462	52	6
Wis. (2)	1,044,857	48	—	1,123,975	52	11
Wyo. (1)	105,858	61	3	66,573	39	—
Total	47,616,957	54%	426	40,781,426	46%	112

Source: News Election Service

slightly less-affluent Passaic County. Bluer-blood Bergen County, a suburb of New York City, gave him an equal share of its vote. In blue-collar Camden County, outside Philadelphia, Bush won about 52 percent.

The low-visibility Democratic Sen. Frank R. Lautenberg, who won re-election with 54 percent, also did very well in these sections of the state. He ran far ahead of the top of the ticket in carrying Bergen, Middlesex and his native Passaic County with 54–56 percent of the vote in each. He swept Camden County with 60 percent of the vote.

Dukakis also lagged behind the typical Democratic performance in working-class areas in Ohio, another state that Bush won handily, with 55 percent. Dukakis won Lorain County outside of Cleveland with about 53 percent of the vote, which was an improvement over Walter F. Mondale's narrow loss in 1984 but was off the 62.6 percent pace for the average Ohio Democratic candidate in the county. Bush turned in a hefty 58 percent victory in middle-class Montgomery County (Dayton), in which the average Ohio Democratic vote, according to the NCEC, is 56.6 percent.

As in New Jersey, the incumbent Senate Democrat, unabashed liberal Howard M. Metzenbaum, was doing quite well among counties populated by so-called Reagan Democrats. He matched Bush in Montgomery and breezed to a 62 percent victory in Lorain.

In Michigan, another state that hasn't voted Democratic since 1968, the Bush victory profile resembled that of New Jersey and Ohio. Bush captured blue-collar voters in Macomb County, outside of Detroit, which normally vote 50.9 percent Democratic, according to the NCEC model.

"Our challenge is to apply the lessons of the state races to the national races," said Al From, the executive director of the Democratic Leadership Council, a centrist group of Democratic elected officials. From played down the idea that the party must move explicitly to the right and suggested that it must somehow reconstitute the "tough-minded liberalism" of candidates such as John F. Kennedy in promoting economic growth and a strong defense.

REAGAN'S ROLE

Outside of Louisiana and Texas, the area west of the Mississippi River was relatively fertile territory for Dukakis. He was very competitive in California, where he received a higher percentage of votes than any Democrat since Lyndon B. Johnson in 1964, and he carried Oregon and Washington, only the second Pacific Northwest double for a Democrat since Franklin D. Roosevelt accomplished it in 1944. Dukakis also carried the upper Farmbelt states of Iowa, Minnesota and Wisconsin, which have a reformist tradition that mixes well with Dukakis's style. Across the Pacific, Dukakis won Hawaii, the sixth victory for a Democratic nominee there in eight elections.

Dukakis's respectable showings in Colorado, Montana, North Dakota and South Dakota were comparable to Jimmy Carter's strength in 1976; like Carter, he lost all four states.

The residue of approval for Reagan and a very strong tradition of voting Republican in most of these states may have helped Bush stem further inroads by Dukakis. The Vice President devoted little campaign time to this region, and he trailed Reagan's totals in all 18 western states. But he did at least as well as President Ford did in 15 of them.

The 77-year-old Reagan proved to be an indefatigable trouper for Bush and for many of the Republican Senate candidates locked in tight races. In the final seven days of the campaign, Air Force One touched down in California, Illinois, Michigan, Nevada, Ohio, Texas and Wisconsin. The President's Nov. 7 flight to California for Election Eve rallies in Long Beach and San Diego, in fact, was his second California political foray within the week and his fourth since the Republican convention in August.

All told, Reagan logged more than 25,000 miles, appearing at 35 campaign events in 16 states, said White House chief of staff Kenneth M.

Duberstein, who characterized the President's efforts on behalf of his successor as "unprecedented."

Reagan devoted little time to firming up the party base in the Deep South.
After convention appearances in New Orleans, he made one trip to Florida
and two to Texas. Instead, he focused heavily on the industrial heartland,
where defecting blue-collar voters have voted Republican in recent presidential races. The President traveled twice to Illinois, Kentucky, Michigan,
Missouri and Ohio, and also touched base in New Jersey, Pennsylvania and
Wisconsin.

Wherever possible, Reagan's events were staged on college campuses or
before audiences packed with students. The idea, Duberstein said, was to
capitalize on Reagan's "special chemistry" with younger voters and to do
something about "the Reagan Democrats [who] were deserting George Bush
in droves" at the beginning of the summer.

Whether Bush can become a Republican torchbearer like Reagan is unknown. But his victory keeps the Democrats out of the White House for
another four years, denying them that national forum to resurrect the party's
battered image.

"The only way you can turn that around effectively is to have a Democratic President, but how do you get there?" Democratic party elder Richard
Moe asked. He suggested that the party needn't go through a cathartic soul-
searching akin to the period that followed its 1980 debacle, but he added
that Democratic activists must address the fact that the party's liberal image,
especially on social issues, must be modified if it is to compete successfully
in presidential elections.

"A lot of Democrats," he said, "still have not recognized that."

The Year of Living Dangerously: Congressional Elections in 1990

ROBERT BIERSACK

If it is difficult to read a single message into a presidential election, it is even more difficult to interpret mid-term elections, when 435 House seats and 33 to 34 Senate seats are up for grabs. During the 1990 campaign, journalists frequently spoke of an anti-incumbent revolt. On Election Day, a few incumbents were defeated, but the overwhelming majority were reelected. Political scientist Robert Biersack, an expert on congressional campaign finance, provides an explanation for the success of incumbents, but he also notes some evidence of voter dissatisfaction in 1990. His article may portend a more competitive environment for the 1992 congressional elections.

On November 7, 1990 liberal Democrat Paul Wellstone awoke in Minnesota as the only one of thirty-one challengers nation-wide to win a Senate race, while a few hundred miles away in Madison Wisconsin another liberal Democrat, Bob Kastenmeier, found himself one of fifteen members of the House of Representatives to lose a bid for re-election. House winners included Socialist Bernie Sanders in Vermont while all three Senate open seats were held by Republicans of generally conservative views.

The jumbled Congressional elections of 1990 will be remembered as one of the least competitive Senate campaigns in recent history with four Senators running unopposed. (But try telling that to Rudy Boschwitz who lost to Wellstone, or to Bill Bradley (D) of New Jersey who nearly lost to a virtual unknown.) 1990 will also be referred to as the year in which anti-incumbent sentiment was strong enough to strike fear in the hearts of many House members in both parties, and defeat more Congressmen than the elections of 1986 and 1988 combined.

We can begin an effort to understand the 1990 elections with an examination of the general trends that structured this campaign. First, while 1988 was a successful year for the Republican presidential candidate, George Bush's election did not bring Republican voters into the process at other levels. For the first time since 1944, fewer Americans voted in the presidential election in 1988 than voted four years earlier. More importantly for our purposes, while Bush was winning the White House, the Republican party suffered a net loss of three House seats and one Senate seat, the first Congressional loss during a presidential victory since 1960. By contrast, Republicans had a net gain of thirty-three House seats in 1980, and fourteen in 1984 when Ronald Reagan was winning the Presidency.

The common expectation that the President's party loses seats at the mid term is based in part on additional voters who support the winning presidential candidate and therefore his party, often resulting in Congressional gains. Since there appear to have been few additional voters and no extra Congressional seats won by Republicans in 1988, 1990 might be expected to show fewer losses for the president's party simply because 1988 did not show any gain.

HOUSE RECRUITMENT IN 1990

The first indication of the type of Congressional campaign to expect comes as potential candidates decide whether or not to make the race. Given that "quality" challengers are defined as those with political experience and name recognition usually stemming from previous state or local elected office, the decision to run for Congress against an incumbent poses considerable risks. Often the candidate must relinquish the position he or she holds making the Congressional race an all or nothing proposition. With House re-election rates reaching 98 percent in 1988, the political environment would presumably need to be substantially in your favor before you would be willing to take the risk of becoming a challenger. Neither party could realistically claim those conditions in late 1989. There were few new members of Congress from either party whose strength had not been tested, and general economic and political conditions did not significantly favor either party. It is not surprising, then, to find that in the winter of 1989–90 relatively few "quality" challengers were announcing campaigns for Congress in districts where the incumbent would be seeking re-election.

In addition, potential Republican challengers face a considerably different judgment about the value of holding Congressional office than do Democrats. There was no expectation in 1989 that the Republican party could obtain a majority in the House in the 1990 election, or for that matter in the foreseeable future. Given the overall shift in policy influence from the federal to state and local governments in this era of deficits and Gramm Rudman budget restrictions, the prospect of giving up an influential state or local position to become a junior member of a permanent minority in the House might represent a questionable career move in the eyes of Republican officeholders.

As a result of these conditions, only 18 of the 326 major party general election challengers in 1990 held any other public office at the time of the election. Twenty-one others were former officeholders. While some political conditions would change during the course of the campaign (particularly rising anti-incumbent sentiment stemming from budget stalemate, pay raises for members, etc.) the universe of candidates who might take advantage of these conditions was small and weak and for the most part unable to exploit the situation. There were fewer officeholders running as challengers in 1990 in both parties than there were in 1988, and 1988 was not considered a good year for challengers either.

RECRUITMENT FOR 1990 SENATE CAMPAIGNS

The decision to run for a Senate seat is considerably different, and the pool of "quality" challengers who choose to make the race is usually much larger than in House campaigns. The demands of a statewide campaign, along with the added influence and prestige that comes from being one of one hundred members raises the value of the office so much as to insure good candidates most of the time. Membership includes many former governors, other statewide elected officials, and former members of the House who clearly view a Senate seat as a significant step on the career ladder. For Republicans in the House the decision to seek a Senate seat may be easier because it represents an opportunity to move away from the frustration of being a member of a small minority.

1990 was thought to have been a very successful year for Republican Senate recruitment. Three Republican incumbent Senators chose to retire (McClure in Idaho, Armstrong in Colorado, and Humphrey in New Hampshire) but well known House members moved quickly to run for those seats. Their high profile in these small states meant they would face minimal primary challenges from within Republican ranks allowing them to concentrate fundraising and campaign resources on the general election. Elsewhere, several prominent House Republicans chose to challenge Democratic Senators. Lynn Martin in Illinois, Claudine Schneider in Rhode Island, Tom Tauke in Iowa, and Patricia Saiki in Hawaii sought to exploit perceived weakness in Democratic incumbents who were either making their first re-election bid or, in Rhode Island, were thought to be vulnerable for other reasons. William Schuette of Michigan also chose to challenge a Democratic incumbent, although in this case initial estimates suggest that the Senator Levin was less vulnerable than the others.

Democrats, on the other hand, were completely unsuccessful in attempts to enlist House members or other prominent statewide figures to challenge Republican Senators. At least some attempt was made in Virginia, Oregon, Indiana, Minnesota, and North Carolina to encourage well known individuals with current or previous political experience to make the race, but none of the specific recruitment efforts were successful. Candidates with experience and statewide recognition did come forward in some of these states, but they did not represent the first choice of Democratic leaders nationally. Moreover, no Democratic House member or current statewide officeholder chose to seek the three open Senate seats.

The relationship between national political and economic conditions and Senate campaigns is complicated by the importance of individual candidacies and state circumstances in ways that don't affect House races. Thus while Democrats failed in some cases to recruit their strongest challengers, they benefited in other states from a surprising lack of competition. Four Senators faced no major party opposition at all (Pryor (D-AR) Nunn (D-GA) Cochran (R-MS) and Warner (R-VA) and five others (Stevens (R-AK) Kassebaum (R-KS) Thurmond (R-SC) Gore (D-TN) and Simpson (R-WY) faced opponents who spent less than $20,000 on their campaigns, making them effectively unopposed. In the two previous Senate elections (1988 and 1986) all incumbents faced at least some major party opposition and only one ran against a challenger who spent less than $20,000. We should note that there were an unusually large number of incumbents running for re-election in 1990 (32) because only three members chose to retire and because two appointed members (Coats (R-IN) and Akaka (D-HI) were running for the first time.

CAMPAIGN RESOURCES

Once the field of candidates has been defined, Congressional campaigns in recent years have focused on amassing campaign resources—primarily money. In an era of candidate-centered politics, where each campaign is independently conducted and the primary means of communication with voters are capital intensive (e.g., TV and direct mail), substantial financial resources are thought to be necessary for a successful effort.

Table 1 provides an overview of Congressional campaign finance in the 1990 election cycle. It lists the amount of money raised by each type of campaign, along with the relative reliance of candidates on certain sources of funds. We can see from the table, for example, the substantial fundraising advantage held by Republican Senate candidates who were not incumbents. Republican open seat candidates outraised their opponents by more than two to one in the type of election which is typically the most competitive. The table also points out the disparities in sources of funding. In the House, for example, none of the Democratic campaign types received at least 50 percent of their resources from individual contributions, while all three types of Republican campaigns (incumbents, challengers, and open seat) received at least 50 percent of their funds from this source. In addition, non-incumbents of both parties are highly dependent upon their own personal resources, with one of every four dollars raised by Republican House challengers coming from the candidate.

Disparities between types of campaigns can also be seen by comparing the amount spent by "typical" campaigns in each category. Table 2 gives the median spending for each type of campaign and compares that value with spending in 1988 Congressional races.

TABLE 1. Sources of Receipts for Congressional General Election Campaigns January 1, 1989–December 31, 1990

	NUMBER OF CANDIDATES	RECEIPTS (IN MILLIONS)	PROPORTION FROM Individuals	PACs	The Candidate
Senate					
Democrats	34	$85.67	66.49%	23.74%	4.33%
Incumbents	17	$63.58	67.82%	26.75%	0.00%
Challengers	14	$19.26	63.76%	14.54%	15.84%
Open Seats	3	$2.83	55.12%	18.73%	23.32%
Republicans	33	$92.64	63.68%	21.88%	5.51%
Incumbents	15	$55.18	69.50%	22.07%	0.00%
Challengers	15	$30.04	57.36%	17.44%	16.98%
Open Seats	3	$7.42	45.96%	38.41%	0.00%
House					
Democrats	413	$142.83	39.61%	48.34%	5.10%
Incumbents	249	$111.35	37.98%	52.64%	1.61%
Challengers	132	$14.61	47.78%	30.25%	17.93%
Open Seats	32	$16.87	43.27%	35.63%	17.01%
Republicans	394	$105.95	52.43%	32.87%	7.48%
Incumbents	159	$70.00	50.86%	41.14%	0.53%
Challengers	206	$22.95	56.38%	11.29%	25.36%
Open Seats	29	$13.00	53.92%	26.46%	13.38%
Other	164	$0.96	61.46%	8.33%	18.75%

Source: Federal Election Commission

TABLE 2. Median Campaign Spending by General Election Candidates through December 31 of the Election Year (in millions of dollars)

	1988	1990
Senate		
Democrats		
Incumbents	$2.70	$2.41
Challengers	$2.36	$1.32
Open Seats	$2.62	$0.54
Republicans		
Incumbents	$3.21	$1.92
Challengers	$0.61	$1.85
Open Seats	$2.85	$1.65
House		
Democrats		
Incumbents	$0.29	$0.34
Challengers	$0.06	$0.07
Open Seats	$0.45	$0.48
Republicans		
Incumbents	$0.34	$0.37
Challengers	$0.06	$0.07
Open Seats	$0.45	$0.46

TABLE 3.   Cost per Voter Senate General Election Candidates by Size of State

VOTING AGE POPULATION	COST PER VOTING AGE POPULATION		
	1986	1988	1990
8 million or more	$0.98	$0.78	$1.16
(number of states)	5	5	2
4–8 million	$1.14	$1.35	$1.66
(number of states)	3	6	7
2.5–4 million	$1.61	$1.63	$1.73
(number of states)	8	6	6
1.5–2.5 million	$1.80	$2.04	$1.56
(number of states)	9	3	7
800,000–1.5 million	$0.74	$3.03	$2.81
(number of states)	1	5	6
less than 800,000	$4.95	$5.42	$4.53
(number of states)	8	8	7
Overall	$1.44	$1.37	$1.74
	34	33	35

Table 3 shows Senate spending controlling for voting age population where the states have been grouped by size. The table clearly shows that as state population declines, the amount spent on Senate campaigns per potential voter increases.

MAJOR SOURCES OF FUNDS—PAC's

We have seen in Table 1 that different sources of funding are more important to different types of campaigns. Certainly the most controversial of these sources in recent times have been PAC's—representing employees of corporations, members of unions, trade associations, and individuals who join together because of a concern for one or more public issues. These organizations, commonly referred to as special interests, contribute to political campaigns in order to gain access to the policy making process, express their positions on issues and help elect like-minded individuals, and/or to encourage their members to become more active in politics (Sorauf, 1988).

Whatever the reasons for their participation, the 4,000 or so PAC's currently on the books (about 3,000 are really active in making contributions or expenditures) have become the focal point in the debate on campaign finance reform. They have reached this level of scrutiny because they are the most visible source of campaign funds in Congressional campaigns although they are only the largest source for House Democratic incumbents. This visibility stems in part from the concentration of resources among PAC's, with the largest 50 committees (1.2 percent of all PAC's) making 34.6 percent of all PAC contributions and expenditures, compared with the great diversity and complexity of the other large source of funds, i.e., contributions from individual people.

In 1990 PAC's continued a pattern of behavior which has been evolving over the past several election cycles. As the likelihood of success for non-incumbent candidates declined during the 1980's PAC's in general concentrated more of their resources in support of incumbents. Figure 1 shows the proportion of PAC contributions to all House candidates given to incumbents from 1978 to 1990. What had begun as a relatively modest 60 percent given to incumbents in 1978 has grown steadily until by 1990 more than $8 of every $10 PAC's gave to House candidates were contributions to sitting members. It is difficult to determine whether candidates succeed (or legislation is passed) because PAC's contribute disproportionately, or whether PAC's contribute because certain candidates will probably win (or are likely to vote a certain way on legislation).

In fact, PAC support of incumbents in 1990 was in some respects even more pervasive than these numbers indicate. Throughout the recent period of greater concentration on incumbents, one type of PAC, labor organizations, continued at least some significant level of support for non-incumbent House candidates. In 1988, for example, labor PAC's gave 31 percent of their House contributions to non-incumbents (nearly all of them Democrats). In many cases, these contributions were made early in the campaign to challengers and open seat candidates who appeared to have some chance for victory, under the assumption that early support would stimulate additional contributions and add to the viability of the candidate. By 1990, however, the picture is substantially different, even for labor committees.

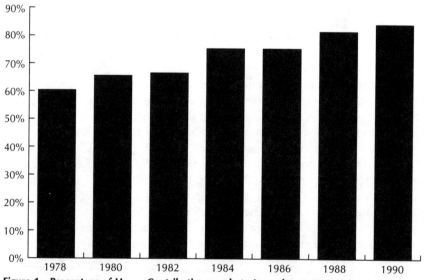

Figure 1—Percentage of House Contributions made to Incumbents 1978–1990

Only 23 percent of labor contributions to House campaigns through the end of November, 1990 went to non-incumbent candidates. This limited support was especially apparent in the early stages of the campaign. By the end of March Democratic House challengers had raised only $3.6 million compared with $6.2 million raised by Democratic challengers at the same point in 1988. The proportion of those receipts coming from PAC's also declined from 17 percent in 1988 to 15 percent in 1990.

The importance of these numbers may be seen more clearly by looking at the situations faced by specific candidates in late March of 1988, and comparing them with their 1990 counterparts. Tom Ward, for example, was mounting a challenge in the 3rd district of Indiana in 1988. By the end of March, he had raised over $178,000, with nearly $128,000 coming from PAC's. These contributions had come from 62 different committees, 43 of which were labor PAC's. Labor contributions represented about $104,000 or about 58 percent of all Ward's receipts up to that point. This reliance on institutional support is very unusual for House challengers, but there were five other districts in which Democratic challengers had received more from PAC's than from any other source at the end of March, and three others where PAC contributions were substantial and nearly as large as contributions from individuals.

In the same district in March of 1990 Tim Roemer was seeking nomination to challenge incumbent Republican John Hiler who had survived Ward's challenge. Roemer's reports through March showed receipts of $133,000, substantial for this early stage but still $45,000 less than the 1988 challenger. Moreover, only $52,800 of Roemer's funds had come from PAC's. Of the 47 committees who had contributed, only 9 were labor organizations representing a total of $23,800. Nationally in 1990, two challengers had more PAC contributions than individual, and two others approached equal proportions.

PAC's were less aggressive in 1990 in other ways as well. During the 80's they had become more active in making independent expenditures in Congressional campaigns. These expenditures are made directly by the PAC, without consultation or cooperation of the candidate involved. They can involve anything from direct mailings advocating the election or defeat of a candidate to purchasing air time and producing ads supporting or opposing a particular individual. Once the province of ideological or single issue groups, independent expenditures had become more popular in the late 80's as large PAC's sought ways to use their resources beyond the limited contributions to candidates allowed by law.

Table 4 lists the largest independent spenders in Congressional campaigns in 1988 and 1990, and shows the considerable decline in PAC involvement in this activity. Whereas in 1988 a total of $6.9 million was spent independently by PAC's, the 1990 total was just more than $3.9 million. Further, of the five largest PAC's in terms of this activity in 1988, only one increased independent spending in 1990, and another virtually withdrew from this process completely. While spending was less, it was not necessarily unim-

TABLE 4.   PAC's Making the Most Independent Expenditures in Congressional Campaigns, 1988–90

	1988	1990
Auto Dealers and Drivers For Free Trade	$1,435,672	$532,415
National Association of Realtors	$1,322,421	$1,099,585
National Committee to Preserve Social Security and Medicare	$1,132,952	$402,666
American Medical Association	$825,376	$6,700
National Right to Life PAC	$208,247	$508,450
Total Spent by All PAC's	$6,909,021	$3,965,470

portant in all races. Certain campaigns generated considerable interest, and the largest amount ($460,000) was spent in New Hampshire on behalf of Bob Smith, the Republican candidate in the open Senate race there.

Strategically, then, PAC's seem to have seen 1990 as a year with no opportunities for any "aggressive" behavior, either in direct contributions to non-incumbent candidates or mounting independent campaigns on a large scale.

PARTIES

Another important source of financial and other support for Congressional campaigns are the major party organizations, with their Congressional campaign committees and other national, state, and local organizations who work to elect members of the party. The general pattern of financial support coming from these organizations has closely paralleled their own institutional development in the age of capital intensive campaigns (Herrnson, 1988; Cotter et. al., 1989). While their overall electoral goal is perhaps more straightforward than those of PAC's—parties pretty clearly want to maximize the number of seats they control—there are constraints on their behavior that sometimes work to limit their effectiveness. Thus, while we might expect these organizations to be the most likely to support non-incumbent candidates, the control over the committees themselves that is exercised by members of Congress constrains the party campaign committees to some extent (Herrnson, 1989; Jacobson, 1986). In addition, the relative availability of resources forces these organizations to make judgments about the electability of their candidates and allocate in such a way as to maximize their impact.

Table 5 provides an overview of direct party support of candidates in 1990 Congressional elections. This support comes in two forms, contributions to the campaign and what are called "coordinated expenditures." These are activities undertaken by the party organization directly (rather than giving cash to the candidate to spend) which may be done in coordination with the

TABLE 5.   Party Direct Support of Congressional Campaigns, 1988–90

		DEMOCRATS		REPUBLICANS	
		Contributions	Expenditures	Contributions	Expenditures
Senate					
Incumbents	1990	$267,833	$3,127,666	$305,064	$3,702,110
	1988	$168,107	$2,024,936	$234,273	$3,575,133
Challengers	1990	$188,800	$1,782,880	$473,521	$3,575,635
	1988	$221,594	$2,972,106	$322,858	$4,574,582
Open Seats	1990	$53,500	$282,611	$80,555	$443,608
	1988	$103,035	$1,520,355	$151,600	$2,105,001
House					
Incumbents	1990	$300,773	$1,240,608	$436,908	$741,773
	1988	$416,919	$1,300,256	$940,006	$1,264,901
Challengers	1990	$235,175	$1,302,353	$693,132	$922,889
	1988	$510,320	$963,519	$1,041,710	$1,772,067
Open Seats	1990	$405,557	$724,498	$897,888	$1,335,960
	1988	$328,467	$564,199	$659,418	$1,123,524

campaign. The law limits coordinated expenditures, based on a formula in-cluding an inflation adjustment. In 1990, national congressional campaign committees could spend up to $25,140 for each House general election candi-date, and the state party could spend a similar amount. In the Senate, expen-diture limits are based on state population, ranging in 1990 from $50,280 in the smallest states to $605,270 in Texas. Once again, the national committee and the state have separate coordinated expenditure limits.

Table 5 suggests a shift away from direct candidate support on the part of Republican committees, with amounts contributed and spent declining for Republicans in many types of campaign. Chuck Alston has reported in Congressional Quarterly Weekly Report that for the National Republican Congressional Committee this represents a policy change in which "money was instead diverted to hire veteran consultants to manage specific programs, such as an incumbent protection program run by consultant Eddie Mahe . . . and a TV strategy directed by Larry McCarthy." Alston reports that "(t)he new strategy grew out of a study of 1988 House races in which the NRCC spent the full amount the law allows ($60,280 in today's dollars), . . . 'We found out it didn't have a huge impact' " (Alston, 1990).

Parties have also often been innovators in campaign finance. When their resource base exceeds the amount they are permitted to contribute to their favored candidates, or spend on their behalf, they seek ways to use these re-sources to their best advantage within the constraints of the Federal Election Campaign Act. For example, national party committees may make contri-butions to House candidates only up to $5,000 per election (primary and general) while the state party may make an equal contribution. In recent years, however, national organizations have extended this limit by having the Senatorial Campaign Committee make contributions to certain House candidates, using their own separate $5,000 limit. Thus for candidates in the general election, it is possible to receive a total of $30,000 in contributions from national party committees ($5,000 for the primary and $5,000 for the general from the National Committee, the Senatorial Campaign Committee, and the Congressional Campaign Committee). This contribution limit has been further extended by state party organizations making contributions to House candidates in other states. As a result, in theory at least, an additional $500,000 could be given to a single candidate by party committees throughout the country ($10,000 from each of 50 states). While it would be unlikely that many state committees would be in a position to make significant out of state contributions when candidates at home crave support, this opportunity has been used effectively by both parties in special elections, where there are a small number of campaigns underway at a particular time.

Party committees at the state and national level can also make a total of $50,280 in coordinated expenditures on behalf of each general election candidate. National committees have demonstrated their financial strength here by persuading many states to allow the national organization to make the state's allotted expenditures as well as their own.

Parties are in some respects more restricted in the way in which they can contribute to Senate campaigns. Here a single limit exists for contributions ($17,500) from the combination of the National and Senatorial Campaign Committees. This restriction is balanced by the allowance in the law for greater "coordinated expenditures" made by party committees in coordination with campaigns up to a limit based on state population and indexed for inflation. These expenditure limits vary from about $50,000 in the smallest states to just over $1 million in California, with the state party having an equal spending limit.

It is in the context of these Senate campaigns, however, that party organizations have shown their greatest ingenuity in 1990. Unable to provide direct contributions to candidates in excess of the $17,500 limit, the National Republican Senatorial Committee found a way to utilize its extensive list of contributors for the benefit of Republican Senate candidates. The party created "joint fundraising committees" called the Republican Senatorial Inner Circle, which could solicit contributions for the party and its candidates, dividing the cost and proceeds according to an agreed upon formula. In this way the NRSC was able to help candidates raise an additional $1.6 million they might not have received otherwise.

In addition, state and local party organizations are permitted to spend moneys in support of state and local candidates that are outside the bounds of Federal restrictions. While these expenditures may not directly affect a federal election, greater electoral success for state and local candidates might be expected to indirectly affect federal races as well. The NRSC transferred a total of nearly $3 million in 1989–90 to the federal committees of state parties in states with 1990 Senate races. Thus while the traditional methods of supporting Senate candidates (contributions and coordinated expenditures) totaled about $7.8 million for the NRSC through late November of 1990, the Committee was able to spend or generate an additional $4.6 million that might benefit those Senate candidates.

MONEY AND VOTES IN 1990 CONGRESSIONAL ELECTIONS

Having reviewed the patterns of recruitment and fundraising undertaken in the 1990 Congressional elections, one is led to some specific expectations about the outcome. We might expect, for example, that the lack of significant numbers of "quality" challengers in either party, along with the conservative, incumbent based behavior of several major actors in campaign finance would result in an election much like those of 1986 and 1988. In those years, approximately 98 percent of all House incumbents who sought re-election were successful, and the vote percentage received by the average incumbent was well beyond the 60 percent generally considered to indicate a "safe" seat.

That the 1990 House elections cannot be characterized in these terms suggests first that the relationship between funding of campaigns and outcomes of elections is less obvious and determinant than some would claim. While financial competition was hard to find in most cases, 15 House incumbents lost, more than the total in the previous two elections combined. The results also provide some specific evidence of the existence of an "anti-incumbent" sentiment among the electorate which was discussed so extensively in the media in the fall.

One measure of the closeness of many House races, and the difference between 1990 and earlier years can be seen in Table 6. It lists the number of incumbents who received less than 60 percent of the general election vote in each year beginning in 1982. First, the number of "close" races for incumbents of both parties was substantially higher in 1990 than it had been in the previous two elections. Moreover, while the years 1982, 84, and 86 follow a pattern consistent with theories of Congressional elections in which one party has a favorable set of overall political circumstances and is able to take advantage of those events, 1990 was an equally bad year for incumbents of both parties, at least as measured here.

TABLE 6.   Number of House Incumbents Receiving Less than 60 Percent of the Vote

	1982	1984	1986	1988	1990
Republican	85	20	39	29	56
Democrat	41	77	23	31	61

Another anomaly in 1990 Congressional voting which may suggest general voter antipathy is the unusually large percentage of the vote received by third-party candidates in several states. In California, for example, third-party candidates received at least 5 percent of the general election vote in 20 districts. In four of those districts the winning candidate actually received less than 50 percent of the total votes cast. In 1988, only 3 California districts reported third-party vote in excess of 5 percent. In New York state third-party candidates received at least 5 percent in 17 districts, compared with 3 in 1988 who reached similar levels.

Some have found these results gratifying in that they challenge the common assumption that financial barriers to electoral competition were the cause of the limited electoral turnover in the House. Certainly naive models of electoral outcomes based totally on financing (Common Cause's definition of "financially competitive" races, for example, where competitiveness is defined by the ratio of challenger spending to incumbent spending) have difficulty explaining 1990 results. In the 58 House districts in 1990 where the incumbent received 55 percent or less of the vote, 21 were "financially competitive" according to Common Cause, while 37 (nearly two thirds) were not. But these models are also inconsistent with the findings of political science that spending by challengers is a very important correlate of election result virtually no matter what the incumbent spends. They also ignore non-electoral turnover in the House, new members who are elected when an incumbent retires or chooses to run for another office. (While 15 House incumbents lost in 1990, a total of 44 new members were elected. This represents about 10 percent of the total membership changing in just one election.)

In the Senate, the strength of individual candidates and the specific political conditions in each state often overwhelm the general trends that affect campaigns at other levels. How much of Paul Wellstone's victory can be attributed to anti-incumbent sentiment and how much to the chaos in the state Republican party resulting from a sex scandal involving the gubernatorial nominee is hard to determine. Even the most extreme "send them a message" outcome, the close vote for Bradley in New Jersey had much to do with attitudes toward the new Governor's tax policy. What is certainly true in both of these cases, and in other close Senate races as well, is that campaign money was not the determining factor in the outcome.

While the results of the 1990 Congressional election may expose the simplistic analysis of those who see campaign finance as the source of most political stagnation and other evils, it might be wise to consider what might have been. If the events which encouraged dissatisfaction among the electorate had occurred six months earlier, encouraging more candidates to consider a challenge, the results may have been even more dramatic. Moreover, it remains to be seen whether this sentiment will be maintained, adding to the already uncertain environment for 1992 when many Congressional districts will have changed as a result of redistricting.

9. Reforming the Electoral System

Critics of the U.S. system of elections maintain that the process is too expensive, too lengthy, and too biased. U.S. elections are the most costly in the world, and many argue that the money to fund campaigns comes with strings attached. The presidential campaign usually takes two or three years, and House members are involved in a perpetual campaign for reelection. Finally, the early presidential primaries may create systematic biases against certain types of candidates. Democrats who favor a strong defense are unlikely to do well in dovish Iowa, and Republicans who favor increased government revenues will likely fare poorly in anti-tax New Hampshire—the two most important states in the presidential selection process.

Although there are many proposals to reform the U.S. electoral system, there is little consensus among those who wish to change it. Some propose minor changes in the rules concerning the allocation of delegates to the national conventions. Others suggest more sweeping reforms of the presidential prenomination process, such as holding regional or national primaries, and radically restricting or expanding the money available to candidates during the campaign process. Some propose major reforms of the presidential general election process, including limiting the types of advertising and the independent spending by political groups, and abolishing the Electoral College.

Reformers also suggest changes in the way we elect members of Congress. Many focus on campaign finance, where proposals include banning political action committees (PACs), expanding or restricting the role of parties or individual contributors, and providing public funds. Others want to limit negative campaigning by limiting the types of advertisements that candidates can use. Most recently, reformers have suggested limiting the numbers of terms that members of Congress can serve.

Often reform proposals reflect the political interests of those who propose them. For example, Bush's proposal for campaign finance reform includes eliminating corporate and labor PACs, which give substantial funds to Democrats, but maintaining ideological PACs, which generally favor Republicans. The House Democratic proposal for campaign finance reform would increase the role of small contributors, a group who the Democrats believe (perhaps mistakenly) is more likely to contribute to their candidates than to their Republican opponents.

The readings in this chapter include several reform proposals, as well as two arguments against proposed reforms. In the first selection, James

Lengle indicts the current system of choosing the party nominees for president. He examines a series of possible reforms, finally endorsing a proposal for randomly selected time-zone primaries.

The next two readings debate the merits of the Electoral College. Stephen Wayne notes that the system does not function as the framers had intended, and that it creates the possibility of a winner who has received fewer popular votes than the loser. Although this has not occurred in this century, in both the 1960 and 1976 elections a shift of a few thousand votes in a few states could have had this result.

Ronald Rapoport argues that the Electoral College fulfills an important role. Small states are overrepresented in Congress, but underrepresented in the Electoral College. Moreover, the Electoral College deters third-party candidates who lack a strong regional base, thus preserving the stability of the two-party system. Rapoport argues that direct popular election might result in runoff elections, which might weaken the legitimacy of the winner.

In 1974, Congress responded to revelations of financial improprieties in the Nixon campaign by amending the Federal Election Campaign Act to regulate the funding of presidential elections. Candidates seeking each party's nomination are now limited in the amounts they can spend in certain states and in the overall campaign. Such reforms were intended to level the playing field, allowing lesser-known candidates to emerge. Tony Corrado argues for closing one loophole in this system of regulations: the ability of candidates to form PACs. These candidate PACs, ostensibly formed to aid other candidates within the party, are increasingly used to cover the costs of early campaigning and to keep consultants on retainer.

Mark Green advocates reform of the funding of congressional campaigns. In his race for Senate in New York in 1986, Green faced an incumbent who was able to raise far more money. He advocates a number of changes, including capping PAC contributions and candidate expenditures, regulating "soft money," and providing public financing.

The final two readings debate the merits of a reform proposal that gained popularity during the 1990 campaigns. As public dissatisfaction with Congress and some state legislatures grew, pollsters found support for limiting the number of terms that incumbents could serve. Some states passed limits on terms for their state legislatures, and others may vote on such proposals in 1992. Hendrik Hertzberg argues that limiting the terms of incumbents in Congress would provide new blood, eliminate the powers of seniority, and create a more responsive Congress.

In contrast, Charles Kesler cites the views of the Framers in arguing that term limits deprive citizens of their right to reelect incumbents that they support. Limiting terms would weaken Congress in its dealings with the bureaucracy and deprive the legislature of the wisdom and institutional memory that veteran members provide.

Reforming the Presidential Nominating Process

JAMES I. LENGLE

Nearly all political scientists who study the presidential nomination process feel that some types of reforms are needed, but they differ widely on which reforms they think should be adopted. Some favor a single national primary, others regional primaries, still others favor increasing the role of party officials in the process. Political scientist James Lengle has written widely on the presidential nomination process. He is convinced that recent reforms of the nomination process have failed to achieve their stated objectives, and in the process have seriously weakened the parties. Here he discusses some of the problems with the current system and suggests possible reforms.

Few elections match the excitement, suspense, and significance of an American presidential nominating campaign. The race commands the attention of the nation and the world, as citizens everywhere await weekly primary results and delegate totals, speculate endlessly about who's ahead and who's behind, and watch two contenders emerge from the pack and inch inexorably closer to their party's nomination and to the most important political office on the face of the earth, the U.S. presidency. The national and international significance of the event, however, is marred by the spectacle of an irrational, unfair, and dysfunctional process.

Nowhere are the combined flaws of the system better illustrated than by Iowa's and New Hampshire's life and death grip over the fate of contenders. The Iowa caucuses and the New Hampshire primary traditionally begin the delegate selection process. Because of the extensive coverage afforded these states by the media, winning or doing better than expected in Iowa and New Hampshire transforms long shots into instant front runners and generates sufficient momentum either to propel a candidate toward the nomination (e.g., McGovern, 1972; Carter, 1976; Reagan, 1980) or to sustain him through the remaining primaries (e.g., McCarthy, 1968; Bush, 1980; Hart, 1984). The power of Iowa and New Hampshire to shape the eventual outcome is substantiated by the track record of recent winners: every Democratic and Republican nominee between 1972 and 1984 finished first or second in these early contests. And history repeated itself in 1988, as Vice President George Bush (R) and Governor Michael Dukakis (D-Mass) won their respective party nominations after winning in New Hampshire,

Source: Portions of this article appeared in the June 1988 issue and is reprinted with permission from *The World & I*, a publication of *The Washington Times Corporation*, copyright © 1988.

and as Senator Robert Dole (R-Kan) emerged as the only serious (albeit, short-lived) challenger to Bush after winning in Iowa.

Candidates who fare badly in Iowa and New Hampshire are doomed at the start. A poor showing leads to bad press or no press, fewer contributions, a demoralized campaign staff, the disintegration of the campaign organization, and an early exit from the race. Here again, the evidence is overwhelming: of the twenty-eight Democratic and Republican contenders from 1972 to 1988 who finished third or worse in both states, twenty-four were eliminated shortly thereafter. Of the four who survived the Iowa and New Hampshire "veto" (Governor George Wallace, (D-Ala), 1972; Senator Henry "Scoop" Jackson, (D-Wash), 1976; Reverend Jesse Jackson, 1984, 1988; Senator Al Gore, Jr., (D-Tenn), 1988), only one, Jesse Jackson, managed to stay in the race until the end.

To confer such power over presidential recruitment on these two states is absurd. First, neither state is politically, socially, and economically representative of the country and of both political parties at-large. Thus, candidates are forced to test their popularity, themes, and issue positions before an atypical partisan audience and the nation is asked to accept the results as a meaningful expression of the party will. For the Democratic party to protect the privileged status of Iowa and New Hampshire in its rules is particularly irrational because both states have voted Republican in at least eight of the last ten presidential elections. Moreover, states with populations more representative of the party membership and of crucial importance in the Electoral College, such as New York, Illinois, Pennsylvania, Ohio, New Jersey, and California, often find themselves with no choice and influence if the race ends early or with limited choice and influence from a menu of candidates served up by their atypical brethren in Iowa and New Hampshire.

Second, such small states exercising such disproportionate influence over presidential recruitment makes a mockery of the notion of popular control, because success and failure in both states is based on so few votes. In 1976 Jimmy Carter was transformed from dark horse to nominee by appealing initially to only 34,000 voters (11,000 in Iowa and 23,000 in New Hampshire)—or to fewer people in two states combined than currently live in Hilo, Hawaii. In 1984, Gary Hart was similarly transformed overnight on the basis of five voters per caucus in Iowa and 38,000 voters in New Hampshire. Meanwhile, candidates only slightly less popular in Iowa and New Hampshire are routinely dealt a fatal blow. In the 1980 GOP race, Senator Howard Baker was eliminated on the basis of just 7 fewer voters per caucus than George Bush. For Democrats to accept a process dominated by Iowa and New Hampshire "bosses" is particularly ironic, because they have spent the last twenty years trying to rid the process of "party bosses."

How a process dominated by a small band of atypical party members from two states conforms to basic democratic notions of political equality, majority rule, and popular control is never explained. The defense of the current arrangement is found elsewhere. It is often argued that "face-to-face" campaigning in Iowa and New Hampshire is qualitatively better than "media and tarmac" campaigning in the other forty-eight states. In Iowa and New Hampshire, partisans get to meet and evaluate the candidates personally. In other states, candidate evaluations and votes are based primarily on political advertising. For defenders of the status quo, democracy and the party are better served by retail politics, even if the audience is unrepresentative, than by wholesale politics.

The argument, however, stops short of offering any measures of a "qualitatively better" campaign. If turnout is any indication of interest, face-to-face campaigning seems to be only marginally better at engaging the public politically because turnout in Iowa and New Hampshire, although slightly higher than most other states, is still embarrassingly low. In 1988, 89 percent of the voting-age population in Iowa stayed at home the night of the caucuses, and 66 percent of New Hampshire's voting-age population failed to vote in the primary. Such low turnout is neither a testimony to face-to-face campaigning nor a tribute to the purported civic-mindedness of the citizens of both states. Moreover, no study or poll to date shows that citizens in Iowa and New Hampshire who meet the candidates personally are more knowledgeable about the candidates and issues than residents of other states whose communications from the candidates is limited to political advertising.

Other supporters of the current process defend Iowa's and New Hampshire's privileged positions by touting the clean politics and geographical compactness of both states. Both factors, they argue, make the process fairer by enhancing the prospects of less well-known candidates. These same supporters, however, never define "clean" politics, never identify those states that revel in dirty politics, and never explain why candidates whose qualifications and experiences add up to relative anonymity should be given an advantage.

Support for the present system of primaries and caucuses derives almost exclusively from its openness. Based on aggregate vote totals, one can hardly argue. In presidential nominating campaigns from 1956 to 1968, fifteen states held primaries and twelve million people participated in the delegate selection process per year. Since 1972, the number of primaries has increased to over thirty and participation has increased to twenty-six million per election.

Appearances, however, are deceiving. Turnout in Democratic primaries in 1976 (sixteen million) was twice the Democratic turnout in 1968 (eight million), but nearly nine million Democratic votes cast in 1976 were meaningless because the race effectively ended after Carter defeated Morris Udall in Wisconsin and Henry Jackson in Pennsylvania. Thus, despite more voters, the 1976 campaign was decided by fewer voters than the one in 1968. Because the 1980 and 1988 Democratic and Republican campaigns were also decided well before the end of the primary season, millions of votes cast late in primary season amounted to millions of worthless votes.

Second, but more importantly, popular participation in delegate selection is a myth. In primary states, turnout rates vary normally between 15 percent and 25 percent. In caucus states, turnout is even lower, ranging usually between 1 percent and 5 percent. Thus, as the campaign shifts from state to state, 75 percent to 99 percent of the voting age population routinely abstain from the process.

Worse still, turnout is heading lower. Democratic turnout since 1972 provides a useful gauge for measuring this trend, because every Democratic campaign was hotly contested. In 1972, the first year of the current primary-based nominating system, average turnout per Democratic primary was 20.3 percent. By 1988, the average had dropped to 15.1 percent. In fact, despite extensive efforts to encourage participation since 1972, average turnout rates in 1984 and 1988 were actually lower than those in 1960 and 1968, the last two competitive Democratic nominations contested under the party-based system. Needless to say, this lack of participation undermines the mandate of the nominee, the notion of popular control, and the legitimacy of the process.

Although primaries and caucuses provide the opportunity for public participation, primary and caucus results do not reflect the voice of the party membership because those who turn out are not representative of the party at-large; liberal ideologues tend to be disproportionately over-represented in the Democratic process and conservative ideologues tend to be disproportionately over-represented in the Republican process. Of course, liberal Democrats and conservative Republicans do not win every primary, caucus, and nomination because the magnitude of the bias shifts from state to state and year to year depending on conditions and the issues. But it is more than just coincidence that George McGovern won the 1972 Democratic nomination, that Walter Mondale, Gary Hart, and Jesse Jackson led the pack in 1984, and that Michael Dukakis and Jesse Jackson emerged as the two front runners in 1988. In fact, even in the conservative South, liberals outnumber conservatives in Democratic primaries. In 1984, Mondale, Hart, and Jackson, the three most liberal candidates in the Democratic field, won 75 percent of the southern vote on Super Tuesday. In 1988, the liberal bias was again evident as Dukakis and Jackson won more than 50 percent of the vote cast by Democrats in the South on Super Tuesday.

The conservative bias in Republican campaigns is also apparent. Ronald Reagan fell just 200 delegates short of defeating President Gerald Ford in 1976 and then went on to win back-to-back nominations in 1980 and 1984. In 1988, conservatives Jack Kemp (R-NY) and Pierre DuPont (R-Del) did not fare too well against George Bush. Bush, on the other hand, campaigned as a converted conservative disciple of Reagan, and conservative television evangelist Pat Robertson won one less state primary and caucus than Senator Robert Dole.

Low turnout also magnifies the power of single-interest groups over the process and the candidates. In a primary with two candidates and a turnout of 20 percent, a candidate with the support of only 10 percent of the party membership can capture first place with 50 percent of the primary vote. In a multi-candidate field, the support of only 5 percent of the party is needed to win. In caucus states, victories can be delivered by 1 percent of the party membership in a two-man race and by even less in a multi-candidate field. Consequently, small but organized groups, such as teachers, evangelicals, environmentalists, gays, etc. carry great weight in the process and exact the full attention of most of the contenders. Because of low and biased turnout, primaries and caucuses distort the public will rather than reflect it and create an illusion of popular control that masks a much more elitist and unrepresentative set of decision makers.

Since the proliferation of primaries in 1972, the number of candidates seeking party nominations has more than doubled. Moreover, the range of choice has expanded to include certain kinds of candidates who might have been unacceptable in the previous era, such as ideologues (George McGovern, Ronald Reagan, Jack Kemp), party outsiders (Jimmy Carter, Gary Hart, John Anderson), and non-politicians (Jesse Jackson, Pat Robertson, Al Haig). Larger and more diverse fields means more choice, and choice is essential to democracy.

More choice is certainly good, but meaningful choice from among quality candidates is even better. Unfortunately, the current system falls short of providing the optimal.

As noted earlier, the field of contenders is winnowed quickly, and the nominee is routinely chosen before the end of the primary season. Thus, the dynamics of the process creates three classes of voters: those at the beginning of the process who have a full range of choice, those during the middle stages who have a limited range, and those at the end who have no choice at all. In 1988, the GOP race was essentially over on the first official day of delegate selection, Super Tuesday, March 8, when George Bush won 16 of 17 contests. The fact that the GOP field was larger than it used to be is probably little consolation to Republicans in approximately 30 states who had no choice at all in their party's most important decision.

The ultimate test of any nominating system is its ability to attract and elect the most qualified, talented, and experienced politicians of each generation. Unfortunately, the current process deters the kinds of people who should be encouraged while encouraging the kinds of people who should be deterred.

To succeed in primaries and caucuses, candidates must start their campaigns early because it takes time to build an organization and to raise money. Lengthy presidential campaigns, however, create a serious dilemma for political officeholders with presidential ambitions: they must either relinquish their office or neglect their constitutional responsibilities.

Jimmy Carter, Ronald Reagan, and Walter Mondale were unemployed when they won the nomination. Their success was not lost on Gary Hart and Howard Baker, both of whom gave up their Senate seats in order to run in 1988. In fact, Hart might have become the fourth nominee in a row to win an out-party nomination while unemployed were it not for his alleged affair with Donna Rice. A nominating system that rewards the unemployed over the employed or forces the employed to become unemployed is perverse to say the least.

Not all presidential aspirants give up their seats in order to run, but full-time campaigners are forced to be part-time officeholders and full-time officeholders are forced to be part-time campaigners. Senator Dole's 95 percent voting record in 1987 undoubtedly cost him valuable time on the campaign trail in his race against George Bush, while Congressman Richard Gephardt's 18 percent voting record may have cost him valuable points with his constituents. A nomination process that punishes responsibility and encourages negligence is equally perverse.

Lastly, and most importantly, some of the country's ablest and most qualified officeholders have been reluctant to run because of the financial, organizational, and personal costs imposed by the system. When the nominating system inhibits America's more qualified and experienced politicians from running while encouraging those less qualified and experienced, the country unnecessarily forfeits the best for less when nothing less than the best should suffice.

Our current system of presidential nomination is intended to be a compromise between two competing theories of democracy, direct versus representative. On paper, a system that divides the power of presidential recruitment between party members and party leaders is probably better than one that centralizes it in either group. Unfortunately, what looks good on paper has failed in practice, because the design achieves neither the popular control of direct democracy nor the enlightened deliberation and peer review of representative democracy.

To return to a pure form of representative democracy such as the conventions of old which were tightly controlled by party and elected officials in smoke-filled rooms is unfeasible given public ambivalence toward parties and a political tradition that extols open and popular decision-making. To move toward the other extreme, a pure form of direct democracy in the manner of a direct national primary is equally unacceptable, because it would weaken even further our political parties and would destroy the federal character of the nominating process.

A third alternative is a system of time-zone primaries. Primaries and caucuses are grouped by time-zone and scheduled one month apart on the first four Tuesdays of March through June. The immediate effect of time-zone primaries is to eliminate Iowa's and New Hampshire's permanent advantage and political clout in the process. If the dates for the four sets of time-zone primaries are randomly selected by lot every four years, no state or group of states always benefits from being first to select delegates or is always disadvantaged by being last. Political power is distributed more equally among states and party members, enhancing the worth of everyone's vote. Within each time-zone, of course, the power of states to attract the candidate's time and resources would vary reliably by size of state delegations. Larger states would receive more attention from the candidates and the media than smaller states. Thus, state power in time-zone primaries would be based on the importance, representativeness, and loyalty of a state's population and not on scheduling because delegate formulas are tied to state population and past party support.

In a system of time-zone primaries, momentum and winnowing would still occur, but survival and elimination are based on millions of votes in a large number of states rather than thousands of votes in two states. Moreover, faced with a more representative audience, candidates are forced to broaden their message rather than to kowtow to activists and single interest groups on a state by state basis. They would also be pressed to address national and regional as well as state and local issues.

A series of time-zone primaries also would reduce the prospects of relatively unknown candidates and enhance the prospects of politicians with national reputations and distinguished careers. Long-shot candidates would have neither the name recognition nor the resources to fare as well as front-runners in ten to twelve primaries held on a single day. If one believes that politics is a profession, and that political skills increase with the length and range of political experience, then a system that favors front-runners and deters long shots is a virtue rather than a vice. If a bias is to exist, and no nomination system is ever neutral, should it not consciously be designed to the advantage of both the party and the public by rewarding the skills, qualities, and experiences that produce both a winner and an effective president? Moreover, the social, economic, and political diversity of each time zone enhances the prospects of quick starts or dramatic comebacks for a broader range of front-runners. A system of time-zone primaries is certainly not perfect, but it does maintain some of the virtues of the current system while eliminating most of its major defects.

No process in any democracy is more important than its system of leadership recruitment. To pretend our current system works in spite of its flaws is to succumb to blind optimism, political inertia, and twisted logic and to gamble with the American presidency. It's time to face reality and reform the process so that its performance can match its promise.

Let the People Vote Directly for President

STEPHEN J. WAYNE

Although no candidate in this century has won election in the Electoral College after losing the popular vote, it has happened in the past and could happen in the future. Such a minority president would face popular discontent and have a difficult time building coalitions in support of his or her programs. Political scientists Stephen Wayne and Ronald Rapoport have written widely on presidential elections. Wayne argues for the abolishment of the Electoral College because it is antiquated and undemocratic, while Rapoport believes that the Electoral College continues to serve the vital function of maintaining a political balance between small and large states.

On November 8, Americans will vote for president. They will participate in a ritual and a function that is vital for a democracy, one that links the people to their government.

For a democracy to work, every vote should count equally and the majority should win. Yet, as far as George Bush and Michael Dukakis are concerned, every vote does not count equally and the person who is preferred by the most voters may not be elected.

The culprit, of course, is the Electoral College. Designed more than 200 years ago by people who believed a direct popular vote for president was neither wise nor feasible, it has maintained its archaic form despite wholesale changes in the political system—including the development of parties, expansion of suffrage, direct election of senators, and more equal legislative representation for all.

The Electoral College was proposed as a compromise between the large and the small states and the proponents of a stronger national government and a more decentralized federal system. It was designed to facilitate the selection of a well-qualified president in a manner that did not jeopardize the independence of the office and was consistent with a republican form of government.

The idea was to have electors, equal in number to the state's congressional delegation, choose the president, with a majority required for election.

The electors were supposed to exercise their own judgment in casting their votes. The advent of political parties around the turn of the century, however, quickly turned electors into partisan agents who voted for their

Source: Stephen J. Wayne, author of *The Road to the White House*, is a Professor of Government at Georgetown University.

party's nominees. Moreover, the movement toward popular election of the president has rendered the electors as individuals irrelevant.

The system is an anachronism. It does not work as intended, nor does it accord with the growing nationalization of American politics. Voters do not understand the indirect method of election. Most believe they are voting directly for president. The names of the electors do not even appear on the ballots in most states.

The problem is not only deception and electors performing as robots. It is worse. Electors can actually undermine a popular mandate if they have the chutzpa to do it.

Sixteen states and the District of Columbia have laws that require electors to vote for the candidate who wins the popular vote, but it is questionable whether these laws conform to the Constitution. Eight electors have failed to vote for their party's nominees over the years, and it could happen again. The fear is not massive defections but, in a very close election, tremendous pressure put on a few people to change their vote.

The basic problem with the system, however, and the principal reason that it should be abolished is that it is undemocratic in conception and in practice. All votes are not equal. Those living in the largest states and the smallest states have an advantage.

The large states benefit not only because of the number of electoral votes they cast, but because the votes are cast in a bloc. There is no minority representation within states.

By giving an edge to the larger states, the Electoral College also benefits groups that are geographically concentrated within those states and have cohesive voting patterns.

There is a slight off-setting gain for the very smallest states. Each receives a minimum of three electoral votes regardless of size, thereby increasing the voting power of sparsely populated states. In general, states in the Far West and East are aided by the Electoral College, but those in the South, Midwest, and Rocky Mountain areas are hurt by it.

Additionally, the system works to the benefit of the two major parties and to the detriment of minor parties, which find it difficult to accumulate enough votes to win an election.

To have any effect, third-party support must be geographically concentrated, as George Wallace's was in 1968 and Strom Thurmond's was in 1948 (both Southerners), rather than evenly distributed across the country, as Henry Wallace's was in 1948 and John Anderson's in 1980.

A direct popular vote would eliminate these biases. It would better equalize voting power both among and within the states.

The large, competitive states would lose some of their electoral clout by the elimination of winner-take-all voting. Party competition within the states and perhaps even nationwide would be increased. Candidates would be forced to wage campaigns in all fifty states. No longer could an area of the country be taken for granted. Every vote would count in a direct election.

More extensive campaigning by the presidential candidates might produce two other desirable outcomes. It should improve turnout. It might also tie the presidential contest more closely to congressional elections, thus improving the chances for cooperation between the two institutions when the government got under way.

Finally a direct popular vote would preclude the possibility of electing a nonplurality president. We have done that twice in our history, once in 1876 and again in 1888.

In both those elections, the two candidates who won a majority of the Electoral College failed to win even a plurality of the popular vote. This could happen again. We must not allow that to occur. If government is to be based on the consent of the governed, then popular will must prevail.

The Electoral College:
Still the Best Alternative

RONALD B. RAPOPORT

Some pundits warn that the November 8 election could shock Americans: just possibly the candidate who most voters choose as president will be denied victory by the Electoral College.

But this unlikely prospect should not be misused to spark opposition to a venerable and useful institution of U.S. politics.

The Electoral College sprang from a thorny debate at the 1787 Constitutional Convention. It represented a middle ground between the popular election of the chief executive (rejected as too radical), and election by the Congress (deemed contrary to the separation of powers).

Instead the framers granted each state a share of the "electoral votes" equal to its number of House and Senate seats combined, and stipulated that the candidate who won a majority of electoral votes would enter the White House.

Only twenty-five years later this imperfect institution underwent major reform (the Twelfth Amendment to the Constitution), and further proposals for reform or abolition have popped up ever since.

Are these demands warranted?

The Electoral College fulfills a vital balancing role in the American system by offsetting the advantage small states enjoy in Congress—another product of compromise at the Constitutional Convention.

Although each state receives a share of seats in the House of Representatives proportionate to its population, all states—large or small—claim two senators. Rhode Island and Vermont send just as many senators to Washington as California or New York.

The Electoral College squares this unfairness by enhancing the clout of voters from large states in presidential elections.

At first glance this seems implausible. After all, Alaska with only 534,000 people controls three electoral votes, and California with twenty-seven million has forty-seven. This means that there are more than three times as many people per electoral vote in California as in Alaska.

But, the fact that all states but Maine allot their electoral votes on a winner-take-all basis—and have with few exceptions since 1836—offsets the apparent small state advantage. Thus carrying California by a one vote margin entitles the lucky candidate to a rich harvest of forty-seven electoral votes; a second-place finish yields none.

Source: Ronald Rapoport, an expert on electoral behavior, is a Professor of Government at The College of William and Mary.

In fact, carrying California by even a thin margin thus yields a greater electoral reward than sweeping the twelve smallest states, plus the District of Columbia.

Because large states tend to be socially diverse and electorally competitive, their advantage is enhanced. Political scientists estimate California voters are almost three times as attractive campaign targets as those in Washington D.C. Such numbers have certainly impressed Republican bigwigs, who have chosen five of their last eight nominees from California.

The main beef leveled at the Electoral College is the chance of an unrepresentative outcome—that is the College could produce a winner who actually received fewer popular votes. In 1876 and again in 1888 candidates with clear popular victories lost the presidency because they failed to win most of the electoral votes.

While the last time this happened was a century ago, some pundits claim that Republicans enjoy an electoral college "lock." In other words, Republicans are certain to win popular vote majority in just enough states with sufficient electoral votes to win the White House: even if the majority of voters nationally choose a Democrat.

Yet this logic is wrong. In states where the Republicans do boast a solid base, they will pile up large popular vote margins, yet such victories will not bring a disproportionate share of electoral votes.

A Republican candidate could skunk his rival in Utah, for example, but still win only four electoral votes. Moreover, a candidate who barely won the largest states, and capturing all their electoral votes, would be all but assured of victory.

It is precisely these close contests in which victory is problematic. Neither Republicans nor Democrats can count on disproportionate success in the large states. Hair's breadth victories have a way of evening out.

Yet, even those who remain convinced that the Electoral College could cheat the voters out of their first choice offer no suitable alternative.

Directly electing presidents, under a system requiring the winner to garner a majority of the popular vote, would insure frequent runoffs—that is a second round of voting between the two leading candidates needed to produce a clear winner.

After all, in only half of the presidential elections since 1948 has any candidate received 51 percent of the ballots cast.

Growing prospects of a runoff would weaken the two-party system by enticing third-party candidates—and others from factions of the Democratic and Republican parties who had lost the nomination—to enter the race in hopes of preventing a clear winner in round one.

They would hope to strike a bargain with the leading contenders for their endorsement in the runoff. The option of requiring only 40 percent to win without a runoff would weaken the winner's claim to represent a majority, and would in any case not guarantee against a runoff.

As the old saying goes: "If it ain't broke, don't fix it."

Presidential Candidate PACs and the Future of Campaign Finance Reform

ANTHONY CORRADO

In the 1988 presidential nomination process, candidates of both parties formed their own political action committees, or PACs. Although these PACs were ostensibly formed to help other candidates within the party, they were in fact appendages of the candidate's campaign, paying the salaries of consultants before the official start of the campaign, paying for travel by the candidate, and enabling the candidates to hone their direct-mail lists for future fund-raising. Political scientist Tony Corrado has just completed a book on the funding of Presidential campaigns. Here he argues that candidate PACs are a loophole that should be closed, for they provide a mechanism for candidates to avoid spending and contribution limits.

On January 28, 1977, one week after the inauguration of President Jimmy Carter, Ronald Reagan discovered a new loophole in the federal campaign finance laws. On this date Reagan established Citizens for the Republic, a political action committee, as a means of disbursing $1.6 million in surplus funds from his unsuccessful 1976 presidential campaign. The committee's original purpose was to assist conservative Republican candidates and state and local party organizations. But Reagan, who served as chairman of the PAC, and his advisers soon realized that the PAC could also be used to conduct a wide range of campaign-related activities that would help prepare the way for another presidential bid in 1980.

Between 1977 and 1980, Citizens for the Republic spent $6.27 million. Only 10 percent of this amount ($674,386) was contributed to federal candidates. Most of the PAC's funds were used to hire staff and consultants, develop fundraising programs, recruit volunteers, subsiize Reagan's travel and public appearances, and host receptions on his behalf. In short, Citizens for the Republic served as a shadow campaign committee, providing Reagan with the resources needed to launch his successful 1980 run for the White House. But since the PAC's avowed purpose was to assist other candidates and since Reagan was not a candidate while he served as chairman of the PAC, none of the funds raised or spent by the PAC counted against the contribution and spending limits imposed on his campaign. The committee thus provided Reagan with

Source: Anthony Corrado is an Assistant Professsor of Government at Colby College. He previously served on the staffs of the Carter, Mondale and Dukakis presidential campaigns.

a means of spending more than $6 million outside of the limits of federal law.

Reagan's approach dramatically changed the way in which presidential candidates finance and organize their campaigns. Since 1980, "pre-candidacy" PACs have become a common feature of the presidential nomination campaigns and now constitute one of the biggest loopholes in the federal campaign finance system. Over the course of the last three elections, sixteen presidential aspirants established a PAC prior to becoming a candidate. These committees spent more than $40 million, none of which was disclosed on campaign spending reports. Most of this amount, at least $25.2 million, was spent in anticipation of the 1988 election as ten of the fourteen major party candidates formed PACs to begin their quest for the nomination (Michael Dukakis, Jesse Jackson, Albert Gore, and Gary Hart did not take advantage of this option).

The number of "pre-candidacy" PACs has increased significantly in recent elections because a PAC provides a prospective candidate with a means of circumventing almost every major provision of the Federal Election Campaign Act. This legislation, adopted in the wake of the Watergate scandal, completely restructured the campaign finance system in an effort to end the corruptive influence of large contributions by "fat cat" donors and to curb the rising costs of presidential campaigns. To accomplish these goals, the act required full public disclosure of a campaign's finances, set a limit of $1,000 on individual contributions, placed strict ceilings on campaign expenditures, and established a system of public financing for presidential primary and general election campaigns.

These changes in the campaign finance system fundamentally altered the strategic environment of the presidential selection process and encouraged candidates to develop new organizational and financial approaches in pursuing the nomination. These new approaches were in part a response to the conflicting strategic and operational demands that grew out of the reforms. Some provisions of the law, such as the individual contribution limit, compel candidates to begin campaigning early. This limit forces candidates to generate the funds for their campaigns through small donations of $1,000 or less. As a result, a candidate must begin to raise money long before the primaries begin due to the long lead time needed to amass the millions of dollars needed to finance a nationwide campaign.

Other provisions of the law, especially the state and overall spending limits, encourage candidates to delay the start of their campaigns and restrict their activities in the pre-primary period. A candidate who begins to campaign early in the election cycle may reach the spending limit before the end of the selection process or may reach the spending limit in a state before election day, and have to cut back on anticipated expenditures to avoid violating the law. Such a candidate risks defeat at the hands of a less extravagant opponent who has not approached the limit and can therefore spend more money in the late stages of the race. No candidate wants to face this situation. Consequently, most presidential hopefuls look for ways to avoid spending substantial sums of money in the initial stages of a campaign.

The campaign finance regulations thus present candidates with a fundamental strategic problem: how to conduct the early campaigning required by the system yet avoid violating the expenditure limits. In recent elections, presidential aspirants have learned to solve this problem by exploiting the opportunities offered by a pre-candidacy PAC.

By establishing a PAC, a candidate can avoid the stringent financial limits of the Federal Election Campaign Act and defy the intent of federal lawmakers. First, since a PAC is considered to be a legally separate committee from a candidate's campaign organization, the monies raised and spent by a PAC do not have to be disclosed on a candidate's financial reports. A candidate can therefore rely on a PAC to avoid the strict public disclosure required of federal candidates.

Second, a PAC can accept contributions of up to $5,000 a year, as compared to the $1,000 per election allowed a presidential campaign committee. A candidate with a PAC can therefore receive up to $20,000 from an individual ($5,000 a year for each of the four years in a presidential election cycle), instead of the $1,000 mandated by law. And the individual who gives to the PAC may still donate the maximum amount to the candidate's campaign committee since it is legally separate from the PAC.

Third, federal law places no limit on a PAC's spending. A candidate may therefore spend huge sums through a PAC without having to worry about overall or state spending ceilings since the funds disbursed by a PAC are not counted against campaign spending limits, so long as the committee's publicly-stated purpose is to assist other candidates and help build party organizations.

Presidential PACs have had a major impact on the effectiveness of the campaign finance reforms. Consider, for example, the activities of the leader of the PACs, George Bush's Fund for America's Future. This committee, established on April 25, 1985, with then Vice-President George Bush as its honorary chairman and Lee Atwater as its Executive Director, raised and spent more than $11.2 million before the 1988 election. Approximately two-thirds of this amount was received in contributions in excess of $1,000, donations which would have been illegal if given directly to his campaign. This included contributions from more than 200 "fat cats" who donated at least $10,000 each to the committee. The PAC's purpose was supposedly to assist other Republican candidates, but the committee contributed only $844,000 to other federal candidates. Most of the money was used to finance "pre-campaign" activities.

The PAC hired a national staff of about fifty persons who coordinated the formation of steering committees and volunteer organizations. It also hired political organizers in Iowa, New Hampshire, and Michigan to begin to recruit the nucleus of a campaign organization in these crucial early primary states. The PAC also developed direct mail fundraising programs, prepared policy papers, and conducted polls. Yet none of its expenditures were applicable to the Bush campaign's spending.

Bush's chief opponents, Senator Robert Dole and Congressman Jack Kemp, also took advantage of the PAC alternative. These committees raised substantial amounts of money, but neither of them could match Bush's fundraising prowess. Dole's Campaign America raised $6.1 million prior to the 1988 election, while Kemp's Campaign for Prosperity raised about $4.1 million. Bush therefore entered the presidential race with a $5 million advantage over Dole and a $7 million advantage over Kemp. Given this head start, it is not surprising that he easily wrapped-up the nomination in the first weeks of the primary campaign.

Over the past decade, campaign finance reform has been a major issue on the congressional agenda. The debate, however, has been dominated by the issues associated with the financing of congressional elections. The experience with presidential candidate PACs demonstrates that, if a truly effective program of reform is to be developed, the Congress must broaden its focus to encompass the problems that have emerged in the funding of presidential nomination campaigns.

In developing future reform proposals, Congress must acknowledge the limits of its ability to restrict political behavior. Instead of simply increasing the restraints imposed on candidates and adopting stringent ceilings that fail to reflect political reality, lawmakers should emphasize compliance and respect for the law. While some of the regulations should be strengthened, Congress must consider easing or completely abolishing some of the current regulations in order to reduce the strategic and operational demands imposed on candidates. The regulations should allow candidates to generate the resources they need to conduct a viable campaign within the framework of their campaign committees. This is the crucial first step towards improving the system and discouraging the use of pre-candidacy PACs and other unregulated organizations since it resolves the strategic problems that induce candidates to circumvent the law. Such a regulatory approach can be achieved by adopting a number of specific reforms.

First, Congress should improve the information available to the public by strengthening the disclosure provisions of the Federal Election Campaign Act. Each candidate should be required to disclose the financial activities of any PAC or other political organization with which he or she is associated. Even if these funds do not legally qualify as campaign-related contributions or expenditures, candidates should reveal their association with a PAC and report its financial activities. This will help to ensure that the public is aware of any pre-candidacy PAC operations and thus provide for increased scrutiny and more informed decision-making by the voters.

New regulations should be set forth to define more clearly the criteria for determining whether a PAC's activities are "campaign-related" and therefore subject to the limits applicable to presidential campaign committees.

Currently, the regulations provide a narrow definition that is easily avoided. By broadening the scope of this definition, the funds spent by a PAC on activities that are clearly campaign-related or of direct benefit to a campaign (e.g., the development of fundraising lists) will be regarded as a campaign contribution or expense subject to the contribution limits or spending ceilings that govern presidential campaigns.

Congress should also adopt a number of reforms that would reduce the operational pressures that encourage candidates to form PACs and channel unregulated monies into their campaigns. Most importantly, the spending ceilings imposed on presidential campaigns must be revised. These limits have not had a major effect on campaign spending; indeed, few candidates have ever reached the overall ceilings. To the extent that they have restricted the expenditures of some contenders, this has only served to convince candidates in subsequent elections to create PACs so that they can spend money outside of the limits and nullify any potential effect of the law. The state spending ceilings, which were primarily adopted to provide lesser-known candidates with an opportunity to compete against better-known challengers, should be abolished and the overall limit should be raised significantly in recognition of the real increase in the costs of campaigning. Currently, the ceiling is increased on the basis of the Consumer Price Index, but this index does not account for the substantial increase in the costs of campaigns that have resulted from rising advertising expenses and new campaign technologies. Consequently, the amount a candidate may legally spend becomes less realistic with each election.

Finally, Congress should increase the individual contribution limit so that candidates can generate the funds needed to finance their campaigns without having to begin fundraising far in advance of the election. At a minimum, the contribution limit should be indexed to reflect the rate of inflation and rounded to the closest $100 increment. This simple reform would increase the individual contribution limit from $1,000 to approximately $2,500. This would help to eliminate the artificial pressure to begin fundraising early that is generated by the low contribution limit.

Securing passage for some of these proposals may prove to be difficult since Congress is wary of "de-reforming" campaign financing. But unless this approach is adopted, candidates will continue to raise and spend unlimited amounts of money through pre-candidacy PACs and an effective system of campaign finance regulation will never be achieved. After all, as Reagan and Bush demonstrated, the "PAC Man" strategy can win elections.

Take the Money and Reform

MARK GREEN

Throughout the 1980s and into the 1990s, Congress has routinely considered many proposals to reform the system of funding congressional elections. Critics have charged that PACs buy congressional votes, and that "soft money" allows wealthy individuals to purchase more access to members of Congress. For a variety of reasons, no comprehensive reform has been enacted. Writer and politician Mark Green advocates limiting PAC money, regulating "soft money," and providing public funds for Congressional candidates.

Has the pro-democracy movement finally reached America? Congress is actively considering the most significant reforms since Watergate in the way we fund and elect legislators, and for much the same reason. Apparently the kindling of democracy needs an occasional match of scandal, and not since Watergate has there been such a confluence of incendiary revelations about the money chase in Congress, from the dubious financial transactions of Jim Wright and Tony Coelho to Charles Keating and the S&L disaster. So the Senate this week and the House soon thereafter will take up such long-discussed reforms as a limit on campaign expenditures, free TV time, public financing, and less "soft money," PAC money, and "bundled" money.

The problem of pay-to-play politics is now beyond dispute. Consider these fault- and trend-lines of the congressional culture:

- Alan Cranston and Alfonse D'Amato each spent as much to be elected to the Senate in 1986 as John Kennedy spent to be elected president in 1960: $13 million. Senators raise an average of $3,000 every working day for six years to run for reelection.
- In 1988 PACs favored incumbents over challengers by seven-to-one; after election, incumbents had more funds left over than their challengers spent in toto.
- A survey of 114 members by the bipartisan Center for Responsive Politics found that 20 percent of respondents *admitted* that contributions influenced their votes.
- In 1986 Senator Rudy Boschwitz, Republican of Minnesota, gave all of his $1,000+ contributors a booklet of blue "special access stamps" and ordered his staff to expedite letters with those stamps.
- A freshman Texas congressman has a box in his office for lobbyists to drop $5,000 and $10,000 checks.

Source: *The New Republic*, May 14, 1990. Reprinted by permission of *The New Republic* © 1990, The New Republic, Inc.

- In the past election cycle, a congressman was more likely to die (seven) than lose (six).

Clearly there is a fundamental problem eroding democracy: the infection of public values by market values. There is an unspoken consensus in this country in favor of parallel systems of power—a capitalist economic system and a democratic political system. No one argues that everyone should have an equal balance in the bank, but everyone agrees that all should have a equal vote at the ballot box. This structure collapses when those with unequal wealth in the economy gain similarly unequal influence in government. In the end, money may trample democracy as we are left with a Congress filled with millionaires and heirheads.

Interviews with both members and donors reveal a widespread agreement on the costs of a system that combines legislatively interested money with legislators interested in money. "I can't say that PACs are buying these elections," says former Senator William Proxmire, "but you would have to be a fool to believe they aren't buying something." Members become, in Senator Robert Byrd's phrase, "full-time fund-raisers and part-time legislators," leading to a Congress of unelected staff and absentee politicians. Meanwhile, women and men without wealth or access to it are discouraged from seeking office—the "silent casualties" of the current system, as Judge J. Skelly Wright called them.

The steady rise in money and the decline in voting may be causally connected as voters come to understand how their franchise has been diluted by dollars. And as Representative Dan Glickman of Kansas notes: "Because Democrats and Republicans take money from the same sources, it's harder to differentiate between the parties." (Sixty-four House Democrats, for example, voted for more capital gains tax breaks at a time when the gap between rich and poor is the largest in forty years.)

In terms of the prospects for effective change, the political planets seem to be in alignment. The S&L debacle and other congressional scandals have altered the chemistry in the Senate and the country. After a decade when the Senate did not investigate a single one of its members, seven senators are currently under ethics scrutiny. Suddenly Senators Dave Durenberger and D'Amato, two of those being investigated, have announced they are in favor of the public funding of campaigns (the writer filed the ethics complaint that led to the current investigation of D'Amato. See "Al's Pals," TNR, October 30, 1989); and Republican Senator Warren Rudman of New Hampshire, vice chair of the Senate ethics panel, says he's now leaning in favor as well. (All three opposed the last Congress's pro-reform Byrd-Boren bill, which at its peak gained the support of fifty-three senators.) And President Bush, judging from his speech last June on this subject, is rhetorically closer to Ralph Nader than Ronald Reagan. "Today's special interest political action committees and their $160 million war chests," he said, "overshadow the great parties of Thomas Jefferson and Abraham Lincoln."

At the same time, all four congressional leaders claim to be either enthusiastic or open-minded. Speaker of the House Thomas Foley and Senate Majority Leader George Mitchell say it is a top priority. House Minority Leader Bob Michel announced last December for the first time he'd consider a spending limit, and Senate Republican leader Bob Dole expressed interest in an oxymoronic "flexible cap," a limit on expenditures that can be adjusted upward only if the candidate receives small in-state contributions.

Privately, members say some reform is likely this year, but not necessarily serious reform. For the planets, though aligned, are still miles apart due to reasons of hypocrisy, complexity, and partisanship.

Bush and Dole say they oppose public funding of congressional campaigns, despite the fact that they (with Reagan) received more than $100 million in public financing in the eighties for their national bids. Many Democrats, who for years railed against evil "special interest PAC money," now balk at reducing the role of funds that disproportionately favor the incumbent party (i.e., them).

Each of the 535 experts in Congress, of course, has his or her own views on flexible caps, lobbyists' bundling, "soft money," matching funds, pre-emptible time, tax credits, etc., etc. And the parties have staked out contrasting positions: Republicans want less PAC money, more party money, and no caps or public funds; many Democrats oppose PAC and party reform yet favor caps and public funds.

Real campaign finance reform will be enacted only if Democratic philosophy and Republican frustration combine to ensure that our democracy isn't governed merely by those who win an alms race. This means, at a minimum, putting a ceiling over and a floor under campaign resources so we again have reasonably competitive elections. Two essential floors include public funding and free or cheap TV; two essential ceilings include caps on spending and soft money.

Public funding. Representative Al Swift, Democrat of Washington, who co-chairs the bipartisan House Task Force, says he's all for public funding. But you'd never know it from talking to him: "There are only three groups against it—incumbents, challengers, and the public." Wrong. The public favors it, according to a Greenberg-Lake poll, by 58 percent to 33 percent. And as a challenger who was outspent $13 million to $2 million in a Senate race, I'm convinced that a system of publicly matched small gifts would make it possible for non-heirs to compete on more equal terms with well-endowed incumbents. With supporters like Swift—and Republican opponents complaining about giving taxpayer money to grubby politicians—no wonder public funding has fallen off the radar.

Enter Senators John Kerry, Bill Bradley, and Joe Biden, who are determined to force the issue in the Senate by proposing a public funding amendment to the leading bill. They should especially push two arguments. First, there's the cost to taxpayers of the existing *private* financing of public elections. The bailout of the Lincoln S&L alone is four times the annual cost of total general election campaign financing. Second, the best real-world argument for public funding is not only the presidential funding process, but also the twelve states and several cities already successfully implementing it.

In New York City, candidates were able to raise up to $100,000 from individual contributors and faced no ceiling on overall expenditures. In the 1985 Democratic primary, for example, Ed Koch outspent his leading opponent ten-to-one. The Campaign Finance Act of 1988 put a stop to this, establishing matching funds for smaller gifts, a $3,000 contribution limit, and a $3.5 million spending limit. The 1989 city elections showed the act to be a success, evening the playing field among contestants and generating bipartisan praise from David Dinkins, Koch, and Rudolph Giuliani.

Still, direct public funding is in neither the central Senate measure, the Boren-Mitchell bill, nor reportedly the current Foley draft. So unless Public Citizen's million-dollar media and grass-roots campaign boosts Kerry's version, the odds are long that our system for electing presidents and mayors will be good enough for members of Congress.

Free or cheaper TV or mail. "Why not . . . require that, near election time, both great parties be allowed, without expense, an equal amount of time on the air, to the end that both sides of all issues be fairly and adequately presented to the people?" The speaker was Frank Knox, the Republican vice presidential nominee in 1936, and he was talking about radio.

Today, TV and radio advertising typically consume half of all campaign expenditures. Candidates become incessant panhandlers in order to enrich private companies for the use of the public airwaves to educate the public in public elections. So Senators John Danforth, Rudman, and Dole, noting that TV ad costs doubled in the past six years, are pushing for subsidized electronic advertising of a kind that is common in Europe. Indeed, of twenty-one democratic countries studied by the American Enterprise Institute, eighteen provided free TV time to political parties (Norway, Sri Lanka, and the United States were the only ones that did not).

The final form can vary greatly: the time could simply be made far cheaper. It could go directly to candidates in thirty- and sixty-second increments, or in five-minute increments with the requirement that only a talking candidate could appear; in TV/radio markets with many congressional districts, such as New York City and Los Angeles, candidates unhappy with wasting 90 percent of their ad time on voters in other districts could convert the electronic value of their time into targeted mail; or candidates able to verify a threshold of small gifts could get them matched by public funds and earn a "Candidate Communications Voucher" that could be redeemed at a TV station or the post office.

According to the best calculations, the "opportunity cost" of 120 minutes of general election TV time for House candidates and 210 minutes for Senate candidates would be $200 million. Either stations would absorb this cost as the precondition of a scarce lucrative license ($200 million is under one percent of TV's 1986 ad revenues of more than $22 billion) or it would be paid out of public funds (from an increased check-off on income tax forms of $3).

When President Bush told a group of public interest advocates last June that he opposed public funding of congressional races, Joan Claybrook of Public Citizen asked him, "What about cheaper TV time or mail?" "Oh, that's a possibility," he answered. Of course, subsidized electronic advertising is a form of public funding. But since the money goes directly to voter education, and not a politician's war chest or pocket, Bush, like many key swing Republicans and Democrats, is sympathetic. Odds: perhaps one in three.

A cap on expenditures or PAC gifts. In 1974 Congress put a lid on House spending, but the Supreme Court's 1976 *Buckley* v. *Valeo* decision ruled the $140,000 cap to be an unconstitutional infringement of "speech." In what Senator Mitchell (a former federal judge) called "one of the most weakly reasoned, poorly written, internally contradictory court opinions I've ever read," the six-justice majority reasoned that in politics the right to spend was equal to the right to speak; ergo, limits on spending were limits on speech. We always knew that in politics "money talks," but most non-lawyers thought that was a problem, not a principle.

Justice Byron White, in a dissenting opinion, predicted that "without limits on total expenditures, campaign costs will inevitably and endlessly escalate." Score one for the Whizzer: since the decision, the average cost of winning a Senate seat has increased ten times. If spending keeps doubling, as it did from 1982 to 1988 ($2 million to $4 million), the average cost of a Senate seat would be $16 million by the year 2000.

Under *Buckley*, Congress could still persuade candidates to accept a cap voluntarily in exchange for other benefits, such as public matching funds. But not if Senator Mitch McConnell, Republican of Kentucky, has his way. "There is no chance that a bill will become law that contains spending limits," he says, reflecting the view of Ed Rollins, head of the Republican Congressional Campaign Committee, that the Republican challengers should preserve the option of vastly outspending Democratic incumbents. One wonders why. It's hard to think of many examples of when Republican challengers won such races, though it's easy to come up with hundreds of Democratic incumbents who financially buried Republicans. Perhaps the party of privilege just can't let go of its spending habits.

A general expenditure cap would indirectly reduce the problem of PAC contributions with strings attached. There's a PAC cap in the Boren-Mitchell bill of 12 percent of receipts, which would have reduced PAC funds in Senate races in 1988 by two-thirds. With Bush, Dole, Mitchell, and Foley behind some PAC lid, its odds are no worse than even.

Regulating soft money. "Soft money" is non-federal money given to state parties that ends up influencing federal races. There are at least two reasons that *The New York Times* calls this phenomenon "sewer money": Charles Keating Jr. and the '88 presidential election. Although federal law limited

Keating to $1,000 individual donations and $25,000 overall, he gave $1.3 million to various candidates, as well as to state parties and voter drives, which in turn spent the funds in ways that allegedly helped federal candidates. Similarly, at the presidential level, although Bush and Dukakis each took $44.5 million checks from the Treasury on the condition that they accept no private funds, their fund-raisers were coaxing $100,000-level donors to give what turned out to be a total of $100 million to state parties, which spent the money to help their respective tickets. This is called a loophole.

Common Cause believes that a campaign finance bill that allowed soft money would be more loophole than law. While Boren-Mitchell would nearly ban such funds, state party chairmen, especially Democrats, are militantly opposed: Texas Democratic chairman Bob Slagle thinks "Mitchell-Boren could be writing the epitaph on the tombstone of state parties all over the country." California's Jerry Brown calls a ban unconstitutional. This conflict between Common Cause and the Democrats is likely to produce a compromise that imposes some ceiling on such gifts (say, $20,000) with full disclosure.

If the current campaign finance system doesn't fall this year, even given partisan obstacles like McConnell and Rollins, it's hard to know when it will. The public wants change. Members are embarrassed that they both have to genuflect for gifts and endure comedic taunts. (Jay Leno: "Did you hear the latest S&L scandal? They wasted millions on extra bonuses, trips, and carpets when they *knew* the money had been earmarked for corrupt senators. Outrageous!") Donors too are getting weary: one major Democratic contributor in New York told me he was astonished when a freshman senator called for help in 1989—"and he was up for re-election in '94!"

Last month in Manhattan five Soviet visitors and several Americans cross-examined each other on the state of each country's democracy—our venerable and imitated yet imperfect one and their new, groping, flawed one. The Soviets expressed shock at how the quantity of money and ads so often seemed to determine the winner in our elections. In Moscow, they pointed out, candidates for Peoples Deputy more equally competed by leafletting, rallying, doorbell ringing, and debating, including at least one debate on television. You have to hope Congress will have more pride than to let our great republic take lessons in campaign fairness from the Soviet Union's toddler of a wannabe democracy.

Twelve Is Enough

HENDRIK HERTZBERG

The anti-incumbent mood in the 1990 Congressional elections was most evident in proposals to limit the terms of members of Congress. California and Colorado passed referenda limiting the terms of their state legislators, and there was some talk of trying to impose such limits on members of Congress. Writer Hendrik Hertzberg supports this proposal, for he believes that it would make for a more responsive Congress, but Charles Kesler sees several disadvantages in term limitations. In the readings that follow they debate this issue—a debate that is likely to continue in many state houses across the country for the next several years.

Before you automatically reject the proposal now making the rounds for a twelve-year limit for members of Congress as a dreadful idea—an anti-democratic, anti-political, mechanistic "reform" that like so many other "reforms" would most likely end up making things worse, a bit of mischievous tinkering with the precious Constitution that has served us so well for 200 years, a misguided gimmick that ignores the *real* problem (PACs, polls, gerrymandering, special interests, negative ads, cowardly politicians, ignorant citizens, whatever) and is probably nothing but a Republican plot anyway—before you agree with all these dismissals and turn your attention to more pressing matters, consider three numbers.

Number number one: 37.1. Yes, it's a voter turnout figure, the op-ed writer's best friend. This particular figure represents the percentage of American over-eighteens who bestirred themselves to go to the polls in 1986, the last time the citizenry was invited to vote for members of Congress without the added glitz of a presidential contest. Compared with the turnout in any other arguably democratic country—France, Nicaragua, Norway, Hungary, El Salvador, Israel, Turkey, Italy, Lithuania, you name it—this is pathetic. It was the lowest since 1926, not counting 1944, when World War II made voting inconvenient for large numbers of people. And the public's true interest in House elections is even lower. According to *Congressional Quarterly*'s Rhodes Cook, if you factor out districts where there was a contest for governor or U.S. senator to lure people out, the turnout was a scandalous 27.6 percent. Only the most perverse elitists argue that this state of affairs is anything but a symptom of extreme political ill health.

Number number two: 98.3. This is the percentage of incumbent members of the House of Representatives who won their "races" for re-election in

Source: *The New Republic*, May 14, 1990. Reprinted by permission of *The New Republic*, © 1990, The New Republic, Inc.

1988, up from 98 percent flat in 1966. According to a recent study by David C. Huckabee of the Congressional Research Service of the Library of Congress, this number has remained in the 90s since 1974, and it is currently the highest it has ever been since the middle of President Washington's first term. And because more incumbents now choose to run than ever before, the re-election rate for the House as a whole is now in the 90s, too—92.4 percent last time out, to be exact. In the 19th century this figure tended to hover somewhere between 40 percent and 70 percent, once dropping to as low as 24 percent (in 1842); it hit the 70s after World War I and has been climbing more or less steadily ever since.

The 98.3 figure actually understates the political stasis of the House. Of the 409 incumbents who ran for re-election, six were defeated in November. But five of these had been tainted by one sort of scandal or another. So the grand total of representatives who lost their seats as a consequence of what we normally think of as politics—that is, a process in which the electorate chooses between competing sets of programs and policies—was exactly one.

Number number three: 36. This is how many years a single party, the Democrats, has controlled the lower house of the national legislature of the United States. By contrast, the British House of Commons has changed hands four times since 1954, the French Chamber of Deputies three times, the West German Bundestag five times, the Canadian House of Commons five times, and the Indian Lok Sabha three times. When it comes to one-party legislative dominance in serious countries, only Japan, Mexico, South Africa, and the Soviet Union are even in our league. And in the last two, unlike in the United States, the ruling party is a pretty good bet to lose the next election. No moral equivalence intended, of course. Or deserved.

In the light of numbers two and three, the wonder is that number number one is so high. In the overwhelming majority of congressional districts, voting is increasingly an irrational act. Why bother, when 85 percent of the incumbents are getting more than 60 percent of the vote in their districts, when the *average* incumbent is getting 73.5 percent, when sixty-three members are returned with Brezhnevian majorities exceeding 94 percent? Except in the handful of districts where there are open seats or close races, voting may still make sense as a civic sacrament—as a way of refreshing one's soul with a sense of belonging to a democratic community—but it makes no sense as a form of political action. Better to spend the hour or so it takes to vote writing checks and sending them off to candidates in contested districts.

Against this background, the idea of a twelve-year limit begins to acquire a certain logic. Such proposals are neither new nor flakily marginal. A limit on congressional service was considered at the founding constitutional convention (which laid it aside as "entering too much into detail"), and the idea has won the support, over the decades, of a bipartisan list of luminaries including Abraham Lincoln, Harry Truman, Dwight D. Eisenhower, and John F. Kennedy. The current campaign for a constitutional amendment that would limit service to six two-year terms for House members and two six-year terms for senators (with an exemption for the present crew of incumbents, of course) is led by Senators Gordon Humphrey, Republican of New Hampshire, and Dennis DeConcini, Democrat of Arizona. Their ten co-sponsors span the Senate's ideological spectrum, from Jake Garn on the right to Nancy Kassebaum in the center to Tom Daschle on the left.

Even so, truth in packaging compels the admission that the current push is basically a Republican scam. All but three of the Senate co-sponsors are Republicans. The twelve-year limit was endorsed in the 1988 Republican platform. The letterhead pressure group promoting the idea, something called Americans to Limit Congressional Terms, is run out of a Republican political consultant's office and consists mostly of Republican ex-congressmen and state legislators (though it does include a few Democrats, of whom the most distinguished is former eight-term Representative Donald M. Fraser, now mayor of Minneapolis). Republicans are understandably eager to support any lunatic notion that holds out the promise of helping them break the Democratic stranglehold on Capitol Hill. But this just might be one of those rare cases where the narrow self-interest of the Republican Party is congruent with the public good.

The arguments for the term limit are surprisingly persuasive, especially where the House is concerned. Almost all of them are variations on a single theme: breaking the Gordian knot of entrenched incumbency, which distorts our democracy from the polling place clear up to the Senate and (especially) House chambers. Out in that fabled land beyond the Beltway, the term limit would mean that at least once every twelve years (and probably more frequently), every citizen would get a fighting chance to vote in a genuinely *political* congressional election, which is to say one that would turn not on the goodies that good old Congressman Thing has procured for the district or the Social Security checks he has expedited or the campaign funds he has raised or the newsletters he has franked, but rather on the competing political visions and programs of parties and candidates. But the most interesting, and salutary, effects of the limit would be the ways in which it would change the political ecology of Congress itself.

A twelve-year limit would necessarily bring an end to the much-reformed but still pervasive and undemocratic rule of seniority. The House Speaker, the chairmen of important committees, and the other potentates of Congress have long been elevated by a decades-long, quasi-feudal process of favor-trading, personal alliance-building, ladder-climbing, and "getting along by going along." The term limit would leave Congress little choice but to elect its chiefs democratically, on the basis of the policies and the leadership qualities of the candidates. Like the Speakers of many of our state legislatures, these leaders would tend to be vigorous men and women in their forties and fifties—people in the mold of Bill Gray, Stephen Solarz, and Henry Hyde. The Dingells and Rostenkowskis would remain where they belong, on the back benches of private life. This would be an important gain. And the frequent turnover of leaders—one who served more than six years would be a rarity—would be a spur both to brisk accomplishment and to attentiveness to the concerns and needs of the country.

The seniority system occasionally produces good leaders as well as bad ones, but there is no denying that it is grossly biased in favor of the most politically sluggish and unchanging parts of the nation. A swing district—one marked by close elections, and the robust debate and clamorous participation that close elections bring—has a hard time keeping somebody in office long enough to survive the glacial process by which congressional power is accumulated. It is precisely such districts that are most likely to elect representatives alive to the cutting-edge problems that most urgently require action. Systematically disempowering these districts and the people representing them, as the current arrangement so efficiently does, is insane.

A Congress invigorated by frequent infusions of new blood would be a more responsive, more democratic, more varied place. So would a Congress whose majority regularly changed from one party to the other, which a term limit would unquestionably promote. However bad this might be for the short-term partisan interests of Democrats like me, it would be good for the long-term interests of the country—and the party, too. Critics of the term limit idea argue that it would "weaken" Congress: and so it would, but in ways that would strengthen both its most useful functions and democratic governance in general. The one-party Congress has become a world unto itself, and the long period of Republican control of the presidency and Democratic control of Congress has produced an insidious mentality on Capitol Hill. The leaders of the Democratic congressional majority, veterans of decades of supremacy in their own little universe, no longer constitute an opposition. They conceive of themselves as ins, not outs—as leaders of one-half of a permanent coalition government. They may imagine that their own fiefdoms are secure, but their party is reaping almost all of the penalties of incumbency and almost none of the benefits. The foundations of Democratic congressional dominance are being relentlessly undermined, and once the structure topples, as eventually it must, rebuilding it will seem as hopeless a task as destroying it does now. A Congress shaped by a term limit would have a different and healthier mentality. During periods when it was controlled by the party that also controls the White House, it would be energetic in pursuit of that party's program; when in opposition, it would—for a change, and just as energetically— oppose.

The many Americans who deplore the decline of political parties in this country ought especially to welcome the term limit idea. By routinely undermining the totally independent, totally personal power bases that long-serving senators and representatives are able to build and maintain under the current system, and by dramatically increasing the number of elections fought on the basis of national issues, the term limit would enhance the strength and coherence of both national parties.

The term limit would mean that at any given moment something like sixty or seventy representatives, and perhaps half that number of senators, would be ineligible to run again. To critics of the proposal, this is one of its worst features. The lame ducks, say the critics, would be "unaccountable" and unresponsive to their constituents' wishes. But Congress's problem is hardly that its members are insufficiently obsessed with re-election, insufficiently attentive to polling data, and insufficiently ardent in pursuit of district pork barrel. The broader public good could only benefit from having a cohort of comparatively disinterested legislators, relieved from re-election pressures and free to consult their consciences as well as their pollsters and contributors. The critics add that the lame ducks might fall prey to corruption, legal or illegal. This phenomenon is not exactly unknown under present arrangements. But it would not be more likely to happen if most of the departing members are still relatively young and still ambitious. Why should they feather their nests at the cost of their reputations?

It's true, as the critics also say, that the term limit would deprive Congress of the services of legislators whom experience has made wise. This would be a real cost. But it would be a cost worth paying to be rid of the much larger number of timeservers who have learned nothing from longevity in office except cynicism, complacency, and a sense of diminished possibility. And it's not as if the job of being a congressman is so difficult that it takes decades to master. It's easier than being a first-rate schoolteacher, for example, and no harder than such jobs as president, governor, or mayor—all of which are regularly performed very well indeed by people who have had no on-the-job experience at all.

In any case, the senators and representatives obliged to seek other employment after twelve years will not vanish from the face of the earth. They will be available for service in the executive branch, in industry, in advocacy groups, and in the academy. Few will become lobbyists, because the turnover on the Hill will quickly make their contacts obsolete and their influence unpeddlable. Many will run for other public offices. Representatives will run for senator, senators will run for representative, and both will run for president, governor, mayor, and state legislator. The result will be more and better competition for these jobs, too. This would not be such a bad thing. Membership in Congress would no longer be a life calling or a lifetime sinecure, but this would not be such a bad thing either. A shot at Congress would be an attractive option for the young and ambitious, for the old but still energetic, and for men and women in midlife who want something more meaningful than whatever success they have earned elsewhere. There would be no shortage of candidates. Though harder to keep, the job would be easier to get.

A Gallup Poll taken in December found that 70 percent of the American public favor the idea of a term limit. This is uncannily close to the percentages of the public that (*a*) think Congress is doing a lousy job and (*b*) keep on voting to re-elect the same old incumbents. Opponents of the term limit say that if voters are so fed up with Congress, there is a simple way for them to do something about it without tinkering with the Constitution: "Throw the rascals out," as *The Chicago Tribune* suggests. So why don't they? "The explanation," writes my friend Michael Kinsely ("Voters in Chains," TNR, April 2), "is that the voters are lazy hypocrites." Maybe they are, but that's not the explanation. A given voter can vote to throw out a maximum of one rascal—three if you count senators. The problem is not individual incumbents; it's chronic incumbency, and trying to solve it by removing one's own incumbent is like treating tuberculosis with a cough drop. To tell a voter he can solve the problem of chronic incumbency by voting against his own representative is to recommend a particularly fruitless form of single-issue politics. The public's disgust is with Congress as an institution, and defeating one member out of 535 won't revamp Congress any more than firing the Deputy Assistant to the President for Scheduling would revamp the White House.

Thanks to seniority, voting to remove a long-serving congressman necessarily means voting to replace him with someone who will have less power. It therefore means voting to deprive one's district (and oneself) of clout. That's fine if you truly think your representative is a rascal. But what if you simply think he's a mediocrity?

There has to be a better way, and the twelve-year limit just might be it. The movement for it deserves the support of all who think Congress is broke and needs fixing—even those who, unlike me, don't think the limit itself is a particularly good idea. Let's be realistic: the chances a term limit amendment will actually get enacted are pretty remote. Congress, for obvious reasons, is not likely to pass it, and the other route—a constitutional convention called by two-thirds of the state legislatures—has never been successfully traveled. But the movement to impose a limit, if it catches fire, could throw enough of a scare into the Congress we've got to induce it to make changes—in campaign financing, PAC spending, access to television, mandatory campaign debates, and so on—that would accomplish most if not all of the same salutary results. The term limit movement is potentially like the nuclear freeze movement of the early 1980s. As a policy blueprint the freeze proposal left a lot to be desired. But the movement did a world of good by forcing the Reagan administration to offer serious arms control proposals of its own, most of which the Russians eventually accepted. The freeze movement was a cri de coeur. So is the term limit movement. Listen, Congress.

Bad Housekeeping: The Case against Congressional Term Limitations

CHARLES R. KESLER

Everyone complains about Congress, but nobody does anything about it. Frustration with our national legislature, which is by almost every measure widespread among the American public, is about to be exploited by a national movement to throw the rascals out—the rascals, in this case, being incumbent congressmen and senators who have so mastered the art of reelection as to be thought unremovable by conventional means. The most widely touted solution to the problem is the extreme one of adding an amendment to the Constitution limiting the number of terms that members of the House and Senate can serve.

This notion appears to have been first circulated by the same informal network of radio talk-show hosts who were instrumental in rallying public opposition to last year's congressional pay raise. The idea has found support in public opinion polls and is being pressed by a new organization, Americans to Limit Congressional Terms (ALCT), that operates out of the offices of Republican political consultant Eddie Mahe and whose board includes both prominent Democrats and Republicans.

It is the latter party that stands to benefit most from limiting the years a congressman can serve, inasmuch as it is the Republicans who suffer under the rule of a more or less permanent Democratic majority in the House and Senate. In fact, term limitations were endorsed in the 1988 Republican platform. It is hardly surprising, therefore, that conservatives, too, are seizing the issue. In the symposium on conservatism for the 1990s featured in the Spring 1990 issue of *Policy Review*, almost a third of the contributors called for some sort of limitation on congressional terms.

98-PERCENT PARADOX

This movement builds on the public's mounting dissatisfaction with a Congress that is seen not only as unresponsive but also as incompetent and corrupt. Indeed, in light of the chronically unbalanced federal budget, Congress's reluctance to perform even its minimal duty of passing a budget (balanced or not) without resort to omnibus continuing resolutions and reconciliation acts, the 51 percent salary increase for its members that it tried to brazen through without a rollcall vote, the generous privileges it extends to its members (large staffs, multiple offices, free travel allowances,

Source: Reprinted with permission from the Summer 1990 issue of *Policy Review*, the flagship publication of The Heritage Foundation, 214 Massachusetts Ave. NE, Washington, DC 20002.

It is a violation of the law to reproduce this selection by any means whatsoever without the written permission of the copyright holder.

frequent mailings at public expense, liberal pensions), the corruption-tinged resignations of former House Speaker Jim Wright and former Democratic Whip Tony Coelho, the metastasizing scandal of the Keating Five—in light of all these things, it is a wonder that congressmen get reelected at all.

And yet that is the paradox. Despite a deep dissatisfaction with Congress as an institution, the American people are reelecting their congressmen (that is, members of the House) at the highest rates in history. In the 1986 and 1988 elections, more than 98 percent of incumbent congressmen seeking reelection were returned to office. By now we have all heard the jokes about there being more turnover in the British House of Lords or in the Soviet Politburo than in the U.S. House of Representatives. The interesting question is, Why? What has happened to transform what the Framers of the Constitution envisioned as the most democratic, turbulent, changeable branch of the national government into the least changeable, most stable of the elective branches? And to come around to the question of the moment, will limiting the number of terms a congressman or senator can serve do anything to remedy the problem?

ANTI-FEDERALISTS: "VIRTUE WILL SLUMBER"

This is not the first time in American history that a limit on the reeligibility of elected federal officials has been proposed. At the Constitutional Convention in 1787, whether the president ought to be eligible for reelection was extensively debated, although always in close connection with the related questions of his term of office and mode of election. With the invention of the electoral college and with his term fixed at four years, it was thought to be productive of good effects and consistent with his independence from the legislature to allow the president to be eligible for reelection indefinitely; and so it remained until the 22nd Amendment was added to the Constitution. But what is less well known is that the Constitutional Convention also considered limitations on the reeligibility of the lower house of the legislature. The so-called Virginia Plan, introduced by Edmund Randolph, would have rendered members of the House ineligible for reelection for an unspecified period after their term's end. The period was never specified because the Convention expunged the limitation less than a month after it had been proposed.

Nevertheless, the question of limiting congressional terms lived on. It was taken up vigorously by the Anti-Federalists, the opponents of the new Constitution, who urged that "rotation in office" be imposed not so much on House members as on senators, whose small numbers, long term of office, and multifaceted powers made them suspiciously undemocratic. The AntiFederalists built upon the legacy of the Articles of Confederation, which had required that members of Congress rotate out after serving three one-year terms within any five-year period. Quite a few critics of the

Constitution attacked the unlimited reeligibility of the president, too, but the brunt of their criticism fell upon the Senate. In their view, it was a fatal mistake to neglect "rotation, that noble prerogative of liberty." As "An Officer of the Late Continental Army" called it in a Philadelphia newspaper, rotation was the "noble prerogative" by which liberty secured itself, even as the Tudor and Stuart kings had ignobly wielded their "prerogative power" in defense of tyranny.

The current appeal for limits on congressional office-holding echoes the major themes of the Anti-Federalists 200 years ago. One of the most rigorous of the Constitution's critics, the writer who styled himself "The Federal Farmer," put it this way: "[I]n a government consisting of but a few members, elected for long periods, and far removed from the observation of the people, but few changes in the ordinary course of elections take place among the members; they become in some measure a fixed body, and often inattentive to the public good, callous, selfish, and the fountain of corruption." After serving several years in office, he continued, it will be expedient for a man "to return home, mix with the people, and reside some time with them; this will tend to reinstate him in the interests, feelings, and views similar to theirs, and thereby confirm in him the essential qualifications of a legislator." Were the people watchful, they could recall him on their own and substitute a new representative at their discretion. But they are not sufficiently vigilant. As Patrick Henry warned at the Virginia ratifying convention, "Virtue will slumber. The wicked will be continually watching: Consequently you will be undone."

FEDERALISTS: THE PEOPLE ARE NOT FOOLS

The Anti-Federalist arguments were rejected by the advocates of the new Constitution. However, it is only for the presidency that the authors of the most authoritative defense of the Constitution, *The Federalist*, give a detailed refutation of the scheme of rotation in office. In *The Federalist*'s view, there is "an excess of refinement" in the notion of preventing the people from returning to office men who had proved worthy of their confidence. The people are not fools, at least not all of the time, and they can be trusted to keep a reasonably sharp eye on their representatives. So far as history can confirm such a proposition, it seems to pronounce in favor of *The Federalist*. Throughout the 19th and most of the 20th centuries, American politics was not characterized by a professional class of legislators insulated from the fluctuations, much less the deliberate changes, of public opinion. In the 19th century, it was not unusual for a majority of the membership of Congress to serve only one term; congressional turnover consistently averaged 40 to 50 percent every election. Occasionally it reached 60 or 70 percent.

The young Abraham Lincoln, for example, served only one term in the House of Representatives, in keeping with an informal rotation agreement he had negotiated with two Whig Party rivals in his district. Such agreements were not uncommon, and betokened a vigorous intraparty political life as well as keen competition between the parties: no party wanted its officeholders to betray an unrepublican ambition. But ambition was controlled informally by rotation within a party's bank of candidates so that the party and the country enjoyed the best of both worlds—a circulation of capable and experienced men through public office, with the possibility of keeping truly exceptional ones in office if circumstances demanded it.

Accordingly, even the most distinguished congressmen and senators of the 19th century pursued what by today's standards would be frenetic and irregular political careers. Henry Clay, famous as "the Great Compromiser," was sent thrice to the Senate to serve out someone else's term (the first time despite his being less than 30 years old); served two years in the Kentucky assembly, the second as its speaker; was elected seven times (not consecutively) to the House and three times was chosen speaker, although he often resigned in mid-term to take up a diplomatic post or run (unsuccessfully, three times) for president; and was elected twice to the Senate in his own right. Daniel Webster was elected to five terms in the House (not consecutively) and four terms in the Senate, in addition to running once (fruitlessly) for president and serving more than four nonconsecutive years as Secretary of State under three presidents. John C. Calhoun was elected to four terms in the House, served seven years as Secretary of War, was elected twice to the vice presidency, and then served two years of Robert Hayne's (of the Webster-Hayne debate) Senate term, two Senate terms in his own right, one year as Secretary of State, and four more years in the Senate.

By the way, the ALCT's proposed constitutional amendment, which would limit members of Congress to 12 consecutive years in office (six terms for representatives, two for senators), would have had no impact on Clay's nor Calhoun's career but would have disabled Webster, who was elected three times in a row to the Senate.

THE SWING ERA ENDS

But the larger and more important point is that today's entrenched Congress is a product of the great changes in American politics that have occurred since the late 19th century, particularly the weakening of political parties and the great increase in the size and scope of the federal government. Serving in Congress has become a profession over the past 100 years. The average (continuous) career of congressmen hovered around five years at the turn of the century, already up significantly from its earlier levels; today, the figure has doubled again, with the average member of the House serving about 10 years. In the century after 1860, the proportion of freshmen in the House plummeted from nearly 60 percent to around 10 percent, about where it remains today. This gradual professionalization of Congress owes something to the gradual increase of power in Washington, which made it more attractive to hold office; and still more to the seniority system, introduced in the House after the famous revolt against the power of the Speaker around 1910. With the seniority system in place, districts had great incentives to keep their representatives serving continuously. But the contemporary problems of incumbency are something else again. Since 1971, when House Democrats voted in their caucus to elect committee chairmen by secret ballot rather than follow the rule of committee seniority, the perquisites of seniority have declined, in part. Yet congressional reelection rates have risen. If it is not the advantages of seniority that account for today's almost invulnerable incumbents, then what is it?

Since the Second World War, reelection rates have been very high, averaging more than 90 percent; they have risen even further recently, approaching 100 percent in the last few elections. The political scientist David Mayhew identified the key to the incumbency problem as "the vanishing marginals," that is, the decline over the past 40 years in the number of marginal or competitive House districts. (A victory margin of 50 to 55 percent makes a district marginal, that is, capable of being won by a challenger.) In 1948 most incumbents won narrowly, getting less than 55 percent of their district's vote. Twenty years later, three-fourths of the incumbents received 60 percent or more of their district's vote, making these essentially safe seats for the winning congressmen. So, not only are more incumbents than ever winning, they are winning by bigger margins than ever before.

Explanations for the decline in marginal districts have not been scarce. First, there is the effect of gerrymandered congressional districts, which tend to be drawn in such a fashion as to lock in incumbents of both parties. Researchers have shown, however, that marginal districts declined just as sharply in the 1960s in states that did *not* redistrict as in those that did; so gerrymandering cannot be the principal culprit. Then there is the effect of incumbency itself—the franking privilege, free publicity stemming from benefits delivered to the district, prodigious sums of money contributed by political action committees, all of which make possible the greater name recognition that is supposed to discourage unknown and underfunded challengers. As the rates of incumbent reelection have climbed, therefore, one would expect an increase in incumbents' name recognition. But, as John Ferejohn and other analysts have shown, the data do not bear this out: incumbents are no better known now than they were before the marginal districts started vanishing. For all of the incumbents' advantages in name recognition, this factor cannot be the crucial one in explaining the decline in competitive House districts.

FACELESS BUREAUCRACY'S FRIENDLY FACE

In his arresting book *Congress: Keystone of the Washington Establishment*, the political scientist Morris Fiorina puts his finger on the nub of the problem. During the 1960s, congressmen began to put an unprecedented emphasis on casework or constituent service and pork-barrel activities as a way to ensure their reelection. The new emphasis was made possible precisely by "big government," the federal government's expansion of authority over state and local affairs that began dramatically with the New Deal and accelerated during the Great Society. As the federal bureaucracy expanded, more and more citizens found themselves dealing directly with federal agencies—the Social Security Administration, the Veterans Administration, the Equal Employment Opportunity Commission, the Environmental Protection Agency, and so on. To penetrate the mysteries of the administrative state, to find a friendly face amid the "faceless" bureaucrats and a helping hand among so many seemingly determined to do injustice in particular cases, citizens began increasingly to turn to their congressman for succor.

And they were encouraged to do so, particularly by the younger and more vulnerable congressmen who had come into office in the great Democratic waves of 1964 and 1974. Eventually, however, almost all congressmen caught on to the "new deal" made possible and necessary by the increased reach of Washington. The beauty of the new politics was that the same congressmen who were applauded for creating new federal agencies to tackle social problems also got credit for helping their constituents through the labyrinths of these impersonal bureaucracies. In Fiorina's words: "Congressmen take credit coming and going. They are the alpha and the omega." The more ambitious of them exploit the paradox shamelessly: the more bureaucracy they create, the more indispensable they are to their constituents. To which one must add: the longer they've been around Washington, the more plausible is their claim to know precisely how to aid their constituents with the bureaucracy.

It is clear that knowledge of these bureaucratic folkways is more important to voters than ever before. But it requires only a very small number of swing voters, perhaps only 5 percent or so, to transform a district from being marginal or competitive into being safe (thus increasing the incumbent's vote from, say, 53 to 58 percent). To explain the disappearing marginal districts it is therefore necessary only for a very small sector of the electorate to have been won over to the incumbent by the constituent service and pork-barrel opportunities opened up by an activist federal government. To this group of voters in particular, perhaps to most voters to one degree or another, the congressman's job is now thought to be as much administrative as political. The spirit of nonpartisan, expert administration—central to modern liberalism as it was conceived in the Progressive Era—is gradually coloring the public's view of the House of Representatives, transforming it from the most popular branch of the legislature into the highest branch of the civil service.

If this is true, the congressman's expertise is a peculiar sort, involving as it does interceding with civil servants (and appointed officials) in the spirit of personal, particularistic relations, not the spirit of impersonal rule following associated with the civil service. Nonetheless, he is expected to keep benefits and services issuing to the district, just as a nonpartisan city manager is expected to keep the streets clean and the sewers flowing. And to the extent that ombudsmanship is a corollary of bureaucracy (as it seems to be, at least in democratic governments), his casework partakes of the spirit of administration rather than of political representation.

HAMILTON'S "SORDID VIEWS"

Given the origins and nature of the problem with Congress (really with the House of Representatives, inasmuch as Senate incumbents remain beatable), it is apparent that limiting congressional terms to 12 years will do little or nothing to remedy the situation. Any new faces that are brought to Washington as the result of such an amendment will find themselves up against the same old incentives. They will still be eligible for reelection five times. How will they ensure their continued political prosperity without seeing to constituents' administrative needs? If anything, these new congressmen will find themselves confronting bureaucrats rendered more powerful by the representatives' own ignorance of the bureaucracy; for in the administrative state, knowledge is power. It is likely, therefore, that the new congressmen will initially be at a disadvantage relative to the agencies. To counter this they will seek staff members and advisers who are veterans of the Hill, and perhaps larger and more district-oriented staffs to help ward off challengers who would try to take advantage of their inexperience. Is it wise to increase the already expansive power of bureaucrats and congressional staff for the sake of a new congressman in the district every half-generation or so?

The proposed limitation on congressional terms would also have most of the disadvantages of the old schemes of rotation in office that were criticized by the Federalists. Consider these points made by Alexander Hamilton in *Federalist* No. 72 (concerning rotation in the presidency, but still relevant to rotation in Congress). In the first place, setting a limit on office-holding "would be a diminution of the inducements to good behavior." By allowing indefinite reeligibility, political men will be encouraged to make their interest coincide with their duty, and to undertake "extensive and arduous enterprises for the public benefit" because they will be around to reap the consequences. Second, term limits would be a temptation to "sordid views" and "peculation." As Gouverneur Morris put it at the Constitutional Convention, term limits say to the official, "make hay while the sun shines." Nor does a long term of eligibility (12 years in this case) remove the difficulty. No one will know better than the present incumbent how difficult it will be to defeat the future incumbent. So the limits of his career will always be visible to him, as will the temptation to "make hay" as early as possible.

A third disadvantage of term limits is that they could deprive the country of the experience and wisdom gained by an incumbent, perhaps just when that experience is needed most. This is particularly true for senators, whose terms would be limited even though Senate races are frequently quite competitive (recall 1980 and 1986) and that the Senate was precisely the branch of the legislature in which the Framers sought stability, the child of long service.

DISTRACTION FOR GOP

For conservatives and Republicans, the pursuit of a constitutional amendment to limit congressional terms would act as a colossal distraction from the serious work of politics that needs to be done.

The worst effect of the incumbents' advantage in the House is to have saddled America with divided government since 1968 (excepting Jimmy Carter's administration, which was bad for other reasons). Professor Fiorina estimates that if marginal districts had not declined, the Republicans would have taken control of the House five times in the past quarter-century—in 1966, 1968, 1972, 1980, and 1984 (he did not evaluate the 1988 results). Because the marginals did decline, the Democrats, trading on the power of their incumbent members, retained control of the House throughout this period, despite the success of Republican presidents who were elected.

It would be unfair, of course, to blame the Democrats' popularity wholly on the decline in marginal districts. The GOP has not done well enough in open-seat elections to rely on the incumbency effect as the all-purpose excuse for its inability to take the House. But it is a fair conjecture that the ethos of administrative politics works to the Republicans' disadvantage even in those districts lacking a Democratic incumbent. Which is not to say that Republican incumbents don't look out for themselves; they do. But the spirit of casework and pork-barrel cuts against the grain of conservative Republican principles, and so it is hard for Republican candidates to sound like Republicans when they are preaching the gospel according to FDR and LBJ. More to the point, it is difficult for the Republican Party to articulate why people ought to consider themselves Republicans and ought to vote a straight GOP ticket under these circumstances.

The attempt to limit congressional terms would do nothing to relieve Republicans of these tactical disadvantages. What is needed is not a gimmick to stir up political competition, but the prudence and courage to take on the strategic political questions dividing conservative Republicans and liberal Democrats. By (among other things) reconsidering the scope and power of the federal government, by opposing the extension of centralized administration over more and more of American life, Republicans could inaugurate robust political competition. President Reagan and the Republican Party were successful at this in 1980, when the GOP gained 33 seats in the House and took control of the Senate. But they seem to have neglected those lessons in succeeding elections.

By the 1992 election, when reapportionment and redistricting have taken hold (and assuming a generous number of retirements), there could be 100 House districts without an incumbent. To win these the Republicans will require not just the better party organization they have been assiduously building, important as that is, but also a moral and political argument against what, to borrow the 18th-century vocabulary, could be called the corruption of the national legislature and of national politics generally—not corruption in the sense of criminal venality, but in the sense of insulating our legislators from the currents of national political opinion, and encouraging them, and their constituents, to subordinate the public good to their own private welfare.

In this fight, congressional term limitations would be at best a distraction. If the American people want to vote all incumbents out of office, or just those particular incumbents known as liberal Democrats, they can do so with but the flick of a lever. All they need is a good reason.